Words of Destiny

SUNY series in Hindu Studies

Wendy Doniger, editor

Words of Destiny

Practicing Astrology in North India

CATERINA GUENZI

SUNY PRESS

Cover image: "An astrologer. Watercolour by an Indian artist, ca. 1825."
Credit: Wellcome Collection. Attribution 4.0 International (CC BY 4.0)

Translated by Renuka George and Caterina Guenzi.

Published by State University of New York Press, Albany

Printed in the United States of America

For information, contact State University of New York Press, Albany, NY
www.sunypress.edu

Library of Congress Cataloging-in-Publication Data

Name: Guenzi, Caterina, author.
Title: Words of destiny : practicing astrology in North India / Caterina Guenzi.
Other titles: Discours du destin. English
Description: Albany : State University of New York Press, 2021. | Series: SUNY series in Hindu studies | Includes bibliographical references and index.
Identifiers: LCCN 2020024801 | ISBN 9781438482019 (hardcover : alk. paper) | ISBN 9781438482026 (pbk. : alk. paper) | ISBN 9781438482033 (ebook)
Subjects: LCSH: Hindu astrology—Social aspects—India—Vārānasi (Uttar Pradesh) | Predictive astrology. | Astrologers—India—Vārānasi (Uttar Pradesh)
Classification: LCC BF1714.H5 G7813 2021 | DDC 133.5/9445—dc23
LC record available at https://lccn.loc.gov/2020024801

10 9 8 7 6 5 4 3 2 1

To Carlo and Margherita

Et tantost que li enfant naissent, si font escrire le jour et l'eure et le mois. Et ce font il pour ce que il font tuit leur fais atout devinaille, quar il sevent moult d'[art magique] et de nigromance et d'astronomie et d'autres enchantemens dyaboliques.

—Marco Polo, *Le devisement du monde: Livre d'Ynde*

As soon as a child is born, whether it be male or female, the father or mother writes down its birth—that is, what day it is born, what month, what moon and what hour; and they do this because they place all their faith in astronomers and diviners who know a lot about enchantments, magical arts and geomancy; there are also some who know astronomy.

—Marco Polo, *The Description of the World: The Book of India*

Contents

Illustrations

Figures

Tables

Acknowledgments

This work is the fruit of a long gestation period—over fifteen years spent between Italy, India, France, and Great Britain (not to mention journeys across constellations and planetary orbits)—and was supported by a large number of people and institutions. Among the institutions that made this research possible, I would particularly like to thank the École des Hautes Études en Sciences Sociales, the Centre d'études de l'Inde et Asie du Sud, the University of Sienna, the Oriental University of Naples, the Fonds Louis Dumont for research in social anthropology, the Fyssen Foundation, and the Institut Français in Pondicherry. The doctoral thesis that was adapted to produce this book was awarded the Krishna Varma medal (the recipient is chosen by the Institut d'études indiennes at the Collège de France).

It is impossible for me to cite all the people who participated, directly or indirectly, in the different phases of this work, from gathering ethnographical material, analyzing texts, developing ideas, to its writing and rewriting. I would first like to express my gratitude to the astrologers in Banaras who welcomed me into their homes and offices, and introduced me to their clients, in particular: Gyanvati Pandey, Shree Kanth Shastri, Neelkanth Shastri, Kameshwar Upadhyay, Dina Nath Tiwari, B. P. Mehrotra, Nagendra Pandey, Ram Chandra Pandey, Chandrama Pandey, and Chandra Mawli Upadhyay. To show my appreciation for them, and because they are somewhat "public figures" in the city, their names are not anonymized in this book. Sunita Singh, who started out as my research assistant and went on to become a colleague and lifelong friend, shared the work in the field, day after day, and has become an astrological expert in spite of herself. Sushila and Virendra Singh's family took me into their home and treated me like a daughter during fieldwork, and conscientiously encouraged my progress in Hindi. Beyond my studies at university Paris III–La Sorbonne Nouvelle, where I did my bachelor's and master's in Indian studies, my knowledge of Sanskrit progressed thanks to Professor R. C. Panda, from the Department of Sanskrit Literature at Banaras Hindu University. He helped me translate certain passages of the Sanskrit astrological texts. I also thank my Bharata Nāṭyam teachers in Banaras, Mala and Prem Chand Hombal, whose family theater company and house in the forest were a real landmark, and at times a refuge during my staying in Banaras. During my last fieldwork, Simon Georget agreed to accompany me to do a photo report on astrologers. Some of the photographs reproduced in this work are expressions of his gaze, and I thank him for his participation.

Jean-Claude Galey and Pier Giorgio Solinas, advisors of the doctoral thesis "Destin et divination: Le travail des astrologues de Bénarès" that I defended at the École des Hautes Études en Sciences Sociales in 2004, followed the progress of this work from its infancy in Sienna to its final versions in Paris. Jean-Claude Galey's encouragement and support were crucial to this manuscript becoming a book, and I would like to express my deep gratitude to him. Among the researchers who made a fundamental contribution to this study by their teaching, rereading, or discussions, I would like to mention Nalini Balbir, Daniela Berti, Kamaleshwar Bhattacharya, Shelah Bloom, Véronique Bouillier, Catherine Clémentin-Ojha, Silvia D'Intino, Gérard Fussman, Agathe Keller, Charles Malamoud, Claude Markovits, Aïssatou Mbodj, Elisia Menduni, Christopher Minkowski, Gilles Tarabout, Sophie Vasset, David Gordon White and Francis Zimmermann. I am deeply grateful to them, even if I bear sole responsibility for any mistakes and imprecisions in this work. Renuka George was patient enough to share with me the galactic journey of the translation of this book from French into English; Francie Crebs helpfully added a finishing touch. Finally, I would like to thank Maurice Godelier for publishing this volume in the collection Bibliothèque de l'anthropologie he directs at CNRS Éditions, and Wendy Doniger for encouraging the publication of its translation as part of the SUNY series in Hindu Studies.

The publication of this book will certainly gladden and reassure all those close to me, the friends and family who followed the torturous evolution of this work and feared they would never see it completed. I thank them warmly for their affection, patience, and kindness. Simon, Néroli, and Anita, who were involved in my earlier gestations, know how long and difficult the delivery of this book was. I thank them for their maieutic teachings.

Introduction

In his inaugural speech "A Tryst with Destiny," to proclaim the birth of India as an independent nation and the end of British colonization, Nehru uttered the famous sentence: "At the stroke of the midnight hour, when the world sleeps, India will awake to life and freedom." With his admirable eloquence, Nehru transformed a somewhat curious fact of Indian Independence into a lyrical, even epic image. Why midnight? Why perform such a solemn and institutional event at the dead of night? Indeed, despite the evocative force of India's awakening while the rest of the world is asleep, one cannot but note that it was midnight only in India and not, for example, in England, where it was still daytime. Few are aware of the reasons that led "Mother India," the Indian nation, to give birth to the "Midnight's children" of Salman Rushdie's novel. The reasons for this choice are explained in an article written by Nehru's first secretary, H. V. R. Iyengar, on the occasion of the fiftieth anniversary of Independence, and published in the daily newspaper *The Hindu*.[1]

The British Empire, represented by the viceroy Lord Mountbatten, had fixed the date for the transfer of power for August 15, 1947. Nonetheless, before accepting this date, several members of the Indian Constituent Assembly consulted a committee of astrologers to ensure that the moment was propitious, that the nation would be born under happy auspices. According to these experts, August 14 was more favorable than August 15. However, as the British government had committed to promulgating Pakistan's independence on the fourteenth, and Lord Mountbatten was to go to Karachi that morning, it was impossible to advance the declaration. In addition, the date of August 15 had already been announced to the British Parliament. It was finally Sardar K. M. Panikkar, a historian and writer from Kerala educated at Oxford University, who suggested the solution to the conflict between the pragmatic requirements of the British and the celestial constraints. Having demonstrated his diplomatic skills on this momentous occasion, Panikkar went on to become one of India's ambassadors after Independence. He suggested that the Constituent Assembly gather on August 14 at 11:00 p.m., but that the oath be sworn at midnight. Hence, by this chronological compromise the date set by the British was respected, but without contravening the astrological directives.

However anecdotal it may seem, this event perfectly illustrates the convergence within a single institution, the Indian Constituent Assembly, of the values of independence, modernity, and secularism embodied in the progressive leader Nehru, and the traditional Brahmanical values that stipulate the prerequisite of an astrologer's opinion in order to ensure the success of any undertaking. In this case, the creation of a nation.[2] This episode could be read as a discrepancy, a contradiction, between the "content" of the proclamation of Independence, promoting an enlightened and democratic India, and its "form," driven by an obscurantist India with its local "superstitions." Nehru can be seen as having ceded to the pressure exerted by some of the particularly conservative members of the Constituent Assembly. Nonetheless, looking more closely at his speech, the title to start with, one notices that India's future is not represented solely in political terms, and the idea of a transcendent destiny, determined by superior powers, is crucial to the message he addresses to the Indian people. Although any inaugural speech pronounced before a nation is necessarily rhetorical, the words Nehru chose are far from inconsequential:

> At the dawn of history India started on her unending quest, and trackless centuries are filled with her striving and the grandeur of her success and her failures. Through *good and ill fortune* alike she has never lost sight of that quest or forgotten the ideals which gave her strength. *We end today a period of ill fortune* and India discovers herself again. . . .
>
> The *appointed day* has come—*the day appointed by destiny*—and India stands forth again, after long slumber and struggle, awake, vital, free and independent. The past clings on to us still in some measure and we have to do much before we redeem the pledges we have so often taken. Yet the turning point is past, and history begins anew for us, the history which we shall live and act and others will write about.

> It is a *fateful moment* for us in India, for all Asia and for the world. A *new star rises*, the star of freedom in the east, a new hope comes into being, a vision long cherished materialises. May *the star never set* and that hope never be betrayed![3]

British colonization is described as *a period of ill fortune*, Independence Day was *appointed by destiny*, and India's future is a *new star* rising in the east. Of course, Nehru's speech also contains numerous passages that evoke the ideas of freedom, responsibility, struggle, and work, and we are in no way contesting Nehru's secularism here by attributing an occult astrological significance to his words. Nehru was quite simply an outstanding orator who knew how to address the nation. His representation of a change of era in transcendent and fatalistic terms corresponds, on the one hand, to a diplomatic strategy—a means of not explicitly accusing the British colonizers—but also, on the other hand, to the use of a language familiar to his Indian audience. And for the latter, misfortune and suffering, just like happiness, are to be understood in the context of a vaster cosmic arrangement.

Whether they apply to a nation, an individual, or a family, the ideas of destiny, good and bad luck, days set by fate, more or less favorable periods, and stars rising in the east are central to this work. The research presented here strives to show that what occurred at the proclamation of Independence was in no way an "accident." Nehru's speech should not be read as the persistence of a vestige of superstition that would erroneously have crossed the threshold of government institutions, fortuitously slipping into India's modernity but destined to disappear with the spread of technological progress and scientific discoveries. Astrology is a scholarly tradition deeply rooted in Indian society, with particularly lively ramifications in contemporary India. This work sets out to examine the processes of adaptation, interpretation, and rewriting this Brahmanical discipline underwent in urban India at the turn of the twenty-first century, as I observed it in Banaras and over the course of repeated fieldwork carried out between 1995 and 2008. By revisiting the journey that led me to choose this subject, I will clarify the approach and the analytical perspectives developed in this work.

I had just arrived in Banaras; it was 1995. I had decided to spend five months in this town to carry out my first fieldwork: the subject was not yet clearly defined. I did not speak a word of Hindi and having spent a few weeks there on an earlier visit to India, I was both intrigued and terrified. The recent reading of *Banaras: City of Light* by Diana Eck and *Death in Banaras* by Jonathan Parry had reinforced my contradictory feelings. These two monographs, when read close together, are a good illustration of the combination of light and death, purity and corruption, spirituality and pragmatism that makes the reputation of Banaras.

While I was considering how I could carry out my survey on a subject as vast as arranged marriages and personhood in Banaras (a subject I finally abandoned), noticing my worry and confusion, the family I was staying with—Christians from Kerala—advised me not to waste my time on futile questions and to go and consult an astrologer. This would ensure the successful outcome of my studies and my good health in the coming months. They invited me to join them when they next visited the astrologer to have him calculate their newborn baby's horoscope. With no inkling that the meeting with an astrologer could "actually" influence the direction my studies would take, I accepted their invitation, thinking this recreational hiatus would at least bring me some relief and momentarily distract me from the "real" issues of ethnographic research.

Brahmanand Colony, a fairly upmarket residential area in the south of Banaras, is taking shape in the zone to the west of the Durga temple.[4] Gyanvati Pandey sees her clients in one of the two rooms of the flat she occupies with her mother, two brothers, her younger sister, and paternal grandfather on the first floor of a three-story cement building. When we arrived, Gyanvati's brother signaled to us to wait outside on the veranda, as his sister was busy with other clients. Half an hour later we were invited into the room. Her face almost completely hidden behind a shawl that covered her head, with an ease born of practice, this twenty-five-year-old woman rolled and unrolled the two long scrolls covered in diagrams and numerals that made up the horoscope of the couple that had come to consult her. Gyanvati indicated we should sit (on the floor, like everyone else, as there was no furniture in the room), and she continued her consultation. The sick eighty-three-year-old grandfather, *dādājī*, lying beside her on a mattress, muttered *mantra*s (sacred formulae) incessantly, while Gyanvati's youngest sister, Madhu, came and went, serving tea and biscuits. The brother, Manesh, chatted with the people waiting their turn outside and, from time to time, entered the room to inform his sister of a client's arrival or departure.

About twenty minutes later, when she had finished with the couple, Gyanvati finally addressed my hosts, in Hindi as she spoke no English. She asked them who I was and where I came from. When she heard I was Italian, her eyes lit up. She left the room to return a few moments later with a photograph showing an Indian man, with a moustache, standing at the entrance to Gardaland, an amusement park located near Lake Garda, in Italy. Surprised and amused by this photo, I later discovered that the gentleman was Gyanvati's father, Murlidhar Pandey. In Banaras he had met some people from Bergame who were passionate about astrology and, a few years before, they had invited him to give classes and hold astrological consultations in Northern Italy.

Murlidhar Pandey was a Shakadvipi (*Śākadvīpīya*) Brahmin, descended from nine generations of astrologers. He had left his village in the Rohtas district of Bihar to study philosophy and astrology at the Sanskrit University in Banaras (*Sampūrṇānanda Saṃskṛta Viśvavidyālaya*) and at Banaras Hindu University (BHU). After obtaining two master's degrees in philosophy and a PhD in astrology, he was employed as an astrologer at the Banaras Hindu University hospital and was paid by the Central Government in Delhi. As a tenured astrologer, Murlidhar Pandey not only held consultations at the hospital, he also carried out a clinical study called "Study on the Astrological Basis of Cardiorespiratory Diseases with Special Reference to Diagnosis, Prognosis, and Prevention." As he was highly reputed as a medical astrologer, Murlidhar Pandey often traveled to Bihar, Madhya Pradesh, Delhi, Calcutta, and Bombay (and of course, to Italy) for consultations. During these trips, his wife stayed behind in Banaras with the three youngest children, while the two eldest daughters accompanied him to cook his meals and take care of his other household arrangements. Over the course of these travels, Gyanvati, the second daughter, who was less occupied with household activities than her older sister, developed an interest in astrology, which she cultivated by helping her father prepare the horoscopes. When her father suddenly died in 1992, she knew how to calculate horoscopes and she joined Sanskrit University in Banaras to obtain a master's degree (*ācārya*) in astrology (*jyotiṣa*). Nonetheless, her inexperience, her youth, and most probably the fact that she was a woman did not allow her to replace her father in the government job he occupied at the hospital, and the position was terminated. Gyanvati began to hold consultations at home and her income was the family's only source of income, supplemented by her father's pension.

After showing me her father's photograph, Gyanvati noted the details of my birth and those of my hosts' newborn baby and told us to come back a week later. As I found the price of a complete horoscope too high—one thousand rupees[5]—just for the amusement this astrological excursus would provide me, I asked her to prepare a simplified birth chart for two hundred rupees. So the following week I received my astrological birth chart with its "guidelines": Jupiter (*Guru*) in a very strong position (*prabal*) favored studies, but I had a marriage *yog* (astral combination) for 1996 or 1998, after which I was to spontaneously abandon my studies to dedicate myself to family life. In any event, I had to procure a gold ring with a seven-carat *gomed* (hessonite) to be worn for the first time on a Wednesday, between 1:00 p.m. and 3:30 p.m., on the middle finger of my left hand. Gyanvati gave me the prescription written on letterhead that read:

Gyanvati Pandey
Sanskrit Sahityacharya & Jeotishacharya[6]
Life Member of Indian Red-Cross Society

D/o Late Dr. Murlidhar Pandey[7]
World Renowned Astrologer
MA (Philosophy)
PhD (Astrology and Human Destiny)
CENTRAL COUNCIL FOR RESEARCH IN AYURVEDA & SIDHA
DEPT. OF KAYACHIKITSA INSTITUTE OF MEDICAL SCIENCES
S.S. HOSPITAL, FACULTY OF AYURVEDA
BANARAS HINDU UNIVERSITY
VARANASI (UP)

Contact for:
Mental and Emotional Problems, Nervous Troubles, Psychophysical and Chronic Diseases, Conflict of Married Life,
Education of Abnormal Children,
Service and Business, Your Personal Matters, and
Effective Planet Stones

Gyanvati was one of Banaras's few women astrologers. As one can see from her letterhead, her authority as an astrologer was based on her father's legacy. Nonetheless, if the father had not died, and the family had not needed the money, Gyanvati would probably never have become a professional astrologer. She would have been married much earlier than the age of twenty-nine, which was very late according to Indian standards. And after her marriage, her life would have been entirely dedicated to "domestic concerns" (as she had in fact predicted for me and as had actually happened, in her case, after the age of twenty-nine). For all these reasons, Gyanvati used to repeat that she did not want to marry, as she was afraid that she would have to give up her occupation and her studies.

Gyanvati saw her profession of astrologer both as a family tradition she was proud to continue and as a personal vocation, as she was the only one of the five children who was passionate about studying, astrology in particular. In addition, she told me that because of the planetary configurations present in her horoscope, her father had predicted she would become an astrologer and had always encouraged her to pursue her studies in this field.

While pursuing the family tradition, this young astrologer also wanted to assert her autonomy from her father's work in the field of "medical astrology": she wanted to specialize in women's reproductive health. She planned do a doctorate at Banaras Hindu University, focusing on a study of the astral configurations that affect the menstrual cycle, pregnancy, delivery, and other gynecological questions.

A few weeks after my first meeting with Gyanvati, the room where she had received us as clients was to become my bedroom. I had in fact thought of going to live with Gyanvati's family when I discovered that they belonged to the caste that, for different reasons, had become the object of my fieldwork. They were Shakadvipi (*Śākadvīpīya*) Brahmins, a community of Brahmins of Iranian origin, traditionally associated with the cult of the Sun (Sūrya) and the occupations of astrologer (*jyotiṣī*), Ayurvedic doctor (*vaidya*), and tantric priest (*tāntrika*).[8]

The close cohabitation with the family placed me in the situation of participating observer, rather than that of observing participant, as required by anthropological methodology. Indeed, it was less by observation than by practice that I came to understand that this family's daily life was punctuated by astrological norms that dictated what is "auspicious" (*śubh*) and what is "inauspicious" (*aśubh*). For Gyanvati, I was not just a "disciple"; I was also her "younger sister," which made me a receptacle for constant behavioral advice. With the benevolence of an older sister and the authority of a teacher, Gyanvati instructed me in the color of the clothing I should wear depending on the day of the week—white on Monday, the day of the Moon; red on Tuesday, the day of Mars, and so forth—the time at which I should leave the house for an interview to go well, the direction in which my feet should point when I did my astrology homework, the appropriate day to leave on a train journey, and so on. Respecting Gyanvati's rules, although impatiently at times, allowed me to understand that astrology concerns every aspect of daily life and regulates every type of human behavior.

As a result of this fieldwork experience, I began to see astrology less as an esoteric or spiritual knowledge, as one tends to in the West, than as a highly pragmatic thought system, anchored in daily life and clearly focused on the resolution of concrete problems. Similarly, Gyanvati and her father's positions within Banarsi society,[9] their university degrees (MA and PhD) in astrology, and the post of astrologer at a public hospital proved that the profession of astrologer in Banaras plays a decisive role in the functioning of the society.[10]

Approaching Astrology: Standpoints

> In societies in which divination is not, as it is in our own, considered a marginal, even aberrant phenomenon, where it constitutes a normal, regular, often even obligatory procedure, . . . Divinatory rationality in these civilizations does not form a separate sector, an isolated mentality, contrasted with modes of reasoning that regulate the practice of law, administration, politics, medicine, or daily life; it is coherently included in the entire body of social thought and, in its intellectual processes, it observes similar norms, just as the seer's status in the functional hierarchy seems very closely linked with those other social agents responsible for collective life.
>
> —Jean-Pierre Vernant, *Mortals and Immortals*

My anthropological interest in the work of astrologers took shape after I realized that, in India, astrology enjoys institutional recognition and is not a marginal system of thought. In Banaras, astrology is taught at two universities, as well as at the thirty-odd Sanskrit colleges in the town. Hindus systematically seek an astrologer's opinion before they arrange a marriage, perform a ritual, build a house, or buy a piece of land. In addition, when they face economic or professional difficulties, family conflicts, health problems, or when it comes to any major decision, for example, concerning the children's education, financial investments, travel, or career, both Hindus and Muslims alike often seek advice from an astrologer.

To apply Jean-Pierre Vernant's words to the context of Banaras, one can say that in this town of North India, following astrological recommendations is "a normal, regular, often even obligatory procedure," particularly for the Hindus, and astrological thought "is coherently included in the entire body of social thought and in its intellectual processes." Astrological rationality does not constitute "a separate sector, an isolated mentality," and the status of astrologer "in the functional hierarchy seems very closely linked with those other social agents responsible for collective life."[11]

With regard to the interaction of astrology with other types of knowledge, to start with one can note that *jyotiṣa*—the textual tradition in Sanskrit literature dealing with astronomy, astrology, and divination—is recognized as a valid and useful knowledge system by the representatives of religious orthodoxy, that is to say, the Brahmins. Hence, there has been no rupture in the Hindu world between religion and astrology: astrology is a constitutive part of every Brahmin priest's (*purohit*) intellectual background. The dates for performing rituals and celebrating Hindu religious festivals are calculated on the basis of astrological principles. In addition, the interpenetration of astrology and religion seems obvious as the planets are fully recognized deities in the Hindu pantheon; they are worshipped through propitiatory and appeasement rituals and their anthropomorphic images are present in numerous temples both in North and South India.

Second, it is important to note that in the Brahmanical tradition, over the centuries, there has been no epistemological break between "astronomy" (*gaṇita*) and "astrology" (*phalita jyotiṣa*, *horā*), between scientific theory on the one hand and divinatory or predictive speculation on the other. Both these approaches to the study of the stars are seen, even today, as two branches of the same knowledge, *jyotiṣa*, the science that studies "celestial light" (*jyotis*), including as well other types of divination such as the interpretation of omens (*saṃhitā*).

Third, astrology plays a crucial role as auxiliary knowledge for other applied sciences like ritual, architecture, agronomy, or Ayurvedic medicine. *Jyotiṣa* serves to establish the "auspicious moments" (*muhūrta*) that ensure the success of activities such as performing a ritual, constructing a house, starting the harvest, or beginning medical treatment.

Nonetheless, astrology is not only an integral part of "traditional" Brahmanical culture. In contemporary India it remains an important feature of the lifestyle of the urban middle class and elite who see themselves as the representatives of "modernity." In Banaras, as elsewhere in the country, the most voracious consumers of horoscopes are civil servants and their families, businessmen, politicians, celebrities (Bollywood actors, cricket players, et al.), university professors, engineers, doctors, lawyers, and computer engineers. Astrology is particularly appreciated in these circles. It guides the decision-making process in the daily lives of well-off urban families in matters of career, travel, financial investment, identifying matrimonial partners, choice of schools for children, and so forth. It is also seen as knowledge that is more scientific in nature than religion. It combines seamlessly with technological and computer innovations, tablets and smartphones, viewed as expressions of "modernity" in today's India. Because horoscopes are based on mathematical operations and can be calculated using software, and astrological services can be accessed by the internet in India, as well as the United States or Australia, it is seen as an innovative type of knowledge, both global and cosmopolitan, highly emblematic of the modernity of the contemporary world.

Today, astrology is taught at several Indian universities alongside Sanskrit studies, history, and philosophy as well as physics, engineering, and statistics. With its polymorphous epistemological status that allows it to hover between religion and science, in Banaras astrology seems to be flourishing. Indeed, it is seen as a discipline capable of reconciling scientific rationalism and religious devotion, empirical observation of natural phenomena and the appeasement of supernatural beings, technological innovation and the celebration of ancient rites, pragmatic management of daily problems and conformity with a transcendent order.[12]

The institutional recognition of astrology in India today may be startling, since the validity of this discipline was widely rejected in the West. On the one hand, ecclesiastical dogma condemned astrology as a pagan belief, connected to magic and incompatible with the principle of free choice and divine omnipotence, and on the other, astrology was deemed contradictory to the development of the modern scientific paradigm. From the seventeenth century onward, in the West, astrology was expelled from every institutional field and mainly confined to esoteric and occult circles.[13] The comparative perspective proves particularly pertinent in this area because Western astrology and Hindu astrology share a common theoretical matrix, Greco-Babylonian astrology, which developed and metabolized in different ways in each of these civilizations.

Today, in the West, astrology is not considered an *intellectually* legitimate subject. It represents a marginal and "superstitious" belief that cannot be taught at universities as it is considered antinomic to the principles of philosophical and scientific rationality, which form the basis of our "paradigms of thought."[14] It is confined to horoscopes in newspapers, social conversations around the qualities and shortcomings of the signs of the zodiac, or to the personal "business" astrologers, who are generally seen as charlatans, indulge in.

The status of "irrational belief" attributed to astrology is established both by the exact sciences and by the social sciences. In what concerns the former, we have only to mention the statement signed by 186 scientists, eighteen of whom were Nobel Prize winners, published in 1975 in the magazine *The Humanist*. In this statement, astrology is defined as a "belief based on magic and superstition" that contributes "to the growth of irrationalism and obscurantism," as it is "simply a mistake to imagine that the forces exerted by stars and planets at the moment of birth can in any way shape our futures. . . . Neither is it true that the position of distant heavenly bodies make certain days or periods more favourable to particular kinds of action, or that the sign under which one was born determines one's compatibility or incompatibility with other people."[15] Social sciences also see astrology as an irrational belief.[16] According to the definition T. W. Adorno provides in his essay *The Stars Down to Earth and Other Essays on the Irrational in Culture* (1994), dedicated to analyzing the content of the astrological column in the *Los Angeles Times*, astrology is a "pseudo-rational belief," an irrational belief that contains a semblance of rationality or a "secondary superstition," where the occult, as such, plays only a marginal role, but one that is objectified and socialized.

Given the epistemological status astrology enjoys within the dominant paradigm of contemporary Western thought, it is "normal" and "rational" for a researcher in the exact or social sciences to afford it little credit. This does not mean there are no researchers or academics who believe in astrology, but merely that scholarly institutions (research laboratories, universities, higher education establishments) do not recognize it as "*legitimate knowledge*," and to state in a scientific publication that astrology is true and valid would be reprehended.[17] My research falls within this paradigm of thought, to the extent that I do not afford astrology the status of a subject endowed with scientific and universal truth, and I do not believe in astrology myself.

Nonetheless, I would like to clarify that this statement is not made as a deontological precaution. The very fact that I do not believe in astrology played a fundamental role in the choice of this research subject. Indeed, my interest in a study of astrology in Banaras did not develop *despite* my lack of personal belief, but precisely *because* I did not believe in it and have always considered it "normal" not to believe in astrology. What led me to approach a study of astrology in India was the desire to try to understand how a subject that plays a secondary role within the Western intellectual paradigm, and is considered a "belief" with no rational foundation, can be seen as rational within another paradigm of thought where it enjoys such high institutional status that it is taught at schools and universities. So, what interests us here is not how true astrology is in itself but the value of the truth this knowledge is invested with within a certain society. In this work, astrology is seen neither as an irrational belief, nor as a superstition, but as a field of "knowledge," and we will try to understand the meaning and rationality of this knowledge in the context within which it is practiced.

Astrology in South Asia: The Current State of Research

Although treatises on horoscopes and divination represent a very prolific area of Sanskrit literature, and the importance of astrology in Indian society is well known to every specialist of the region, astrology has long occupied a marginal position in South Asian studies. In part, this marginality can be attributed to the interstitial position astrology occupies as a subject. Its empirical foundation is too weak to set it among the "sciences" like astronomy, mathematics, chemistry, or the natural sciences. Because its theological, ritual, or devotional aspects are only optional, it is not recognized as a full-fledged religious subject. Its language is too scholarly and technical to arouse the interest of anthropologists, too abstract to be seen as an applied science like medicine, law, or architecture, and too arid and dogmatic to be appreciated by specialists of literary and philosophical studies. Hence astrology does not easily fit into the academic disciplinary divisions that exist within the human and social sciences.[18] So although popular works on "Indian," "Hindu," or "Vedic" astrology, for enthusiasts or practitioners, continue to proliferate and represent an important proportion of the sales in Indian, European, and American bookshops, there are still very few studies that provide a historical or anthropological view on astrological practices in the past or today.[19]

Indian astronomy, on the contrary, has always been clearly and univocally affiliated to the disciplinary field of the "sciences." Because of the ideological issues related to the dating of Indian celestial observations—their antiquity could invalidate the date of Creation established in the Bible—India's astronomy was the focus of fervent Orientalist debates in the eighteenth and nineteenth centuries.[20] During the colonial period, Indian astronomy received special attention as, for the British administration, the teaching and transmission of scientific knowledge was one of the privileged instruments of government of the colonized nation. In an attempt to discover whether the Indians were more or less skilled in a science comparable but of course inferior to that known to the Europeans, the publication and translation of astronomical treatises (*siddhānta*) were strongly encouraged, not only by the European Orientalists but also by Indian scholars involved in projects of intellectual cooperation.[21] The interest in these treatises continued into the postcolonial period, a time when the history of astronomy was fully recognized as a part of the Indian nation's scientific heritage, and it continues to be of lasting interest to historians of science from all horizons as is evident in the regular publication of reference works in this area.[22]

Although in Sanskrit literature, astronomy, astrology, and divination are in fact three branches of a same discipline, *jyotiṣa*, few authors have approached a study of the astral discipline in its totality, attributing equal importance to divinatory content as to mathematical and scientific data.[23] The contribution made by David Edwin Pingree, the historian of science, has been invaluable in this area. Seeking to respect the holistic nature of the discipline, he produced a monumental review and critical edition of the astrological and divinatory manuscripts, thus laying the groundwork for a new field of study.[24] Despite the mine of materials his research reveals, and the stimulating questions it raises, one can regret that few philological and historical works have since contributed to illuminating the innumerable areas of the history of astral sciences that remain unknown. Pingree's approach is, in fact, that of a historian of science who, with his vast erudition, examines the process of transmission of astral literature not only within the Indian tradition but also between the Indian and the Babylonian, Greek, Latin, Persian, and Arabic worlds. Nonetheless, one could approach the Indian corpus from other analytical standpoints. To take one example, the question of the connections and conceptual exchanges between astronomy, astrology, and divination remains largely unexplored (how were these branches articulated at a theoretical level and when, how, and why would Brahmin pandits specialize in one or the other?). Although Pingree describes over one hundred thousand manuscripts, we still know too little about the social identity of their authors, the conditions under which they were produced, and the practical use they were put to.[25] Some significant progress in this huge field of study was recently made by Christopher Minkowski, Michio Yano, Bill Mak, Marko Geslani, Martin Gansten, and Kenneth Zysk. Because of their publications, one may hope that new generations of scholars interested in the history of Indian astrology and divination will come in the next decades.

Art historians who have studied the iconographic representations of the planetary deities have made an important contribution to the study of exchanges between astrology and other fields of knowledge in India.[26] Indeed, from the first centuries of our era onward, the planets described in the treatises on horoscopy have been progressively included in the Hindu pantheon to become gods in their own right that are to be appeased and propitiated. Through an analysis of epic and ritual literature describing the planetary deities and their worship, as well as their sculpted representations in temples, these studies reveal how astrological ideas were assimilated and translated into ritual and devotional practices.

As a subject that plays a major role in the life of the Hindus, astrology has also aroused the interest of anthropologists, although ethnographic studies in this area are surprisingly rare, particularly given the visibility of this social phenomenon. One notes that it is only very late, around the 1980s, with the publication of works of Steven Kemper, Judy Pugh, and R. S. Perinbanayagam[27] that astrology comes to be considered a subject worth studying in the field of South Asian anthropology. These studies are noteworthy as they lift astrology out of the field of "superstition" and bring it into the domain of culture. Nonetheless, their ethnographic description is not as thick as one would expect. The analysis of astral cosmology is mainly approached from a symbolic and disembodied anthropological perspective, in which the work of the astrologer in local society is only briefly touched upon. Since then, apart from the studies by Karin Kapadia and Gilles Tarabout that usefully examine certain astrological practices in Tamil and Kerala society, respectively, the state of research has not evolved as much as one could have hoped given the wealth of South Asian material available.[28] Most anthropological studies dealing with astrology in the Indian world are concerned with the structure of the Hindu calendar that regulates the festivals and activities that punctuate the year.[29] But the social and professional identity of astrologers, the usage horoscopes are put to, the manner in which consultations are conducted, the cult of the planets, the use of precious stones for therapeutic purposes, and many other features, have been little investigated.[30] Although certainly still partial and imperfect, the research presented here is an attempt to fill these gaps, in the hope that other studies in different regions of India will complete the data and analyses gathered here and provide other perspectives on them.

In this work, astrology is apprehended as a knowledge that is *practiced*. The theory of astrology, as described in Sanskrit and Hindi literature, thus interests us to the extent that it becomes a *discourse* that enables the orientation of choices and is translated into *acts* that seek to resolve concrete issues. This approach will allow us to see how astrologers adapt ideas and techniques based on canonical theoretical treatises to the complexity of life in contemporary urban India.

Astrology in Banaras: In the Field

Banaras, today officially known as Vārāṇasī, is a town with about 1,200,000 inhabitants located on the banks of the Ganges River in the eastern part of the state of Uttar Pradesh. A quintessential pilgrimage site, the town of the God Śiva, where Hindus from the whole country go to die in order to obtain liberation (*mokṣa*) from the cycle of reincarnations, Banaras is said to have remained perpetually in *satya yuga*, the primordial golden age. Thus, the constant traffic jams, daily power cuts, roads destroyed by the monsoon, air and water pollution, and acts of extortion committed by the Brahmin priests when they conduct religious acts are so many tests for a devotee, whether inhabitant or pilgrim, who considers this holy town immune to the effects of *kali yuga*, the degenerate era of the contemporary world.[31] As the ethnologist who carries out fieldwork is also to some extent motivated by a form of devotion, I will now try to describe my own *yātrā*, or pilgrimage, to meet astrologers in Banaras.

The ethnographical material presented here was gathered over the course of several field studies conducted in Banaras between 1999 and 2008.[32] During these visits, we mainly used three methods of data collection: questionnaires and interviews; observation, recording and transcription of astrological consultation sessions; translation of texts in Sanskrit or Hindi dealing with astrological theory, the cult of the planets, and other divinatory techniques.[33]

When referring to the means used to collect ethnographic material (apart from the textual works), the use of the pronoun "we" is not merely rhetorical. Sunita was my constant companion. Seated silently and attentively amid the clients in astrologers' offices, looking very "professional" with our notebooks, tape recorder, and video camera, we were sometimes overcome by fits of giggles, brought on by a joke about the astrologer's new hairstyle whispered into the other's ear, or because we suddenly realized, at the same instant, in the middle of an interview, that I had worn my *kurtā* back to front. We spent hours on our bicycles, stuck in traffic jams under the scorching sun, trying to wriggle out from between the scooters, rickshaws, small school buses, roasted peanut vendors, herds of buffalos, and carts of vegetables, both of us exhausted at the idea of having to cross the city to meet an astrologer whose address we had but who may not be at home when we got there. We ate huge dosas (rice pancakes) together at Kerala Café, or went to the confectionery shop, Ksheer Sagar, for a bowl of saffron and pistachio yogurt to restore ourselves after a few hours spent standing in front of the Saturn temple or in the alleys in the center of the town filled with hordes of pilgrims. We spent mornings sitting at the foot of a tree on the green Banaras Hindu University campus, just beside the Astrology Department, noting the details of the interview we had conducted with a professor or a researcher at the department. We spent whole nights locked in a room, in front of a computer taking advantage of the electricity, to continue the transcriptions of the videos of the astrological consultation sessions, interrupting our work every now and then to listen to and sing the latest Bollywood hit. We spent days at Ayurvedic, homeopathic, or "allopathic" doctors' offices to try to discover whether, beyond the *pūjā* and precious stones the astrologers had advised, there was another way to cure my raging fever or the abscess that made my leg swell up. For the "fieldwork" we were always together, Sunita and I. Born the same year, a few months apart, at opposite ends of the world—one in Milan, the other in Banaras—we met at the age of twenty-two in Banaras. We worked together for over ten years, sharing not only the difficulties and satisfactions of the fieldwork but also a warm friendship that filled everything I learned in India over those years with meaning. (Nonetheless, I am obviously entirely responsible for any errors or omissions related to the development of the data gathered over the course of the fieldwork.)

We met with about fifty astrologers (*jyotiṣī*), only two of whom were women, and asked them to fill in a questionnaire on their family and socio-professional identity.[34] The qualitative study, however, was carried out using a limited sample of about a dozen astrologers whose professional practice we followed more closely.[35] The method we adopted when working with these astrologers mainly consisted of recording their astrological consultation sessions—usually with a video camera, sometimes a tape recorder—transcribing the content and seeking further details on each case. We then asked the astrologer to clarify the astrological diagnosis, the client's situation, or the type of remedy prescribed. Sometimes we also contacted and visited the clients, whose addresses we obtained from the astrologers.

Among the fifty astrologers we met, the criterion that dictated our choice of those whose professional practice we wanted to follow closely and regularly was the number of their clientele. An affluent clientele was a particularly significant element for us, as it provided a guarantee of the social legitimacy these professionals enjoyed, as well as allowing us to observe astrologers who were constantly active and at work. As the focus of our survey was not astrological theory in itself but its practice, we concentrated on specialists appreciated for their skill and professional expertise, rather than those renowned for their theoretical knowledge and recognized as famous scholars by a limited circle of cultivated Brahmins.

Another criterion that led us to focus our study on certain astrologers rather than others was, quite pragmatically, the astrologers' attitude to our presence in their consulting rooms. The astrologer needed to be completely at ease with our filming the consultations and had to be available to answer our questions about the cases we recorded. Certain astrologers seemed to be very distrustful and our "curiosity" made them uncomfortable, while others reacted enthusiastically to the idea of being filmed and interviewed throughout their professional day. They enjoyed taking the time to explain all the details of the case we had witnessed.

Our work was evidently facilitated by this latter attitude, and it is mainly this group that is represented in this book. Beyond their natural generosity, these astrologers' willingness to welcome us into their consultation rooms was probably also motivated by the fact that a Westerner with a video camera, filming divinatory declarations, confers a certain prestige and international brilliance upon an astrologer in the eyes of his clients. Nonetheless, this availability also reveals the good faith with which these professionals carry out their work and, moreover, their confidence in the value of their services. Our gaze was a constant examination and judgment of the "truth" of the diagnoses formulated, and the "efficacy" of the treatments prescribed. Accepting our filming of the consultations and our analysis of the contents of the recordings implied that we would possibly have proof of the astrologer's incompetence or dishonesty. But this thought does not seem to ever have crossed the minds of the professionals with whom we worked.

Over our months of assiduous participation in the consultations, for some astrologers we became an integral part of their professional team. Along with the ritual specialists, the secretary, the tea boy, and all the staff that gravitate toward the astrologer, there were also the two ethnographers, one with a video camera, the other with a sound recorder and a notebook. A significant development in this respect is the fact that when my last fieldwork was coming to an end, the astrologer Shree Kanth Shastri asked Sunita to become his assistant. Although Sunita has no specific training in astrology, her familiarity with the astrologer's daily work and her ability to develop empathetic relationships with the clients led the astrologer to ask her to continue to be a part of his professional team, and to learn the profession of astrologer.

When astrologers allowed us to film the consultations, the clients, for their part, never seemed uncomfortable with our presence in the consultation room and they rarely asked us about our work (what seemed to interest them more was to discover whether we were married or single women, or whether I knew Sonia Gandhi). Dialogues between clients and astrologers are not designed as a private and confidential interaction, and most astrological consultations are public sessions that everyone can attend.

Divinatory sessions are very rarely one-to-one discussions. Generally people go to an astrologer as a group: the husband and wife, with or without the children, a parent and a child, a brother and sister, an uncle and his nephew, two or three friends, and so on. During a consultation, it is normally the "companion" who questions the astrologer while the owner of the horoscope, or the person who is having his hand read, just listens, as if there were a sort of modesty involved in the revelation of a destiny. In addition, the owner of the horoscope is often not even present at the consultation and it is close family or friends who ask about his destiny on his behalf. As we will see in many examples throughout this study, women most often go to see the astrologer with the horoscopes of different members of the family, to ask for advice for their children or husbands. Women and men represent a more or less equal proportion of the astrologer's clients, but the women who go generally do so to show the horoscope of someone close to them. On this subject, one astrologer said, "Hindustani women have this quality (*guṇ*), they always want their children to follow the right path, the husband to do the right thing, family members to do the right thing, that's why they go to the astrologer, because they want to know what should or should not be done." Astrology is a means by which women try to enhance their power of intervention in the family situation.

With regard to the social background of astrologers' clients, to start with one must distinguish between those who consult an astrologer on a regular basis, for all kinds of problems, and those who only consult on an occasional basis, for specific reasons. The first category includes families belonging to the middle and upper classes, generally living in urban areas. They have every newborn baby's horoscope calculated and they go to an astrologer regularly to resolve problems or make choices. These clients generally have a high level of education (high school diploma or university degrees) and do not necessarily live in Banaras: they are often families who come from other urban centers in North India, or large Indian metropolises, specifically to consult one of the sacred town's astrologers

In the second category we find poor or low-caste families, who live in Banaras or the surrounding villages and who do not have a horoscope. This type of client uses astrological consultation only in specific circumstances, for example, when they have to arrange a marriage or plan to buy a piece of land. When dealing with this type of client, astrologers use methods of divination other than the horoscope, for example, reading the almanac or geomancy. For common problems and everyday difficulties, these poorer families usually consult an "exorcist" (*ojhā*, *sokhā*) or a "sorcerer" (*tantr-mantr*) instead of an astrologer. These practitioners, who generally belong to the lower castes (particularly the exorcists), attribute their clients' misfortunes to malevolent ghosts (*bhūt-pret*) and acts of sorcery (*ṭonā-ṭoṭkā*) rather than to planetary influences.[36]

Nonetheless, the distinction between different categories of specialists and the distinction between the two categories of clients is in no way rigid. Like exorcists and sorcerers, most astrologers use "tantric" treatments: remedies that are supposed to be efficacious thanks to the supernatural powers (*siddhi*) the specialist who prepares them possesses. They are very economical in comparison to other astrological services and are hence often requested by the poorest families, who may consult an astrologer solely for this type of remedy. Although the more specifically astrological services—reading the horoscope or the hand, identifying "auspicious moments" to undertake new enterprises, prescribing precious stones, and so on—are hence the prerogative of middle- or upper-class clients, astrologers are nonetheless frequently consulted by a poor and low-caste clientele, for whom the diagnostic part of the consultation is greatly reduced and the astrologer's intervention generally consists of preparing a tantric remedy.

This study focuses on professionals who define themselves as *jyotiṣī*. They display this title at the entrance to their office or their home, or on their visiting card, and are recognized as such by their clients. In Banaras, there are some practitioners, generally Brahmins, who have a hybrid identity between astrologer, exorcist, sorcerer, or tantric specialist and who combine a very imperfect notion of astrology with ghost possession, sorcery, and tantric remedies. Over the course of our fieldwork, on several occasions we followed the work carried out by some of these specialists, but we finally decided not to include them in the reflections that make up this study, as their usage of astrological knowledge is very limited. A more fundamental reason for their exclusion was because their clients do not address them as *jyotiṣī*, "astrologer," nor do these specialists claim this professional identity.

In this research we describe methods and techniques commonly employed by the *jyotiṣī*s of Banaras to diagnose and resolve problems. Although individual astrologers may prefer some divinatory techniques or treatments over others, according to our survey, there are no salient differences that may point to the existence of separate "schools" in the way of exercising the profession of astrologer.

All the Banarsi astrologers included in this study are Hindus. Actually, we did not choose to restrict this survey to Hindu professionals, but during the fieldwork we realized that there were no Muslim professional astrologers. Although there are Muslim scholars (*maulvī*) in the town who know, and sometimes even practice astrology, they do not consider themselves, nor do others consider them, "astrologers" (*najūmī*, in Urdu). Hence we chose not to include them in the professional category that is the focus of our study.[37] Within the Islamic tradition, astrology occupies a highly controversial position—it is not taught at Koranic schools as it is at Sanskrit colleges—and in Banaras, Muslim practitioners of divination generally use techniques other than astrology.[38] Nonetheless, although we are keen to distinguish between (Hindu) astrologers and Muslim practitioners of divination, it is important to underscore that when it comes to consulting a specialist of divination, the inhabitants of Banaras do not seem to make communitarian choices. Hindu astrologers have Muslim clients, just as Muslim practitioners have Hindu clients. Astrologers adapt their services to the client's religious identity (and to the client's social and economic situation). Thus, they obviously do not prescribe the celebration of Hindu rituals for a Muslim client, but they do advise them to wear precious stones or tantric amulets. In the same manner, specific consultation methods are designed for Muslim women who find it difficult to go to an astrologer—either because they cannot go out of their homes, or because their family does not believe in the use of astrology. Some Muslim women consult their astrologer solely by correspondence, without ever meeting him personally, while others may see him in their homes, but surreptitiously, as in the case of an astrologer who was told to introduce himself as a homeopathic doctor in order to be allowed to enter certain Muslim homes.

Note on Transliteration, Translation, and Terminology

In this study, I have used three systems of transcription or transliteration. Toponyms, personal names, authors, and editors are generally transcribed according to their anglicized form with no diacritic signs or italics: thus we have Shree Kanth Shastri and not *Śrī kaṇṭha śāstrī*, Chowkhamba and not *Caukhambā*. Nonetheless, the name of the authors of Sanskrit treatises, as well as the names of the Gods, are transliterated with diacritic signs. The standard method for Devanagari transliteration (IAST) is followed for Sanskrit and Hindi. Nevertheless, depending on whether we are citing a Sanskrit text or a conversation in Hindi, a same word may appear

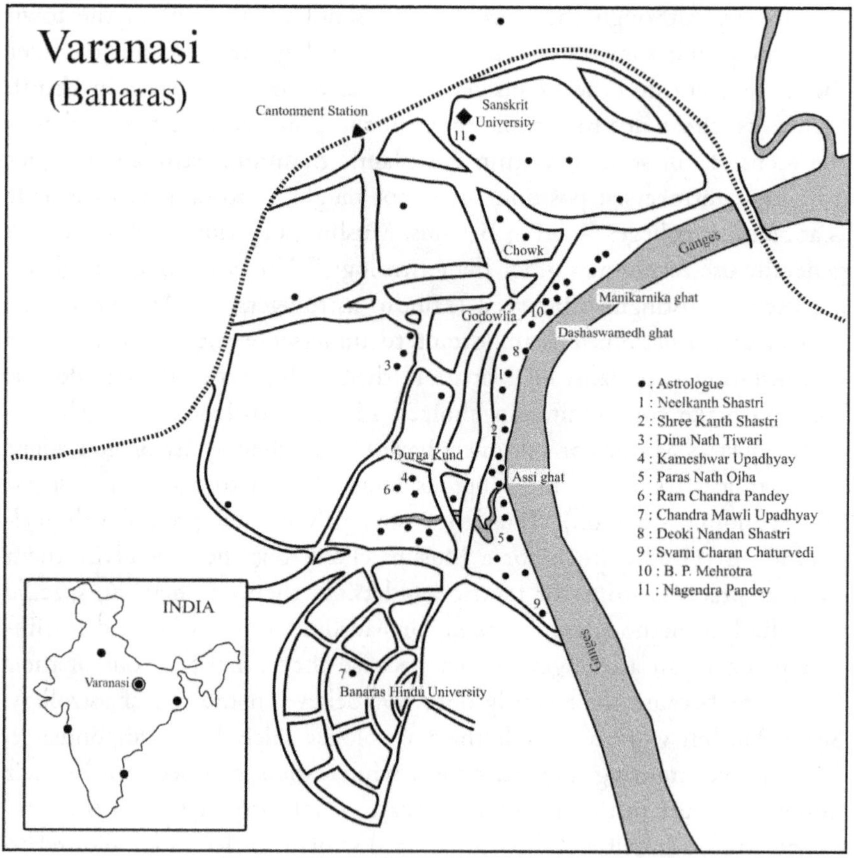

Figure 1. Location of the fifty astrologers participating in the field study and identification of those whose practice was observed.

differently transliterated in this book, according to the context in which it is mentioned: thus, for example, the word *yog*, "planetary conjunction," is transcribed as *yoga* (Sanskrit transliteration) in the translations of passages of Sanskrit astrological treatises and as *yog* (Hindi transliteration) when it is used in dialogues between astrologers and their clients. The English plural marker "s" is added to Sanskrit and Hindi words when these are used in a sentence in English. Otherwise, when mentioned in parentheses as original-language terms, their uninflected form is preferred.

I am responsible for all translations from Sanskrit and Hindi unless otherwise indicated. Some fundamental terminological choices need to be clarified, though. Today, in Banaras as elsewhere in India, the Sanskrit word *jyotiṣa* and its vernacular variations are commonly used to refer to "astrology." Thus, a *jyotiṣī*, "he who knows *jyotiṣa*," is an astrologer; university degrees in *jyotiṣa* prepare students for the profession of astrologer. Nonetheless, from a textual and historical viewpoint, the word *jyotiṣa*—from *jyotis-*, "celestial light"—refers to a composite discipline that includes mathematics (*gaṇita*), astronomy (*siddhānta*), astrology (*horā* or *phalita*), and divination (*saṃhitā*). In order to take this semantic ambiguity into account, the word *jyotiṣa* will be translated as "astral sciences" (or astral discipline) when it is used in the context of Sanskrit literature and as "astrology" in the other cases. As we will see in the following chapters, far from being an accident of language, the semantic evolution of the term *jyotiṣa* expresses configurations of knowledge and power that took shape in South Asia from the colonial period onward.

Part I

Institutions

Figure 2. The *jyotiṣa* tree and its branches. Illustration taken from the *Jātakapārijāta* of Vaidyanātha, a Sanskrit treatise on natal horoscopy (Chaudhary 1953, 3).

The roots of the *jyotiṣa* tree are (*from left to right*): the Ṛgveda, the Atharvaveda, the Sāmaveda, the Yajurveda, the Upaniṣads, the Purāṇas, and the Tantras. The *jyotiṣa* trunk develops into three branches (*from left to right*): *saṃhitā* (divination), *horā* (horoscopy), and *siddhānta* (astronomy and mathematics). The leaves on each branch are divided into the following:

Saṃhitā:

Treatises on breath (*svara-granthāḥ*).
Discussion of oneirology (*svapna-adhyāya-prakaraṇam*).
Examination of falling lizards (*palli-patana-vicāraḥ*).
Treatises on predicting rain (*vṛṣṭi-vicāra-granthāḥ*).
Effects of good or evil omens as a result of trembling in different parts of the body (*aṅga-sphuraṇa-śubha-aśubhaṃ phalaṃ*).
Treatises on the examination of earth, sites, buildings, and so on (*bhū-śodhanādi-vāstu-granthāḥ*).
Collections of treatises on appeasement rituals (*śānti-grantha-rāśayaḥ*).
Collections of treatises on presages (*śakuna-grantha-rāśayaḥ*).
Study of the auspicious and inauspicious influence of the movement of the planets (*graha-cāra-vaśa-śubha-aśubha-viṣayāḥ*).
Treatises on signs, presages, and marvels (*adbhuta-utpāta-lakṣaṇa-granthāḥ*).
Treatises on physiognomy (*sāmudrika-śāstri-granthāḥ*).
Study of the cost of cheap and expensive substances (*vastu-samargha-mahārgha-vicāraḥ*).

Horā:

Collections of treatises on natal horoscopy (*jātaka-grantha-rāśayaḥ*).
Collections of treatises on the Perso-Arabic art of casting horoscopes (*tājika-grantha-rāśayaḥ*).
Compilation of treatises on the horoscopy of queries (*praśna-grantha-samūhā*).
Collection of horoscopy treatises on auspicious moments (*muhūrta-grantha-rāśayaḥ*).
Studies of lost birth horoscopes (*naṣṭa-jātaka-viṣayāḥ*).
Treatises on the composition of almanacs (*pañcāṅga-nirmāṇa-granthāḥ*).

Siddhānta:

Collections of concise astronomical manuals (*karaṇa-grantha-rāśayaḥ*).
Study of the "bowstring" or the sine (*jyām-iti viṣayāḥ*).
Algebraic studies (*bīja-gaṇita-viṣayāḥ*).
Studies of differential calculus (*calana-kalana viṣayāḥ*).
Studies of arithmetic (*pāṭi-gaṇita-viṣayāḥ*).
Studies of "arc trigonometry" (*cāpīya-trikoṇam-iti viṣayāḥ*).
Geometrical studies (*rekhā-gaṇita-viṣayāḥ*).
Lessons on the spheres (*gola-adhyāyaḥ*).
Studies of "triangles" (*trikoṇam-iti viṣayāḥ*).
Studies of the geometry of the spheres (*golīya-rekhā-gaṇita-viṣayāḥ*).

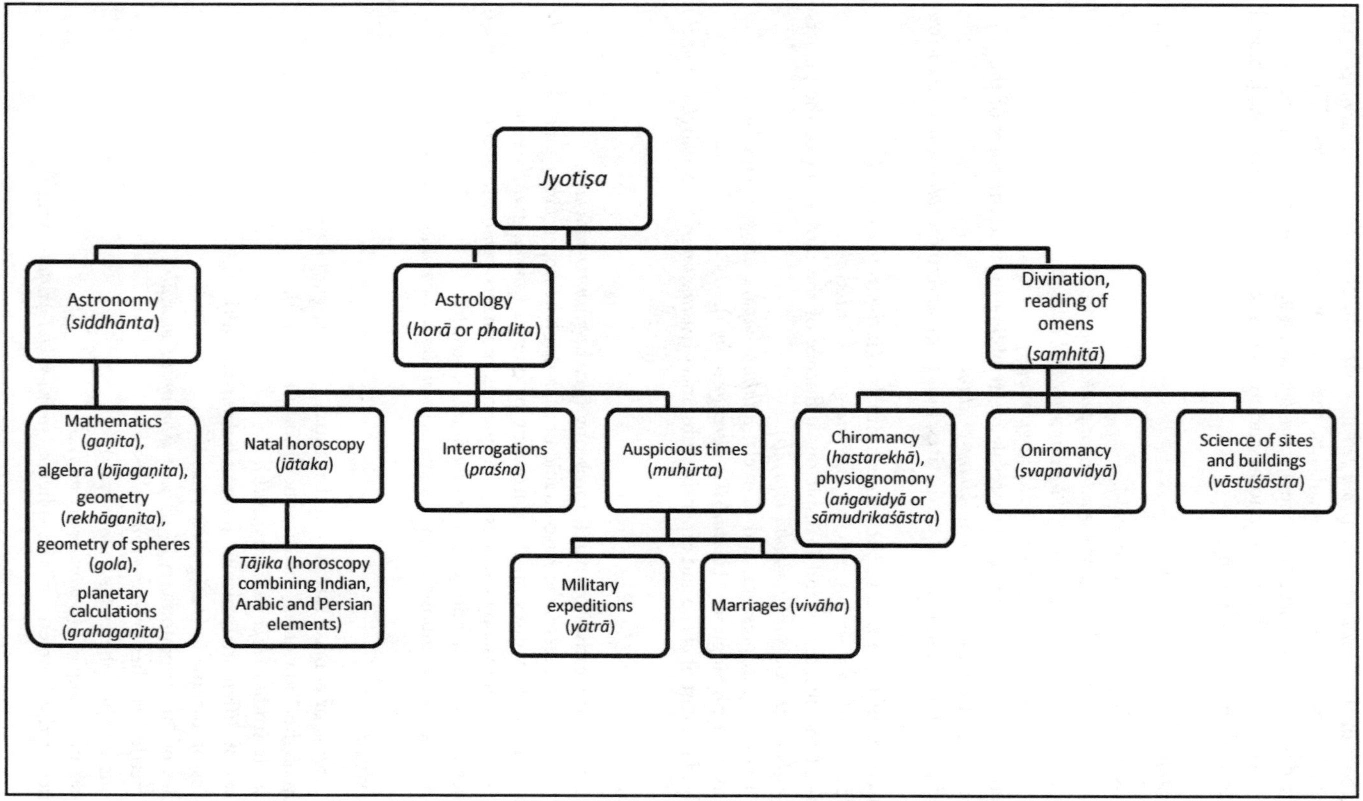

Figure 3. The divisions of the astral discipline. Figure by the author.

1

The Many Branches of a Tree

Jyotiṣa as a Scholarly Tradition

Ideas are to objects as constellations are to stars.

—Walter Benjamin

For someone not familiar with *jyotiṣa*, it may be difficult to think together subjects as different as lunar eclipses, the shape of an elephant's feet, trigonometric calculations, the preparation of a perfume, the theory of planetary aspects, the eruption of rashes on a person's skin, the sexagesimal division of temporal units, and lizards falling. This list may rather remind the reader of the famous Borgesian classification purportedly found in a certain Chinese encyclopedia entitled *Celestial Emporium of Benevolent Knowledge* (Borges 1942) and cited by Foucault as an example of a taxonomy "breaking up all the ordered surfaces and all the planes with which we are accustomed to tame the wild profusion of existing things" (Foucault 1970 [1966], xv). According to standard academic categories of knowledge, these different subjects fall within the competence of disciplines as far removed as astronomy, zoology, mathematics, cosmetology, astrology, or medicine. Nonetheless, in Sanskrit literature these subjects are investigated within a single discipline, *jyotiṣa*, and are described and studied within a literary corpus designed as *jyotiḥśāstra*.[1] The first part of this research intends to examine how, despite the variety of subjects dealt with and the diversity of investigative methods employed, *jyotiṣa* developed over time and continues to be practiced today as a discipline. As we will see, the epistemological identity of *jyotiṣa* is expressed in Sanskrit through terms such as *aṅga*, *vidyā*, *śāstra*, *vijñāna* that are used, at different periods and in different contexts, to refer to *jyotiṣa* as an authoritative form of knowledge.[2]

While, in most studies conducted by Sanskrit scholars, astral sciences and other scholarly traditions are approached as "knowledge systems" (Pollock 2008), here we choose to look at *jyotiṣa* as a "discipline," a category that has a specific analytical fecundity for our study.[3] To start with, the idea of discipline highlights the institutionalized, standardized, and normative dimension of knowledge, more than its theoretical coherence or systematicity; second, this idea makes it possible to articulate the intellectual, institutional, and social aspects of knowledge around a single axis, thus connecting materials as diverse as textual sources, historical documents, and ethnographic data.

The three chapters that make up the first part of this book will consider *jyotiṣa*, respectively, as a *theoretical discipline* described in Sanskrit literature (chap. 1), as an *academic discipline* taught at universities (chap. 2), and as a *professional discipline* practiced by specialists (chap. 3). These three dimensions of the astral discipline should be viewed conjointly. As we shall see, while on the one hand the theoretical complexity of *jyotiṣa*, as it is formulated in the texts, impacts its social implementation, on the other hand, institutional settings and social configurations define the validity of the discipline on the basis of constantly changing criteria and thus affect the manner in which the texts are written, read, and interpreted.

Furthermore, to approach *jyotiṣa* as a discipline implies not viewing it as an isolated subject, circumscribed by impermeable borders. Even if, as Christopher Minkowski observes, "Jyotiṣ was practiced at some remove—in method, assumptions, even in the form of textuality—from the pre-eminent *śāstras*, the sciences of language analysis (*vyākaraṇa*), hermeneutics (*mīmāṃsā*), logic-epistemology (*nyāya*), and moral-legal-political discourse (*dharmaśāstra*)" (2002, 495), it is also true that the astral sciences developed historically and continue to be practiced today in dynamic interaction with ritual, devotional, medical, and architectural ideas. The interdependency between *jyotiṣa* and these fields of knowledge exists both at the conceptual and the operational levels. The first type of interdependency is attested by the existence of numerous technical concepts that, despite their semantic variations, substantially connect astral sciences with other areas of thought. One only needs to mention the concepts of *graha*, *doṣa*, *yoga*, or *ariṣṭa* that play a crucial role not only in astrological but also in medical, tantric, and devotional literature, although their meaning varies from one field to another.[4] A functional interdependency is explicitly formulated in the texts as, from the outset, *jyotiṣa* was envisaged as a pragmatic discipline to ensure the success of ritual, therapeutic, or agricultural activities. The representation and worship of planetary deities is also an "interdisciplinary" subject described not only in astrological treatises but also in iconographic, ritual, devotional, and tantric literature.

David Pingree's monumental work (1970–1994) of classifying, identifying, and dating astral literature, and his critical editions of the *Yavanajātaka* (Pingree 1978a; YJ) and the *Vṛddhayavanajātaka* (Pingree 1976), represent a valuable starting point for the history of *jyotiḥśāstra* in India. These studies allow us not only to situate the Sanskrit astrological texts in relation to each other, but also to understand their development in the light of the exchanges between different civilizations. Few areas of the history of knowledge show, as *jyotiṣa* does, such a wealth of intellectual exchanges between Babylonian, Greek, Latin, Arabic, Persian, and Sanskrit sources. In India as elsewhere, this form of knowledge develops over a long process of borrowing, translations, and interpretations that Pingree's invaluable research allows us to follow in all its details.[5] Nonetheless, as Francis Zimmermann remarks in his review of Pingree's critical edition of the YJ (1978a), "in this commentary the *internal* comparisons of Sanskrit literature are subordinated to the *external* comparison between India and its neighbours. . . . [The] analysis of the Sanskrit terms in their Sanskrit context is somewhat sacrificed to the search for sources and borrowings" (Zimmermann 1981, 300). By describing the impact of stereotyped nomenclatures of Ayurvedic medicine on the classification system established in the horoscopy treatises, Zimmermann (1981) opens up a research path that has been little explored since, which consists of studying the interactions between literature on the planets and other domains of knowledge found in Sanskrit literature.[6] In the wake of this research, rather than underscoring the borrowing of external elements, the present work is more interested in the "local" anchorage of astrological knowledge, or its cultural and social rootedness in the South Asian region.

The exchanges with ritual, medical, and cosmological systems of knowledge are of particular interest to us here as a means to understand the criteria that support the intellectual legitimacy of the astral discipline. In both ancient texts and contemporary debates this legitimacy is most often based not only on criteria that exist within the discipline, like the respect for textual authority, but also on the relationship—of complementarity, contradiction, or reciprocal influence—between *jyotiṣa* and other forms of knowledge accepted as valid or true. We will see that as early as the first centuries of our era, the authors of treatises on the art of casting horoscopes (*jātakaśāstra*) attempt to reconcile the theory of planetary influences with another Brahmanical doctrine that serves to explain human destiny, the theory of karma (chap. 5). About *jyotiṣa* and Purāṇas, Minkowski has shown that the question of compatibility (*avirodha*) or incompatibility (*virodha*) between the models of the cosmos described in the astronomical treatises (*siddhānta*) and the cosmology of the Purāṇas raised questions for the authors of the early modern period and was vividly debated during the modern period (Minkowski 2001 and 2002). Another subject, also central to the conflictual discussions between the British administrators and the Brahmin pandits in Banaras, is the relationship between astrology and modern science. Even today in Banaras it is the driving force behind academic research projects that seek to confirm the compatibility between astrology and biomedicine (chap. 2).

Making no claims of being exhaustive, this first chapter identifies the periods in Sanskrit literature when the limits of *jyotiṣa*'s field of investigation were defined, and the astral discipline underwent a process of positioning, repositioning, and adaptation with regard to other types of knowledge. This investigation based on textual history lays the groundwork for the following chapters and helps us grasp the terms of the debate concerning the institutionalization of *jyotiṣa* in universities, from the colonial period to date. It also throws light on the complexity of contemporary astrological practices at the crossroads of the religious and medical fields.

An Auxiliary Discipline

Just as the term "discipline" means not only a subject of learning but also a branch of knowledge included in a configuration of different types of knowledge, the term used in Vedic literature to describe the astral science is *aṅga*, which means both "limb" and "body." From the outset *jyotiṣa* is referred to not only as a "body" of knowledge on its own but also, and primarily, as a "limb" attached to a larger body of knowledge, the Vedas. Along with phonetics (*śikṣā*), grammar (*vyākaraṇa*), etymology (*nirukta*), meter (*chandas*), and the science of instructions dealing with the execution of rituals (*kalpa*), *jyotiṣa* is one of the six auxiliary disciplines of the Vedas, known as *vedāṅgas* ("limbs" of the Vedas).

The astral discipline is characterized as much by its object of study—the "celestial light" (*jyotis-*) and the "rules of time" (*kālavidhāna*)—as by its function in relation to the Vedas. This function is clearly stated in the *Jyotiṣavedāṅga* (JV) or *Vedāṅgajyotiṣa*, the oldest treatise on *jyotiṣa* that has come down to us. It was probably composed close to the year 400 BCE, but it describes older astronomical data. As stated in the JV, the study of celestial bodies and the identification of a calendar system are "for the purpose of determining the proper time for sacrifices" (*yajñakālārthasiddhaye*) (RJV 3, YJV 2).[7] According to a passage in this text:

> The Vedas indeed go forth for the sake of the sacrifices (*yajña*), and sacrifices are prescribed in accordance with time (*kālānupūrvya*); therefore, only he who knows *jyotiṣa*, the science of proper time (*kālavidhānaśāstra*), knows the sacrifices. (YJV 3; RJV 36)

Astral science is thus established as heuristic knowledge, knowledge in the service of the Vedas, the science of sacrifice. Although it plays an auxiliary role, *jyotiṣa* is in no way conceived as an accessory or a marginal discipline.[8] On the contrary, from Vedic times onward, a relationship of reciprocal interdependency is established between ritual science and the astral discipline: just as *jyotiṣa*'s raison d'être lies in supporting rituals, rituals cannot be carried out without the help of the science of time. Thus today, just as in the past, every Brahmin priest has to study *jyotiṣa* in order to be capable of identifying the auspicious times for all kinds of rituals to succeed—festivals, *saṃskāras* (perfective life cycle rites), domestic rites, and so forth.

In the *Jyotiṣavedāṅga* auspicious moments are identified using a five-year lunisolar cycle (*yuga*). According to Achar (1997), this temporal unit may be an echo of the fivefold structure (*pāṅkta*) of Vedic sacrifices.[9] Despite its concise form and somewhat obscure passages, the JV is the only treatise that provides a systematic presentation of astronomical data from the preclassical period, and it can be seen as the first ancestor of the lunisolar calendars (*pañcāṅga*) that are still calculated and published in different regions of India today. It also contains a system for dividing up the year (*saṃvatsara*) into two six-month halves (*ayana*) that correspond respectively to the Sun's passage through the northern (*uttarāyaṇa*) and southern (*dakṣiṇāyana*) hemispheres; the six seasons (*ṛtu*); the lunar months (*candramāsa*); the lunar fortnights or syzygies (*parva*, *pakṣa*), respectively, "dark" (*kṛṣṇa*) or "luminous" (*śukla*); the division of the lunar synodic month into thirty sections (*tithi*); and the addition of the intercalary month (*adhimāsa*). Moreover, the JV describes the Moon's passage through twenty-seven sections of the ecliptic, each measuring 13°20', called *nakṣatra*s or lunar mansions, that play a key role in the definition of auspicious times for ritual activity.[10] Different deities are associated with each *nakṣatra* and their ritual role is clearly indicated:

> According to those who know the *śāstra*s (*śāstrajña*), the deities (*devatā*) of the *nakṣatra*s should indeed replace the name of the sacrificer (*yajamāna*) while performing sacrifice.[11] (RJV 28; YJV 35)

Table 1. Correspondence between *Nakṣatra*s (Lunar Mansions) and Vedic Deities (RJV 25–27; YJV 32–34)

Nakṣatra	**Deity**
Kṛttikā	Agni
Rohiṇī	Prajāpati
Mṛgaśīrṣa	Soma
Ārdrā	Rudra
Punarvasū	Aditi
Puṣya	Bṛhaspati
Āśleṣā	Sarpa
Maghā	Pitṛ
Pūrvaphalgunī	Bhaga
Uttaraphalgunī	Aryaman
Hasta	Savitṛ
Citrā	Tvaṣṭṛ
Svātī	Vāyu
Viśākhā	Indrāgni
Anurādhā	Mitra
Jyeṣṭhā	Indra
Mūla	Nirṛti
Pūrvāṣāḍhā	Āpas
Uttarāṣāḍhā	Viśve devāḥ (all Gods)
Śravaṇa	Viṣṇu
Dhaniṣṭhā	Vasu
Śatabhiṣaj	Varuṇa
Pūrvabhadrapadā	Aja ekapāda
Uttarabhadrapadā	Ahir budhnyaḥ
Revatī	Pūṣan
Aśvinī	Aśvin
Bharaṇī	Yama

While the JV is the only treatise specifically dedicated to the astral discipline before the classical period, numerous passages in Vedic literature deal with celestial phenomena and reveal an interest in the manner in which astral bodies affect human affairs.[12] Although in these passages astral discourse is not systematic and does not constitute a "discipline," a specialized field of knowledge is recognized by the name *nakṣatravidyā*, "knowledge of the *nakṣatras*" (*Chāndogya Upaniṣad* 7.1.2, 7.7.1), and practitioners of this subject are described as *nakṣatradarśa*, "observers of *nakṣatras*," "stargazers." In the Saṃhitās and the Brāhmaṇas a privileged relationship is established between the position of the Moon among the *nakṣatras* and the success of human activity.[13] This is true of sacrifice—particularly the rite of *agnyādhāna* (establishing sacrificial fires), which must absolutely be performed under favorable *nakṣatras*—as well as of weddings and agricultural activities.[14] According to the ṛgvedic hymn that describes the marriage between Sūryā and Soma (10.85), the offering of goods to the groom's family must be carried out when the Moon is in Aghā *nakṣatra*, and the bride must go to the husband's home just after the wedding, during Arjunī *nakṣatra*.[15] Thus, according to the *Taittirīya Brāhmaṇa* (2.13), land must be labored when the Moon is in Anurādhā *nakṣatra*.[16] The different *nakṣatras* are classified as being either *puṇya* "auspicious" or *pāpa* "malefic" (*Taittirīya Brāhmaṇa* 1.5.2.1, 3.1.2.8), and each of these constellations is associated with a Vedic deity. It also describes forms of astrolatry: propitiatory rituals called *nakṣatreṣṭi* are dedicated to the lunar mansions and consist of offerings of sacrificial oblations, accompanied by invocatory formulae (Dumont 1954).

In some divinatory treatises composed around the beginning of our era, like the Buddhist treatise *Śārdūlakarṇāvadāna*, the Jaina *Sūriyapaṇṇatti*, and the somewhat earlier *Gārgīyasaṃhitā* or *Gārgīyajyotiṣa* (Mitchiner 1986; Geslani et al. 2017), the *nakṣatravidyā*, "science of the lunar mansions," of the Vedic period takes the form of an actual lunar astrology in which individual and collective destinies are studied on the basis of the *nakṣatra* where the Moon is located (Pingree 1981, 68–69; Mak 2019b: 53). From the eighth century onward, it develops into a specialized branch of the astral discipline called *muhūrtaśāstra* that focuses on identifying the "auspicious times" (*muhūrta*) for undertaking human activities. Sanskrit treatises on *muhūrta* describe auspicious times for performing different types of rituals such as sacrifices (*yajña*), rites of passage in the life cycle (*saṃskāra*), royal consecration (*rājābhiṣeka*), or installation of divine images (*devapratiṣṭhā*). The range of activities regulated by the science of *muhūrta* also includes military expeditions (*yātrā*), agriculture (*kṛṣi*), and rituals to mark the foundation of a site (*vāstu*) or a house (*gṛha*). As we will see, even today's lunisolar calendars (*pañcāṅga*), published in different parts of India, apply the concept of *muhūrta* to a wide range of human activities that are not just ritual and agricultural but also commercial, artistic, therapeutic, intellectual, or procreative.

Through the science of *muhūrta*, *jyotiṣa* grew into an auxiliary discipline serving several types of knowledge and skills such as architecture, medicine, or performing arts, where the successful accomplishment of activities is subject to undertaking them when auspicious astral conditions prevail. Thus, for example, the *Carakasaṃhitā*, one of the founding treatises of Ayurvedic theory, indicates that the study of medicine must commence during Puṣya, Hasta, Śravaṇa, or Aśvinī *nakṣatra* (*Carakasaṃhitā* 3.8; see also *Suśrutasaṃhitā* 2.4); the *Suśrutasaṃhitā* discourages doctors from beginning a therapeutic treatment during Kṛttikā, Ārdrā, Āśleṣā, Maghā, Mūla, Pūrvaphalgunī, Pūrvāṣādha, Pūrvabhadrapadā, and Bharaṇi *nakṣatra*s (*Suśrutasaṃhitā* 2.29.18–19).[17]

Originally focusing on the study of the calendar, lunar mansions, and auspicious times, during the first centuries of our era *jyotiṣa* becomes a full-fledged and complex textual discipline (*śāstra*) containing numerous interconnected branches and subbranches.

Cosmological Associations

In the first centuries of our era, the assimilation of horoscopic theory, a system to investigate human destiny borrowed from the Greeks, gives rise to a radical transformation within the astral discipline. As Pingree's works have shown, the Hellenistic and Brahmanical worlds came into contact in the satrapies of Northwestern India during the first centuries of our era, and many elements of the Greco-Babylonian astrological theory were incorporated into Sanskrit. The *Yavanajātaka*, "Horoscopy (*jātaka*) of the Greeks (*yavana*)," composed in 149/150 by Yavaneśvara (The Lord of the Greeks) at the court of Ujjain (Ujjayinī), is, according to Pingree, the translation of a lost Greek treatise, written in Egypt at the beginning of the second century. Although Yavaneśvara's treatise has not come down to us, we have the versified and adapted version, the *Yavanajātaka* by Sphujidhvaja, composed in 269/270 (Pingree 1978a).[18]

Along with a third text attributed to Satya that is now lost, both treatises by Yavaneśvara and Sphujidhvaja introduce a new astrological technique into India based on the observation of the movement of the planets (*graha*)—including the Sun and the Moon—through the twelve zodiacal signs (*rāśi*) and the twelve houses of the zodiac (*bhāva*). Planets that only played a very minor role in the Sanskrit literature before the beginning of our era occupy a major position in astrological speculation in the first centuries (Yano 2003 and 2004). Along with astrological techniques, mathematical and astronomical ideas like the division of the ecliptic into 360 degrees and the sexagesimal fractions for the measurement of arcs and temporal units seem to have been introduced into India with the translation of Greek treatises (Plofker 2009, 49). Nonetheless, these new methods do not replace the lunar astrology of the *nakṣatra*s and the chronological divisions described in the *Jyotiṣavedāṅga* but are integrated into the existing system.

Throughout the process of transmission of horoscopic treatises, the allochthonous theoretical matrix is progressively transformed and developed taking cultural and social specificities of the Indian context into account. Yavaneśvara and Sphujidhvaja's treatises already contain numerous adaptations to Hindu culture. In these works the Hellenistic theory of horoscopy is enriched, not only by the twenty-seven *nakṣatra*s and other elements of Vedic astral knowledge but also with passages referring to the theory of rebirth; the four *varṇa*s classes (*brāhmaṇa*, *kṣatriya*, *vaiśya*, and *śūdra*); the different sects of Hindu and Buddhist ascetics; iconography relating to Śiva, Lakṣmī, and other deities; as well as Ayurvedic medical categories. These adaptations are to proliferate in the astrological literature that follows, with the Greco-Babylonian framework of the horoscope theory progressively adopting a Hindu form. Thus, the planets are described with anthropomorphic features and iconographic attributes that make them similar to Hindu Gods. They go from being seven (Sun, Moon, Mars, Mercury, Jupiter, Venus, and Saturn) to nine, the *navagraha*s (nine planetary deities), following the introduction of the two pseudo-planets Rāhu, the demon of the eclipse, and Ketu, the personification of comets (Markel 1995).[19]

The process of adapting and appropriating the Greco-Babylonian theory of horoscopes within Sanskrit literature also appears in the development and refinement of horoscopic techniques such as the calculation of longevity (*āyurdāya*), the system of the subdivision (*varga*) of signs, the theory of aspects (*dṛṣṭi*), and the system of *daśā*s (planetary periods), which acquire specific characteristics and particular importance in Indian astrology. Other technical innovations are also introduced through contributions from Perso-Arabic astrology (*tājika*), tantric astrology, or regional astrological schools based in Kerala or Tamil Nadu.

The successful "graft" of the matrix of allochthonous horoscopy onto Hindu culture cannot be explained solely by the progressive adaptations within astrological theory but should also be examined in light of some conceptual affinities that link horoscopic theory to the cosmology of Vedic ritual. Thus the Greek principle of melothesia, according to which the signs of the zodiac are associated with different parts of cosmic man, perfectly matches the Vedic idea of the association between the different parts of the body of the primordial man (*puruṣa*) and cosmological elements. This idea is expressed in the very first verse of the *Jyotiṣavedāṅga* where the body of Prajāpati, primordial man, is said to be made up of temporal divisions of the five-year lunisolar cycle (*yuga*):

> Purified, saluting with [bent] head the presider (*adhyakṣa*) over the cycle (*yuga*) lasting five years (*pañcasaṃvatsara*), Prajāpati, whose body is made of days (*dina*), seasons (*ṛtu*), semesters (*ayana*), and months (*māsa*) [I shall systematically tell the movement of the luminaries]. (RJV 1; YJV 1)

In horoscopic theory, just as in Vedic ritual, a vast network of correspondences is established between the celestial macrocosm and the human microcosm. In the *Yavanajātaka*, a network of correspondences connects the zodiacal signs, the parts of the body, the planets, the directions, the five elements, the weekdays, the principles of existence (*sattva*), the humors (*doṣa*), the qualities (*guṇa*), the sexes, the social classes (*varṇa*), positions at the royal court, colors, relations of kinship, months of gestation, plants, moods, the letters of the alphabet, minerals, metals, as well as different types of objects (*dravya*) and houses. This system of correspondences is gradually extended throughout the transmission of astrological treatises to include categories such as the seasons, the senses (*indriya*), the deities, the savors (*rasa*), the Vedas, animals, the regions of India, occupations, clothes, precious stones, cereals, trees, diseases, and others. According to this cosmology every element belonging to a category is associated with one or several elements belonging to other categories. Thus, for example, the planet Mars is related to the zodiacal signs Aries and Scorpio, the color red, the element fire, the bilious humor, the quality *rajas*, the *varṇa kṣatriya*, and so on.

The astrological principle by which connections are established between series of elements belonging to different orders of the cosmos shows a certain isomorphism with the theory of Vedic ritual. As Louis Renou remarks in his article "Connexion en védique, cause en bouddhique," Vedic thought is defined as a system of correlations: "correlations between the microcosm and the macrocosm, between the ritual world and the mythical world, between the human order and the divine order" (1978, 149). The correlation between different levels—the human and the divine, the microcosm and the macrocosm—occurs "due to the connection," *nidānena*, as the word *nidāna* means "a connection based on the identity between two things located at two different levels" (Renou 1978, 151).[20] In *Instant et cause*, Lilian Silburn gives a detailed description of the system of cosmological connections established within the Brahmanical sacrificial system, where Prajāpati's body is linked to the sacrificial altar, the meter of the prayers, the seasons, and the directions (1989, 62–86). According to Brian K. Smith, the systematic effort to establish connections (*nidāna*, *bandhu*) between different cosmological elements represents the very principle that defines "Vedic religion": "As the history of scholarship amply attests, the predominant feature of that religion is an apparent preoccupation with the 'discovery' or constitution of linkages between what others regard as wholly discrete objects, acts or entities. . . . Making connections has served as the defining feature of Vedism as a whole" (1989, 30). Through an analysis of the Vedic cosmogonies, the author attempts to show the correspondences between the cardinal directions, the divisions of the day, the seasons, the Vedas, the meters, metaphysical powers, the *varṇa*s, the Gods, the *ṛṣi*s, animals, the parts of the body, chants, hymns of praise, ritual specialists, and other categories. Vedic thought can be seen as characterized by a principle of "resemblance" thanks to which "*essential affinities*" are established between different entities, objects, powers, activities, and cosmic levels (Smith 1989, 47).[21] In the same manner, a relationship of "resemblance" connects the cosmological elements within astrological thought, and these are grouped around semantic clusters familiar to Indianists. Thus ignorance, the *tamas guṇa*, the *śūdra varṇa*, the color black, the role of the slave, old age, the God Yama, suffering, waste, all define a semantic field around the planet Saturn (Guenzi 2005).

Division into Branches

Because of the conceptual innovation that comes with the assimilation of Greco-Babylonian astral sciences at the beginning of our era, a process of differentiation progressively emerges within the astral science. Genethlialogy or natal astrology (*jātaka*), astronomy (*siddhānta*), as well as divination or reading of omens (*saṃhitā*, "collection" or "compilation") appear as distinct fields of knowledge. Nonetheless, up to the fifth century, there seems to be no clear distinction between the three genres or branches, and the texts of this period, or at least those that have come down to us, are essentially eclectic, even when they can be identified as belonging to one of the aforementioned categories. Thus the *Gārgīyasaṃhitā* (or *Gārgīyajyotiṣa*), a treatise on divination composed at the beginning of our era or earlier, contains data relating to Vedic lunar astrology, astronomical calculations dealing with the movement of the planets, astrological ideas dealing with planetary influence on human affairs, as well as a wide range of divinatory methods related to the reading of vegetal, animal, and meteorological omens (Mitchiner 1986; Geslani et al. 2017). In the *Vṛddhayavanajātaka*, a horoscopy treatise composed by Mīnarāja around 300–325 or later (Mak 2018), astral speculations about the movement and influence of the planets are followed by eight chapters dedicated to the reading of presages: oneiromancy, cynomancy, signs of death, and so on (Pingree 1976). The *Paitāmahasiddhānta*, dating from the beginning of the fifth century, and the oldest *siddhānta* that has come down to us, is also a hybrid treatise, with some chapters dealing with astrology and others describing astronomical or mathematical data (Pingree 1981, 17).[22]

Two major events mark a fundamental shift in the history of astral knowledge in the sixth century. One is the founding of the Āryapakṣa, one of the most important schools of astronomy in the Indian tradition, based on the *Āryabhaṭīya*, the treatise on astronomy and mathematics by Āryabhaṭa (b. 476). The other decisive event of this period, which is more relevant to our topic, is the work produced by Varāhamihira, the famous sixth-century astronomer-astrologer, an unquestioned authority who is still constantly quoted by today's astrologers. Varāhamihira composed a vast and exhaustive work that occupies a crucial place in the history of astral sciences. Unlike the authors who preceded him, he established a clear distinction between the different branches of astral knowledge and, unlike most of those who follow him, he approached *jyotiṣa* as a complete discipline, not limiting himself to studying any specific branch of it. Born at the beginning of the sixth century in the kingdom of Avantī, Varāhamihira descended from a family of Maga Brahmins, a group of priests of Iranian origin, specializing in the cult to Sūrya, the Sun God.[23] His interest in celestial phenomena and his acceptance of an allochthonous and non-Brahmanical science conveyed by the Greeks (*Yavana*), whom he described as *mleccha*s (barbarians, outcastes), may be related to his heterodox social background.[24]

By systematizing the works of the authors who preceded him, Varāhamihira established the canons of a complex and organized discipline, consisting of numerous branches and subbranches. In a passage of the *Bṛhatsaṃhitā* (BS) he describes the divisions of *jyotiṣa* in the following manner:

> Astral science (*jyotiḥśāstra*) is made of several divisions (*bheda*), subjects (*viṣaya*), and three main branches (*skandha*). The subject in its totality has been named "collection" (*saṃhitā*) by the sages; the branch named *tantra* deals with planetary movement (*grahagati*) through mathematical calculations (*gaṇita*); the second branch is called *horā*, and the third *aṅgaviniścaya* (knowledge of body's parts). (BS 1.9)[25]

Although Varāhamihira is still cited today as the authority who established the divisions of the discipline, over the centuries the names of certain branches have undergone variations and new specializations have emerged (see figure 3). We should note that in this passage, the term *saṃhitā* is employed to mean the astral discipline in its totality, as a "collection" of various subjects, just as in Garga's treatise, both titles *Gārgīyasaṃhitā* and *Gārgīyajyotiṣa* are found to be synonymous. In the following centuries, however, the term *saṃhitā* comes to indicate the branch of *jyotiṣa* (called *aṅgaviniścaya* in the preceding passage) specializing in the reading of omens, and the same Varāhamihira uses this meaning in other passages of the same text.[26] During this period, the synonymy between *jyotiṣa* and *saṃhitā* nonetheless deserves to be underscored, in that it shows that these early authors saw astral knowledge as a composite discipline.

The division of *jyotiṣa* into branches structures Varāhamihira's entire literary production, and each of his works is dedicated to a specific section of the discipline. On the field of study he calls *siddhānta*—or *gaṇita*, *tantra*, *karaṇa*—he writes the *Pañca-siddhāntikā*, a treatise that describes "five (*pañca*) astronomical treatises (*siddhānta*)"—*Pauliśa*, *Romaka*, *Vāsiṣṭa*, *Sūrya*, and *Paitāmaha siddhānta*s—composed between the first and sixth centuries of our era (Neugebauer and Pingree 1970–1971).[27] Despite recognizing the unequal value of these five treatises from a scientific viewpoint (*Pañcasiddhāntikā* 1.4), Varāhamihira's doxography aims at circumscribing a field of investigation marked not only by continuity and transmission but also by evolutions and developments. Varāhamihira's comprehensive and didactic approach to the study of astronomy applies also to the branches of astrology and divination. In his horoscopic treatise the *Bṛhajjātaka*, Varāhamihira explains that his work is a "small boat in the form of a treatise" that allows one to cross the "vast ocean" (*mahārṇava*) of astral literature (BJ 1.2). The didactic purpose can be seen in his writing of detailed or "extended" (*bṛhat*) versions of his treatises, as well as synthetic or "abridged" versions (qualified as *laghu*, *samāsa*, *sūkṣma*, or *svalpa*), the latter probably destined for oral study.[28] Thus, in the field of natal horoscopy (*jātaka*), we have the "Complete Book of Horoscopy" (*Bṛhat-jātaka*) and the "Concise Horoscopy" (*Laghu-jātaka*); in the field of divination (*saṃhitā*), the "Major Collection" (*Bṛhat-saṃhitā*) and the "Minor Collection" (*Samāsa-saṃhitā*).

The second chapter of the *Bṛhatsaṃhitā* describes the qualities and skills of a good astrologer (*sāmvatsara*) and indicates the different areas of study that must be mastered by a practitioner. As for the astronomical branch of learning (*graha-gaṇita*), described in *siddhānta* treatises, the astrologer should know how to calculate

> . . . ages (*yuga*), years (*varṣa*), semesters (*ayana*), seasons (*ṛtu*, corresponding to two-months periods), months (*māsa*), fortnights (*pakṣa*), day and night (*ahorātra*), *yāma* (1/8th of a day = three hours), *muhūrta*s (1/30th of a day = forty-eight minutes), *nāḍī* (1/60th of a day = twenty-four minutes), *prāṇa*s ("breath," corresponding to the time requisite for the pronunciation of ten long syllables), *truṭi*s (the time separating two eyes blinking), the smaller units composing a *truṭi*, as well as other divisions of time and space (*kṣetra*). (BS 2.3)

> He should also know the reasons (*kāraṇa*) for the existence of four systems of measurement (*māna*) [of time], that is,

> solar (*saura*), terrestrial (*sāvana*), sidereal (*nākṣatra*), and lunar (*cāndra*), [as well as the reasons explaining] intercalary months (*adhimāsa*) and the difference between solar and lunar months (*avama*). (BS 2.4)

> In spite of the differences (*bheda*) in astronomical treatises (*siddhānta*) regarding the end of semesters (*ayana-nivṛtta*, the solstitial points), [the astrologer] should be able (*kuśala*) to demonstrate in a visible way that the latitudes (*aṃśaka*) of sun rising (*abhyudita*) and the conjunctions (*samprayoga*) described on the *samamaṇḍala* ("prime vertical," or the great circle passing through the zenith, as well as the east and west points on the horizon) correspond to the observation (*dṛggaṇita*) made through the "shadow instrument" (*chāyā-yantra*) and the water clock (*jala-yantra*). (BS 2.7)

The branch of astronomy described by Varāhamihira also includes calculating sixty-year cycles (*ṣaṣṭyabda*), eclipses (*grahaṇa*), planetary orbits (*kakṣyā*), the earth's rotation around its axis (*bhūbhagaṇa*), latitude (*akṣa*), and other parameters that enable the measurement of the movement of the stars in space and time, using instruments (*yantra*) (BS 2.3–12). These subjects are investigated over the centuries in the five principal "schools" (*pakṣa*) of astronomy—*Brāhma*, *Ārya*, *Ārdharātrika*, *Saura*, and *Gaṇeśa*—differentiated mainly by the method of calculating divisions of time within the cosmic cycles (*kalpa*).[29] The almanacs published today in the different regions of India still refer to one or the other of these schools.

While Varāhamihira employs terms like "computation" (*gaṇita*), "measure" (*māna*), "demonstration" (*pratipādana*), "cause" or "processes" (*karaṇa*) to characterize the branch of astronomy, in his description of astrological divisions (*horāśāstra*) he favors terms such as "prediction" (*ādeśa*), "comprehension" (*parigraha*), "identification" (*nirdhāraṇa*), as well as "fruit" or "effect" (*phala*). The following are the subjects included in the astrological or horoscopic (*horāśāstra*) branch, and their role in an astrologer's training:

> In *horāśāstra* [are included] the understanding of the strength (*bala*) and weakness (*abala*) of the planets (*graha*) in the zodiacal signs (*rāśi*) and their divisions (*bhāga*): *horā*s (half sign),

> *dreṣkāṇa*s (a third of a sign), *navāṃśa*s (a ninth of a sign), *dvādaśāṃśa*s (a twelfth of a sign), and *triṃśāṃśa*s (a thirtieth of a sign); the identification of different types of planetary strength, according to their direction (*diś*), place (*sthāna*), time (*kāla*), and movement (*ceṣṭa*); the understanding of natural dispositions (*prakṛti*), bodily elements (*dhātu*), substances (*dravya*), castes (*jāti*), functions (*ceṣṭa*), and other characteristics [of planets and zodiacal signs]; the assured prediction (*pratyayādeśa*) about the conception (*niṣeka*), the time of birth (*janmakāla*), prodigious births (*vismāpana*), as well as immediate deaths (*sadyomaraṇa*), life's length (*āyurdāya*), planetary periods (*dāśa*) and subperiods (*antardāśa*), *aṣṭakavarga*s (eighth divisions [a system of prediction based on planetary transits]); effects (*phala*) of planetary conjunctions (*yoga*), such as royal conjunctions (*rājayoga*), lunar conjunctions (*candrayoga*), conjunctions between two planets (*dvigrahayoga*), and so on, as well as celestial conjunctions (*nābhasayoga*)[30] and others; according to the zodiacal sign, the house (*bhāva*), and planetary aspects (*avalokana*), [the astrologer should predict] death, the way to other worlds, and previous existences (*anūka*); auspicious and inauspicious (*ṣubhāśubha*) omens (*nimitta*) concerning immediate interrogations (*praśna*) as well as [auspicious moments] for marriages (*vivāha*) and the performance of other rituals (*karman*). (BS 2.17)

Without explicitly naming them, this passage evokes the three subdivisions of astrology (*horā*, *phalita*) that are to develop in the following centuries (see figure 3). They are genethlialogy or natal horoscopy (*jātaka*) that studies the effect of the astral configurations at the time of birth; horary astrology or the astrology of interrogations (*praśna*) that studies the signs (astral, terrestrial, or corporeal) detected at the time one asks a question to the astrologer; and then elective astrology, or the astrology of "appropriate moments" (*muhūrta*) that studies the auspicious astral conditions and omens for the success of rituals and other undertakings.[31] This latter branch further consists of two sections—marriages (*vivāha*) and military expeditions (*yātrā*).[32]

These days military astrology is little used, but until the colonial period it was extremely important, as kings did not start a war or a strategic operation without the astrologer's approval.[33] In his description of the astrologer's skills, Varāhamihira thus provides a detailed enumeration of the subjects that fall within military astrology (*yātrā*) (BS 2.18). This field deals not only with the study of astral configurations but also with the prescription of propitiatory rituals to be performed by the king—sacrifices offered to the planets (*grahayajña*) or other groups of deities (*gaṇayāga*), ablutions to be carried out before starting a battle (*vijayasnāna*, "victory bath"). It also includes the reading of different types of omens: trembling of a part of the body (*dehaspandana*), dreams (*svapna*), the flame in the fire (*agniliṅga*), the movement of elephants and horses (*hastyaśveṅgita*), the proclamations of the army's commanders (*senāpravāda*), their behavior (*ceṣṭā*), and other military events. The astrologer should also be able to determine the planetary conditions for implementing the sixfold strategy (*ṣāḍguṇya*) and methods (*upāya*) of foreign policy;[34] favorable and unfavorable omens (*maṅgalāmaṅgalaśakuna*); suitable terrains for military camps (*sainyaniveśabhūmi*); the color of fire (*agnivarṇa*); the investigation of the appropriate time (*yathākālam*) for the employment of ministers (*mantri*), spies (*cara*), messengers (*dūta*), and foresters (*āṭavika*); as well as strategies for laying siege to enemy fortresses (*paradurgopalambha*). An astrologer to a king needs to master all these features of his art (BS 2.18).

The treatises dedicated to the study of auspicious times (*muhūrta*)—one example being those dealing with military astrology—combine the use of horoscopic techniques with the examination of omens. They thus represent a sort of link between astrology and the third branch of *jyotiṣa*, divination (*saṃhitā*). The latter looks at natural omens (*nimitta*, *utpāta*, *adbhuta*, *śakuna*, *lakṣaṇa*) studied through a thorough examination of the empirical characteristics of astral and meteorological phenomena, vegetal and mineral substances, animal and human characteristics, and manufactured objects. Varāhamihira provides a long list of omens that every qualified astrologer must be able to identify and decipher (BS 2.21). The planetary conjunctions of the Sun, the Moon, the planets, the zodiacal signs, the *nakṣatra*s, and other types of celestial phenomena (eclipses, comets, shooting stars, etc.) are also studied to know the future of kings and kingdoms and the prosperity of populations, harvests, and animals. Among the atmospheric signs, clouds, parhelions, solar and lunar halos, red skies, winds, meteors, rainbows, storms, and lightning should be examined. The characteristics of flowers, creepers, and trees, as well as those of different kinds of soils and precious stones—pearls, rubies, and emeralds—are also included in the *saṃhitā*. Particular attention is paid to the behavior and characteristics of animals—dogs, chickens, sheep, cows, horses, elephants, birds, among others—and to human beings' phenotypic features: their height and the shape of the parts of the body, birthmarks, pimples, and so forth. Among the daily objects that are vectors of meaning, the *saṃhitā* looks closely at clothes, shoes, parasols, beds, seats, lamps, flywhisks, toothpicks, sticks, and crowns.

The signs that can arise from the earth or in the sky are so numerous, continues Varāhamihira, that "it is not possible, for a single person, day and night, to perceive all omens" (BS 2.21). To ensure that the examination is reliable and exhaustive, the author advises setting up a system that could be qualified as "panoptic." The royal astrologer should coordinate the work of four assistant astrologers. Each of them should be responsible for a division of the celestial and earthly environment based on the eight directions (*diś*). The first is thus responsible for recording and examining the omens that manifest themselves in the east and the southeast, the second for those in the south and southwest, the third those in the west and northwest, and the fourth those found in the north and northeast. In this way no omen can escape notice (BS 2.21). Nonetheless, *saṃhitā* does not consist solely of identifying and interpreting omens. The texts relating to this branch also indicate the rules to be followed in areas as varied as the preparation of a perfume, the building of a house, the installation of a divine image, the performance of a propitiatory ritual, the seduction of women, the treatment of tree diseases, or the preparation of adamantine glue.

The Unity of the Discipline

This brief description of the branches that compose *jyotiṣa*, as they are described by Varāhamihira in the sixth century and still referred to today, reveals the highly eclectic nature of this discipline that assembles a wide variety of epistemological approaches and fields of investigation. The image opening this chapter, taken from a recent edition of a horoscopy manual dating from the fifteenth century, the *Jātakapārijāta* by Vaidyanātha (Chaudhary 1953), is a good illustration of the diverse types of knowledge included in *jyotiṣa*. Areas of investigation range from the falling of lizards to arithmetic, oneirology to the study of the movements of the planetary spheres, from geomancy to horoscopy. The tree of *jyotiṣa* is typically polythetic and the parts that constitute it have no general common property, but they are connected in different ways. The specialties included in this discipline hence maintain Wittgensteinian "family resemblances" with each other. The "study of the favorable and unfavorable influence of the movement of the planets" (*grahacāravaśa-śubhāśubhaviṣayāḥ*), for example, is part of the branch of divination, as in this field celestial phenomena are examined as omens comparable to trembling in parts of the body (*aṅgasphuraṇa*), dreams (*svapna*), or lizards falling (*pallipatana*). This divinatory specialty nonetheless also shares numerous properties with the the horoscopic branch, which also studies planetary movements. However, because of the complexity of the calculations and the astronomical categories they draw upon, horoscopic treatises (*jātakagrantha*) are also connected to the astronomical study of the movement of celestial spheres (*gola*). In turn, this subject shares epistemological and conceptual properties with geometrical (*rekhāgaṇita*) and algebraic (*bījagaṇita*) studies, among others.

To formulate this differently, using Wolf Lepenies expression, one could say that *jyotiṣa* contains "three cultures" or scientific cultures as the exact sciences, the humanities and social sciences, and the natural sciences are all three constitutive of the astral discipline.[35] Without seeking to establish rigid frontiers, we could say that the three branches of *siddhānta*, *horā*, and *saṃhitā*, respectively, represent these three scientific cultures. The first develops the mathematical and geometrical rules, the second questions the relationship between human beings, the society and the cosmos, while the third investigates the empirical properties of vegetal and mineral substances, animal species, human bodies, atmospheric phenomena, and so on.

Although there are major epistemological, methodological, and conceptual differences between the three branches of *jyotiṣa*, its unity and cohesion as a discipline are visible at several levels. To start with, it is important to emphasize that, historically, the different branches do not develop autonomously. The introduction of horoscope theory at the beginning of our era gives the development of astronomy a major impetus with an aim to making horoscopes more precise. Most astronomical treatises (*siddhānta*) contain a section, generally the last, on measurements that are of astrological relevance. These include planetary conjunctions, the position of the planets and the Moon in relation to the *nakṣatra*s, and so forth. "Scientific" and "divinatory" rationality are not seen as antagonistic and incompatible and often progress conjointly. We should note that the mathematical rules governing combinatorial calculus are formulated for the first time in the chapter of the *Bṛhatsaṃhitā* dedicated to the preparation of perfumes (*gandhayukti*) (chap. 76), in which Varāhamihira seeks to calculate how many perfumes can be produced by choosing a number *k* of substances from a number *n* of substances (Hayashi 2003).[36] In the same chapter Varāhamihira also develops the first "numerical diagram" (*aṅkayantra*) or magic square of Indian tradition, a concept that is to be further developed by Indian mathematicians from the premodern period onward (Hayashi 1987).[37]

The different branches of *jyotiṣa* are also connected to each other by technical terms used throughout the discipline, although their signification may vary depending on whether they are used in the fields of astronomy, astrology, or divination. Thus, in the *siddhānta*, the term *muhūrta* means a temporal unit of forty-eight minutes, while in astrological and divinatory treatises it more generally means any moment that is auspicious for undertaking an activity. In an astronomical sense, the term *lagna* indicates the point of intersection between the horizon and the ecliptic, and in its astrological sense, the first house of the horoscope that plays a fundamental role in human destiny. One technical signification does not necessarily exclude another; on the contrary, the semantic shift is often visible, but depending on the type of treatise a particular meaning prevails. Thus, if we take the term *rāśi*, which in astronomical treatises means a 30° curve of the ecliptic, in horoscopic and divinatory treatises it means the zodiacal signs with their iconography (Aries, Taurus, etc.). Similarly, the *nakṣatra*s are both 13°20' divisions of the ecliptic and the twenty-seven "wives of the Moon," or the constellations that exert a more or less favorable influence over human activity.[38]

Besides these conceptual and terminological connections, the cohesion between the different branches of the astral discipline is to be understood at a practical rather than an epistemological, theoretical, or textual level. The history of scientific production in the field of *jyotiḥśāstra* shows the scarcity of authors who, like Varāhamihira, composed works in all three branches of the discipline, as the conceptual and methodological complexity was more conducive to specialization in one or another field of investigation.[39] In terms of social practice, however, every astrologer has to master mathematical, astronomical, and divinatory concepts to be able to satisfy clients' requests. Calculating the yearly calendar, identifying suitable times for human activities, foreseeing eclipses, preparing horoscopes, reading meteorological and natural omens, as well as the other tasks astrologers have accomplished over the centuries, demand skills drawn from different fields of the astral discipline.

All the learning indispensable to the practice of the profession of astrologer is to be found in the almanac (*pañcāṅga*), the astrologer's daily work tool. This text combines the quantitative dimension of time, defined in astronomical terms, with the qualitative dimension of time, formulated according to astrological principles and rules of divination taken from the *saṃhitā*. We will investigate the practice of astrology throughout this work, but we felt it was important to start by underscoring that the coherence of *jyotiṣa* as a theoretical discipline, with its complex ramifications and its diverse methods and objects of investigation, cannot be understood if it is not seen from the professional astrologer's perspective with the need to provide answers for all sorts of daily problems.

Local Knowledge

Because of the close relationship with practice that characterizes this discipline, the development of *jyotiṣa* should be studied in the light of the historical, social, and regional context in which the profession of astrologer/astronomer is exercised. Before going on to examine the case of astrologers in Banaras, it would be useful to emphasize that the spread of *jyotiṣa* as a theoretical discipline is neither constant nor uniform in South Asia, and is constantly evolving. The value attributed to each branch of the astral discipline varies greatly in each period. Thus, we saw that military astrology (*yātrā*) played a crucial role during Varāhamihira's time and was one of the main branches of the discipline. In the same manner, in the royal courts of the ancient and medieval periods, *saṃhitā*—the examination of omen—was considered indispensable to the proper functioning of the kingdom (Inden 1985; Geslani 2018). These branches play a far less important role today, as the "patron" (*yajamāna*) who ensures the astrologer's survival is no longer the king ordering collective predictions—regarding the kingdom, the army, the regions, and populations—but middle- or upper-class families concerned with individual or family issues, and astrologers can generally satisfy these demands by reading the horoscope and the almanac.[40] Horoscopy (*horā*, *phalita*) has become the dominant branch today, more popular than mathematics (*gaṇita*) and astronomy (*siddhānta*), as the latter offer few professional openings when they are studied in Sanskrit and practiced outside the framework of "modern science."

One specialty in the field of divination based on *saṃhitā* is nonetheless extremely popular today, *vāstuśāstra*, the science of architecture and building sites. This knowledge is not mentioned in the classical treatises as a "branch" (*skandha*) of *jyotiṣa* but is considered such by contemporary astrologers, to the extent that for some it is a full-time activity. The popularity of *vāstuśāstra* is certainly linked to the explosive urban development that Indian cities and their suburbs have experienced over the last decades, along with the vast financial investments in real estate made by the upper or middle classes. Before or after acquiring a property, it is common practice for a family or an entrepreneur to have it examined by an astrologer. The latter is responsible for studying the good or bad omens present in the earth or the building (house, flat, office, factory, etc.) in order to prevent or eliminate any kind of negative influence (Guenzi and Singh 2009). Given the ever-rising demand for expertise in this field, several Indian universities that deliver degrees in *jyotiṣa* have begun to offer classes specializing in *vāstuśāstra*.[41] For the last ten years there has been a huge increase in the popular literature on the subject, both in vernacular languages and in English.

The development of the different branches of the discipline also varies depending on the social and historical conditions prevailing in different regions. Thus, for example, because of its position on the northwestern border of India, Gujarat has been the cradle of major exchanges with Greek and Arabic astrological knowledge. It is in this region that "Greek horoscopy" (*yavanajātaka*) was assimilated and spread, at the beginning of our era, through the satrapies established by Alexander. From the thirteen century onward, a type of horoscopy with a wealth of Perso-Arabic features developed in the peninsula of Saurāṣṭra, where there was widespread cohabitation with Muslim traders (Pingree 1997a). Known as *tājika*—from the Pahlavī *tāzīg* (Arab)—this specific form of natal horoscopy (*jātaka*), a combination of Indian and Perso-Arabic theories written in Sanskrit, was to spread over the following centuries through the courts of the Mughal Empire, thus reaching the different regions of India (Minkowski 2014; Gansten and Wikander 2011; Gansten 2012 and 2017).[42] Another characteristic of the Gujarati astral tradition, and its acceptance of non-Brahmanical worlds, is the involvement of Jain monks in the composition of texts on *jyotiṣa*. This is confirmed both in the ancient period in the field of *saṃhitā* and during the medieval period, under Caulukya's reign, by authors of treatises on *muhūrta*s (Pingree 1981).

From the viewpoint of regional conformations, Kerala is well known for sophisticated developments in the field of mathematics (*gaṇita*) that occurred in Mādhava's school (*guru-paraṃparā*) between the fourteenth and the seventeenth centuries.[43] The *jyotiṣa* practiced in this region is also marked by the importance attributed to the *praśna* (horary) branch, as attested not only by the textual production of the last centuries but also the specific usage of this divinatory technique in temple management (Tarabout 2002a, 2007, and 2012). In Tamil Nadu, a specialty in the field of divination known as *nāḍī jyotiṣa* was developed on the basis of a textual corpus containing a collection of horoscopes written on palm leaves, probably composed from the seventeenth century onward (Gansten 2003). From a conceptual perspective, this literature shares numerous features with the *jātaka* treatises, but it differs in that, rather than illustrating the theoretical rules of genethlialogy, it presents a sequence of individual horoscopes. The astrologer has to identify the text that corresponds to his client among a series of horoscopes that are already written and ready for use. Although today *nāḍī jyotiṣa* is presented (and sold to tourists) as a ("ancient") Tamil tradition, the textual corpus it draws upon was written not only in Sanskrit but also in other South Indian languages, which suggests an origin common to the whole Dravidian region (Gansten 2003).[44] As we will see, a similar horoscopy technique based on the same principle also exists in North India and refers to the *Bhṛgusaṃhitā*, a treatise probably composed around the sixteenth century, containing a collection of thousands of individual horoscopes (Pingree 1981). The regional variations in astral and divinatory knowledge, however, remain largely unexplored, both from the historical and anthropological perspectives, and we hope that future research will shed some light on the numerous aspects of local forms of *jyotiṣa*.

In addition to regional developments, there are certain towns or districts where astral and divinatory studies flourished during a particular period. The vitality of a local tradition is often related to the presence of particularly prolific families of *jyotiṣī*s who transmitted their knowledge down through the generations. Pārthapura, on the Godavari River in today's Maharashtra, is one example of this. Between the fourteenth and seventeenth centuries two lineages of Brahmins (belonging to the Bhāradvāja *gotra*) engendered several important authors—Jñānarāja, Sūryadāsa,

Gaṇeśa, Vīreśvāra, and others—whose works marked the history of the astral sciences during the early modern period (Pingree 1981; Minkowski 2002). A teacher's reputation could also turn a place into a thriving training center for young *jyotiṣīs*. This is the case of Nandigrāma, in Gujarat, which in the sixteenth century became an important center for *jyotiṣa*, attracting disciples from other Indian regions thanks to Gaṇeśa Daivajña's great renown (b. 1507). The latter is the author of the *Grahalāghava*, a manual of astronomy (*karaṇa*) suggesting new computing methods, simplified in comparison to those presented in the *siddhānta*s—and which became so popular that a new *pakṣa* (school of astronomy) was founded on his methods (Plofker 2009).[45]

The vitality of a local tradition was also strictly linked to the presence of generous patrons committed to promoting the *jyotiṣīs*' work. While today this patronage mainly exists within institutions and universities, in the past Hindu *mahārāja*s and Mughal emperors played a fundamental role in the development of local astronomers' or astrologers' activities. Numerous treatises on the different branches of the astral discipline were composed under King Paramāra Bhoja, who ruled over Dhārā (Malwa) in the first half of the eleventh century, by the king himself and by the *jyotiṣīs* employed at his court. The best-known case of patronage is however that of the *mahārāja* Jayasiṃha (Sawāī Jai Singh II), sovereign of the royal courts of Amber and Jaipur in the first half of the eighteenth century. This enthusiastic and learned promoter of the astral sciences had five astronomical observatories built under his patronage in the cities of Delhi, Jaipur, Ujjain, Mathura, and Varanasi and supported the collaboration between Hindu, Muslim, and Jesuit astronomers whom he invited to his court. To encourage exchanges between the various scientific traditions, he financed the translation of Arabic and Latin treatises into Sanskrit (Pingree 1999). Just as Jayasiṃha supported the work of Muslim astronomers, over a long period the Mughal sovereigns promoted the work of Brahmin *jyotiṣīs* who were regularly employed at their courts (Minkowski 2014). An exemplary case is that of Emperor Akbar, the patron of scholars from every horizon. Under his patronage the work of the very prolific Nīlakaṇṭha, who was appointed "royal astrologer" (*jyotiṣarāja*), flourished, as did that of his brother Rāma, the author of the famous treatise *Muhūrtacintāmaṇi* (Pingree 1997a; Minkowski 2014).

Nīlakaṇṭha and his brother Rāma, descendants of a family from Dharmapura on the River Narmada, settled in Kāśī (Banaras) where they composed their works in the second half of the sixteenth century, a time when the town was governed by King Ṭoḍaramalla, one of Akbar's ministers. They were no way unique, as from the sixteenth century onward Kāśī became a center that attracted *jyotiṣīs* from other Indian regions. The history of astral literature shows several lineages of Brahmin *jyotiṣīs*, most of them from Maharashtra, moving to Banaras to train with a teacher. They then went on to found their own lineage of astronomers and astrologers in the town.[46] From the sixteenth to the eighteenth centuries, Banaras fulfilled the three conditions that encourage a local concentration of *jyotiṣīs*: the presence of families specializing in the field, the reputation of learned teachers, and patronage. As in other fields of Brahmanical knowledge, the town progressively developed as an intellectual capital. As we will see in the following pages, this reputation only increased under British domination, while major changes were taking place in the transmission and production of astral knowledge.

In this chapter we looked at the theoretical and textual aspects of *jyotiṣa*, highlighting the main stages of its constitution and ongoing development into a complex discipline made up of branches and subbranches. The presentation revealed a science that is epistemologically complex, combining concepts of mathematics, geometry, astrology, ritual, medicine, cosmetics, and zoology. This heterogeneous group of methods and fields of investigation, though, acquires its coherence when approached from the perspective of the astrologers' work. The cohesiveness between the branches of the discipline as well as their evolution, the introduction or the disappearance of specializations, makes sense in light of the social context in which the astrologer acts as a practitioner and adviser.

2

Professors and Prophecies

Astrology at Universities in Banaras

Astrologia vero partim naturalis, partim superstitiosa est.

—Isidore de Séville, *Etimologíae*

The science of astronomy is the most famous among them, since the affairs of their religion are in various ways connected with it. If a man wants to gain the title of an astronomer, he must not only know scientific or mathematical astronomy, but also astrology.

—Al-Biruni, *India*

Astrological Perspectives on the Study and Diagnosis of Cancer (*jyotiṣ ke dvāra kainsar rog kā vicār evam nidān*) is the title of the two-day workshop organized by the Department of Jyotish (*jyotiṣa vibhāg*) at Banaras Hindu University (BHU) on March 16–17, 2007. About one hundred scholars, including professors, readers and lecturers from North Indian universities and Sanskrit colleges, graduate students, high school teachers, as well as a few doctors from the Faculty of Ayurveda at BHU, joined together to discuss issues concerning the prevention, diagnosis, and treatment of cancer.[1] By examining the relationship between celestial configurations and human diseases, the aim of the conference was to revivify research in the field of "medical astrology" (*cikitsīya jyotiṣa*). The studies presented at the conference were published in an edited volume (Pandey and Mishra 2008) with a foreword by the then vice chancellor of BHU, Panjab Singh:

> Sanskrit language is a reservoir (*bhaṇḍār*) of the knowledge (*jñān*) of our ancestors (*pūrvaj*), sages (*ṛṣi*), and great sages (*mahāṛṣi*). How the applications (*upayog*) of this knowledge can benefit ordinary people (*janasādhārāṇ*), this is what learned men (*vidvān*) after meeting here all together should reflect upon. The effort made in this sense by the Department of Jyotish is praiseworthy. Thanks to astrological knowledge, the probability of getting cancer or other frightful diseases is known in advance; for sure, at a preliminary stage, the treatment is much easier; that is how poor people (*nirdhan log*) in our country will get rid of much cost and suffering. I hope that the Department of Jyotish in the future will continue to develop this kind of research for the well-being (*hit*) of ordinary people (*ām log*). (Pandey and Mishra 2008, iv)[2]

The words of the vice chancellor locate astrological knowledge midway between two very distinct ways of knowing: that of the *ṛṣi*s, the ancient sages of Vedic India who possessed divine and revealed knowledge, on the one hand, and that of contemporary biomedical research, on the other. Connecting these forms of knowledge, one ancient and revealed, the other "modern" and empirical, astrology is said to prove its "usefulness" (*upayog*) for the "masses" (*janasādhārāṇ*), the "underprivileged" (*nirdhan log*), and "ordinary people" (*ām log*).

In this chapter, looking at the case of Banaras, we will examine the process by which *jyotiṣa* became an academic discipline that continues to be practiced as such today. We will examine the social negotiations and ideological conflicts that accompanied the institutionalization of this Brahmanical knowledge at universities. The preface to the aforementioned edited volume is a perfect illustration of some of the questions we will look at in these pages. We will see that what characterizes *jyotiṣa* as a university subject is its reference to a dual paradigm of legitimacy: religious, divine, and revealed on the one hand, and scientific, empirical, and secular on the other. This framework, which we could call an "epistemological double bind," is central to debates on the institutionalization of this discipline from the colonial period to date, and it appears in the arguments put forward both by the detractors and supporters of *jyotiṣa*, or researchers working in this discipline. Because it provides a cosmic template for articulating mathematical calculations and Hindu devotional practices, astronomical observations and ritual observances, *jyotiṣa* plays a crucial role as a system of knowledge at the crossroads of two major ways of organizing and explaining the world in colonial and post-colonial India: modern science and Hinduism.

Debating "Useful Knowledge"

In Banaras, *jyotiṣa* is taught at two universities: the Sampūrṇānanda Saṃskṛta Viśvavidyālaya or Sampurnananda Sanskrit University (SSU), and Kāśī Hindū Viśvavidyālaya or Banaras Hindu University (BHU). Both establishments deliver bachelor's, master's, and doctoral degrees in *jyotiṣa*.[3] At SSU, the Department of Jyotish is part of the Faculty of "Vedas and Vedāṅgas," while at BHU it is included in the Faculty of "Sanskrit Studies and Religious Sciences" (*Saṃskṛtavidyā dharmavijñāna*).[4] The astral discipline has been taught at both these universities since their establishment. A short presentation of the historical conditions under which these universities were founded—and *jyotiṣa* was instituted as an academic discipline—will give us a better perspective on the recent events related to the creation of "Vedic astrology" departments under the government program promoted by the Hindu nationalist party, the Bharatiya Janata Party (BJP), in the early 2000s.

The founding of SSU and BHU is intimately connected to Banaras's reputation as a center for Sanskrit culture and Brahmanical orthodoxy.[5] Despite their diversity, both the Benares Sanskrit College, which in the twentieth century became part of the SSU, and BHU played a major role in Indian history as centers where Hindu religious traditions were nationalized, standardized, and institutionalized.[6] The educational project underlying the creation of these two establishments envisaged Sanskrit culture as the highest expression, not only of Hinduism but also of Indianness. As a Sanskrit and Brahmanical tradition, *jyotiṣa* was included in the programs of both these establishments at the time of their creation. Nonetheless, due to the epistemological complexity of the astral discipline, the institutionalization of *jyotiṣa* took specific forms that differentiated it from other Brahmanical disciplines.

The Benares Sanskrit College was founded in 1791, under British patronage, by Jonathan Duncan, the Resident of the East India Company in India. It was created to preserve and cultivate "the Laws, Literature and Religion of that [Hindu] nation, at this centre of their faith [=Banaras]."[7] Duncan attributed the highest authority on religious, legal, and literary matters to the Brahmins of Banaras and sought to preserve, institutionalize, and control their knowledge (Dalmia 1997; Dodson 2007). To do this, the traditional methods of learning based on the transmission of knowledge from teacher to disciple (*guru-śiṣya paramparā*) had to be transformed (Kumar 1997). The personal relationship between the teacher and the disciple was to be replaced by institutions delivering standardized classes and degrees. The process of adapting traditional forms to the new methods nonetheless encountered numerous obstacles and gave rise to problems related to pedagogy and corruption. But of greater interest to us here is how colonial authorities and Brahmin pandits came into conflict with regard to decisions relative to the organization of the syllabus. For the colonial authorities who wanted to reform and restructure traditional Sanskrit learning, the teaching of *jyotiṣa* was to raise thorny questions.

In the program established by Duncan at the Sanskrit College in 1791, "Jyotish" is described as a discipline dealing with "Astronomy, Geography and pure Mathematics" (Nicholls 1907 [1848], 3). Astrology and divination are not mentioned whereas, as we saw in the first chapter, they are an integral part of the astral discipline as it is described in Sanskrit treatises. According to the British administrators, the astronomical and mathematical branches of *jyotiṣa*—*siddhānta* and *gaṇita*—represented the highest expression of the scientific and rational spirit of Brahmanical culture. The study of these subjects was hence to be encouraged. The colonial administrators used this knowledge as a didactic tool that could bring about the "engraftment" of modern science and "useful knowledge" in India.[8] Astrology and divination, however, were seen as superstitious and irrational beliefs, the most insignificant and degenerate expression of the Brahmanical tradition.[9]

During the first decades of the nineteenth century, the British supervisors of the Sanskrit College realized that not only were the pandits delivering classes on all the branches of the astral discipline, but the astrological subjects—*phalita* and *saṃhitā*—were among the most popular with the students. Thus, in his report written in 1839, the superintendent of the Sanskrit College remarked:

> The study of Mathematics is at a very low ebb and I fear but little improvement can be hoped, for the pupils appear to evince scarcely any desire for strictly scientific attainments; *their chief object appears to be the acquisition of Astrology and they learn little of Algebra and Astronomy with the view of using them in Astrological computations.* I have endeavoured to introduce Geometry amongst them, but hitherto without success. The bias in favour

> of astrological researches, which is so prevalent among the students is much to be regretted. (Nicholls 1907, 83; our italics)

Questioned on the reasons why students were more interested in astrology, the pandits teaching *jyotiṣa* explained that unless they mastered the astrological subjects, the students would obtain "neither subsistence nor respect." On this subject the report quotes the words of one of the pandits teaching at the Sanskrit College:

> That science the reading of which will procure money by which support is obtained will be ardently studied by the students; the people of Hindustan ask questions on Phuludeshi [= *phaladeśa*] or Phalagranth, *i.e.* Astrology, and give something for the answer, therefore astrology is read; without reading Astronomy (Siddhanta) and Algebra (Ganita), Astrology cannot be understood, therefore the Siddhantas and Ganita are studied by all called Yotish [*jyotiṣī*]. *But those who study Siddhantas (Astronomy) alone cannot by means of it obtain a livelihood and therefore do not give their minds to it.* (Nicholls 1907, 88; our italics)

For the colonial administrators astrology represented an obstacle to the spread of what they called "Useful Knowledge" or modern science, but for the students it was an eminently "useful" science as it allowed them to earn a living. The evangelist John Muir, influenced by the educational reforms of the 1830s, banned the teaching of astrology, despite its popularity, at the Sanskrit College in 1845.[10] According to Muir, the pandits teaching Jyotish were to limit "their predilections to arithmetic, algebra, mathematics and astronomy" (Young 1981, 53). As Young observes, banning astrology was the only draconian measure Muir imposed in his management of the institution. The astrology class was reintroduced when the Sanskrit College was given the status of university after independence, in 1958.[11]

While, for the British, the teaching of *jyotiṣa* was problematic due to the ambivalence of this discipline that consisted both of "scientific" knowledge and "belief," the nationalist leader and founder of Banaras Hindu University, Pandit Madan Mohan Malaviya, saw this epistemological ambivalence as the strength of the astral discipline. He placed it at the heart of a pedagogical project where the study of the Hindu *śāstra*s was combined with that of the modern sciences. While most universities established in India by the British government in the nineteenth century had been instruments of colonial power in which only "Western knowledge" was taught, BHU was founded in 1916 with the aim of creating a university where Hindu thought and Indian knowledge in the different fields of art, literature, and the sciences could be promoted in the spirit of a dialogue with European knowledge (Renold 2005).

In this context, the teaching of *jyotiṣa* was perfectly coherent with the plans for the new university designed by Malaviya, not only because it enabled the creation of a connection between modern science and the Sanskrit tradition but also because of the "pan-Indian" nature of this discipline. The canonical treatises (*jyotiḥśāstra*) had been composed, transmitted, and used in both the North and the South of India, and had circulated transregionally. As Christopher Bayly remarks in *Empire and Information* (1996), astrologers actively contributed to the process of nationalizing traditions during the colonial period:

> With the slow improvement of communications, soothsayers and astrologers moved out into the back-lands and the camps of the migrant tribals and low castes, bringing the almanac and the horoscope to new audiences. In this way they helped "bring them within the pale of Hinduism," as one observer put it. . . . The Indian astral sciences were continuing to extend their hegemony over the "little tradition" of necromancy and divination just as the pioneer peasants conquered the jungle and hill fastnesses. . . . the ancient Indian astral knowledge became a source of pride for an emerging national consciousness. (1996, 263)

As a vehicle for propagating the "great Sanskrit tradition" to the detriment of "minor local traditions" of divination and necromancy, the astral discipline was thus to contribute to the emergence of a "national consciousness."

In his initial project for the creation of the university, developed at the beginning of the twentieth century, Pandit Malaviya recommended that *jyotiṣa* be one of the main subjects taught at the department of Vedic studies (Vaidik College) and that an astronomical observatory be attached to the department in order to encourage a dialogue between Sanskrit tradition and scientific research.[12] In the early years of its existence, *jyotiṣa* classes were taught at the College of Theology and the College of Oriental Learning. While at the former they were part of the training in

Sanskrit studies, at the latter the *jyotiḥśāstras* were taught conjointly with astronomy and European mathematics. Despite Pandit Malaviya's efforts to bring the Sanskrit and European sciences together in a single course, due to a shortage of students, the Department of Oriental Learning was merged with the Department of Theology to become today's Faculty of Sanskrit Vidya Dharma Vijnan or "Sanskrit Studies and Religious Sciences."[13] Since then there has been no university degree combining *jyotiṣa* and the scientific disciplines taught at the departments of physics, mathematics, or chemistry. However, as we will see, the connection between the astral discipline and modern science is still regularly asserted today in university researchers' speeches and publications, as well as in government policies promoted by the Hindu nationalist party.

Astrology as a Vedic Science

The role of *jyotiṣa* as an academic discipline, capable of combining scientific knowledge and Hindu religious traditions and thus serving the nationalist agenda, was reasserted and reformulated at the turn of the twenty-first century. In 2001, the Indian government led by the Bharatiya Janata Party (BJP) launched a campaign to promote the creation of "Vedic astrology"—or "Jyotir Vigyan"—departments at Indian universities. The University Grants Commission (UGC), the national agency responsible for determining and maintaining standards of teaching, examination, and research in universities, as well as for attributing research and teaching funds under the Ministry of Education, published a ministerial circular called "Guidelines for Setting Up Departments of Vedic Astrology in Universities."[14] The circular states that "there is an urgent need to rejuvenate the *science* of Vedic Astrology in India, to allow this *scientific knowledge* to reach society at large, and to provide opportunities to get this important *science* even exported to the world" (author's italics). Universities were invited to submit proposals for establishing departments that would provide teaching and training in Vedic astrology, leading to certificate diploma, undergraduate, postgraduate and PhD degrees.[15] Funds were allotted for staff, including a professor, a reader, two lecturers, a librarian, and a computer specialist, as well as for facilities such as a library, an observatory, and a "Computer Lab & Horoscope Bank."[16] The Vedic astrology classes were intended for "students, teachers, professionals from *modern streams* like doctors, architects, marketing, financial, economic and political analysts, etc."[17]

After this call for funding proposals was published, forty-one universities in sixteen Indian states applied, and nineteen received funds.[18] A lively debate ensued among the political class and within Indian public opinion: the UGC's decision was widely condemned as an expression of policies backed by the BJP, the Hindu nationalist party in power, with an aim to "saffronize" (saffron is the BJP's color) or "Hinduize" the public education system.[19] In addition, opponents to the UGC decision argued that in a country where over 40 percent of the population is illiterate, and where some universities cannot even afford electricity in the classrooms, the government surely has more urgent priorities than financing the creation of Vedic astrology departments.[20] A few renowned scientists and intellectuals demanded that the Supreme Court suspend the UGC decree. They contested the legitimacy of this decree that, by defining Vedic astrology as "scientific knowledge," contravened Article 51A of the Indian constitution, according to which the state has a duty to promote "the scientific temper" among its citizens. Despite this protest movement, in 2004, the Supreme Court pronounced a judgment in favor of the UGC, declaring: "the teaching of 'Jyotir Vigyan' can under no circumstances be equated with the teaching of any particular religion . . . ; the courts are not expert in academic matters and it is not for them to decide as to what course should be taught in university and what should be their curriculum."[21] Without entering further into the political debate, our aim here is to show how the argumentation behind this finance decree is meant to reinforce the legitimacy of astrology as a university discipline.

Let us first note that although, during the colonial period, *jyotiṣa* had been included in the government education system as a branch of Brahmanical knowledge, it is now described as a "scientific subject." Here, we note a terminological slippage from *śāstra* (treatise, theory) to *vijñān* (science): the discipline traditionally known as *jyotiḥśāstra* becomes "Jyotir Vigyan" (*jyotirvijñān*) in the UGC's formulation. This choice implies a fairly radical epistemological shift, because as Pollock (1985) observes, while the concept of *śāstra* gives absolute priority to theory over practice, to rules over their practical application, the concept of *vijñān* refers to an exact knowledge, based on empirical observation. This new terminology is also used at a local level, in Banaras. Teachers and researchers at the departments of jyotish at universities in Banaras, not only mobilized to defend the legitimacy of the new astrology departments financed by the UGC,[22] but in 2003, they also founded the *jyotiṣa vijñān samiti*, the "Academy of Astral Science," as well as the yearly journal *jyotiṣa vaijñānikī*,

"Scientistic *jyotiṣa*." Both these initiatives are clearly meant to characterize astrological research in universities as "scientific." The aforementioned research on cancer is an example of the work encouraged in this context.

Although it is described as scientific knowledge, however, the discipline taught at the new departments is by no means secular. The type of astrology the Hindu nationalist party would like to encourage at universities is, in fact, defined as "Vedic." This adjective has an ideological value that deserves to be examined. It imprecisely describes the astral knowledge taught today at universities because, as we saw in the first chapter of this work, *jyotiṣa* from the Vedic period is fundamentally luni-solar astronomical knowledge that mentions neither planets nor zodiacal signs, nor horoscopes, nor other divinatory techniques used by today's astrologers. The choice of this attribute should thus be understood in the context of the campaign for the promotion of "Vedic sciences" led by the Hindu nationalist right in India, as well as against the background of the Hindutva diaspora in the United States and the United Kingdom. An example of this is the much-debated distribution of "Vedic mathematics" manuals in secondary schools.

Although the educational policies concerning "Vedic science" promoted by the Hindu nationalist party over the last two decades adopt new forms, they reuse and reinterpret an older ideological program, developed within the Hindu reform movements during the colonial period. As Gyan Prakash shows in his work *Another Reason: Science and the Imagination of Modern India* (1999), in the nineteenth century and at the beginning of the twentieth century, numerous Hindu intellectuals and religious reformists mobilized to make science an essential feature of the national Indian identity. With this aim, not only did they promote the spread of scientific culture in schools, but they reread, reinterpreted, and rewrote the sacred texts (*śāstra*) emphasizing their "scientific" and "rational" content. The Hindu elites educated at British schools then began to reformulate the Sanskrit treatises in terms that conformed to the language of Western science and the positivist theories, while identifying an "archaic Hindu science" in which they claimed the laws of modern science were formulated implicitly and symbolically. Hinduism was thus described as a "science-grounded religion." Prakash shows how the founder of the Arya Samaj, Dayananda Saraswati, and other militants involved in the same movement, strove to prove the value of the truth of Vedic texts, based on their compatibility with the scientific rationality of Western science:[23] unlike the Bible in which creationism contradicts every scientific law, they showed how the Vedas conforms to scientific theory. Vedic sacrificial fires are hence explained as ritual practices developed to purify the air of germs and to prevent the spread of disease. Vedic deities are interpreted as speculations on the physical and chemical properties of the universe, as in the case of Vāyu, the Wind God, who is described as being nothing more than an investigation into the "gaseous envelope," made up of molecules of air charged with energy that is the atmosphere.[24]

While certain discourses pronounced by the Hindu nationalists over the last two decades seem to be a revival of the program to "Hinduize" the sciences and to make Hinduism more "scientific," as it was developed in the colonial period, there is nonetheless a fairly radical shift with regard to the positions on the status of astrology. For example, it is interesting to note that the Arya Samaj reformists, who saw the Vedas as the authentic foundation of orthodox Hinduism, harshly condemned astrology, considering it a corrupt degeneration of the Hindu science, a superstition to be eradicated.[25] By defining astrology as a "Vedic science" worthy of being taught at universities, the representatives of the BJP and a number of contemporary astrologers who use this appellation on the contrary elevate this knowledge to a central position within "orthodox" Hinduism. The reasons that could explain this reappraisal of astrology are complex and will be examined in the following chapters, but what we seek to emphasize here is that this phenomenon cannot be reduced to a product of nationalist Hindu rhetoric or to communalist strategies.

Looking at the bibliography of popular astrology over the last few decades, one notes that the appellation "Vedic astrology" was first used in the Anglo-Saxon countries from the 1990s onward, and progressively replaced the earlier titles of "Hindu astrology" or "Indian astrology."[26] In the last three decades, the number of manuals of Vedic astrology published by Indian, American, and British publishers has steadily increased, along with a proliferation of internet sites selling horoscopes, online consultations, remedies, or journeys to India, in the name of Vedic astrology.[27] The quest for identity in the Hindu diaspora, as well as the growth of "New Age" and other Western religious movements that seek the spiritual or mystic in so-called oriental civilizations, have made Vedic astrology a very lucrative commodity. The adjective "Vedic" seems to satisfy the expectations of the Hindus, for whom the Vedas represent the very essence of Hinduism; meanwhile, for Western consumers of astrology, "Vedic" is synonymous with "spiritual," "ancient," "revealed," or "esoteric," and not necessarily "Hindu."

It is not thus surprising that the UGC circular explicitly formulates the idea that Vedic astrology departments fulfill the "urgent need . . . to get this important *science* even exported to the world." In a television interview following the publication of the circular, chairman of the UGC and former vice chancellor of BHU Hari Gautam, stated that the aim of these departments was to train *certified persons* in the field of Vedic astrology and ritual Brahmanical knowledge (*karmakāṇḍ*) so as to provide them job opportunities abroad. Like the priests trained in the Agama schools in Tamil Nadu studied by Fuller (2003), people who have obtained a degree in Vedic astrology can thus satisfy the demands of the Indian diaspora in the United States and United Kingdom for horoscopes and consultations.

So far, we have seen that the legitimacy of these new astrology departments is affirmed through a dual discourse: on the one hand, the authority of science is evoked to characterize astrology as a modern, rational, and universal knowledge; on the other, the reference to the Vedas proves its autochthonous, original, and authentically Hindu nature. Both divine and secular, revealed and empirical, ancient and modern, universal and Hindu, in the BJP spokespersons' discourses, astrology reconciles "religion" and "science," "tradition" and "modernity," "spirituality" and "materialism." But how do researchers and teachers at the departments of jyotish at universities in Banaras translate this paradoxical characterization into practice? We will return to these questions after a presentation of the organization of these departments.

Departments at Work

The departments of jyotish at BHU and SSU fulfill three basic functions: training students, publishing an annual university almanac, and advancing research. Each establishment has about eighty students registered for a bachelor's, master's, or doctoral degree.[28] Although registration is nominally open to anyone, with few exceptions the students are all male and Brahmin, and the teaching staff consists exclusively of male Brahmins.[29] The social composition of the student body studying literature (*sāhitya*), logic (*nyāyā*), grammar (*vyākaraṇa*), or *dharmaśāstra*—taught at the other departments of Sanskrit studies—is relatively more heterogeneous and includes several women and non-Brahmin students. Questioned about this, a few *jyotiṣa* students at BHU and SSU explained that although the only department in the Faculty of Sanskrit Studies officially reserved for Brahmin men is that of Vedas, the astrology course "is held as forbidden" (*varjit mānā gayā hai*) to women and non-Brahmins. Whether formally established or respected de facto, why do these criteria of social selection only apply to the departments of jyotish and Vedic studies? What differentiates these two disciplines from the other Sanskrit sciences? The answer to these questions is not necessarily to be found in the hierarchies between the sciences, or in a higher degree of purity, sophistication, or orthodoxy of knowledge reserved for male Brahmins. It is, in fact, career opportunities rather than the nature of the knowledge involved that determine the social composition of the student body. While the syllabi followed in the fields of grammar, philosophy, literature, or other scholarly disciplines lead only to professional opportunities in teaching, Vedic studies and astrology are preparation for priest or astrologer careers, which, following the established conventions, are practiced only by Brahmin men.

We must however distinguish between Vedic studies and *jyotiṣa*. While according to the texts and in current practice, a woman or a non-Brahmin cannot occupy the function of priest (*purohit*), the norms regulating the profession of astrologer are losing their rigidity today. Teachers at departments of jyotish are keen to emphasize that as astrology "is a science," astral studies are open to everyone, with no gender or caste restrictions, and anyone who has the skill can exercise the profession of astrologer. As we will see in the following chapter, while retaining its connection to the status of Brahmin, the professional identity of astrologers today also includes characteristics specifically found in the liberal professions and it is hence possible for anyone who is technically qualified to practice this profession. Although they are still a rarity in Banaras, more and more non-Brahmins and women are practicing this profession in other Indian towns. Access to academic degrees in *jyotiṣa* nonetheless remains largely limited to Brahmin men, given the high level of Sanskrit required and the degrees' connection to the priestly occupation. In addition, the "pollution" traditionally associated with the profession of astrologer could compromise the reputation of an unmarried girl or woman who chooses this course of study.[30]

University teaching does not replace traditional methods of learning the discipline but rather reinforces them, giving rise to a mixed system. Regarding access to training, as we have seen, traditional criteria based on caste and gender exist alongside academic admission standards. Similarly, regarding training methods, attending classes and passing exams coexist with the system based on the "relationship between teacher and student" (*guru-śiṣya sambandh*). Students address their teachers as *gurujī* (Respected Teacher) or *paṇḍitjī* (Respected Pandit) and touch their feet as a sign of respect. In addition to their presence in the classroom, they regularly visit their teachers' homes, where they continue their theoretical training, observe astrological consultations, and sometimes help with household tasks (*sevā*).[31] By observing consultations, the student learns how to apply abstract rules, formulated in the texts, to clients' specific, individual cases and how to establish a diagnosis and identify the appropriate remedies to resolve concrete problems.

Because of their complementarity, both academic training and study at a teacher's home are both held as necessary. While the former focuses on textual learning and provides a degree objectively certifying the acquisition of theoretical skills, the latter gives students the experience required for the everyday practice of their profession. However, both students and teachers agree that intensive and prolonged study with a guru provides a more complete education than university teaching, as it exposes the student to both theory and practice, while at a university only the doctrines are taught. In their view, academic training is a necessary requirement mostly because of the rising number of unqualified practitioners that open offices and claim the title of astrologer. This is a growing threat, and the certified education provided by a university is viewed as a way to protect the profession of astrologer from charlatanism.

Furthermore, students appreciate university degrees because they open up a wider range of professional opportunities than those offered by a personal apprenticeship with a guru. In particular, they provide access to government jobs—joining the civil service is something to which large numbers of young Brahmins aspire. Those who have a degree or a doctorate have access to teaching positions at high schools or universities, or they can apply for the highly coveted position of *dharm guru* (or religious teacher) in the army.[32] In the private sector, university degrees are extremely useful for young astrologers who want to go abroad (and we met several of them) since skill certification is required not only by diasporic Hindu communities but also by international spiritual organizations that offer teaching and other services in "Vedic astrology." Schools and universities affiliated, for example, with the Maharishi Mahesh Yogi Foundation, an organization with centers all over the world, regularly recruit astrologers for their "Jyotish and Yagya" (or "Vedic astrology and Vedic ritual") programs, and some BHU alumni have been integrated into these structures. In India, although the most common professional prospect for an astrologer is to set up an independent office, some graduates have found jobs at companies that require expertise in *vāstuśāstra* (a branch of astrology dedicated to creating a suitable organization of workspace), or with mobile phone service providers who sell astrological services. Others have created internet sites to provide online horoscopes or consultations or have set up offices at a luxury hotel or in a shopping mall. According to the director of the Department of Jyotish at BHU in 2005, Shrinivas Tiwari, thanks to ever-increasing and diverse professional opportunities, "no *jyotiṣa* graduate is unemployed today." Although we were unable to statistically verify the validity of this statement, BHU students seem to share this optimism toward their professional future, and the graduates we met are employed as teachers or work as full-time astrologers.

In comparison to the traditional methods of teaching the discipline, based on the teacher's authority and oral transmission, university classes concentrate on the texts and writing. Most of the teaching and examinations focus on sections of *jyotiḥśāstra* treatises, as we can see from the *jyotiṣa* bachelor's and master's degree programs at BHU provided in the annex at the end of this volume. However, although according to the authoritative treatises, the astral discipline is divided into three branches—mathematics/astronomy (*gaṇita/siddhānta*), astrology (*phalita* or *horā*), and divination (*saṃhitā*)—the bachelor's and master's courses are only divided into two branches: mathematical astronomy (*gaṇita*) and predictive astrology (*phalita*). The study of treatises on divination like the *Bṛhatsaṃhitā*, the *Samarasāra*, or the *Vāsturatnākara* are an integral part of the students' training, but divination (*saṃhitā*) is not considered a full-fledged academic specialization. It is approached instead as a part of the astrological training (just as astronomy is seen as a section of mathematics [*gaṇita*]).

Besides studying canonical texts of astral literature (*jyotiḥśāstra*), students are trained in practical exercises (*prayoga*) to learn how to use ancient and modern astronomical instruments (*yantra*), as well as in the calculation of almanacs (*pañcāṅga*). The almanac is a crucial tool for every astrologer and the departments of Jyotish not only train students in this field but also publish an annual almanac to be sold to the town's practitioners and inhabitants. For this reason, in addition to the teaching staff that consists of professors, readers, and lecturers, these departments employ a team of researchers working full-time on the composition of almanacs. The *Dṛk siddha pañcāṅga*, the almanac calculated annually by the astrologers of SSU, has been published since 1876, while the *Viśva pañcāṅga* prepared at BHU has been published since 1927. While they share the same lunisolar calendar system, these almanacs are composed according to two different methods (*paddhati*). In the SSU almanac, planetary movement is calculated on the basis of a direct observation (*dṛś*) of celestial phenomena, while the BHU almanac uses mathematical tables (*sārāṇi*), drawn up following the principles of *Sūryasiddhānta*. Thus the BHU almanac is said to be "composed by the ṛṣi" (*ṛṣi praṇīt*) and hence "certified by the textual authority" (*grantha pramāṇit*), while the SSU almanac is said to be "proved by empirical observation" (*dṛśya pramāṇit*, *dṛśya siddha*). Despite the epistemological differences between these two methods, the temporal discrepancy between the two almanacs is no more than a few *ghaṭi* (unit corresponding to twenty-four minutes), but this can nonetheless have a crucial impact when it comes to identifying the *muhūrta*s, or auspicious times for undertaking ritual activities.[33]

The researchers of the *pañcāṅga* unit carry out the innumerable mathematical calculations that serve to produce the annual almanacs manually, on huge sheets of paper. While this "artisanal" method serves to maintain the tradition, it also probably constitutes a means of preserving the jobs of the civil servants that would otherwise become superfluous. The external observer is struck by the excruciating slowness of the process, all the more so as the manuscript data are subsequently entered, one at a time, into a computer equipped with special software designed for the composition and printing of almanacs. Beyond the mathematical calculations, the SSU team of *jyotiṣī*s also carries out a direct observation and measurement of the planetary movements. For this purpose, an open-air astronomical observatory (*vedhaśālā*) was set up at SSU in 1991, dedicated to the memory of the nineteenth-century astronomer Sudhākar Dvivedī. It is equipped with six masonry instruments (*yantra*), copies of those Sawāī Jai Singh II had had built in the eighteenth century (Sharma 1992).[34] The department's researchers and students make regular use of this observatory to conduct their experiments (*prayoga*).

Research and Rewriting

The third function of departments of jyotish, in addition to teaching and calculating almanacs, consists of promoting and developing research. The department's teachers and researchers regularly publish new editions of the classical treatises on different branches of *jyotiḥśāstra*, with a translation and/or commentary in Hindi.[35] They also develop research programs dealing with themes related to the current preoccupations of Indian society. They thus organize conferences and seminars, the results of which are published in journals or edited volumes. Over the last few years, for instance, the Department of Jyotish at BHU has developed research on how to apply meteorological and botanical principles, set out in the divinatory treatises (*saṃhitā*), to agriculture. Or a statistical survey about the stability of marriages, carried out by confronting the horoscopes of spouses so as to identify planetary conjunctions showing sterility or fertility, adultery or faithfulness, divorce or widowhood, and so on.[36]

As mentioned at the beginning of this chapter, astrological research into modern diseases—such as cancer, diabetes, AIDS, or cardiovascular problems—is another rapidly expanding field of research. A former director of the Department of Jyotish at BHU, Ram Chandra Pandey, explains in an article that the aim of astrological research is not to replace medical research but to provide complementary tools that can encourage the prevention and treatment of incurable diseases: "While medical diagnoses deal with maladies that are already there, astral science can predict in advance any arising disease" (Pandey 2003, 8). Unlike biomedicine, which focuses on studying *how* diseases evolve, develop, and are transmitted, astrological research seeks to provide instruments to understand *when* diseases are likely to strike and the *type of people* predisposed to suffer from them, according to the planetary situation at the time of their birth.

Over the last decades, "medical astrology" (*cikitsakīya jyotiṣa*) has become a privileged field of investigation within *jyotiṣa*, and some Indian universities deliver diplomas certifying a specialization in this area. In 2009 the departments of jyotish at BHU and at Lal Bahadur Shastri Rashtriya Vidyapeetha, a university in Delhi obtained funding from the University Grants Commission (UGC) to conduct long-term research projects to study cancer and heart-related diseases. Another project on asthmatic diseases received financial support from the UGC in 2011. Numerous publications dealing with the relationship between astrology and disease have appeared over the past few years, in the academic field as well as in popular literature.[37] A close examination of some academic publications will illustrate how the theory described in the classical astrology treatises is reformulated today, so that it can meet new epistemological standards and changing social needs.

To start with, it is important to underscore that there is no such thing as "medical astrology" in Sanskrit treatises. In astral literature, reflections on the relationship between the body, health, diseases, and celestial phenomena do not constitute a specific branch and do not form a separate textual corpus but rather are scattered over numerous passages in the treatises on horoscopy.[38] Physical pathologies are not treated as a category distinct from other types of suffering—such as accidents, poverty, hunger, death, exile, dishonor, drug dependency, or the loss of status and power—that can occur over the course of a person's existence. Predictions dealing with diseases are mixed into other subjects. By separating research on disease from that dealing with other types of suffering, contemporary astrologers make horoscope theory conform to the epistemological model of biomedicine, according to which physical pathologies constitute a field of investigation to be considered separately from other types of events in human existence. Similarly, from an etiological viewpoint, the ancient treatises establish no clear distinction between natural causes (e.g., a dysfunction of the three humors), supernatural causes (attacks by harmful spirits, Gods or their assistants, curses, etc.), and causes that one could qualify as "social" (poverty, conflict with enemies, attacks by people belonging to other castes) as planetary configurations indicate (or give rise to) all sorts of pathological agents. In contemporary academic works in the field of medical astrology, however, only natural causes are taken into account and connections with Ayurvedic theory are emphasized (Sharma 2008; Jha 2008).

Research in the field of "medical astrology" consists primarily of identifying the passages in the ancient horoscopy treatises that describe the relationship between planetary movements and human physiology. Researchers pay particular attention to Sanskrit verses describing conception, birth, malformations, masculine and feminine phenotypes, diseases, psychic problems, longevity, signs of death, and so on. The fundamental principle behind iatro-astrological theory is melothesia, the correlation between heavenly bodies and the parts of cosmic man's body (*kālapuruṣa*, "the embodiment of time"). This principle, established in horoscopy treatises written from the first centuries of our era onward, allows us to connect the components of the celestial macrocosm with the human microcosm. Each planet, zodiacal sign, or lunar mansion is connected to a part of the body. Although of Greek inspiration, the astral melothesia described in horoscopy treatises includes many categories belonging to Ayurvedic medical theory such as the three *doṣa*s ("humors"), the seven *dhātu*s ("tissues"), the *rasa*s ("savors"), or the *guṇa*s ("qualities") (Zimmermann 1981). In the *Jātakapārijāta*, a medieval treatise by Vaidyanātha containing a wealth of medical material regularly used by astrologers today, melothesia is also applied to the nosological field, and each planet is associated with a series of pathologies or psychophysical problems, as well as all kinds of accidents caused by natural or supernatural agents (JP 2.75–83).

Other horoscopic principles beyond melothesia elaborate an astrological diagnosis. The sixth, eighth, and twelfth houses of the horoscope show the likelihood of disease, accidents, wounds, and death and should be carefully analyzed. Astrologers search for "planetary conjunctions of diseases" (*roga-yoga*[39]), which indicate the horoscope owner's predisposition to developing certain pathologies. These are a few examples:

> When Sun is in the ascendant (*lagna*) and is aspected by Mars, the native is afflicted with tumors (*gulma*), consumption (*kṣaya*), and asthma (*śvāsa*) (JP 6.62a); when Sun is in the sixth house, in conjunction with a malefic planet and aspected by a malefic planet, the person suffers of an excess (*ulbaṇa*) of bile (*pitta*) (JP 6.68a); when the Lord of the sixth house is in the ascendant, in conjunction with a malefic planet, the body of the person will have ulcers (*vraṇa*) (JP 6.70a).
>
> When Sun, Moon, Mars, and Saturn are, respectively, in the eighth, sixth, second, and twelfth house, the strongest planet among them will cause the loss of an eye (*anetratā*) because of a humor (*doṣa*) in excess; if the same planets are, respectively, in the ninth, eleventh, third, and fifth house, and are not aspected by benefic planets, this gives an injury to the ear (*śravaṇa-upaghāta*); if they are in the seventh house, this gives teeth deterioration (*rada-vaikṛtya*). (BJ 23.10–11)

In publications by university researchers, passages dealing with the relationship between planets and human bodies are not only cited and enumerated, they are also subjected to various modifications in an attempt to update the ancient authors' knowledge from a linguistic, conceptual, and methodological perspective. To start with, the Sanskrit *śloka*s are translated, paraphrased, or commented in Hindi. They are also often reconfigured in the form of tables, graphs, or schemas.[40] The discursive and versified style of Sanskrit treatises is thus presented as a systematic and objective sequence of data where the mnemotechnical value of the verses is replaced by the visual efficacy of graphic representations.

A second type of rewriting occurs at the interpretative level and consists of carrying out a "biomedical" exegesis of the astrological treatises. Researchers adopt a hermeneutic approach to reveal the biomedical meaning of the Sanskrit *śloka*s composed in ancient times.[41] With regard to astrological research on cancer, for example, researchers look for passages where polysemic Sanskrit terms are likely to indicate tumoral pathologies. They thus study the astral conjunctions associated with cancer-related pathologies such as the *arbuda* (growth, polyp), *gulma* (glandular swelling), *vraṇa* (lesion, wound, ulcer, abscess, tumor), *tāpagaṇḍa* (painful swelling/enlargement), *vidradhi* (abscess), and *sphoṭa* (growth, tumor) (Tripathi 2008; Upadhyay 2008; Devduta 2006). Using the correlative system mentioned earlier, researchers can carry out specialized studies of the astral conjunctions responsible for certain topical forms of disease like uterine cancer (*garbhāśay-kainsar*) (Chowbe 2008) or blood cancer (*rakta-kainsar*) (Mishra 2008). Although this biomedical interpretation may seriously alter the signification of the Sanskrit passages, it does not compromise the authority of the Brahmanical treatises and is methodologically close to traditional forms of knowledge. It can, in fact, be seen as a contemporary form of "commentary" (*ṭīkā*, *bhāṣya*, *vyākhyā*), which is a very common genre in Sanskrit literature.

A methodological shift, however, can be noted in research projects that develop an experimental approach in order to test theoretical rules formulated in ancient treatises. The influence of certain planetary configurations on health is in these cases examined through the observation of empirical cases. In his study, "Astrological Diagnosis of Breast Cancer" (*stan-kainsar kā jyotiḥśāstra nidān*), Shatrughna Tripathi, a lecturer at BHU's Department of Jyotish, analyzes and compares the horoscopes of thirty women suffering from breast cancer in an attempt to identify the planetary conjunctions likely to engender this type of pathology (Tripathi 2008).[42] In order to collect a statistically significant number of horoscopes, researchers sometimes employ new communication technologies. Thus, in the framework of the project Astrological Diagnosis and Treatment of Heart Disease (*hṛdayarog kā jyotiṣśāstrīya nidān evaṃ upacār*), funded since 2009 by the University Grants Commission, the Department of Jyotish at BHU published an online form addressed to anyone suffering from a cardiac disease (see figure 4 on pages 74 and 75).[43] Another research project carried out by Professor Nagendra Pandey (Department of Jyotish at SSU), in collaboration with colleagues working at the Lal Bahadur Shastri

UNIVERSITY GRANTS COMMISSION,NEW DELHI

MEJOR RESEARCH PROJECT

1. Broad Subject - Astrological Diagnosis and Treatment of Heart Disease

((हृदयरोग का ज्योतिषशास्त्रीय निदान एवं उपचार)

2. Area of Specialization- Jyotish Falit And Siddhantas.
3. Duration - 02 Year,
4. Principal Investigator-

Name:	Dr. Shatrughna Tripathi
Qualification:	Acharya, Ph.D.
Designation:	Assistant Professor,
Address:	
Department:	Jyotish Deptt. SVDV. BHU.Varanasi, UP
Residence:	N1/30/A 8. Nagwa. Varanasi, UP PHONE 0542-6703229,09452186560,
Email:	drstripathi_bhu@ reddifmail.com drstripathibhu @gmail.com

5. Methodology - Only diagnosis and Treatment of heart disease by astrological survey and data collection.
6. Year wise Plan of work -
   first year plan - Data collection of patients and jyotish grahayoga.
   second year - calculation of kundali position and natives present position.

Date 4/10/07,

(Dr Shatrughna Tripathi)
Dr. SHATRUGHANA TRIPATHI (P.I.)
P 01/588
JYOTISH DEPTT. S. V. D. V.
B. H. U., VNS.

Figure 4. Online forms published by the Department of Jyotish of the Banaras Hindu University during a research project on the astrological foundations of heart diseases.

732
5/10/09

सेवा में,

समन्वयक

कम्प्यूटर सेन्टर

का०हि०वि०वि०,वाराणसी

RSY
AB

द्वारा– ज्योतिषविभागाध्यक्ष,

विषय– नेट पर ज्योतिष विभागीय प्रोजेक्ट हेतु data collection के सन्दर्भ में, (P-01/588)

महाशय,

विश्वविद्यालय अनुदान आयोग के द्वारा मुझे "हृदयरोग का ज्योतिषशास्त्रीय निदान एवं उपचार" नामक प्रोजेक्ट प्राप्त हुआ है। जिसका विवरण संलग्न है। निवेदन यह है कि प्रोजेक्ट हेतु data collection के लिए निम्नलिखित विवरण को नेट पर डालने की कृपा करें।

If You have Heart Disease or any problem releted to your heart, pl tel me for free service through the major project at jyotish deptt. BHU,VARANASI,U.P mob. 09452186560. 0542-6703229.

Pl. send me blow detail.

Email **Add.** drstripathi_bhu@ reddifmail.com
drstripathibhu @gmail.com

Name --

Fathers Name ------------------------------

Date of Birth /---------/----------/----------

(Not Certificate date original DOB)

Birth Place -------------------------------------

Birth Time --/------------/-----------**AM/PM**

starting Date of Heart disease –

Name of particular disease-

Date --4/10/09--.

(Dr Shatrughna Tripathi)
Dr. SHATRUGHANA TRIPATHI (P.I.)
P 01/588
JYOTISH DEPTT. S. V. D. V.
B. H. U., VNS.

Attested
04-10-2009
ज्योतिष विभाग
संस्कृत विद्या धर्म विज्ञान संकाय
का० हि० वि० वि० वाराणसी–5

Sanskrit Rashtriya Vidyapeetha in Delhi, applies the same methodological approach to constitute a database including the horoscopes of a thousand patients who were treated at hospitals in Delhi for cardiovascular diseases, diabetes, and psychic disorders. In addition to the analysis of planetary conjunctions, the researchers ask the patients whose horoscopes they are studying to test astrological remedies based on precious stones and formulae (*mantra*) to evaluate the "clinical" efficacy of these methods through statistical studies.[44]

Epistemic strategies developed by academics in the field of medical astrology—the creation of a specialty, the use of graphic systems, the translation of Sanskrit terms into biomedical categories, an empirical and inductive method—aim to make Brahmanical knowledge conform to "scientific" categories and methods. These new ways of establishing a "commentary" of Sanskrit treatises do not however call the authority and epistemological principles established in the classical treatises into question, thus making astrology an exclusive space where Brahmanical truths and scientific knowledge cohabit.[45]

After examining astral knowledge as a textual discipline in the first chapter, and as an academic discipline in the second, in the following chapter we will go on to look at astrology as a discipline practiced by professionals. We will see that astrologers have a hybrid professional identity—a combination of religious authority and techno-scientific skill—that reflects the epistemological eclecticism of the discipline as it is defined in the astral literature, as well as the ambiguity of the position attributed to the teaching and practice of astrology at universities.

A significantly enhanced version of this chapter, including an analysis of the historical background and colonial sources, is forthcoming in the journal *South Asian History and Culture* (Guenzi forthcoming).

3

Sacred Specialists, Modern Professionals

Astrologers between the Temple and the Office

A Syncretic Professional Identity

In Banaras, there is a saying that "every Śiva lingam has its astrologer" (*ek Śiv liṅg, ek jyotiṣī miltā hai*), an expression used to mean that Banaras has innumerable astrologers, like the innumerable lingams that dot the town dedicated to Śiva. There are also sayings like: "There is an astrologer in every alley in Banaras" (*Banāras mẽ galī galī mẽ ek jyotiṣī miltā haĩ*), or "Banaras is the empire of astrologers" (*Banāras jyotiṣiyõ kā sāmrājya hai*). Astrologers (*jyotiṣī*), in fact, occupy a considerable position in this town that is home to about three hundred to four hundred full-time practitioners, and where two universities give institutional legitimacy to their knowledge.[1] Furthermore, in Banaras, academic astrologers are often themselves highly reputed practitioners.

Astrologers in Banaras benefit from the town's reputation as a sacred city and a center for Sanskrit culture and Brahmanical orthodoxy.[2] Clients coming from outside the town see Banaras as a privileged site where ritual practitioners are still capable today of conducting Hindu rites in the proper manner, "according to the rules" (*yathāvidhi*).[3] This reputation for "ritual excellence" contributes largely to the success of local astrologers, as consultations include rituals to be performed by the astrologer himself or by a staff hired by him. Thus people from all over India—particularly the states of Uttar Pradesh, Bihar, and Madhya Pradesh, and major cities such as Mumbai, Delhi, and Calcutta, as well as sometimes from abroad (Gulf countries, United States, Australia), go to Banaras, not just on pilgrimage to acquire spiritual merit, but also to take advantage of the divinatory, ritual, and therapeutic services offered by astrologers. For their part, Banaras's best-known astrologers travel widely, providing their services to wealthy families and companies that ask for their home services all over India.

As we saw in the preceding chapter, besides being described in Purāṇic literature, Banaras's reputation as a sacred town and a center of Brahmanical orthodoxy gained institutional approval from the British administrators during the colonial period. Today, the tourist industry and the mass media contribute to defining Banaras as a cultural and religious capital, and astrologers seem to benefit from the publicity generated by these new industries. Along with temples, ghats, yoga, and music, astrology is one of the main attractions mentioned on internet sites for tourists, dedicated to the town of Banaras.[4] In the list of services five-star hotels in Banaras offer their clients, consulting an astrologer appears beside access to the swimming pool, Ayurvedic massage, and guided visits of the town's temples. Posters in guesthouses and billboards in the streets also remind visitors, who may want to know their future or spend a week learning the principles of the discipline, that they are never far from an astrologer or a "Vedic astrology" center.

The visibility of Banaras's astrologers is also reinforced by their appearances on television channels or at media events described in the press.[5] A typical example is the wedding between the two Bollywood superstars Aishwarya Rai and Abhishek Bachchan. This celebration was the focus of huge media attention in 2006 and 2007, not only because of the spouses' fame but also because of the "planetary flaws" (*graha doṣa*) that the press claimed were present in the horoscope of Bollywood's most popular heroine.[6] Even before the wedding was publicly announced, the "Bachchan clan," known for its conservative stands, made a pilgrimage to Banaras accompanied by the future daughter-in-law. On this occasion a series of rituals were performed by the Bachchan's family's astrologer, Chandra Mawli Upadhyay, a Brahmin from Banaras who teaches at the Department of Jyotish at Banaras Hindu University. He is also a member of the Kashi Vishwanath temple management trust. According to media sources the rituals performed included those intended to neutralize the harmful effects of Mars on Aishwarya's horoscope, to protect her future husband from any kind of accident. The Bachchans' astrologer and other practitioners in the town, who were constantly questioned about the nature and significance of the rituals conducted, were thus the protagonists of numerous articles and reports on the question.[7] Beyond exceptionally popular events like these, their expertise is more commonly referred to in newspaper articles or televised interviews during elections, terrorist attacks, epidemics, or other events likely to affect national or international politics.

The professional identity of Banaras's astrologers should be considered in the context of the "industry of the sacred" that characterizes the holy town's economy, to which a large number of Brahmin families owe their survival. Although not directly involved in the "extremely big business" of pilgrimages and death (Parry 1994), astrologers in Banaras are an important category in the wide range of "sacred specialists" who provide religious services, not only for the town's inhabitants but also for its numerous visitors, pilgrims, and tourists. Astrologers nonetheless seek to distinguish themselves from other Brahmin specialists working in Banaras, like temple priests (*pujārī*), pilgrims' priests (*paṇḍā*), or funeral priests (*mahābrāhmaṇ*). As Parry's (1980, 1986, 1994) studies clearly show, in Banaras and elsewhere in India, these categories of Brahmin practitioners all have a reputation of being corrupt, degraded by their greed and the avidity with which they extort gifts (*dān*) from pilgrims and devotees. Their reputation is also tarnished by the morally negative implications associated with the acceptance of these gifts that are supposed to transfer the donor's sins and impurities to the Brahmin.

Astrologers refuse this type of "poisoned gift." This is a recent evolution as one or two generations ago, some Brahmin castes specializing in astrology—the Bhareriya, Joshi, or Shakadvipi—were known for accepting and receiving the most dangerous and evil type of *dān*: *graha-dān*, "planetary gift." Accepting this kind of *dān* was considered so degrading that, within the caste hierarchy and their own community, the status of these Brahmin astrologers was similar to that of the untouchable castes.[8]

Most of the Brahmins who practice astrology in Banaras today belong either to communities who were once specialized in the acceptance of planetary gifts or, more commonly, from *purohit* (family priests) families belonging to other Brahmanical communities.[9] Among these communities, until a few generations ago, the profession of astrologer was very rarely an occupational specialization and was more a complementary activity priests engaged in. Astrology was an integral part of the intellectual training a household priest followed as he had to be capable of identifying the auspicious times (*muhūrta*) for performing rituals, based on the planetary configurations described in the almanac (*pañcāṅg*).[10]

While claiming a pedigree that dates back to several generations of ancestors skilled in astrology, today's Brahmin astrologers are keen to display a "modern" and "secular" professional ideology: they do not accept *dāns* and often practice their profession in an office setting, with fixed rates and timings, appointments made over the phone, and their university degrees displayed on the walls of the waiting room. While in most cases they act as ritual specialists (*karmakāṇḍī*) as well as tantric specialists (*tāntrik*), astrologers in Banaras insist on distinguishing their occupation from that of the town's other ritual specialists. They describe it as closer to the liberal professions of doctor, lawyer, or architect. They seek to emphasize the "secularism" and "cosmopolitanism" of their work that does not discriminate between clients on the basis of religious belief, caste, or nationality. Hindu or Muslim, Brahmin or untouchable, Indian or foreign, everyone can enjoy the same astrological services.

In the following pages, we shall examine the syncretism that characterizes the professional identity of astrologers in Banaras, to show how the authority of astrologers is asserted today through the constant reference to a double idiom of legitimacy: the incarnation of a Sanskritic and Brahmanical tradition on one side, and on the other the display of a secular and "scientific" way of being modern professionals. The popularity of astrology, particularly among the urban elite, seems to us to be largely based on its syncretic virtue of being a knowledge that reconciles ancient and Hindu religious values with modern, secularized, and scientific values. We will now see how the syncretic qualities of astrological knowledge are embodied in the figure of the astrologer (*jyotiṣī*) in Banaras.

Pandits and Doctors

Most astrologers in Banaras share common characteristics in terms of their social background, training, the type of services offered, or the means of payment. It is nonetheless very difficult to make generalizations applicable to *all* the professionals practicing as astrologers in Banaras, which would allow us to establish characteristics intrinsic to the category of *jyotiṣī* or astrologer. For example, while it is true that astrologers are *generally* Brahmins, they are not *necessarily* Brahmins: of the fifty astrologers we met in Banaras, three do not belong to a Brahmin family.[11] Likewise, while it is true that astrologers are *generally* men, they do not *necessarily* have to be men, as, although rare, there are a few women astrologers in Banaras.[12] Although a large number of astrologers studied astrology at university and obtained a degree in this subject, there are also some who have not followed a certified course and who learned the profession from a teacher (*guru*). These, like other "exceptions," force us to develop a characterization of the astrologer's professional identity that is not based on an "extensional definition," or the description of all those who belong to the astrologer category in Banaras. We will hence develop an "intensional" definition—according to the logical acceptation of the notion—by identifying criteria that allow a certain professional to be recognized as an astrologer. In other words we will attempt to sketch the characteristics that define the professional identity of an astrologer and, for example, allow a member of a trader caste to be recognized as an astrologer, even if most astrologers belong to the Brahmin caste. We will thus see that what characterizes the profession of astrologer in Banaras today is the syncretic cohabitation of two profoundly different work ideologies. One states that the astrologer is a Brahmanical occupation intrinsically connected to priesthood, and the other that it is a modern and secular profession. Each practitioner "doses" and combines these two ideologies differently, but the reference to both is always present. The concomitance of these two ideologies not only allows us to explain the internal variations in the professional category but also helps us understand how the most popular astrologers in the town shape their professional identities.

A first element shows the cohabitation of two distinct professional ideologies among astrologers in Banaras: the honorary titles they use. In their visiting cards, some astrologers put "Pt." or "Pdt." before their name, while others use "Dr.": the first acronym is the abbreviation of "pandit" (*paṇḍit*) and the second of "doctor." Both titles indicate that the owner of the visiting card is "learned": the title pandit designates a person who is trained in Sanskrit studies, knows sacred texts (*śāstra*) by heart, and is recognized as a custodian not only of technical knowledge but also of a certain spiritual and moral wisdom (often associated with the observance of a form of renouncement, such as vegetarianism or sexual abstinence).[13] The title "doctor," conversely, designates a person who has obtained a doctoral degree from a university, without social or moral connotations.

Both these honorific titles that are printed on the visiting card serve to certify that the person is authorized to exercise the profession of astrologer, but each of these certifications has radically different connotations.

The title doctor, in fact, only indicates that the person has acquired a skill recognized by a public higher education institution, but it provides no information on the identity of the "doctor," who could be a woman, a Muslim, a Brahmin, or an Adivasi, as no other attribute, apart from the university qualification, has any bearing on the definition of a "doctor." The knowledge the astrologer possesses is, in this case, connoted as being a technical and objective skill—a "science"—independent of the person's social or religious identity. The honorific title of pandit, on the other hand, is synonymous with "learned Brahmin man" in Banaras: an astrologer who certifies his own professional skill with the title pandit is thus displaying certain elements of his social identity beyond his intellectual faculties and claims to be in possession of a knowledge connected to the Brahmanical tradition.

Among the astrologers we met in Banaras, those who have a doctorate prefer to introduce themselves as "doctor astrologer" rather than "pandit astrologer," although they are Brahmins trained in Sanskrit studies (and could lay claim to the title of pandit).[14] In our opinion, this choice is not due to the fact that university recognition affords an astrologer greater prestige than the status of learned Brahmin, but rather because the title of "doctor" associated with a surname—like Mishra, Tripathi, Upadhyay, Pandey, and so on—clearly states that the astrologer enjoys a Brahmanical pedigree as well. It thus certifies, at the outset, the astrologer's dual legitimacy and qualification to exercise his profession, both in terms of the skills he has acquired as well as in terms of his family tradition.

In Banaras, most "doctor astrologers" hold academic positions in the field of *jyotiṣa*: they are professors, readers, or lecturers working at one of the departments of jyotish mentioned in the previous chapter, or professors recruited by one of the thirty-odd Sanskrit high schools (*Saṃskṛta mahāvidyālaya*) in Banaras, where both branches of *jyotiṣa*—astronomy (*siddhānta*) and astrology (*phalita*)—are subjects included in the curriculum.

In addition to their salaried teaching or research jobs, these astrologers also practice a liberal profession as people consult them regularly for divinatory or therapeutic services. They are nonetheless keen to differentiate themselves from other astrologers, in that they do not ask for payment for the consultations they provide: as government employees, these academic astrologers are not dependent on the money they earn from their consultations for their survival, while "professional" *jyotiṣī* (the

English term "professional" is used in this context in a deprecatory sense) live solely off the payments they receive from their clientele. Academic astrologers say they only accept money spontaneously offered by their clients and have great disdain for astrologers "who demand" (*jo māṅgte haĩ*) payment. According to them, the latter are nothing more than crooks who use astrology for profit.

In reality, just like professional astrologers, academic astrologers are regularly paid by their clients, but as they are not entirely dependent on the fees they charge, they claim higher status.[15] The discourses these astrologers pronounce is evocative of the well-known Brahmanical ideology according to which the Brahmin-priest who is dependent on the gifts offered by the sacrificer (*yajamāna*) is inferior to the Brahmin-teacher who is closer to the ideal of renunciation and autonomy in relation to the social and material world (Heesterman 1985). "Doctor" astrologers see professional astrologers as corrupted and defiled practitioners who use astrology as a business, like the *paṇḍā*s or pilgrims' priests who make a profit out of devotion. Several academic astrologers did not hide their disappointment at the fact that I was *also* interested in the work of professional astrologers.[16]

Besides the coexistence of honorific titles like "pandit" and "doctor," astrologers' hybrid professional ideology can be seen in many aspects of their work: the reasons for going into the profession, the training, the criteria for gaining accreditation to the profession, the place where the service is provided, the duration of the consultation, the relationship to the client, and the methods of payment.

With regard to the reasons for going into the profession, we note that while the majority (in our survey, twenty-nine out of forty) decided to become an astrologer because it was in their family tradition (*pārivarik paramparā*), others entered this field as a matter of personal choice. The first category consists of Brahmin descendants of families that have been practicing astrology and priesthood for several generations as an occupational specialization.[17] The second category includes Brahmins, as well as representatives of other castes. When astrology is not a family tradition, the "personal choice" of specializing in this field involves different—and apparently paradoxical—motivations for Brahmins and non-Brahmins. Brahmins put forward material and economic arguments to justify their choice of this profession, while non-Brahmins describe a spiritual vocation. This is how Devesh Sharma, a Brahmin, explains why he became an astrologer:

> There were no astrologers in my family; my father was a *karmakāṇḍī* (ritual specialist). I didn't like his job as he had to fight like a dog to earn two or three rupees.

When it is not to earn money, in other cases it is to save money. Thus, Brahmin Ashwin Mishra recounts:

> My father was an uneducated farmer. After high school I was admitted to Engineering College, but I didn't have the money to pay for the course. So, I registered at the Faculty of Sanskrit Studies [at Banaras Hindu University] where there is a *jyotiṣa* department . . . it's the only faculty that's free. The five best students in the department receive a scholarship and I was one of them.

The astrologer Siddhartha, a non-Brahmin whose professional pseudonym reflects his spiritual aspirations, also recounts the reasons behind his choice to become an astrologer:

> When I was young, I enjoyed being around *sādhu*s, *saṃnyāsī*s, and astrologers. I became increasingly interested in astrology. It was as if I had an innate gift, I could predict a person's future just by looking at his face. I converted my family to vegetarianism and I abandoned my caste. Baba Saccha Sankar Dash was my guru in Bihar. I spent eighteen years studying, seven or eight with my guru and the rest alone . . .

Similarly, Ram Kumar Mehrotra, who belongs to the Khatri community of Punjab, explains his choice of becoming a professional astrologer as an "astral vocation." Like his father, his career was predetermined by the planetary conjunctions in his horoscope:

> People interested in astrology should have a specific planetary conjunction (*graha-yog*). To make someone an astrologer (*jyotiṣī banāne mẽ*), his Jupiter has to be very strong (*ucca*, "high"). My father was a Pisces, and he had Jupiter in the fifth house. This means that his Jupiter was the lord of the ascendant and occupied the house of learning (*vidyā*), so he was very clever.

> These people necessarily turn to astrology . . . Jupiter is very strong in my horoscope too: it is lord of the house of learning and also present in my house of destiny (*bhāgya bhāva*). My father realized straight away that I could become a good astrologer and he encouraged me to pursue this career.

Brahmins do not need to justify an innate skill, as it is implicitly guaranteed by their status of Brahmin, while non-Brahmins seek legitimacy in terms of a spiritual or astral vocation, thus adding a sort of compensation to their non-Brahmanical social identity.

In what concerns the times and places of consultations, we also note the coexistence of two types of practice. Some astrologers see clients at home and are available at any hour, while others have an office (*kāryālay*), with opening and closing times, and their clients have to make an appointment. Similarly, from the point of view of the payment methods, we note that some astrologers do not have fixed rates and only accept the fee (*dakṣiṇā*) the client wants to offer, while others have a preestablished *fee* table (they use the English word "fee").

Astrologers who do not set fixed rates declare that the remuneration should be left up to the client: each should pay according to his or her wish (*icchā*) and up to his or her means (*yathāśakti*). Many astrologers told us that when payment is not made "happily" (*sukh se*) and does not reflect the satisfaction or means of the client, it has malefic effects on the practitioner who accepts it. The intent with which the client hands over the fee or goods (for example, sweets or clothing) determines the effects the payment will have on the practitioner. When a *dakṣiṇā* (fee) or a *dān* (gift) is given because the person is satisfied and wants to express his gratitude toward the astrologer, it can only be auspicious (*śubh*), whereas a payment made unwillingly or an offering made with ill intent has harmful effects on the astrologer.

The client's "freedom" to give as much as he wants and as much as he can is nonetheless accompanied by the recommendation to pay at least some kind of fee for the service provided: a client who receives an astrological service without paying the specialist is said to be unable to enjoy the benefits of the consultation.[18] On this subject this is what the astrologer Shree Kanth Shastri explained to a client who had not paid for his consultation and who realized that the three amulets (*jantar*) the astrologer had given him were not effective:

> Now I understand why the *jantar*s I gave you don't work, you didn't give any *dakṣiṇā* . . . You know what happened to my guru's guru?
>
> One day, a young man went to my guru's guru and he showed him his hand. Looking at the hand, the guru said to him: "your lines are good, you will have a good life, and you will spend the last part of your life in Kāśī."[19] That very day, while he was walking in the street, the young man met another man, and they got into an argument. The young man hit the other man with a stick and accidentally killed him. The police arrived and began to investigate. They decided to take the young man to prison. In prison, the policemen offered to grant his last wish. So, the young man said, "I want to see my guru." So, he went to his guru and, furious, he complained that the prediction was wrong. The guru replied: "What I told you didn't happen. But did you fulfill your promise, to give me a *dakṣiṇā* of fifty kg. of rice? As you didn't give me a *dakṣiṇā*, what was to have been Kāśī (Banaras) has become *phāṃsī* (hanging)." Understanding the guru's message, the young man gave him the fifty kg. of rice and was taken back to prison. That evening there was a fire in the prison that killed almost all the detainees, but the young man managed to escape; everyone thought he had died so no one looked for him.

Kāśī (Banaras, "the Luminous") may become *phāṃsī* (hanging) for anyone who does not pay for the service provided: we indeed noted that it is very rare for clients not to give any *dakṣiṇā* for the consultation and this "spontaneous" payment normally ranges from fifty to a hundred or two hundred rupees.[20]

Fixed rates called *śulk*, or more commonly *fis* (from the English "fees"), solve all moral issues regarding payment for the service provided. This system of payment is systematically used for the preparation of horoscopes: horoscopes have fixed prices that vary depending on how detailed they are. The price of a "simplified" horoscope—which really only contains the description of the astral configurations present in the sky at the time of birth, is generally around 200–250 rupees, while the price of a "complete" horoscope, which includes the description of the different planetary "periods" (*daśā*) the person will go through over the course of his existence, as well as interpretations and therapeutic advice, costs about 500–550 rupees.[21]

A large number of "professional" astrologers also have fixed rates for consultations and because of this, as we saw earlier, those who do not explicitly ask for payment consider them inferior and corrupted. Some define their rates for a horary consultation "by question" (*prati praśn fīs*)—25 rupees a question, 50 rupees a question—while others charge for the overall consultation—50, 100, 150, or 200 rupees, depending on the astrologer. Nonetheless, the difference from astrologers who do not ask for payment is a question of form rather than substance: just as astrologers who leave the payment up to the client state that their hourly rate should be "up to the means" (*yathāśakti*) of the client, astrologers who apply predetermined rates modify them according to the client's economic situation (*ārthik sthiti*), so that each pays according to his or her means. For the same consultation, the astrologer can decide which rate to apply—fifty, one hundred, or two hundred rupees, for example, depending on the type of client. His clothing, the type of job he has, the area he lives in, and the client's own description of his financial situation generally provide the astrologer with the necessary elements to decide on the appropriate rate. In particular, these differential rates distinguish between Indians, NRI (Non-Resident Indians), and foreign clients and, as a reflection of the standard of living in their country of origin, the latter are supposed to pay anything from double to five or ten times the usual rates Indians are charged.

Temple, Home, and Office

The two professional ideologies described so far—"pandit" versus "doctor," family tradition versus personal choice, home versus office, *dakṣiṇā* versus fixed rates—should not however be seen as criteria that serve to define two categories of astrologers. In Banaras one does not find any practitioner that conforms exclusively to "traditional criteria" or to "modern," "secular" ones. In Banaras, *all* astrologers are both "traditional" and "modern," Hindu and "secular" and each one combines these features in his own personal way.

Let us now look at how the syncretism that characterizes the professional identity of astrologers is expressed in the work of individual astrologers in Banaras. The most popular specialists (at least in terms of the number of clients who come to consult them) in Banaras seem to be those who best reconcile the most rigorous respect for Brahmanical tradition with work methods that emulate the model followed by the liberal professions.

Among the city's most popular astrologers we will mention Neelkanth Shastri and Shree Kanth Shastri, two Bengali Brahmin brothers. Shree Kanth and Neelkanth Chattopadhyay were born in a village on the border of Bihar and Bengal. Their father and grandfather were astrologers and they were sent to study at an ashram in Bhagalpur where they "dressed like *saṃnyāsīs* (ascetics)." They then moved to Banaras and were trained in Sanskrit studies up to the level of *śāstrī* (equivalent to a BA in the British system), in *jyotiṣa* and other branches of Sanskrit learning (Vedic ritual, grammar, logic, etc.).[22] After learning astrological theory, the two brothers were trained for several years as astrologers under the guidance of some gurus of the town.[23] They then begin to practice, but due to the professional rivalry between them their paths diverged, so much so that today almost nobody knows that the town's two most famous astrologers are also brothers.

The older brother, Neelkanth Shastri, born in 1930, is undoubtedly the most famous astrologer in Banaras, and his services are highly valued both by the inhabitants of the poorest areas in the town and by the national economic and political elite. During the 1999 elections, for example, Neelkanth Shastri was sent twenty-seven plane tickets by politicians from all over India, and he spent six months on a sort of election tour. He left Banaras in the month of April and returned in October, having held consultations regarding the election results in the cities of Bangalore, Hyderabad, Bombay, Nasik, Indore, Meerut, Delhi, Bhagalpur, Patna, Ranchi, and Calcutta.

Often dressed in the orange ascetics' tunic, Neelkanth Shastri is a frail man, with delicate features; his hands are long and pinkish, and he has a growth in the middle of his forehead where the "third eye" would be. These signs give him the reputation of being a *bābā* (a term of respect, "father," "wise man") or a "Siddh saint" who has accomplished a lot of *tapas* (penance): the pink color of his hands and the "third eye" are seen as the results of the "fire" produced by his ascetic fervor. Nonetheless, this astrologer also has the reputation of being someone who manages a vast financial enterprise and who, instead of being "outside the world" as expected by the ideals of renunciation, is very much "in the world."

He is rooted in material affairs and involved in a network of social and political relationships that some suspect have ties to drug trafficking and mafia criminality.

The ambivalence of this astrologer's reputation is all the more obvious when we look at the manner in which he organizes his professional practice. Neelkanth Shastri practices his profession at home, in a house located a few hundred meters from the banks of the Ganges, in the Devanathpur neighborhood in the heart of the town. The ground floor of this house serves as an office-temple, where the astrologer receives his clients and performs rituals. He lives on the floor above with his family. His office consists of three rooms set around an arched hall where the temple is located. The three rooms, separated from the hall by luxurious glass doors with varnished wooden frames, are, respectively, the waiting room, Bābā's office, and the office of his elder son, who is also an astrologer. Fifteen meters away in the same *galī* (lane), and connected to the main house, Neelkanth Shastri owns another house, with a second temple that is also used for astrological treatments (his son lives on the first floor of this building, with his family).

From six to eight every morning—except Thursdays, his day off—Bābā offers his services free to all those who come to him. Neelkanth Shastri says he sees his profession of astrologer as a "social service" (*sāmājik sevā*) that he makes available to everyone, the rich and the poor, Hindus and Muslims, Brahmins and untouchables. So, a crowd of poor people, including dyers, cobblers, and sweepers, throng the hall of this astrologer's house every morning, waiting for a free consultation with Bābā and his team of ritual officiants. Neelkanth Shastri does not make any actual astrological diagnoses at these sessions but, with the help of his assistants, he provides ritual treatments, most often tantric in nature, to rapidly solve the problems of people who cannot afford a personalized astrological consultation. The morning's "free" service is followed by paid consultations for well-off clients throughout the day. A consultation with Neelkanth Shastri cost about two hundred rupees in the early 2000s, one of the highest rates charged by an astrologer in Banaras at that time, and it was definitely expensive for most Indian families.

The consultation with the astrologer has to be fixed by making an appointment with Mr. Shrivastava, Bābā's secretary, who sits in a corner of the waiting room answering the telephone and organizing the astrologer's schedule. Any time he has a practical problem to resolve, Bābā calls Mr.

Shrivastava by pressing a bell in his office that rings in the waiting room: the secretary immediately appears in Bābā's office, ready to carry out his instructions—making tea, buying cigarettes, changing an appointment, ushering in another client.

The door to Bābā's room has tinted glass so that those in the hall cannot watch the consultation: only clients who have fixed an appointment are received in this room. Inside, Neelkanth Shastri sits at his desk: the bookshelf behind him is filled with texts in Bengali, Sanskrit, and Hindi, and a briefcase on display just behind his head bears the inscription "International Astrological Conference 2000 A.D.—Under the auspices of the Astrological Research Project & Vishwa Jyotish Vidyapith ('University of Universal Astrology')." To the right of the office there is a rotating globe and a yellow board saying, "Each consultation lasts twenty minutes (*āpkā samay 20 minaṭ*)." Above this hang a large blue clock and an image of the Goddess Kālī.

When he meets clients in his office—usually about ten appointments a day—Neelkanth Shastri carries out a diagnosis by recording the person's astrological data in a large notebook that contains all his cases. In terms of diagnosis, it is important to note that Bābā is the only astrologer who prefers chiromancy over horoscope reading. Astrologers generally consider that because the data recorded in the horoscope are expressed numerically, they are more complete, objective, and clearer than the lines of the hand, and hence in a way not only more "scientific" but also easier to decipher. Palmistry, on the contrary is seen as a difficult science, and its reliability mainly depends on the astrologer's experience and subjective intuition. Although he prefers chiromancy, Neelkanth Shastri approaches it as an objective science, to the extent that he represents the lines on a person's hand on a sheet of paper, as a grid of twelve houses, just like a horoscope. In this manner, in the divinatory services he provides, Bābā emphasizes both his subjective power as a Brahmin who has a "third eye" as well as his objective skill as an astrologer.

After studying the hand for a nerve-wracking fifteen minutes, with the help of a large electric magnifying glass that illuminates and amplifies the lines, the astrologer asks a few questions about the client's situation, without ever being drawn into a lengthy verbal exchange. In this, Neelkanth Shastri differs from most astrologers whose consultations are, on the contrary, rich in divinatory dialogues and conversations of all kinds. He then writes his "prescription" on a postcard that the client is to keep on his person. The card says, "From Pt. Neelkanth Shastri to . . . ," filled in with the person's name and the appropriate remedies for his astrological situation. In particular, the astrologer indicates the type of *pūjā* (worship) the person should have performed, the date on which they should return, and the substances (fruits, flowers, etc.) and money required for the ritual that will be performed in both astrological office temples.

As is the case of most practitioners in Banaras, Neelkanth Shastri's work as an astrologer does not consist solely of identifying the client's astral situation, but it also involves performing rituals and preparing tantric remedies for his treatment. The astrologer (*jyotiṣī*) thus serves as a ritual officiant (*karmakāṇḍī*) and a tantric practitioner (*tāntrik*). To conduct the rituals, Neelkanth Shastri employs a team of ten Brahmins—commonly known as pandits[24]—who work under his guidance every day, performing the necessary rituals. In most cases the astrologer himself only performs the *saṅkalp*—"statement of purpose" in which the deity is invoked—and the actual ritual—repetition of mantras for hours on end—is then carried out by the team of pandits. Normally, Neelkanth Shastri does the *saṅkalp* inside the temple in the hall of his house, and the client then goes to the temple at the other end of the street where the pandits are ready to perform the second part of the ritual that most often consists of reading a sacred text (*pāṭh*) or making a *havan*, an offering of oblations into the fire.

Neelkanth Shastri embodies a range of contrasts: the temple and the office, free services and very expensive consultations, ascetic's clothing and the management of a team of employees. His house in Banaras is a sort of institution where all types of problems are addressed: from dog bite to the construction of a house, marrying a daughter to losing a job, asthma attacks to legal issues.[25]

The professional structure Shree Kanth Shastri created in the Shivala neighborhood, in the southern part of the town not far from the banks of the Ganges, is quite similar to his older brother's. Work is organized around the three axes of "work-office-temple." Shree Kanth Shastri fulfills the threefold role of astrologer (*jyotiṣī*), ritual specialist (*karmakāṇḍī*), and tantric practitioner (*tāntrik*) and has a team of pandits regularly appointed to perform rituals. However, his office is located in a building separate from the astrologer's home, about fifty meters away on the same street. The office serves mainly for consultations and diagnosis, while the therapeutic aspects of astrological treatment are carried out in the house, along with the rituals.

In the mornings, the astrologer works as a ritual specialist (*karmakāṇḍī*) at home while also supervising the work of four to five pandits (ritual technicians) who are permanent staff. The pandits conduct rituals in the courtyard when oblations into the fire (*havan*) are to be offered, or in the temple room located on the floor above, when they are only reciting mantras. After lunch, Shree Kanth Shastri goes to his office where he sees clients. As indicated on his visiting card, it is open in the afternoons and evenings, from "4 p.m. to 9 p.m.—Monday closed."

The functional and temporal complementarity between the home and the office is not always rigidly respected: sometimes people come to the house in the morning and he sees them for a consultation. Shree Kanth Shastri explains that the division between the office and the house is essential as it allows him to protect his own family from the daily encounters with a clientele that is not always respectable and sometimes seeks help with problems concerning sexual relations or violence, which would impair the purity of the home. For this reason, when people turn up at his home in the morning, the only ones he agrees to see are those who belong to the category of clients seen as "trustworthy"—women, a married couple, or a family.[26]

Although like his brother he wears the orange cloth of the ascetic to perform rituals and the pandits' traditional garb—a cream-colored *kurtā* and *luṅgī*—at his office, with his round face and fleshy hands, Shree Kanth Shastri does not share his brother's reputation of being a *bābā* gifted with spiritual power. He seems to be entirely focused on developing the image of a "modern" professional astrologer. During an interview Shree Kanth Shastri also explicitly evoked the idea that today's astrologers are "modern people." Thus, while describing the office of one of his clients, a lawyer, he explained to us: "He put in a table and all the rest (*table-vable*), like today's astrologers (*jaise jyotiṣī log baiṭhte haĩ āj-kal*), like modern people (*modern log*). Thus furnished, the room, which was not very attractive before, became very bright and charming."

To illustrate how Shree Kanth Shastri maintains his image of "modern astrologer," we will start by describing his office as it was in 1999–2000, and we will then compare this with what we found in 2002. The numerous changes the astrologer made over these two years shows how "modernity" constitutes a value in terms of the astrologer's professional identity.

When we first visited him in 1999, above the door to the office there were three blue boards, written, respectively, in Roman, Devanagari, and Bengali script, saying "Prācya jyotiṣ anusandhān kendra" (Center for Research in Ancient Astrology). Below this, the board with Roman characters said "Astrolzer and Karmakandee," followed by the astrologer's name and the address of the office. In addition to the qualifications of *jyotiṣī* and *karmakāṇḍī*, the boards in Hindi and Bengali specified "for all sorts of ritual acts related to astrology" (*jyotiṣ sambandhit sabhī prakār ke kāryõ ke liye*). Next to the entrance that consisted of two moldy white panels, the symbol of the Communist Party of India was splashed across the wall in red paint.

Inside, the office consisted of an entrance that served as a waiting room, furnished with a sofa and a few chairs, a room for the marriage agency Nirṇay (Decision, Choice), and a room for the astrologer's office. Shree Kanth Shastri created the matrimonial agency Nirṇay to supplement his activity as an astrologer: the client fills in an application form providing all the individual and family information concerning the candidate to be married and specifies the qualities he desires the future spouse to possess. For the sum of 350 rupees, the form completed at the agency entitles the candidate's family to a monthly letter containing references to three potential partners, while for 500 rupees, the family will receive three letters a month, each containing four references. The agency had 900 registered clients and had arranged 1,100 marriages in its eighteen years of activity, according to the astrologer. In 1999, it was run by a very old man, who sat behind a table covered in ancient pieces of paper, preparing the numerous handwritten letters to be sent every week to the agency's clients.

In the waiting room, a young pandit (ritual technician) seated behind a table was ready to cater to all the astrologer's needs and to usher in the clients. Shree Kanth Shastri's clientele generally belongs to the middle or upper classes: traders, businessmen, civil servants, bank employees, teachers, and so forth. However, artisans, auto rickshaw drivers, masons, or local unemployed people may also call upon this astrologer, but they generally come to request a tantric remedy rather than an actual astrological consultation. This astrologer has a vast and varied clientele that includes Hindus and Muslims, men and women, residents of Banaras and Indians from other regions (particularly Bengalis, but also people from Delhi or other towns in North India).

Unlike his brother, the length of Shree Kanth Shastri's consultations is not fixed and he sometimes keeps his clients for hours on end: he likes chatting with them, asking them questions, lingering over the details of the planetary configurations, recounting anecdotes, and developing a relationship of trust. In 1999, the price of his consultations was at the client's discretion: when the client was ready to pay and asked, "How much?" Shree Kanth Shastri would reply with expressions like "whatever you like" (*jo icchā ho, kyā icchā ho*) or "give the little you can" (*kam se kam jitnā de sakte hai, vahī āp dījiye*) insisting there was no fixed rate and everyone should pay according to their means, and above all, whatever they wanted. Most clients left about one hundred rupees, but those who had serious financial problems could pay nothing or would leave as little as twenty rupees.

When we were doing our fieldwork in 1999–2000, Shree Kanth Shastri wore heavy black spectacles with a plastic frame in a 1960s style. The first thing we noticed when we saw him again in 2002 was that he was wearing a new, light pair of gilt-framed glasses. In addition, the street dog, covered in fleas, that had hung around the house earlier had been replaced by a well-groomed, purebred golden retriever with shiny fur. The astrologer had taken to sleeping with the dog and it remained beside him during the consultations while its predecessor had been chased off vigorously if it ever dared approach the consultation room.[27] But these were only the first signs of a radical overhaul that involved the astrologer's entire office: outside, the wall had been repainted and the symbol of the Communist Party erased; the Bengali sign (giving the astrologer a regional connotation) had been removed; and on the English board, "astrolzer" had been corrected to read "astrologer." The moldy door panels had been replaced by a tinted-glass door, protected by lacquered wooden shutters. Inside, although they were never switched on, two computers were on display in the matrimonial agency office for the clients who waited their turn on the new, comfortable sofa in the waiting room. In the matrimonial agency room, the old man hidden behind a pile of papers had been replaced by a young girl seated before a typewriter: "Miss Sunita Halder, *manager*" read the new nameplate standing on the agency desk. The whole office was air-conditioned, a rare luxury in Banaras, and above the door to the astrologer's office was a board saying "fee: 200 rupees." A temple had been set up in a room behind the astrologer's desk, making the office completely separate from the house.

This gives us a better idea of what Shree Kanth Shastri meant when he said his lawyer client's office had been organized like those of today's astrologers, "like modern peoples' offices." The image of modernity this astrologer displays in no way implies he has abandoned his traditional identity, and Shree Kanth Shastri continues to wear his pandit's and ascetic's clothes and to provide the same ritual and divinatory services as before.[28]

Most of Banaras's astrologers are not as "modern" and "professional" as Shree Kanth Shastri and Neelkanth Shastri: they do not have a *table-vable office* (office with a table and such like) and they meet their clients seated on a small mattress (*gaddi*) placed on the ground. They have no waiting room, which means that the consultation is always a public affair, overheard by all those waiting their turn; they have no secretary to filter the astrologer's telephone calls, and so forth. But most astrologers do not perform rituals inside their houses either (they ask their clients to have them performed at one of the town's major temples), they do not have a full-time team of pandits at their disposal, and do not wear the ascetic's orange clothes. Most astrologers are hence neither as "modern" nor do they display their traditional Brahmanical identity so patently.

The reason we chose to sketch the portraits of these two brothers is because of their popularity. No other astrologer in town seems to attract as many clients as Neelkanth Shastri and Shree Kanth Shastri but, in addition, their clienteles are extremely diverse, as these astrologers adapt their services to the demands of all sorts of clients.

Other astrologers, on the contrary, have a more specific clientele. This is true of Chandrama Pandey, a professor at the Department of Jyotish of BHU. He sees people at his home, a flat inside the university campus. His clientele consists mainly of the population that lives and works on the campus: professors, researchers, and students, as well as employees and technicians. Kameshwar Upadhyay, a researcher at the same department, has also developed a faithful following at the university, particularly among the doctors, engineers, and lawyers, Brahmins for the most part. His clients also include numerous conservative right-wing Hindus as the astrologer's political commitment to the Vishwa Hindu Parishad is well known and has often made the headlines of the local press.[29] Another colleague at the department, Chandra Mawli Upadhyay, the son of the famous late Rajmohan Upadhyay (director of the Faculty of Sanskrit Studies as well as of the BHU Department of Jyotish from 1960 to 1984), boasts a clientele of national celebrities in addition to his university network. They range from "Big B," Amitabh Bachchan, Bollywood's supreme star, to the politician Mulayam Singh Yadav, who has been chief minister of Uttar

Pradesh three times, and include the multimillionaire businessman Anil Ambani (Reliance Group) as well as the cricket player Sachin Tendulkar. In Banaras, his address book is clearly the most "trendy."[30]

Dina Nath Tiwari, who works with his disciple-associate Kailash Nath Chowbe in the Ramapura neighborhood, holds his consultations for local inhabitants on the ground floor of his house. His clientele consists of policemen, bank employees, artisans, and teachers. The astrologers Shyamadhar Dvivedi and Shiv Dev Shastri have an office in the streets surrounding the Viśvanāth temple, a major landmark for anyone visiting Banaras, and Deoki Nandan Shastri's astrologer's sign hangs on the banks of the Ganges (at Chowsatti ghat), on the ground floor of "Shiv Ganga View," a hotel he owns. All of them have drop-in clients, generally tourists and pilgrims who are passing through the town.

During my last trip to Banaras, in 2008, a new category of astrologer had appeared on the "market" attracting a new type of client. They are specialists who, rather than exercising their profession at home, at an office, or a temple, sell their services at a shop (*dukān*) and use public advertising to attract clients.[31] These shops can be more or less sophisticated, a mere stall or a shop with a shiny facade and air-conditioning, selling all kinds of astrological and apotropaic products: precious gems, *rudrākṣa* (*Elaeocarpus ganitrus*) beads, amulets, bracelets, rings, necklaces, and all kinds of other objects supposed to protect people from evil influences, planetary or otherwise. The astrologer can be the owner or tenant of the shop, or may work there as a sales adviser.[32] Among those that are doing extremely well in Banaras we can mention the Shiv Astrological Hospital–Shiv Research Center on *rudrākṣa* (*Śiv jyotiṣ hāspiṭal–Śiv rudrākṣa anusandhān kendra*) that has four shops in Banaras and one in Mumbai, selling all kinds of apotropaic products and lucky charms.[33] The owner of the chain is "Docteur Anup Kumar Jaiswal," who claims expertise in the fields of astrology, *vāstu* (science of buildings), and gemology. The portrait of this commercial astrologer, his face surrounded by the rays of the sun, seated on a golden throne, the arms of which are decorated with lion's heads, adorns the walls of the town, and he also has auto rickshaws circulating in the town with his portrait displayed on the sides, to advertise his services (see plate 23 in the photo gallery). A low-caste specialist of profitable practices, he is considered a charlatan (*ḍhoṅgī*) and impostor (*dhokebāz*) by several astrologers with whom I had the opportunity to discuss. Nevertheless, all of them do not disdain this type of specialist, and three Brahmin astrologers are not averse to working regularly at his shops. Thus, the astrologer Pandit Ravindra Nath Sharma, descended from a family of astrologers, spends all his afternoons at one of Dr. Jaiswal's three shops near the Sankat Mochan temple. He reads clients' horoscopes and advises them on the products to buy—a "Feng shui golden card" (a lucky charm decorated with animals of the Chinese horoscope), a glass Eiffel Tower for academic success, or ceramic dolphins to attract money.

Before examining the divinatory and therapeutic services provided by Banaras's astrologers in the following chapters, we would like to look for a moment at two fairly atypical astrologers in the panorama of professionals to be found in this town: Paras Nath Ojha and Jitendra Narayan Pandey. These two figures allow us to reveal the widest context of today's Hindu astrological practice, and to return to questions we raised in the first part of this chapter.

In the village neighborhood of Nagwa, at the southernmost tip of Banaras, Paras Nath Ojha's three-story cement house stands like a skyscraper on the edge of a large drain that flows into the Ganges, amid an ocean of clay hovels. Born to an astrologer father in a village in Bihar, Dr. Paras Nath Ojha is a Kanya-Kubja Brahmin practitioner whose clients are mainly foreign, Americans and Canadians in particular. They are not tourists—who would actually find it very difficult to access this part of the town—but foreigners, the majority of whom have never been to India.

Paras Nath Ojha holds a doctorate in *jyotiṣa* from Banaras Hindu University. He says that at the end of the 1980s in Banaras he met a Canadian traveler who had come to study astrology. In the role of guru, Paras Nath Ojha trained the young Canadian, who went on to become an astrologer. When he returned to Canada, the young man invited him to visit. Dr. Ojha says that from 1991 to 1995 he traveled between the United States, Canada, and Europe, and that he was invited to give conferences at several American universities, such as Columbia, Boston University, the University of California, and others. Once he returned to Banaras, with some Canadian associates he founded the Jyotirveda Vigyan Sansthan (*Jyotirveda vijñān saṃsthān*, Association of Astrological Science) in 1996, an association that aims both to help the population of Banaras (particularly the population of Nagwa) "materially" and people from Western countries "spiritually." On the one hand the Jyotirveda Vigyan Sansthan uses its funds to finance a free school for the underprivileged children of Nagwa, and to encourage the construction of cement roads, as the mud road surfaces in this area are impassable during the monsoons. On the other hand, the association organizes the performance of sacrificial offerings of vegetal oblations into the fire (*yajña, havan*) or other forms of *pūjā* (worship) in order to "reduce the crime rate in the United States" or to intervene for the resolution of specific issues concerning Americans or Canadians. The "material" wealth of the West thus serves the people of Nagwa (the astrologer to start with), just as Banaras's "spiritual" wealth is supposed to help the inhabitants of countries that lack effective ritual practices.

In terms of resolving problems faced by Americans or Canadians (which seemed to us to be the association's main activity) the Jyotirveda Vigyan Sansthan does the following: the astrologer receives a fax/email from his associates on the other side of the Atlantic with the temporal and geographical coordinates of the client's birth, along with a brief description of the problem the person is experiencing.[34] Once he has calculated the person's horoscope and identified the planets responsible for the affliction, he draws up a list of rituals appropriate to resolving the problem; he then summons the required number of pandits (ritual technicians).[35]

Five hundred pandits work for this *pūjā* company, the Jyotirveda Vigyan Sansthan. Apart from special occasions such as a rituals conducted to bring about a general improvement in the state of the world, when all five hundred pandits are summoned together, the organization only calls upon fifty to sixty pandits a day. The rituals are performed at the Jyotirveda Vigyan Sansthan headquarters, a building located about two hundred meters from the astrologer's residence. This building contains a secretarial service, a hall, two rooms, and a garden with a raised platform and altar to perform the offering of oblations to the fire.

To give the reader an idea of how the astrologer organizes the pandits' work for concrete American and Canadian cases, we will describe a typical day (January 25, 2000) at the center. At 7:00 a.m. dozens of pandits of all ages—from fifteen to sixty years old—cycle through the Nagwa neighborhood on their way to the organization's headquarters. The astrologer is waiting for them there and he announces the rituals to be performed: in the first room eleven pandits recite the *Rām rakṣā stotra* (praise for Lord Rām's protection) for an American who has a problem paying his taxes; in the second room twenty-five pandits sing the *Durgāsaptśatī* (the seven hundred verses for Godddess Durgā), a sacred reading (*pāṭh*) to help Wallace, a Canadian involved in a court case. The astrologer says he has already performed four or five *pūjā* for him over the past year. In the hall, eleven pandits recite the *Hanumān cālisā* (the forty verses for the God Hanumān) for someone suffering from AIDS in the state of Iowa (USA), and in the garden fifteen pandits offer oblations to the fire for a Canadian woman suffering from cancer and heart problems. The performance of these rituals can last weeks, or even months, depending on the gravity of the cases, and the Americans or Canadians pay hundreds of dollars for this service.

Jitendra Narayan Pandey is chief astrologer of the website Cyber Astro (www.cyberastro.com). His work also involves "global" astrological services. The internet site this astrologer from Banaras works for was created in 1997, by the Indian "Cyber Media India Ltd." (CMIL) group of companies, with the aim of spreading the "ancient principles of Vedic Astrology" throughout the world, using the internet. "Vedic or Indian Astrology is over 5,000 years old and has stood the test of time. Cyber Astro makes these ancient principles more applicable for the New Millennium," says the "About Us" page of the site.[36]

As chief astrologer, J. N. Pandey provides personalized astrological consultations for the site's member-clients and he also organizes the performance of rituals ("Ceremonies") or sends amulets to people by post to protect them from harmful planetary influences. This is how his skills are certified on the website:

> **Dr. Jitendra Narayan Pandey—Chief Astrologer**
>
> Dr. Jitendra comes from a traditional family of Indian Gurus and pundits in Varanasi [Banaras]. From his childhood his father and grandfather trained him in Vedic Philosophy.
>
> He is a graduate from Banaras Hindu University in Astrology. He did his post graduation in Vedic Astrology from the same university. He was selected, as National Scholar by the University Grants Commission of the Government of India in 1992, to conduct research in Vedic astrology at Banaras Hindu University. During his research in the university he also taught Vedic astrology to the graduate students, and he was also the Asst. Editor for the Almanac (Vishwa Panchanga) published regularly by Banaras Hindu University.
>
> He was awarded his Ph.D. (Doctorate of Philosophy) in Vedic Astrology by Banaras Hindu University in 1996. His thesis for Doctorate research was on astrological computations

> for non-luminous planets. Dr. Pandey has been practicing Vedic Astrology and giving predictions since 1989.
>
> He joined Cyber Astro, as Chief Astrologer, in May 1997 and has helped Mr. Majumdar create standard services and products based on Vedic principles that can be marketed on the Net, and be delivered by email anywhere in the world.

This final portrait shows us an astrologer descended "from a traditional family of Indian Gurus and pundits in Varanasi" who also holds a doctorate in astrology from Banaras Hindu University. Yet again, this clearly evokes the idea that astrology is "Vedic knowledge," a prerogative of the Brahmins, and "scientific knowledge" accessible to everyone, just as the profession of astrologer is both a traditional occupation that requires an innate Brahmin pedigree *and* a modern and liberal profession, accredited by the university degrees obtained.

Plate 1. The teaching of astral sciences at the Banaras Hindu University. Photo: Author.

Plate 2. The teaching of astral sciences at the Sanskrit University. Photo: Author.

Plate 3. Making calculations for the annual almanac (*pañcāṅg*) in the Department of Jyotish of the Banaras Hindu University. Photo: Simon Georget.

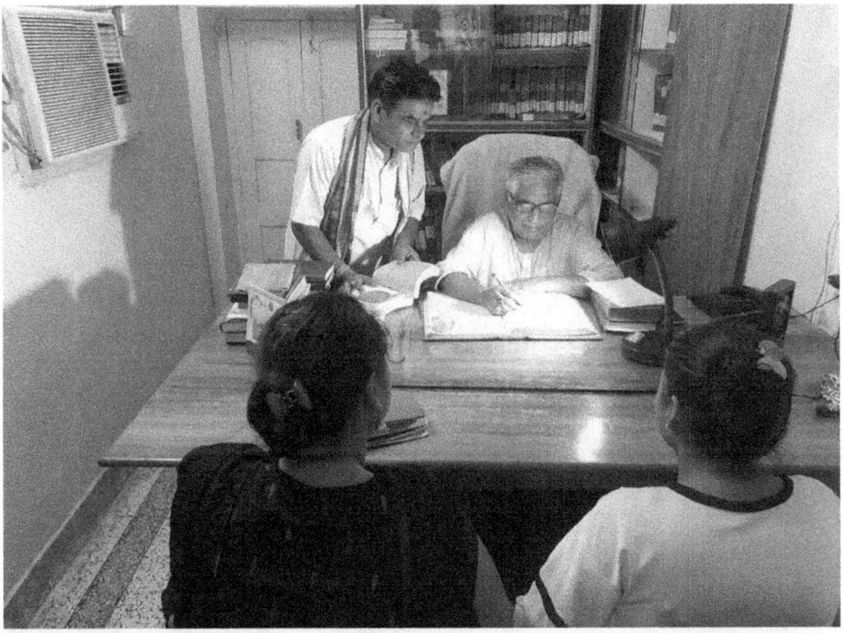

Plate 4. Astrologer Shree Kanth Shastri in his office during a consultation. Photo: Sunita Singh.

Plate 5. The team of ritual specialists working for Shree Kanth Shastri, performing a *havan* for a client. Photo: Author.

Plates 6 and 7. Waiting for a consultation at the astrologer's home. Photos: Simon Georget.

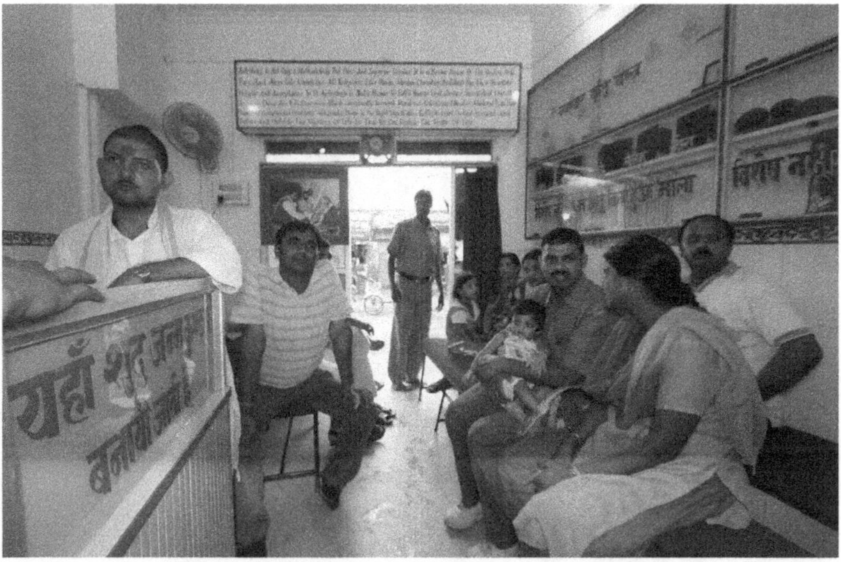

Plate 8. Waiting for an astrological consultation in an office near the Sankat Mochan Temple. Photo: Simon Georget.

Plate 9. How to choose the best daughter-in-law. Photo: Simon Georget.

Plate 10. The horoscope as a scroll. Photo: Simon Georget.

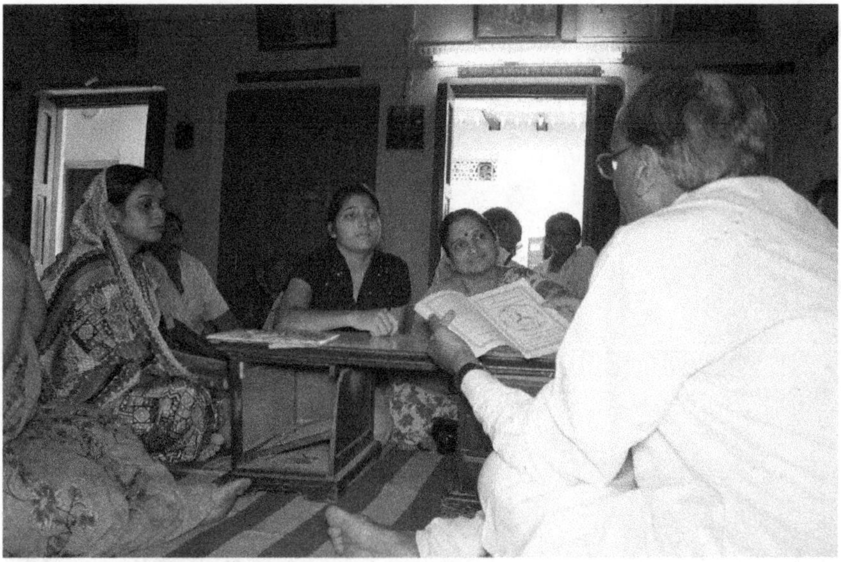

Plate 11. The horoscope as a copy. Photo: Simon Georget.

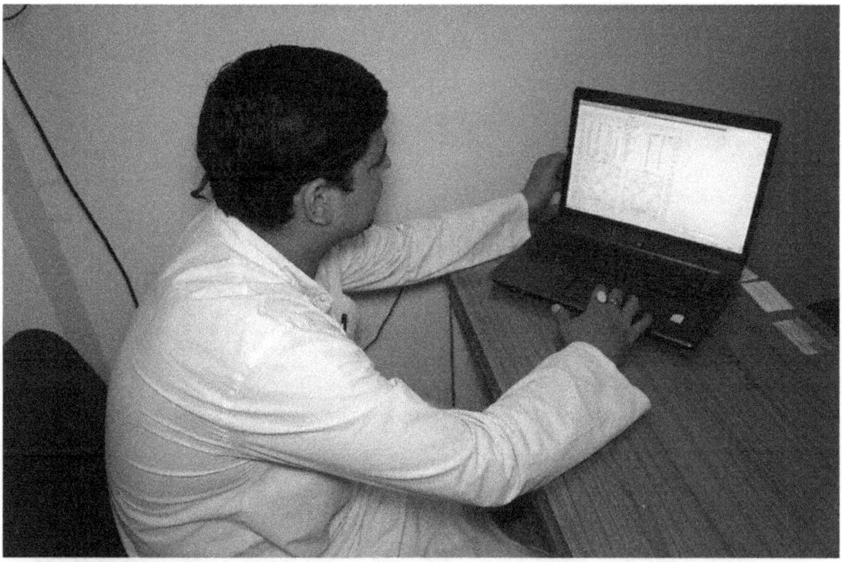

Plate 12. The horoscope via computer software. Photo: Simon Georget.

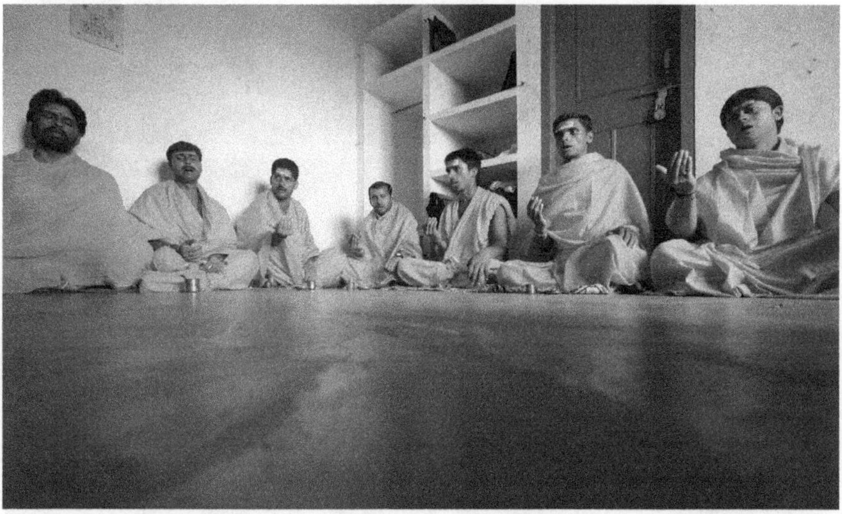

Plate 13. Brahmin ritual specialists performing *japas* (repetition of mantras) for American, Australian, and European clients. Photo: Simon Georget.

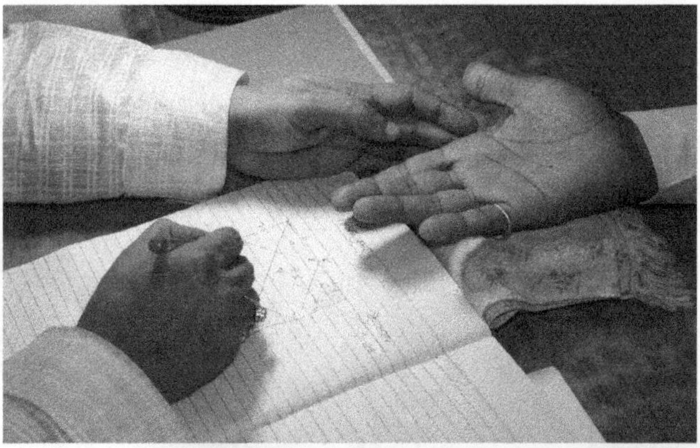

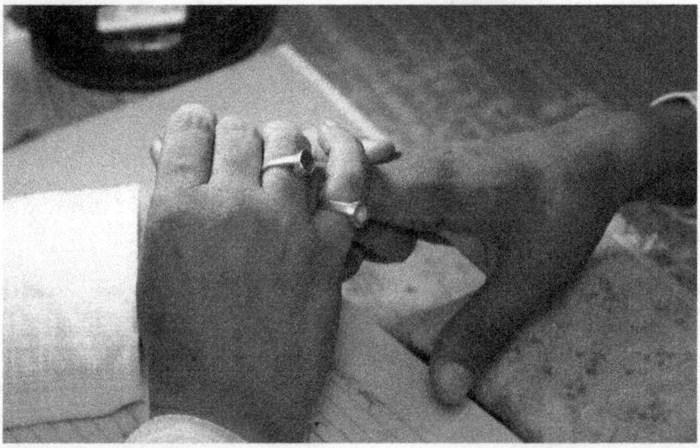

Plates 14-15-16. Hand reading. Photos: Simon Georget.

Plate 17. Astrologer Neelkanth Shastri performs the ritual of *prāṇa pratiṣṭhā* for a *jantar* (amulet). Photo: Author.

Plate 18. A shop selling astrological products. Photo: Simon Georget.

Plate 19. Choosing the right planetary gemstone in a jewelry shop. Photo: Simon Georget.

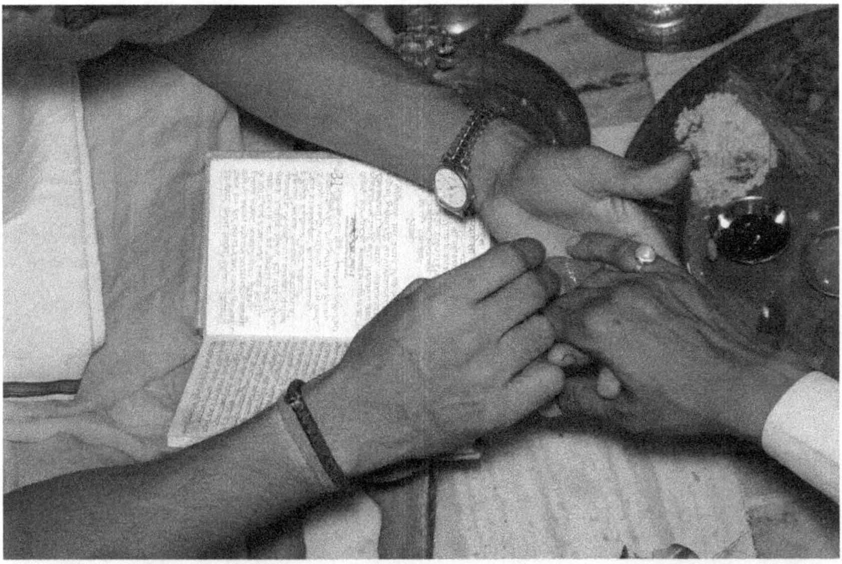

Plates 20 and 21. Performing the ritual of *prāṇa pratiṣṭhā* to make a gemstone ring effective. Photos: Simon Georget.

Plate 22. The billboard installed on a much-frequented road and advertising an astrologer's successful predictions (among these: India's victory in the cricket world cup, the election of Pratibha Patil as president of the Republic, the inclusion of the Taj Mahal among the Wonders of the World, the election of Mayavati as prime minister of Uttar Pradesh, and so on). Photo: Simon Georget.

Plate 23. An autorikshaw advertising a shop selling astrological items. Photo: Simon Georget.

Part II

Readings

4

Horoscopes and Truth

Divinatory Techniques and Their Applications

Astrologers in Banaras employ a varied and composite range of divinatory procedures. Interpreting birth charts, an activity we commonly call "astrology," is only one of the various methods of investigation used during consultations. While drawing up an inventory of the main techniques, the following pages will pay particular attention to examining the articulation between divinatory theory and practice, abstract principles and concrete applications. Rather than analyzing the *knowledge* astrologers possess, this chapter will focus on the study of their *expertise*, the skill they demonstrate during consultations that allows them to provide satisfactory responses to their clients' questions. From this perspective, divinatory techniques will be illustrated *in fieri*, through examples of situations or specific cases to which they are applied.[1] Our considerations will also take into account the reflexive aspect of astrological practice: the discourses specialists develop about the skills they possess.

In order to lay bare the processes at work in astrological consultations, the last part of this chapter will look more specifically at cases that, to an external observer, may seem to be "divinatory failures," that is, astrological diagnoses that do not match the clients' observations. Borrowing the social psychology concept developed by Leon Festinger in *When Prophecy Fails* (Festinger, Riecken, and Schachter 1964 [1956])—the famous book that describes the reactions of a group of believers who realize that the much-awaited, imminent apocalypse does not occur on the predicted date—we will examine cases of "cognitive dissonance" where reality seems to contradict the content of divinatory declarations. From our analytical perspective, failure is not seen as an "accident" *in spite of which* the astrologer and consultant continue to believe in the validity of divinatory knowledge but, on the contrary, as a constitutive element of the divinatory approach, without which astrologers' work would lose its meaning. It is, in fact, in situations where the astrologer is faced with the need to identify an error that the cognitive assumptions of his knowledge are fully revealed. As Jean-Pierre Vernant observes, divination would lose its *raison d'être* if it always foretold the truth:

> Divination infers secure conclusions about events whose outcome, whether desired or feared by the consultant, is always, by definition, uncertain at the start. If the omniscience claimed by the seer were to be fully realized, it would eclipse the function itself of divination, its practical purpose, as well as the chancy character of events, for the consultant does not expect the oracle to predict a future that is already inexorably fixed. (Vernant 1991, 310)

The discrepancy between diagnoses established by astrologers and facts perceived by clients not only contributes the *normal* functioning of divinatory practice but also allows astrologers to more deeply question the social facts mentioned during consultations. As we will see, situations of "cognitive dissonance" become an opportunity to question events highly charged with social expectations, such as arranging a marriage or the question of male versus female offspring.

Let us nonetheless start by presenting the diversity of divinatory techniques astrologers use. As we saw in the first chapter, the astrological branch—*horā* or *phalita*[2]—of astral knowledge (*jyotiṣa*) is divided into three sections (*aṅga*): *jātaka* (genethlialogy or natal astrology), *praśna* (interrogations or horary astrology), and *muhūrta* ("auspicious moments" or electional astrology). These three techniques serve to study the effects of astral configurations on earthly affairs, but each one takes a different temporal moment as meaningful: for natal astrology (*jātaka*) it is birth, for horary astrology (*praśna*) it is the time of the query, and for electional astrology (*muhūrta*) it is the moment of undertaking a particular activity.

Beyond these methods, astrologers also use chiromancy (*hastarekhāśāstra*), physiognomy (*sāmudrikaśāstra* or *aṅgavidyā*),[3] and *vāstuśāstra*, or the "science of sites and building" that studies how the spatial properties of buildings can affect peoples' lives. Even though they do not deal with the movement of the heavenly bodies in the sky, these three areas of divinatory knowledge nonetheless draw upon the language of the stars and are hence considered a part of *jyotiṣa*. In addition, astrologers in Banaras often employ another divinatory technique involving the study of small samples of soil (*miṭṭī*). This practice is partially linked to *vāstuśāstra*, the science of sites and building, and *saṃhitā*, the interpretation of omens, but it also follows its own autonomous interpretative rationales. By analyzing the smell, color, texture, and other properties of samples of soil taken from the site where the client lives or works, the astrologer identifies possible flaws (*doṣa*) likely to have a harmful effect on the life of the people involved (Guenzi and Singh 2009).

Besides the major types of divinatory knowledge mentioned so far, there are others, practiced less systematically and commonly. Breath divination (*svaravidyā*) is a technique related to tantric *yoga* practices. In this case the astrologer answers the client by analyzing the manner in which the breath enters and leaves through his—the astrologer's—nostrils at the moment when the client asks the question.[4] Another technique, oneiromancy (*svapnavidyā*), is generally used to discern whether the client is afflicted by ghosts (*bhūt-pret*) that are believed to appear in the client's dreams.[5] Finally, to complete the list of divinatory techniques we observed in Banaras, we will mention divination by throwing dice (*ramal*) or shells (*kauṛī*), techniques we saw employed by Muslim specialists, but which are not among the Hindu astrologers' skills.

During a consultation, the astrologer can thus choose from several investigative options depending on the type of data he decides to consider significant. It could be the person's date and time of birth, the time at which the consultation takes place, the time when a particular activity should be undertaken, the lines of the hand, the facial features, the way the interior of the client's house is laid out or the type of site where he lives, dreams (the client's or the astrologer's), or the way the astrologer perceives the movement of his own breath when the client asks a question. Practitioners do not see all these techniques as having the same level of objectivity and requiring the same type of training. While horoscopy is seen as a "science" that can be practiced by anyone who has learned the skills—even a computer—chiromancy, studying the soil, or interpreting dreams are considered embodied skills, which are more difficult to theorize. Thus, while horoscopy can be learned at university, the other divinatory methods are more commonly transmitted through a guru-disciple relationship.[6]

There are two ways to use divinatory techniques during consultations. One consists in formulating statements based exclusively on divinatory rules and procedures, through deductive reasoning.[7] Thus, for example, by looking at a person's horoscope, the astrologer infers the person's diseases—past, present, or future—the number of brothers, sisters, and children he has, his personality traits, and so on. The other consists in starting from perceived "symptoms"—the loss of a job, the difficulty in arranging a daughter's marriage, backache, among others—to identify the cause through inductive reasoning. For example, when a client is hurt in an accident or during a fight, the astrologer will examine the position of Mars in his horoscope or hand, since this planet is associated with wounds or violent fights, according to astrological theory. Nonetheless, while for heuristic and descriptive purposes it is useful to state that both these approaches exist and are employed, it would be false to claim that it is actually possible to distinguish, at every consultation, what is revealed by the deductive process rather than the inductive process, as the two are irrevocably intertwined.

Astrologers see the diversity of divinatory procedures as a coherent whole in which any technique, based on a varied category of signs, can contribute to developing a diagnosis. The relationship between the different divinatory methods is complementary rather than exclusive. Thus, reading a palm and a horoscope are two complementary methods, as they tend toward the same goal of knowing what is written in a person's destiny following two different routes. The heavenly pattern written in the horoscope describes, at the "macrocosmic" level, what the lines of the hand say at the "microcosmic" level. Astrologers thus assert that if the calculation of the horoscope and the reading of the hand are correct, there cannot be a contradiction between the content of these readings. Furthermore, divinatory techniques are seen as complementary at an etiological level, as each method specializes in a different category of causes. Astrological techniques serve to identify planetary causes, *vāstuśāstra* recognizes problems at the level of the organization of domestic space, the inspection of samples of soil probes the *doṣa*s (flaws, defects) that affect the site, the interpretation of dreams checks for the influence of the ghosts (*bhūt-pret*), and so on. On this subject, the astrologer Neelkanth Shastri explained that divinatory knowledge is not different from medicine or any other science that includes several methods of analysis and diagnosis:

> Just as doctors use urine examinations, X-rays, electrocardiograms, etc., we astrologers have the horoscope, the lines of the hand, *vāstu*, etc. If, for example, someone is sick, the astrologer should be able to determine (*nirṇay karnā*) through the symptoms (*lakṣaṇ*) whether it is because of the planets (*graha*), the soil (*bhūmi*), external flaws (*bahāri doṣa*),[8] or the surrounding atmosphere (*vātāvaraṇ*) . . . it is up to the astrologer's intelligence (*buddhimattā*) to know how to evaluate all these things simultaneously. . . . One has to proceed gradually, there is no predetermined method (*vidhi*) that tells you how to proceed . . . today science has techniques to carry out analyses of urine (*mūtr parīkṣā*), phlegm (*kaph parīkṣā*), or stool (*viṣṭhā parīkṣā*); in the same way, little by little, we are developing our techniques . . .

In order to show the distinguishing features of each divinatory technique, the following pages combine a study of the textual sources astrologers use—horoscopy manuals (*horāśāstra*), almanacs (*pañcāṅg*), and physiognomy manuals (*sāmudrikaśāstra*)—with an analysis of dialogues between astrologers and their clients during their consultations.

The Horoscope

In Banaras, the words *cakr* or *kuṇḍalī*—both meaning "circle," "ring," "diagram"—are used to refer to different kinds of horoscopes that may be calculated by astrologers:[9] the natal chart drawn upon the basis of the date and time of birth, the astral chart of the time one asks the astrologer a question, the diagram reproducing the lines of the hand or the spatial configuration of land. Thus there are several types of horoscope: the "birth horoscope" (*janm kuṇḍalī, janm cakr*), the "horary horoscope" (*praśn kī kuṇḍalī, praśn cakr*), the "hand horoscope" (*hāth kī kuṇḍalī, hāth kā cakr*), and the "land horoscope" (*zamīn kī kuṇḍalī, zamīn kā cakr*). In this study, we will thus use the term "horoscope" not only to refer to astral charts calculated at a specific time but also in the more general sense of diagram, or series of diagrams, depicting the destiny of a particular subject.

Astrologers calculate horoscopes not only for human beings but also for animals, houses, pieces of land, and other objects. This highlights a first important characteristic of their way of knowing: it goes beyond anthropocentrism. The first example that comes to mind in this respect is that of the astrologer Shree Kanth Shastri's dog, a golden retriever. It had its own horoscope and when it was ill, it was treated with a collar of tantric amulets and precious stones, remedies that provide protection from malefic planetary influences that are commonly prescribed for "human" clients.

Just like living beings, a piece of land, a region, or a state can also have a horoscope. For example, we saw in the introduction that the date chosen for the declaration of India's independence was decided after consultations with a committee of astrologers. The Indian nation thus has a horoscope calculated on the basis of this date.[10] With Taurus as the ascendant (*lagna*) and Cancer as the lunar sign (*rāśi*), the Indian nation's birth chart allows astrologers to provide interpretations and predictions regarding the relationship with Pakistan, election results, or the national cricket team's victories. Similarly, astrologers calculate the horoscope of a piece of land (*zamīn kā cakr, zamīn kī kuṇḍalī*) to know its flaws (*doṣa*) and its qualities (*guṇa*), the profit (*lābh*) it will produce, the type of crops that should be planted, the time it will take to build a house on it, suitable types of activities that can be started there, and so forth. This is how an astrologer explained the importance of calculating the horoscope for a piece of land:

> By examining the horoscope of a land (*zamīn kī kuṇḍalī*) you can see the compactness of the land, its age, fertility, the profits (*lābh*) or problems (*nuksān*) that may arise on the land . . . a land horoscope allows one to know what type of crop (*phasal*) to plant and the appropriate times for cultivation . . . a piece of land is like a woman's womb: it may be fertile or not, and this will change with time . . .
>
> By observing the trees you can see how much the *bhāgya* (fate) of a land may vary . . . on some sites there are trees that live hundreds of years, while on others they die after five years, blown over by the wind as the land is not stable . . . By looking at the horoscope of a site, you can know how long a certain type of tree will live, how long it will take to grow, whether the tree will be large, whether it will provide a lot of wood, whether the wood will be strong . . .

Beyond human beings, animals, land, or houses, horoscopes also refer to social events or processes: court cases, medical therapies, sexual relations, and so on. Astrologers investigate the outcome of any of these events, the conditions under which they would be successful, or the difficulties that might arise, by calculating the horoscope at the time of their undertaking.

However, the horoscope calculated for a human being's birth, known as a *janm kuṇḍalī* (or *janm patrī*), serves as a model for the calculation of most horoscopes. We will now describe the main elements that compose the *janm kuṇḍalī* and then consider the manner in which this basic grammar is employed and applied in different contexts.[11]

In its traditional form, the *janm kuṇḍalī* consists of a scroll, about seven meters long. Ganeśa, the God propitious to beginnings, and hence of course birth, is shown at the top of the scroll.[12] Nowadays, the scroll type of horoscope has largely been replaced by a notebook, with predrawn astrological diagrams, as it is easier to fill in and to consult. Astrologers fill in the scrolls or horoscope notebooks by hand, inserting not only the astral data that corresponds to the person's date of birth but also predictions and advice. However, some clients now have computer-calculated horoscopes produced by specially designed software. Praveen Issar, the founder of "Shubham Computer Astrologers," who holds an MA in *jyotiṣa* from BHU, sells her clients horoscopes calculated using the "Fortune Point" software. During my fieldwork in 2008 I observed that more and more astrologers, particularly those who work at the university, use PDAs (personal digital assistants) during consultations. This allows them to calculate their client's astral theme in just a few minutes, wherever they are.

Every complete *janm kuṇḍalī* is normally divided into three sections: the first is descriptive and illustrates through multiple diagrams the position of the stars at the time of birth and the planetary periods (*daśā*) the person will go through over the course of his or her existence. The second, interpretative, section indicates discursively the effects (*phal*) the astral configurations and the planetary periods will have on the person's life, while the third therapeutic section mentions the remedies (*upāy*) to be applied in order to reduce the negative planetary influences and to increase the positive ones.[13]

The basic diagram upon which every *janm kuṇḍalī* is elaborated is divided into twelve houses of the sky (*bhāva, sthāna*) (see figure 5).[14] In order, these houses are called:

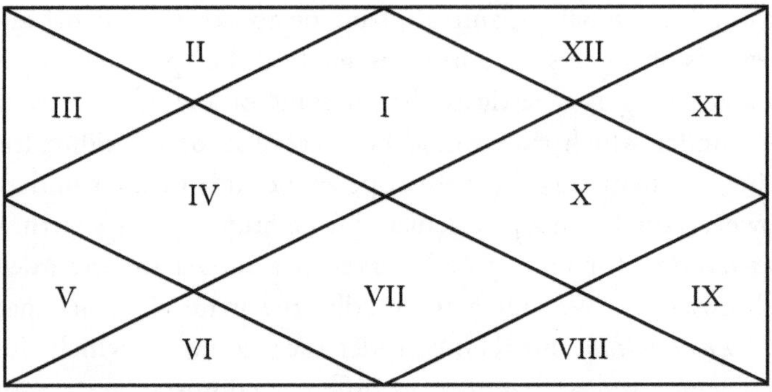

Figure 5. The twelve houses (*bhāva*) of the horoscope.

I. House of the ascendant (*lagna*) or house of the self/body (*tanu*);
II. Second house (*dvitīya bhāva*) or house of family (*kuṭumba*), wealth (*dhana*), speech (*vāc*), eating/possessions (*bhukti*), and eyes (*nayana*);
III. Third house (*tṛtīya bhāva*) or house of siblings (*sahaja*), courage (*vikrama*), servants (*bhṛtya*), and the ears (*karṇa*);
IV. Fourth house (*caturtha bhāva*) or house of relationships (*bandhu*), the mother (*mātṛ*), the home (*gṛha*), happiness (*sukha*), and travel (*yāna*);
V. Fifth house (*pañcama bhāva*) or house of progeny (*suta*), intelligence (*buddhi*), and knowledge (*vidyā*);
VI. Sixth house (*ṣaṣṭha bhāva*) or house of enemies (*ripu*), diseases (*roga*), weapons (*śastra*), dangers (*bhaya*), and wounds (*kṣata*);
VII. Seventh house (*saptama bhāva*) or house of the spouse (*jāyā*) and sexual desire (*kāma*);
VIII. Eighth house (*aṣṭama bhāva*) or house of death (*mṛtyu*) and longevity (*āyus*);
IX. Ninth house (*navama bhāva*) or house of fortune (*bhāgya*), *dharma* (religious norms), teacher (*guru*), austerity (*tapas*), pilgrimage (*tīrthayātra*), and auspiciousness (*śubha*);
X. Tenth house (*daśama bhāva*) or house of work (*karma*), profession (*vṛtti*), the father (*pitṛ*), royalty (*rājya*), and debts (*ṛṇa*);
XI. Eleventh house (*ekādaśa bhāva*) or house of gain (*āya*), cows (*paśu*), and daughters-in-law (*putrajāyā*);
XII. Twelfth house (*dvādaśa bhāva*) or house of losses (*vyaya*).[15]

The twelve houses indicate the constitutive elements of destiny. The first house or the house of the ascendant (*lagna*) represents the owner of the horoscope, the *jātaka* (the one who is born, the native) in his or her totality: his or her body, his or her personality, while the other houses refer to the different parts that compose him or her. They refer to the parts of the body, the members of the family, work, social relationships, material goods, and events (travel, accidents, theft, disputes, disease, sorrow) that are to mark his or her existence.[16] As a classification system of human existence developed and transmitted within Brahmanical culture, it is surprising to find no reference to the caste system in the twelve houses of the horoscope. Although the terms *jāti*—the "birth group," which is often translated as "caste"—and *jātaka*, "horoscopy," derive from the same Sanskrit root *JAN-*, "to be born," they nonetheless convey very different conceptions of human destiny as determined by birth. In fact, as Ashok Kumar Gaur, an astrologer from Banaras and the author of a slim astrological manual—the *Navagraha Rahasyam* (Mystery of the Nine Planetary Deities)—emphasizes, planetary influences do not differentiate between social groups:

> Despite all the differences separating the four *varṇa*s, there is one area where all the *varṇa*s are equal. One could call it "equality before the planets" (*grahõ kī samānatā*). The fundamental reason for this equality is that the planets are not interested in which *varṇa* a person is born into or their professional situation. The nine planetary deities (*navagraha*) exert all their influence (*pūrṇ prabhāv*) in the same way over people from all four *varṇa*s: from the planets' perspective (*dṛṣṭi*), people from every *varṇa* are the same (*grahõ kī dṛṣṭi mẽ cārõvarṇõ ke vyakti ek hī samān hote haĩ*). (1997, 9)

While horoscope theory does not mention belonging to one or another social group as a distinguishing criteria for human destiny, this is not entirely true of gender differences. Women's horoscopes are dealt with in a specific section of the horoscopy treatises, called *strī-jātaka* (women's horoscopy), and, as we will see in chapter 6, the signification of the twelve houses is different for women. For example, the tenth house of the horoscope, indicating professional activity, refers to the husband's profession in most cases.

When the horoscope is calculated for a nonhuman subject, the signification of the twelve houses is adapted to suit the context. Thus, for example in the Indian nation's horoscope, the first house signifies the government, the second wealth, the third the army, the fourth the transport system, and so forth. In the same manner, when looking at the outcome of a surgical operation, the first house shows the success of the operation, the second the cost, the third the nurses and so on. In his study of the the *dēvapraśnam* in Kerala, Gilles Tarabout shows that horoscopes can also be calculated for temples (not a common practice in Banaras): the first house symbolizes the image of the deity and the temple, the second the temple's management and finances, the third offerings, maintenance, the staff, and so on (2002a, 152).

The twelve houses define the different aspects that potentially constitute the person's destiny, while astral conjunctions (*yoga*) indicate what will actually happen in his or her life. Astral conjunctions are determined by the position of the twelve zodiacal signs (*rāśi*)—Aries (*meṣa*), Taurus (*vṛṣa*), Gemini (*mithuna*), Cancer (*karkaṭa*), Leo (*siṃha*), Virgo (*kanyā*), Libra (*tulā*), Scorpio (*vṛścika*), Sagittarius (*dhanus*, "bow"), Capricorn (*makara*, "crocodile"), Aquarius (*kumbha*, "water pot"), and Pisces (*mīna*)—within the twelve houses, as well as by the position of the nine planets (*graha*), Sun (Sūrya or Ravi), Moon (Candra or Soma), Mars (Maṅgala, Kuja, or Bhauma), Mercury (Budha), Jupiter (Bṛhaspati or Guru), Venus (Śukra), Saturn (Śani), and Rāhu and Ketu (the two lunar nodes).[17] The person's destiny is then interpreted by studying the network of correspondences connecting the planets and the zodiacal signs to other cosmological elements like colors, directions, the parts of the body, the members of the family, professional categories, the seasons, qualities (*guṇa*), savors (*rasa*), precious stones, and so on.[18]

Unlike Western astrology that pays a great deal of attention to the symbolism of zodiacal signs, during astrological consultations in Banaras the characteristics of zodiacal signs are rarely mentioned in the interpretation of natal charts and they play a very minor role in comparison to the planets. They serve mainly to identify the strength and the weakness of a planet, which vary depending on the zodiacal sign in which it is located. Astrologers in Banaras focus their interpretation of the horoscope, and the treatments they prescribe, on an identification of the benefic and, more importantly, the malefic influences of the nine planets. Thus, clients are not interested in the characteristics of the zodiacal sign under which they were born; instead they want to know the *planetary* influences under which their existence will unfold. We will have the opportunity to explore the importance attributed to planets, and some of the other specific features of *janm kuṇḍalī*, the birth chart, in the following chapters. Here we will continue our analysis with a presentation of the different divinatory methods used by astrologers in Banaras.

The Question

The diagram representing the twelve houses that we described for the birth chart is also used to calculate the horoscope of a question, a procedure known as *praśna* (question, interrogation, query), or more precisely *praśna gaṇana*, "calculation of the question." The astral theme of the moment when the astrologer is asked the question is supposed to contain within itself all the elements required to provide an answer, and there is no need to consult the birth chart.

This method is used when a person sees an astrologer to ask a specific question or is seeking a solution to a concrete and specific problem, whereas a birth chart is consulted when one wants to know what will happen in several aspects of life. Thus, for example, if a couple goes to an astrologer to know about their eldest son: which field of studies should be encouraged, when will he get married, why does he fall ill so often, and so forth, the astrologer will want to analyze the son's birth horoscope (or hand). If, however, the parents go to the astrologer solely to know whether their son will pass a specific exam, for example, the entrance examination for the faculty of medicine, the astrologer does not ask to see the birth chart. He consults the almanac, the *pañcāṅg*, instead and provides his answer based on an examination of the prevailing planetary situation of the day and the time when the question was asked.

There is however no precise rule to establish when *praśna* should be used and when it is better to look at the birth chart. There are questions that can be analyzed both through the birth chart and the *praśna* horoscope, and it is up to the astrologer to choose one method or the other. A fortiori, if the person does not have a horoscope, the astrologer will tend to use the *praśna* method; in addition, when an unexpected event occurs—for example, a theft, a girl running away from home with a boy, a job offer, and so on—the astrologer is most likely to use the *praśna* method. In Banaras, the divinatory power of *praśna* is used to analyze a single subject per person. Any subject raised after the first query can no longer be investigated by this method as the diagnostic efficacy of the horary horoscope is exhausted by the study of the first issue considered. Once the *praśna* has been calculated to respond, for example, to a client's question regarding his daughter's marriage, the astrologer will no longer be able to provide a correct answer to questions concerning her health (unless he uses other divinatory methods).

The order of priority the person asking a question establishes when formulating a *praśna* is decisive, as everything that is uttered "first" constitutes an object of divination: the first question formulated, the first term used for the question and the first syllable uttered. To explain further, let us look at the case of a man who had come to the astrologer to know whether he should sell or store the potatoes from the February 2002 harvest:[19]

> ♂: Should I put this year's potato harvest in a store (*bhaṇḍār*) or should I sell it (*becnā*)?
>
> J [= *jyotiṣī*, astrologer]: It's better to store it.
>
> ♂: Are you saying that by looking at the lines of my hand or because of the market price?
>
> J: Neither. I'm telling you this from the *praśna gaṇana* . . . there was a *praśna* . . . and I see that you should put it into storage and not sell it. The first question you ask me, and in the first question, the first word you utter, is what I will reply to. In your case it is the word *bhaṇḍār* . . . The very first word that comes out of your mouth when you ask the question is the decisive word: if you had asked me, "Should I sell or put it in a store," I would have advised you to sell, but as you shouldn't sell, the word *becnā* (to sell) was not the first word to come out of your mouth. What you said was the word *bhaṇḍār* (to store) . . .

Not only the first word of the question but also the first syllable uttered in the formulation of the question is loaded with divinatory value. In this respect, the methods of interpretation vary from one specialist to another: some astrologers associate the first syllable with a zodiacal sign and they look at the planets present in the sign at the time the question is asked. Others see the first syllable as corresponding to a planet and they study its position in the horoscope; yet others associate fixed significations with each category of letter (guttural, palatal, cerebral, etc.) and so on.

The questioner himself or herself plays a fundamental role in the way a diagnosis is conducted, to the extent that the answer to the question depends on *what* he asks, *when* he asks it, and *how* he formulates the question.[20] Sometimes, as in the case described earlier dealing with potatoes, the questioner is directly involved in the question under consideration, but this is not always necessarily the case. The questioner's relationship to the subject in question has no relevance from a diagnostic viewpoint. The questioner is in fact a constitutive part of the "signifier" of the question but is not necessarily connected to the "signified," as the question can involve anybody and anything.[21] For example, a family from a village may send a neighbor to the astrologer to know which direction their daughter who has run away has taken, or an uncle may want to know when it will be possible to arrange his nephew's marriage, or a woman may come to ask if the relationship between her younger sister's husband and his lover will continue, and so on.

As the *praśna* method limits the divinatory study to a single object, it allows for it to be examined from every angle, in the slightest details, as we can see from the rest of the consultation regarding the potato harvest:

> ♂: So, *maharāj*,[22] tell us something about the potato situation at the moment . . .
>
> J: About potatoes, I told you, after the month of May, the price will rise.
>
> ♂: After the month of May or until the month of May?
>
> J: No, it will begin in the month of May . . . until the month of May the price will rise a bit, but it's only after the month of May that the price will increase. So, in my opinion you will certainly earn money.
>
> ♂: Coming here I also wanted to know . . . In February will the potato production be sufficient for me to store some and sell some?
>
> J: Of course, it will certainly work. And there's something else, to do with papayas . . . you will do very well from papayas . . . so you should also plant some papayas . . .
>
> ♂: *Maharāj*, I had thought of planting cucumber . . .

J: It will be average, that is to say, you won't lose money, but you won't earn any either . . . it's a better idea to plant papayas, it will bring you money.

The storage of potatoes, the prices of potatoes in the month of May, the abundance of February's harvest, sowing papayas, and so on: the horoscope of the *praśna* allows one to examine the same wealth of details for a *situation* as one can for a *person* based on an examination of the birth horoscope.

Sometimes, rather than choosing the moment when the question is asked, the astrologer prefers to analyze the astral chart of the moment the event under consideration occurred. When, for example, someone runs away from home, the astrologer may choose to study the astral configuration of the time the questioner put the question to the astrologer, or the astral theme of the time when the person left the house. Thus, when a researcher on the Faculty of Fine Arts at Banaras Hindu University went to see the astrologer Shree Kanth Shastri to know why the dean of the faculty, Professor B. S. Katt, had left and had not returned, and where he had disappeared to, the astrologer examined the astral situation prevalent at the moment Professor Katt decided to leave his house on the university campus:

♂: On the thirtieth of last month, without telling anyone, the dean of my department, Professor Katt, left, I mean nobody knew . . . I want to know something about that.

J: On the thirtieth?

♂: Yes, the thirtieth . . . His work was going well, everything seemed to be fine, everything seemed normal, and one morning after having his bath and drinking his tea, at about eleven-thirty, he left without a word to anyone, and he never came back . . . the last person who saw him is a student who was near Vinay Cinema Hall, at about eleven-forty-five; he saw him in an auto-rickshaw, he was alone. On the 30th of last month, at eleven-thirty . . .

J [studying the *pañcāṅg*, the almanac]: So, this was seventeen days ago . . . on the 30th at eleven-thirty.

♂: Yes, seventeen days ago. I had been to see him two or three days before and I learned he had health problems.

J: In the meanwhile, have you lodged an FIR [First Information Report]?

♂: We put advertisements in the newspapers, made appeals on the television; we asked people in the street and people who know him (*parīcit*) . . .

J: He left to end his life, but he hasn't done so, he is alive. . . . He went toward the north (*uttar diśā*) . . .

♂: Toward the north?

J: He hasn't gone very far: Allahabad, Lucknow, Kanpur . . .

♂: So there . . .

J: Yes, in this region, a place between 25–26 degrees latitude . . . the latitude in Delhi is 28 degrees, he can't have gone that far.

♂: You mean he's in the area.

J: Yes, and he's going through a period of mental disturbance, but one isn't mentally disturbed for no reason . . . there must be a reason . . . and I know there is a member (*sadasya*) of his family who is involved, either his wife, or his children, or someone else . . .

♂: So he hasn't gone far? Toward Allahabad, Lucknow, Kanpur . . . and he was involved in a family dispute or something like that . . .

J: Yes, there's always a reason why someone is mentally disturbed . . . he may have problems in the department, but that's not sufficient, there must have also been family quarrels . . .

In this case the date and time were known, the astrologer decided that the time of Professor Katt's departure from the house was more significant, from an astrological viewpoint, than the time of the consultation. Nonetheless, when studying an event that has not yet occurred, it is preferable to look at the astral theme of the time of consultation.

While the birth chart and the question chart are generally used to help the questioner understand the situation he is in, and to make decisions, the branch of astrology known as *muhūrta* deals with the realization of activities that are already programmed and will be undertaken over the course of the year. Hence it is not used to clarify doubts but rather to discover the best circumstances under which the event should be undertaken in order for it to be successful.

Auspicious Times

Electional horoscopy or the branch of astrology concerned with calculating *muhūrta*s, "auspicious times," differs fundamentally from *jātaka*, birth horoscopy, and *praśna*, question horoscopy or horary horoscopy, in that a priori, independently from advisory sessions, it identifies times over the course of the Hindu lunisolar year that are favorable for undertaking certain activities. These "auspicious times" are indicated in the almanacs published each year in the main Indian cities. From an astrological viewpoint, while the interpretation of the horoscope attributes primary importance to the position of the planets in relation to the zodiacal signs and to the twelve houses, when it comes to defining *muhūrta*s the twenty-seven *nakṣatra*s (lunar mansions) play a crucial role.

The auspicious times defined in the almanac concern the performance of rituals and the undertaking of any activity that marks a beginning: thus performing *yajña*s (offering of oblations into the fire), the observance of fasts (*vrata*), *saṃskāra* ceremonies (the sixteen rites of passage in the life cycle, such as shaving the head, marriage, etc.), the beginning of agricultural work, the construction of a house, opening a business, buying a piece of land, leaving on a journey, all are activities that should be undertaken at the appropriate time indicated by an astrologer.

If a ritual is carried out, or an activity undertaken without respecting the *muhūrta*s, it is presumed that the ritual or activity will not be successful (or may even have harmful effects). This was the case of a couple who came to see the astrologer to tell him their son had been badly burned by some boiling milk. After the accident, to relieve the child's pain, the parents had had a *Rudrābhiṣeka yajña* performed, an offering of vegetal oblations into the fire (*yajña*) dedicated to Śiva in the form of Rudra. After studying the almanac attentively, the astrologer realized that the priest who had performed the ritual had not chosen the right *muhūrta*, and he stated that due to this mistake the ritual that had cost the parents six thousand rupees would not have helped alleviate the child's pain.

Respecting the *muhūrta*s signifies ensuring the success of what one undertakes, whether it be performing a ritual like a marriage, undertaking a legal procedure, or the construction of a house. An astrologer explains this idea in the following manner:

> There are times when people get married and times when they don't. People don't just get married when they feel like it. In the same way, if you have bought a piece of land and you want to build a house on it, you need to examine the time when you bought the land, the time when you're going to lay the foundations (*nīv*), the time to lay the first brick (*prastar*) and the other bricks. It is necessary to check that the time when the work is to begin is auspicious, that there are no obstacles (*bādhā vihan*), and that the building of the house can be completed. Sometimes the *muhūrta* is unfavorable and this can create problems in the process of building the house.
>
> Thus, when people have court-related matters, when they have to present a case before the court, they see if the time is favorable or not, and they go to see their lawyer at an auspicious time. They ask me to calculate the astral situation of the time when they are going to deposit the documents with the judge, to see if it is an auspicious time or not. If the time is not auspicious, the person may lose the case or the affair may take a long time.

The almanacs (*pañcāṅg*) published every year in different regions of India list the main *muhūrta*s for the current lunisolar year according to local standards.[23] Judy Pugh (1983c) has carefully examined how *muhūrta*s are identified over a period of four years (1973–1977) in four almanacs distributed in the Banaras region.[24] Her study shows how *muhūrta*s are recalculated every year on the basis of a complex combination of lunar, solar, and planetary time cycles. Among the most meaningful cycles, there are the two solar semesters (*uttarāyaṇa* and *dakṣiṇāyana*),[25] the solar or zodiacal months (*saura māsa*), the astral months (*nakṣatra māsa*),[26] the lunar months (*candra māsa*), the two lunar fortnights (*śukla-pakṣa* and *kṛṣṇa-pakṣa*),[27] the planetary positions (particularly in relation to the twenty-seven *nakṣatra*), the lunar days (*tithi*), the days of the week (*vāra*), and the different times of the day.

Each of these time cycles includes units of appropriate time—auspicious (*śubha*), favorable (*anukūla*), pure (*śuddha*), or "luminous" (*śukla*)—and units of inappropriate time—inauspicious (*aśubh*), unfavorable (*pratikūl*), impure (*aśuddh*), "dark" (*kṛṣṇa*), or "harsh" (*khara*). Hence there are auspicious and inauspicious lunar months, favorable and "harsh" solar months, a "luminous" lunar fortnight and another "dark" one, lucky and unlucky days of the week, and so on. The value of these connotations varies depending on the type of activity to be undertaken (Pugh 1983c). For example, some months are unfavorable for inaugurating a house but favorable for beginning agricultural work.

Astrologers consult the almanac (*pañcāṅg*) to identify the appropriate time to begin an activity—whether it be ritual, professional, agricultural, therapeutic, family oriented, or corporeal (e.g., a pregnancy).[28] The almanac describes the prevalent astronomical and astrological situation for every fortnight (*pakṣa*) of the lunar months of the Hindu year and indicates the *muhūrta*s that correspond to the astral conjunctions.

To understand how *muhūrta*s are described in almanacs, let us look at the *Kāśīviśvanātha Pañcāṅga* (or *Hṛṣīkeśa Pañcāṅga*) (Department of Jyotish 1999–2000, 11).[29] Each page of the almanac lists the "fortnightly *muhūrta*s" (*pakṣe'smin vividhamuhūrtāḥ*, "different *muhūrta*s of this fortnight") according to "lunar days" (*tithi*, astronomically corresponding to one thirtieth of a synodic month): for every lunar day the almanac indicates which planet or planets are in a particular *nakṣatra* and the rituals and activities than can be suitably undertaken at these times. For example, when reading the "bright" (*śūkla*) fortnight (*pakṣa*) of the lunar month of *caitra*,[30] one will see that the first three days of the month, and the eighth and ninth day of the month, do not contain any *muhūrta*, as the astral configurations on these days are not favorable to undertaking any activity. *Muhūrta*s are then described for the remaining lunar days (see table 2).

As we see, the *muhūrta*s indicate the suitable times for several types of undertakings. Among the ritual activities, we find the *saṃskāra*s, the sixteen "rites of passage" in the Hindu life cycle: the ritual to be accom-

Table 2. The *Muhūrtas* during the Bright (*Śūkla*) Fortnight (*Pakṣa*) of the Lunar Month of *Caitra* for the Year 1999–2000 (Department of Jyotish 1999–2000, 11)

Lunar day (*tithi*)	**Planetary configurations (planets and *nakṣatras*)**	***Muhūrtas***
4[a]	Sun in Bharaṇī	Bath after recovering from a disease (*roga-vimukta-snāna*)
5	Moon in Kṛttikā	Sale of a house (*vastu-vikraya*)
6	Mars in Rohiṇī	Bath after delivering a baby (*suti-snāna*) Wear red clothes [for the first time] and the precious stone coral, except for married women (*subhagāṃvinā-raktavastra-pravālaratna-dhāraṇa*)[b] Bleed the veins with a needle to purify the blood (*śirā-mokṣaṇa*)
7	Mercury in Mṛgaśīrṣa	Ritual for having a son and ritual for parting a pregnant woman's hair (*puṃsavana-sīmanta*) Birth ceremony (*jātakarman*) Name giving (*nāmakaraṇa*) Have the child chew betel nut [for the first time] (*śiśu-tāmbūla-bhakṣaṇa*) Place the new born on the ground [for the first time] (*bhūmi-upaveśana*) Weaning (*annaprāśana*) Using a bed or a seat [for the first time] (*śayyāsanādi-upabhoga*) Travel toward the east and the south (*pūrvadakṣiṇadigyātrā*) Architecture (*śilpavidyā*) Taking a medicine (*bhaiṣajya*)

continued on next page

Table 2. Continued

Lunar day (*tithi*)	**Planetary configurations (planets and *nakṣatras*)**	***Muhūrtas***
7	Mercury in Mṛgaśīrṣa	Building a boat (*naukāghaṭana*) Trade (*vipaṇi*) Trading in elephants and horses (*gajāśvakṛtya*) Harvest (*dhānyacchedana*)
10	Venus in Punavarsū	Ritual for having a son and ritual for parting a pregnant woman's hair (*puṃsavana-sīmanta*) Birth ceremony (*jātakarman*) Have the child chew betel nut [for the first time] (*śiśu-tāmbūla-bhakṣaṇa*) Weaning (*annaprāśana*) Using a bed or a seat [for the first time] (*śayyāsanādi-upabhoga*) Sacred thread ceremony for young Brahmins (*vipra-kumārānām-upanayana*) Wear new clothes, precious stones, and gold, except for married women (*subhagāṃvinā-navavastra-suvarna-ratna-dhāraṇa*) Manufacturing ornaments (*bhūṣāghaṭana*) Trading in cows (*gokrayavikraya*) Travel in any direction except toward the west (*paścimāṃvinānyadigyātrā*) Architecture (*śilpavidyā*) Taking a medicine (*bhaiṣajya*) Building a boat (*naukāghaṭana*) Trade in elephants and horses (*gajāśvakṛtya*)

11	Śani in Puṣya	Wear black clothes and a sapphire or other precious stones [for Saturn], except for married women (*subhagāṃvinā-kṛṣnavastra-nīlamādiratna-dhārana*) Trade (*vipaṇi*) Trade in elephants and horses (*gajāśvakṛtya*)
12	Sun in Āśleṣa Rāhu in Maghā	Manufacturing weapons (*śastraghaṭana*) Harvest (*dhānyacchedana*)
14	Mars in Pūrvāphālgunī	Bath after recovering from an illness (*roga-vimukta-snāna*)
15	Mercury in Uttarāphālgunī	Have the child chew betel nut [for the first time] (*śiśutāmbūlabhakṣaṇa*) Enjoying a bed or a seat [for the first time] (*śayyāsanādyupabhoga*) Wearing new clothes, precious stones, and gold, except for married women (*subhagāṃvinā-navavastra-suvarna-ratnadhāraṇa*) Manufacturing ornaments (*bhūṣāghaṭana*) Planting trees and plants (*latāpādapāropana*) Hulling grain (*kanamardana*) Wearing the *tilaka* (*tilaka-vrata*)

a. The fourth, ninth, and fourteenth *tithī*s are considered inauspicious and are called *rikta* (empty): for this reason the *muhūrta*s prescribed on these days do not deal with undertaking an activity, but releasing impurities accumulated over the course of an illness.

b. Several *muhūrta*s contain the clause *subhagām-vinā*, "except for married women." We were not able to elucidate the astral conditions under which this clause is applied. The question is open to future research.

plished for the pregnant woman so that she will have a boy (*puṃsavana*), the ritual of parting a pregnant woman's hair (*sīmanta*), the birth ceremony (*jātakarman*), the naming ceremony (*nāmakaraṇa*), receiving the sacred thread (*upanayana*), and others.[31] Identifying the right time is also important for undertaking commercial activities (selling a house; trading in cows, elephants, and horses), beginning an astrological or medical treatment (wearing red clothes and coral as protection against the influence of Mars, or taking a medicine), departures on journeys, making a valuable object (boat, ornaments), as well as agricultural activities (planting trees, harvesting, hulling grain), and so on.

The almanac provides a diachronic enumeration—day by day, fortnight after fortnight—of the *muhūrta*s that will occur throughout the year. Some *muhūrta*s are nonetheless also grouped synchronically: for a particular ritual ceremony or type of activity, the almanac specifies the lunar months (*candramāsa*), the fortnights (*pakṣa*), and the lunar days (*tithi*) over the course of the year when it is appropriate to perform the ritual or undertake the activity in question. Thus, on the last page, the almanac (Department of Jyotish 1999–2000, 45) specifies all the times of the year when one can undertake the following activities: the head-shaving ceremony (*caula*, *muṇḍana*), laying the foundation for a house (*gṛhārambha*) and moving into a house (*gṛhapraveśa*), beginning a course of study (*vidyārambha*), receiving the sacred thread (*upanayana*), the wife's entry into the husband's home (*vadhūpraveśa*) after her wedding, and the wife's arrival at the husband's home after a visit to her parents (a time called *dvirāgamana*, "second arrival"), laboring the earth with a plow (*halapravahaṇa*) and sowing (*bījopti*), consecrating a pond, a garden or a divine image (*jalāśayārāmasurapratiṣṭhā*), and commercial activities (*vipaṇi*, *vyāpāra*). On this subject, it may be of interest to note that the *muhūrta*s indicated for commercial activities are far more numerous than all the others: while there are about ten *muhūrta*s per lunar year for rituals, there are about fifty for commercial activities.

There are other *muhūrta*s grouped synchronically in the almanac, but instead of indicating the dates, the almanac only specifies the auspicious astrological conditions, depending on the position of the planets in relation to the *nakṣatra*s. The *muhūrta*s mentioned in this category are:

*muhūrta*s for success in business (*krayavikraya muhūrta*)
*muhūrta*s to obtain a government job (*sevākarma muhūrta* or *naukrī muhūrta*)

*muhūrta*s to use the sugarcane machine (*ikṣuyantra muhūrta* or *gannāmil muhūrta*)
*muhūrta*s to use the oil press (*tailikayantra muhūrta* or *telamil muhūrta*)
*muhūrta*s to start music or dance (*saṅgītanṛtyārambha muhūrta*)
*muhūrta*s for royal consecrations (*rājyābhiṣeka muhūrta*) (Department of Jyotish 1999–2000, 5)

As we can see from these examples, *muhūrta*s are calculated particularly for activities that mark a new beginning, an investment, or a new phase of the life cycle. The birth of a child is, par excellence, an event that marks a beginning and the entry into a new life cycle (both for the child and for the family). The almanac thus pays particular attention to determining all the *muhūrta*s that precede and follow the birth of a child. Thus the *Kāśīviśvanātha Pañcāṅga* defines the appropriate days of the week (*sad-vāra*), the appropriate *nakṣatra*s (*sad-bha*), the appropriate lunar days (*sat-tithi*),[32] and the pure ascendant signs (*śuddha lagna*) for the *muhūrta*s that come before and after the birth of a child:

*muhūrta*s for ritual ablutions (*ṛtumatyāḥ snāna-muhūrta*)
*muhūrta*s for conception (*garbhādhāna-muhūrta*)
*muhūrta*s for the ritual carried out to ensure the birth of a boy and for the ritual of parting a pregnant woman's hair (*puṃsavanasīmantayor-muhūrta*)
*muhūrta*s for entering the delivery room (*sūtikāyāḥ sūtīgṛhapraveśa-muhūrta*)
*muhūrta*s for the birth rites (*jātakarman*)
*muhūrta*s for breastfeeding (*stanapāna-muhūrta*)
*muhūrta*s for placing the newborn on the bed [for the first time] (*khaṭvārohana-muhūrta*)
*muhūrta*s for taking medicines to relieve delivery pains (*sūtikākvāthauṣadhibhakṣaṇa-muhūrta*)
*muhūrta*s for the bath after delivery (*sūtisnāna-muhūrta*)
*muhūrta*s for placing the newborn on the ground [for the first time] (*bhūmyupaveśana-muhūrta*)
*muhūrta*s for the first time a newborn goes out of the home (*niṣkramaṇa-muhūrta*)
*muhūrta*s for the naming ceremony (*nāmakaraṇa-muhūrta*)
*muhūrta*s for the child's first solid food (*annaprāśana-muhūrta*)

muhūrtas for the mother's ritual bath one month after the delivery (*jalapūjana-muhūrta*)
muhūrtas for learning the alphabet (*akṣarārambha-muhūrta*) (Department of Jyotish 1999–2000, 5)

Everything that precedes and follows the delivery of a child must be performed or undertaken at the right moment. The very act of delivering a child can be considered an activity that should be undertaken "at the right time," on a special *muhūrta*. This was at least the perception of an engineer who consulted the astrologer Kameshwar Upadhyay when his wife was in the ninth month of her pregnancy. He wanted to know the "right time" (*acchā samay*) for her to deliver the baby so that his son would have the most favorable horoscope. Holding the almanac, the astrologer asked:

J: Tell me the approximate delivery date according to the doctor . . .

♂: Between the ninth and the tenth of the month . . .

J: Listen, this is the problem: if he is born on the ninth, it will fall on a *mūl nakṣatr*[33] . . . what about the eighth? Oh no . . . on the eighth too, from seven onward there is a *mūl nakṣatr* . . . Can she hold on till the tenth? . . .

♂: Yes, till the tenth . . .

J: Then fix it for the tenth, in the morning . . . Until 6:10 a.m. there is still a *mūl nakṣatr*, but then it leaves . . . oh no! In fact, after 6:10 there are no powerful *nakṣatr* (*bal nakṣatr*) and the child will be weak (*kamzor ho jayegā*). I would like him to be born under a strong *nakṣatr* (*bal tagṛā nakṣatra*) . . . so the ninth is better in fact, actually, it's not a problem if there's a *mūl nakṣatra*; you just need to perform the *pūjā* to pacify the *mūl nakṣatr* . . . it won't cost much, you just have an ordinary (*sāmānya*) *pūjā* done, you don't need to throw a party . . . and for the delivery, you have it on the ninth, between 4:00 and 6:15 in the evening, so that the child will have Leo in the

> ascendant (*lagna*), Taurus as his lunar sign (*rāśi*), and a permanent *yog* (planetary configuration) for foreign travel (*videś yātrā kā permanent yog*) . . . the child will have an excellent horoscope from the point of view of his studies too (*vidyā ke dṛṣṭi se*) . . .

A "strong" *nakṣatra* (*bal tagṛā nakṣatra*), combined with an ascendant (*lagna*) and a lunar sign (*rāśi*) that also denote power (Lion and Taurus), plus a planetary conjunction (*yog*) that encourages foreign travel and studies, guarantee the child a "successful" life.[34] This case clearly shows there is not always a clear difference between the three branches of astrological knowledge—*jātaka*, *praśna*, and *muhūrta*—and that there is a common logic behind birth horoscope theory and the other branches. Birth horoscope is only one among the innumerable types of "horoscopes" that can be calculated. In other words, birth is seen as a particular type of beginning, just as every beginning is seen as a particular type of birth.

In the divinatory techniques described so far, the temporal dimension is crucial: we have hence dealt with techniques that are "horoscopic" in the etymological sense of the term.[35] Let us now look at some divinatory methods where factors other than time are taken into account for the calculation of horoscopes (*cakr* or *kuṇḍalī*).

The Hand, the Body

The "horoscope of the hand" (*hāth ki kuṇḍalī, hāth kā cakr*) is based on the geography of the lines (*rekhā*), the mounts (*sthāna*, "places"), and marks (*cihna*) on the palm (*karatala*). Chiromancy is practiced either directly by examining the questioner's hand, by making a handprint on paper using colored paint, or by transcribing the characteristics of the hand as a diagram made up of twelve houses, just like the birth horoscope. Whatever the method chosen, for men, it is the right hand that is studied, and for women, the left.

To describe the main characteristics of the hand, we will refer to the *Sāmudrikarahasya* (The Mystery of Physiognomy; Sharma and Mishra 1999), a short popular treatise on chiromancy and physiognomy, in Sanskrit with a commentary in Hindi and illustrations. It is available in bookshops and at stalls in Banaras (see figure 6).[36]

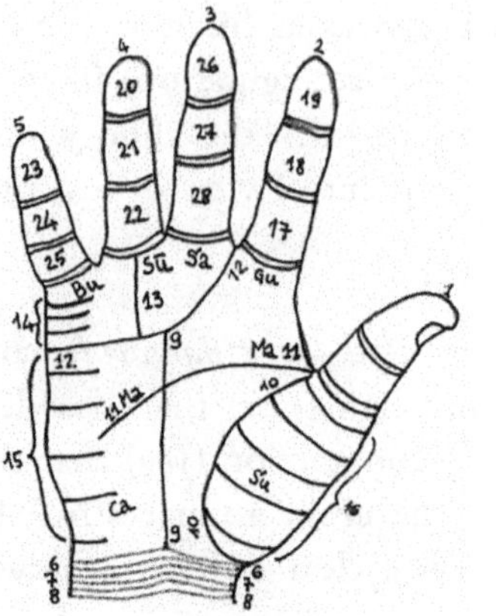

Figure 6. The lines of the hand according to the *Sāmudrikarahasya*, a manual of chiromancy and physiognomy (for ease of reading, the numbers and letters in Hindi have been changed to Roman script).

Fingers (*aṅguli*):
1. Thumb (*aṅguṣṭha*)
2. Index (*tarjanī*)
3. Middle finger (*madhyamā*)
4. Ring finger (*anāmikā*)
5. Little finger (*kaniṣṭhā*)

Bracelet lines (*manibandha-rekhā*):
6. Line of devotion (*bhakti rekhā*)
7. Line of learning (*śāstra rekhā*)
8. Line of wealth (*dhana rekhā*)

Lines of the palm (*karatala-rekhā*):
9. Line of destiny or social mobility (*bhāgya-rekhā vā ūrdhva-rekhā*)
10. Line of the father or *karman* (*pitṛ-rekhā vā karma-rekhā*)
11. Line of the mother or head line (*mātṛ-rekhā vā śīrṣa-rekhā*)
12. Line of longevity or death (*āyu-rekhā vā svānta-rekhā*)
13. Line of merits or knowledge (*puṇya-rekhā vā sarasvatī-rekhā*)
14. Line of marriage or of woman (*pariṇaya-rekhā vā lalanā-rekhā*)
15. Line that shows brothers and sisters (*bhrātṛbhaginī-sūcaka-rekhā*)
16. Line that shows descendants (*santati-sūcaka-rekhā*)

Zones of zodiacal signs (*rāśi-sthāna*):
17. Aries (*meṣa*)
18. Taurus (*vṛṣa*)
19. Gemini (*mithuna*)
20. Cancer (*karka*)
21. Leo (*siṃha*)
22. Virgo (*kanyā*)
23. Libra (*tulā*)
24. Scorpio (*vṛścika*)
25. Sagittarius (*dhana*)
26. Capricorn (*makara*)
27. Aquarius (*kumbha*)
28. Pisces (*mīna*)

Zone of the planets (*graha-sthāna*):
Sū = Sūrya (Sun)
Ca = Candra (Moon)
Ma = Maṅgala (Mars)
Bu = Budha (Mercury)
Gu = Guru (Jupiter)
Śu = Śukra (Venus)
Śa = Śani (Saturn)

The vocabulary of chiromancy clearly reproduces that of horoscopy (list of planets and zodiacal signs), with the lines (*rekhā*) replacing the houses (*bhāva*). The lines of the hand and the houses of the horoscope are made to match: thus, the line of brothers and sisters (*bhrātṛbhaginī-sūcaka-rekhā*) corresponds to the third house ("the house of brothers and sisters," *sahaja-bhāva*); the line of the mother (*mātṛ-rekhā*) corresponds to the fourth house ("house of the mother," *mātṛ-bhāva*); the line of children (*santati-sūcaka-rekhā*) corresponds to the fifth house ("house of children," *suta-bhāva*); the marriage and woman line (*pariṇaya-rekhā vā lalanā-rekhā*) corresponds to the seventh house ("the wife's house," *jāyā-bhāva*); the line of destiny (*bhāgya-rekhā*) corresponds to the ninth house (*bhāgya-bhāva*), and so forth. Using this system of correspondences between lines and houses, the astrologer can translate the features of the hand into a diagram with twelve houses. The different planetary influences are then calculated by examining the zones (*sthāna*): the protuberance of the mounts, the position of marks or lines that show a stronger or weaker influence of the different planets.

Positive qualities or events are generally indicated by a line that is clear and distinct (*svaccha, spaṣṭa*), straight (*sarala*), deep (*nimna*), smooth (*snigdha*), obvious (*vyakta*), unbroken (*avicchinna*), pure (*śuddha*), immaculate (*nirmala*), and so on. A line shows negative qualities and events if it is broken (*chinna-bhinna*), twisted (*ṭeṛha*), dirty (*malina*), in the form of a chain (*śṛṅkhalākāra*), and so forth. The person's age is defined by the longevity line (*āyu-rekhā* or *svānta-rekhā*): depending on whether it ends at the level of the little finger, the ring finger, the middle finger or the index finger, the person will live, respectively, from 0 to 30, from 30 to 60, from 60 to 90 and 90 to 120, the width of a finger being equivalent to about thirty years.[37]

The signification of the different lines and marks varies depending on where they are located: a line in the shape of a triangle (*trikoṇa-rekhā*) indicating prosperity, for example, shows that it will come from the mother's side if it is on the mother's line, and paternal wealth if it is on the father's line. In the same way, the small lines of violence (*hiṃsā-rekhā*) show family conflict if they are located on the mount of Venus (*Śukra-sthāna*), and not completing one's studies if they are near the line of knowledge (*Sarasvatī-rekhā*). This is also true of the planetary zones: the presence of *hiṃsā rekhā* on the mount of Saturn (*Śani-sthāna*), for example, indicates accidents caused by this planet, and so forth.

In general, the hand is supposed to provide the same information as the horoscope: according to astrologers, there can be no contradiction between the lines of the hand and the data in the birth chart as each expresses the same destiny by two different means. Nonetheless, the two methods are thought to be trustworthy in different ways. While the hand is supposed to be more reliable than the horoscope because it unequivocally belongs to the person, the natal chart is seen as a more reliable diagnostic tool than the hand, due to its mathematical language and its high degree of precision that makes it possible to study all the aspects of a person's destiny in greater detail. For this reason, if the client has a horoscope, the astrologer normally examines the horoscope first. However, if the horoscope seems problematic—which is often the case—as it has not been calculated for the right time or because it contains errors, the hand becomes the more reliable divinatory source.

Another feature that distinguishes these two divinatory methods is the fact that while the data in the birth chart are fixed once and for all at the time of birth, the lines of the hand are supposed to change over time. Most astrologers recognize that the lines of the hand change, but the periods under consideration may vary. Thus, according to the astrologer Tar Kesh Joshi, the lines of the hand change over the course of the day: just as the facial features are altered by the events that occur during the day and they change from morning to evening, this is also true of the lines of the hand. For this reason, according to this astrologer, the hand should be read in the morning before it has been affected by external events and when the lines are at their clearest. According to the astrologer Shree Kanth Shastri, the lines of the hand develop and change until the age of twenty-four, by which time all the lines have taken shape and the palm is considered complete. From this age onward, every aspect of the person's destiny is supposed to be visible; nonetheless, even if all the lines are "in place" by the age of twenty-four, they are supposed to change their shape and depth every two or three years. According to most astrologers, every two or three years we can see changes in the lines of the hand; for this reason, chiromancy is supposed to be particularly reliable when it comes to analyzing questions regarding the next few years, rather than the long term.

Time, however, is not the only agent that is supposed to modify the lines of the hand: the astrologer Kameshwar Upadhyay, for example, prescribes a remedy for his clients who are experiencing difficulties. He advises them to massage the palms of the hands and the forehead (as these lines also reveal a person's destiny) with curd, in order to make the lines softer, smoother, and shinier, as he believes this helps reduce the afflictions indicated by the lines. And according to some astrologers, rings set with precious stones worn on different fingers can also modify the lines of a person's hand and hence his or her destiny. From what astrologers say, there is a reciprocal interaction between the conformation of the person's hand and his or her destiny: the hand records the changes in a person's destiny that can be confirmed over time, just as the person's destiny is affected by the changes in the hand produced by external agents like curd or rings set with precious stones, as in the aforementioned examples.

Although according to my survey astrologers do not make charts (*kuṇḍalī, cakr*) for other parts of the body than the hand, these may also be inspected. Thus, a part of the body that is carefully examined is the face, particularly the forehead: following a popular saying, the forehead (*lalāṭ*) is considered the "residence (*nivās*) of destiny (*bhāgya*)." In Banaras it is said that a good astrologer should not need to see the horoscope to know a person's planetary situation, as everything is written on the client's forehead and face. This is the correspondence between the lines of the forehead, the parts of the face, and the planets, as described in the *Sāmudrikarahasya.*

The representation (Sharma and Mishra 1999, 53) in figure 7 shows seven lines on the forehead (*lalāṭa-rekhā*), which from the topmost to the lowest correspond to the planets Saturn, Jupiter, Mars, Sun, Venus, Mercury, Moon, Sun, and Moon. In what concerns the rest of the face, the right and left eyes are, respectively, the "place of the Sun" (*sūrya-sthāna*) and the "place of the Moon" (*candra-sthāna*); the point where the two eyebrows meet is the "place of Venus" (*śukra-sthāna*), the nose is the "place of Mercury" (*budha-sthāna*); the left and right ears are, respectively, the "place of Jupiter" (*guru-sthāna*) and the "place of Saturn" (*śani-sthāna*); the cheeks are the "place of Mars" (*maṅgala-sthāna*).[38]

Figure 7. Face-reading according to the *Sāmudrikarahasya.*

The principles behind the study of the morphology of the human body are set out in the *Bṛhatsaṃhitā* by Varāhamihira, the most well-known Sanskrit text on divination.[39] This is a sort of "encyclopedia" of divination, written in the sixth century, that interprets all kinds of terrestrial and astral omens. Several chapters of this treatise deal with the interpretation of the "signs" (*lakṣaṇa*) revealed by men's and women's bodies.[40] The morphology of male and female bodies is meticulously sectioned and the person's qualities, flaws, social position, fortunes, and misfortunes are studied on the basis of the size, shape, and color of different parts of the body.[41] Let's consider, for example, how the navel (*nābhi*) is painstakingly examined:

> Men with round, protruding, and large navels are happy; a small, invisible, and deep navel produces suffering; an irregular navel, situated in the belly fold, produces pain from a spear (or colic pain) as well as poverty; a nombril twisting [from right] to left leads to dishonesty, while [from left] to right gives intelligence; an oblong navel on both sides gives a long life; an oblong navel on the top makes a man a lord; an oblong navel at the bottom gives plenty of cows; and the navel that resembles the lotus receptacle makes a king. (BS 68.21–23)

In the same way, the morphology of the feet, the calves, the hair, the knees, the thighs, the genitals, the buttocks, the stomach, the waist, the sides, the nipples, the chest, the shoulders, the neck, the armpits, the arms, the fingers, the wrists, the palms, and the nails, all have a signification (BS 68.2–50). In what concerns the face, the different shapes of the chin, the lower and upper lips, the teeth, the tongue, the palate, the mouth, the skull, the moustache, the beard, the ears, the cheeks, the nose, the eyes, the eyebrows, the temples, the forehead, the lines of the forehead, and the hair are all interpreted, along with the proportions between the parts of the body, the complexion, the voice, the strength, the articulations, the waist, the weight, the height, the smell, the "nature" (*svabhāva*), and the manner of walking, sneezing, crying, and laughing (BS 68.51–116).

Despite the unquestioned authority attributed to Varāhamihira's *Bṛhatsaṃhitā*, astrologers in Banaras consider that the science of physiognomy set out in this text is very difficult to apply during consultations, and rather than examining the details of the person's bodily morphology, they prefer to see the client's body as an indication of the planetary influences that dominate the person. The astrologer finds the client's body particularly eloquent when he has some kind of disease: depending on the type of problem affecting the client's body and depending on the part of the body affected, using the system of equivalences established by astrological theory, the astrologer traces the symptoms back to the unfavorable planet and prescribes the appropriate remedy. Thus, for example, the Sun governs the function of sight and the heart organ: if the client is suffering weakness in the eyes, such as severe myopia, or cardiac problems, the astrologer deduces the person has the Sun in an unfavorable position in their horoscope. He will then prescribe having a Sun *pūjā* (worship) performed. In this context, the body is hence examined as a planetary map that reveals the planetary influences without always needing to look at a horoscope.

To conclude this presentation of the techniques of astrological divination employed by astrologers in Banaras, we would yet again like to emphasize the extent to which all the techniques described so far form a divinatory continuum. A minor "divinatory science" is described in the almanac in the section on *muhūrtas* related to the birth of a child: this is the method used to know the effects (*phala*) of the appearance of a child's teeth (*danta-janana*) after the age of one month. The almanac presents a diagram (*cakra*) that describes the corresponding effects depending on the month when the teeth appear (see table 3).

Table 3. The Effects on Children of Developing Teeth from the Age of One Month Onward (*Prathamādi-Māseṣu Bālakānāṃ Danta-Janana-Phala-Bodhaka-Cakram*) According to the *Kāśīviśvanātha Pañcāṅga* (Department of Jyotish 1999–2000, 5)

First month	suicide (*svayaṃnāśa*)
Second month	death of a younger brother (*kaniṣṭhabhātṛnāśa*)
Third month	death of a sister (*bhagininā́śa*)
Fourth month	death of the mother (*mātṛnāśa*)
Fifth month	death of an older brother (*jyeṣṭhabhātṛnāśa*)
Sixth month	pleasure/enjoyment (*subhoga*)
Seventh month	immediate happiness (*tātātsukham*)
Eighth month	prosperity (*puṣṭatā*)
Ninth month	obtaining wealth (*lakṣmīprāpti*)
Tenth month	happiness (*saukhyam*)
Eleventh month	happiness (*saukhyam*)
Twelfth month	obtaining wealth (*dhanasaṃpatti*)

This odontomancy table is a combination of several branches of astrology: it lies between the study of *muhūrta*s—the "first" teeth have to appear at the right time; the study of omens (*saṃhitā*)—the appearance of a tooth is a symptom of something that will happen; physiognomy (*sāmudrikaśāstra*)—the shape the body takes has a significance; and horoscopy (*jātaka*)—not only does it deal with "birth" (*danta-janana*, the "birth" of teeth), but divination over a period of twelve months recalls the twelve houses of the horoscope (some analogies are in fact obvious: the first means the self, the fourth the mother, etc.).

Now that we have presented the main divinatory techniques employed by astrologers in Banaras, we will examine the difficulties that can arise when applying abstract rules to actual cases.

Truth of the Horoscope, Reality of Facts

During consultations, astrologers make constant efforts to apply abstract, textual rules to actual, observed situations, and to read empirical evidence as the expression of astrological principles. Nevertheless, it happens sometimes that the statements made by the astrologer are incompatible with what the clients observe or are experiencing. The astrologer may find himself faced with a contradiction between what the horoscope says and what the clients say. When faced with this incongruity the astrologer has the choice between two options: either he considers the horoscope wrong—that is to say, it was calculated for the wrong time or it contains errors—or he considers that the empirical evidence is fallacious, that is to say, "in reality" things occurred differently from the manner in which they were perceived. As we will see through the analysis of divinatory dialogues, the evidence of facts is seen as far more malleable and subject to caution than the truth of the horoscope. While a correct horoscope is always true, the facts observed and described by clients are open to error: they may conceal a reality that cannot be perceived directly.

In certain cases of incompatibility between the horoscope and the clients' observations, astrologers do not hesitate to question the objectivity of the facts stated by the clients. At first glance this procedure may seem somewhat crude, a sort of manipulation of reality in order to make reality fit the astrological interpretation. But a closer analysis of the cases reveals that the questioning astrologers apply to reality is, in a way, extremely "realistic" and contributes to provide answers to the clients' questions. Let us look at a few examples of how adjustments are made between the evidence of facts and the truth of the horoscope.

During a consultation, looking at a young, sixteen-year-old girl's palm, the astrologer states she will not be married before the age of eighteen. However, the mother says she has already arranged her marriage for the month of March, that is to say, a few months after the consultation. Given this incongruity, the astrologer resolves the discrepancy between his own exegesis and the facts by claiming the girl is not of the age the mother claims:

> J [studying the girl's hand and speaking to the mother]: How old is she?
>
> ♀: Sixteen.
>
> J: Does she have a fickle (*cañcal*) temperament?
>
> ♀: Yes, she has stopped studying.
>
> J: She has three brothers.
>
> ♀: Yes, she has three brothers.
>
> J: She will also have three sons and she will be married in two and a half years.
>
> ♀: But we have already arranged her marriage; it will be performed in March![42]
>
> J: No, her hand says she won't be married before the age of eighteen. Have you already given the money to the husband's family?
>
> ♀: Yes . . .
>
> J: So that means she is eighteen, and not sixteen.

♀: No, I know her date of birth . . . she is sixteen. Now I'm worried . . . This means the wedding won't be celebrated?

J: No, no, don't worry, the marriage will be celebrated . . .

However arbitrary it may seem, the astrologer's doubt about the girl's age is not at all unfounded, as the age of young women in India tends to be highly malleable. The older the girl, the fewer the potential husbands available, and the more likely it is that her age will be reduced by default in order to retain the widest possible selection of marriage proposals. When dealing with questions of marriage astrologers are often distrustful, not only of the girl's stated age but also of the date of birth mentioned in the horoscope.[43] In the case in question, while contesting the astrologer's allegation regarding the girl's age, the mother in no way underestimates the problem raised by the incompatibility between the astrologer's words—the girl will not be married before the age of eighteen—and the facts—the wedding has been arranged. The mother hence begins to doubt the facts that can still be questioned, that is to say, the possibility that the wedding may not be celebrated even though it has been arranged. Here, we see how a subject as delicate as a girl's wedding, with the difficulties and expense it involves for the whole family, can lead both the astrologer and the client to question the "reliability" of the information about the current situation.

Another similar example is provided by the case of a woman who comes to see the astrologer complaining about the weakened state she has been in since the birth of her daughter by caesarean. After carefully analyzing the woman's horoscope, the astrologer wonders how she could have given birth to a girl, when the horoscope clearly indicates the birth of a boy. The astrologer then suspects that she actually gave birth to a boy, but taking advantage of the fact she was unconscious, as she had a caesarean, someone in the hospital took the boy and replaced it with a girl:

> You shouldn't have had a girl; according to the position of Rāhu and Śani in your horoscope, you should have had a boy (*laṛkā honā cāhiye thā*) . . . your *bhāgya* (destiny) in your horoscope is to have boys. As you had a caesarean it is very likely that your son was swapped for a little girl . . . this happens, you know . . . with a caesarean the woman loses consciousness, and without her realizing it, the child is exchanged . . .

The woman denies the astrologer's hypothesis, claiming she was alone in the operating theater. In this case, too, the doubt about the child's identity, insinuated by the astrologer, is a response to a problematic issue like the birth of a girl instead of a boy. If the astrologer takes the liberty of questioning the authenticity of this descendance, and in a way denies the evidence of the facts, it is because he is aware of the questions the birth of a girl raises, particularly when a boy was not only expected but assigned by *bhāgya*, destiny, and hence, in a way, due.

Nonetheless, the "fact" most often questioned by astrologers when there is an incongruity between the perceived evidence and the truth of the horoscope is the time and date of birth. When the information in the horoscope and the client's statements do not match, most astrologers attribute this to the time of birth being wrongly recorded, as an hour or a day's difference can obviously be "fatal" to the person's destiny. As an astrologer said, "The same woman's womb can give birth to a *sādhu-sant* (virtuous ascetic) or a *guṇḍā-badmāś* (hoodlum) . . . it's the same womb, the only difference is the time, the time of birth . . ."

This is the case of the diagnosis concerning Rekha, a seven-year-old child who suffers severe locomotory problems as a result of a delayed blood transfusion when she was being treated for jaundice just after her birth. Rekha cannot walk, nor can she do any kind of physical work. Nonetheless, looking at the child's horoscope, the astrologer notes the presence of a double *rāj yog*, "the king's astral conjunction," indicating success, fame, and prosperity:[44]

> This child has a double *rāj yog* in her horoscope . . . she was supposed to be a wonderful baby (*bahut acchā* baby *honā cāhiye*) . . . according to her horoscope she should have been a high-ranking *administratif officer* . . . this means that either there was some confusion with the birth (*kuch gaṛbaṛ hogā*),[45] or the doctor made a mistake with the time of birth . . . just a few seconds is enough for the horoscope to be completely different . . .

After looking at the child's hand, the astrologer confirms that the hand horoscope (*hāth kī kuṇḍalī*) is completely different from the birth horoscope (*janm kuṇḍalī*): the incongruity between the hand and the birth horoscope, which should not exist under normal circumstances, seems to prove to the astrologer that the latter was calculated for the wrong time.

The use of hand reading to cross-check the validity of a birth horoscope is frequent as, unlike the horoscope, the hand indisputably belongs to the person involved. This is another example of a diagnosis where the planetary information entered in the horoscope and the characteristics of the owner of the horoscope, in this case a young woman, are contradictory:

> J [commenting the horoscope]: Her Mercury is very good (*ucc*), she will be married into a very rich family.
>
> ♀ [mother of the young girl whose horoscope is being studied]: We've been looking for a boy for her for a long time . . .
>
> J: If it didn't happen in 1999, the marriage *yog* (planetary conjunction) will come up again in 2001.[46] She also has the *yog* to go abroad. She will be very successful in life . . .
>
> ♀: But she is not at all successful, she's just failed her twelfth standard exams . . .
>
> J: She shouldn't have failed . . .
>
> ♀: Maybe someone switched the exam results and that's why she failed[47] . . .
>
> ♀2 [wife of ♀'s brother, who accompanied ♀ to the astrologer. She intervenes here to repeat the original version of the facts]: But no one wishes her ill . . . why would they have switched the results?
>
> ♀: She gets angry very quickly . . .
>
> J: She should not get angry, as her horoscope is *Buddh-pradhān* (whose predominant planet is Mercury) . . . she must be skinny (*dublī-patlī*) . . .

♀: She isn't skinny at all!! She is four feet tall and is quite plump (*doharā badan*) . . . nothing you have said so far resembles her at all.

J: According to the position of Śani (Saturn), she must have long hair[48] . . .

♀: No, she has short hair!

J: Well, this horoscope is wrong, she must have been born on the twenty-second and not the twenty-first. Come back with her, I want to see her hand; I will only be able to understand what's wrong with the horoscope once I have seen her hand.

Astrologers use a variety of divinatory techniques to clarify and check an interpretation that does not conform to the facts. When neither the hand nor the horoscope provide satisfactory answers, the astrologer may then look at the horoscope of another family member—the brother, the mother, the father, the husband—as a close relative's horoscope can be responsible for the person's problems.[49] Otherwise, another method frequently employed to cross-check the diagnosis consists of analyzing the astral configuration at the time the astrologer is asked the question, using *praśna kuṇḍalī*. This was the case of a mother who had come to ask the astrologer why nothing he had predicted for her son after studying his horoscope had occurred:

♀: Nothing that you said last year about my oldest son has happened . . .

J: What did I tell you at that time?

♀: That he would have a government job in Calcutta, but nothing like that has happened.

J: What was he doing, medicine?

♀: Yes, a Master of Science . . . and you said he would be married before October, but nothing has happened . . .

J: Yet even now, the *praśna* [the planetary situation at the time the question is asked] confirms what I had told you . . .

♀: But how can it be? I can't understand . . .

J: I assure you the question you are asking me now, at this moment, has a completely positive answer . . . one hundred percent positive, one hundred percent . . .

♀: But I am telling you, nothing has happened, neither the marriage nor the job . . . could we be the victims of *nazar* (evil eye)?

J: You will have to come back to see me with your son's horoscope, I need to look at it carefully again . . .

This dialogue shows a very common interpretive approach: given the failure of the predictions, the astrologer remains within the explanatory universe defined by astrological theory (in this case he returns to the analysis of the birth horoscope); the questioner, however, often draws from other etiological spheres, like the evil eye (*nazar*), sorcery (*ṭonā-ṭoṭkā*, *tantra-mantra*), magic (*jādū*), attacks by ghosts (*bhūt-pret*), and so forth. But they do not refer to these other explanatory idioms to contest the validity of the astrologer's explanation. On the contrary, the clients admit all their suspicions of sorcery so that the astrologer can verify them through the horoscope. Every horoscope shows whether a person is more or less likely to be the victim of sorcery, as this type of problem is indicated by the planets Śani, Rāhu, and Ketu being in a bad position.[50]

The reversals of the order of truth, between the horoscope and the perceived evidence, we have mentioned so far may seem extreme, but these cases are in no way paradoxical: quite the contrary, they fully conform to divinatory principles. The fact of questioning the veracity of what the questioner is saying is, in fact, a standard precautionary principle: before beginning a diagnosis, the astrologer should test the questioner's truthfulness by analyzing the astral theme related to the time at which the question is asked.[51] As the astrologer Shree Kanth Shastri explained:

The first thing one has to do before examining a case is to see whether the person is telling the truth (*sahī bol rahē hai*) or if

> he is lying (*jhūṭh bol rahē hai*). If someone comes to see me and says, for example, "I bought a piece of land on that day and since then I have had problems," I begin by calculating the horoscope of the *praśna* and I check whether the situation is true or not, as there are many people who tell lies. Sometimes they don't understand, they are unable to understand the type of problem they are facing, what it is caused by, they are tormented by doubt. They are unable to formulate the problem correctly. So, to start with, I use the *praśna* to check whether the man is telling the truth or not. Sometimes someone comes complaining they have lots of problems, but no, there's nothing wrong. If we see that they're telling the truth, then we try to understand the situation.

The client may lie consciously or, as in most cases, be unable to see the "real" problems due to the state of confusion and uncertainty he is in. The astrologer should use the same approach in both cases and not trust the evidence of the facts as they are presented or perceived by the client.

Often it is the planetary influence itself that is considered responsible for the client's inability to see the reality of his or her situation. Like an eclipse that conceals the light of the Sun, planetary influence can prevent the person from seeing what is obvious in the horoscope. Thus, one astrologer explained:

> There are lots of people who come to us saying they have been to see several astrologers but they gained no benefit from it (*unko koī phal nahī̃ miltā hai*). Why? Because these people are going through a period (*samay*) that is like that; they are not in a planetary situation that can allow them to see the results . . . it's like the eclipse (*grahaṇ*) . . . an eclipse conceals (*ḍhak kar rakh detā hai*) the very light of the Sun; in the same way, these people live in the shadow (*chāyā mẽ rahate haĩ*) because of the planets . . .

The truth of the horoscope is hence compared to the light of the Sun: just as from time to time the Sun seems to have stopped shining because of an eclipse, similarly, at times the astrologer's observations seem untrue due to the influence of the planets or other factors that veil a person's perception.

Furthermore, when the astrologer casts doubts upon the empirical perception, his view often matches the clients' own suspicions about the existence of things that are not perceptible to the eyes and that the evidence of the facts may conceal.

Facts, as they appear, are often perceived as "suspicious" and the astrologer is asked to verify the feeling of mistrust: for example, receiving a compliment or a gift, being fed by someone—acts that seem benevolent—may conceal charms or acts of sorcery. Thus a doctor went to an astrologer because, after a man had told him he had beautiful hair, he began to have terrible headaches, and he feared they had been caused by the compliment. A woman was extremely worried because since the time someone had come to the house to offer them some rice, the peace of the household had been destroyed and she saw the cause as being the fact of accepting the rice, and so on. Cases of this type are extremely common and the astrologer's task is to study the horoscope and to dissipate or confirm the suspicion regarding the true nature of the facts. Is the gift "really" a gift or "in truth" is it rather . . . something else? The horoscope makes it possible to go beyond empirical evidence.

As a tool that translates each event, person, and thing into a formal language, the horoscope is supposed to make everything visible, at least to the astrologer's eyes. What empirical evidence is likely to hide is, by contrast, necessarily invisible and hence cannot be named: while clients explicitly formulate the fear of being under the influence of such or such a planet, or of going through such or such an astral period, everything related to potential sorcery attacks is almost never explicitly formulated. The expressions employed to express this subject are of the type: "Would someone have done something?" (*kyā kisi ne kuch kyā?*); "Could it be something 'from above'?" (*kyā koī upari bāt hai?*) or "something from outside?" (*kyā koī bahari cīz hai?*).

When faced with the clients' suspicions, the astrologer consults the horoscope: if the planets Śani, Rāhu, and Ketu are not in negative positions, the astrologer reassures the client saying, "There's nothing to worry about" (*koī cintā kī bāt nahī̃ hai*), or "it's nothing" (*kuch nahī̃ hai*). If, however, the planets Śani, Rāhu, or Ketu are in a malefic configuration, then—and this depends on the case or the astrologer—either the suspicion of a sorcery attack or the evil eye is confirmed, or it is replaced by a bad planetary influence. Thus, when a woman went to an astrologer to express her suspicions that her *jeṭhānī* (wife of her husband's elder brother) "had done something to them" and they were unable to open their own shop (*dukān*), looking at the horoscope, the astrologer said:

> No, it's not your *jeṭhānī*, your *jeṭhānī* hasn't done anything, it's because of Śani . . . in reality, the problems you are having are caused by Śani . . . it will last another thirteen months, but after January 2001 it will be over, you will be able to open your shop.[52]

If, however, the astrologer considers that the origin of the misfortune is a sorcery attack, he will prescribe the corresponding protection (generally, a tantric amulet, a *jantar*).

Suspicion of sorcery or external attacks are not the only situations in which the "veracity of the horoscope" is supposed to penetrate and decipher facts perceived as potentially misleading. Any event is, to an extent, likely to be detected through the horoscope, as during an astrological consultation reality is seen as a sort of "epiphenomenon" of what is written in the horoscope.

As an example, let us look at how an astrologer interpreted the case of a man who was suffering from leucodermia (*saphed dāg rog*, "white patch disease") and thought he had developed this disease as a result of a car accident he was involved in, in 1983.[53] Looking at the man's horoscope, the astrologer explained that the white patch disease he was suffering from was not provoked by the accident but was merely one of the manifestations of his serious planetary situation:

> In the planetary situation (*graha sthiti*) you are going through, if you had not had these white patches, you would have lost an eye, and if it wasn't an eye, you would have suffered burns that would have left patches (*dāg*) . . . In any case, some kind of bad accident (*durghaṭnā*) like those I described would necessarily have happened to you (*honī hi thī*). So the car accident is not the reason why these patches appeared; you have the mark (*lakṣaṇa*) of this in your horoscope . . . it could have been something else, but in any case, it was meant to happen.

This interpretation highlights how what is in the horoscope is "necessarily true" as, to use Leibniz's term, it is "true in every possible world."

The life the person is actually living, however, is only "one" of the possible worlds: the white patch disease is only one of the possible manifestations of the "truth" that is the mark (*lakṣaṇa*) of a bad event (*durghaṭnā*) in the horoscope, but this mark could have manifested itself in another "possible world" in the form of the loss of an eye or a burn. What we experience and what we perceive is only one of the possible manifestations of the truth of the horoscope.

The data inscribed in the horoscope allows one to know not only what "really" happens to people but also when the problems "really" begin or end, beyond a person's personal perceptions. Thus a man came to the astrologer saying that since the month of December[54] he had had severe problems (*baṛī pareśānī*), he had gastritis, he had palpitations, he felt anxious (*becain*) and unstable (*asthir*). By studying the horoscope, the astrologer saw that since the month of October, the man had entered a negative planetary period—the Moon's *antardaśā* in Saturn's *mahādaśā*—that would last one and a half years. He explained to the man:

> You feel as if this (*āpko mahasūs huā hai*) began in December, but *actually*, it began in October. Yes, it began in October and not in December . . . the situation (*paristhiti*) you are in now, the anxiety (*becainī*) you are feeling now, began in October and it will remain like this till June . . . after the 15–16 June, little by little you will see it will decrease (*kam honā*), you will see things improve but the problems will remain for one more year, this period (*daśā*) lasts one and a half years; it will remain till the month of February 2001 . . .

Another area that clearly shows how the horoscope is invested with the value of a truth superior to the perception of the facts is the matching of horoscopes (*kuṇḍalī milānā*) before marriages. By examining the horoscopes of the potential couple, the astrologer is supposed not only to detect qualities (*guṇa*) and flaws (*doṣa*) that are not directly "visible" but also to certify the "objective" value of a union through mathematical calculations.[55] While the young couple's—and their families'—perception of reciprocal compatibility can be misleading, either as they do not have sufficient knowledge or due to the illusion engendered by emotions, horoscope matching is supposed to state compatibility or incompatibility through objective criteria that go beyond individual and family idiosyncrasies. Hence, the astrologer's advice is commonly sought for both arranged marriages and love marriages. In the former, as it compensates for the high level of unknown this type of marriage involves—will the couple get on well? Will they like each other? Does the spouse have hidden flaws? And in the latter, because the perception the couple has of the validity of their union is not the result of a reasoned, considered decision—as is the case of arranged marriages—and it hence requires the "rational" and convincing certification of the horoscope.

Nonetheless, the results of horoscope matching can, sometimes, contrast with the families' (or the individuals') wishes. On this subject, the astrologer Tar Kesh Joshi recounted the emblematic case of a marriage that had been arranged between an NRI (Non-Resident Indian) doctor in the United States, whose family was from Banaras, and a woman who was a doctor in Banaras. The *match* seemed perfect: both families belonged to the same caste, both the young people were qualified doctors, the man was older and taller than the woman, and they had both liked the look of each other from the photographs that had been exchanged. Nevertheless, before the marriage was effectively performed (although it had been arranged) the astrologer carefully studied the woman's horoscope and claimed she had a gynecological problem related to the planet Ketu, specifically involving what astrological language calls *gupt rog*s, "hidden diseases," or in other words, genital diseases.[56] When the astrologer informed the doctor in the United States that because of this "hidden flaw" (*gupt doṣ*) visible in the horoscope the woman who was to become his wife would not be able to conceive children, the marriage was canceled.[57]

In all the cases mentioned in these pages, we have seen how the horoscope is supposed to shed light on, complete, or question empirical evidence. What we were trying to show through these examples is the lack of any occult, esoteric, or mysterious dimension in astrology, as it is envisaged and practiced in Banaras. Astrology, as the name *jyotiṣa* (from *jyotis*, "light") confirms, is seen as a language of clarity, truth, certitude, visibility, while common knowledge and ordinary perceptions are considered likely to conceal the mysterious, the occult, and the unknown.

Making due distinctions, the relationship one observes between the truth of the horoscope and the occult nature of common knowledge recalls the relationship Charles Malamoud identifies between ordinary language and the language of the Gods in the Brāhmaṇas. In his chapter "The Gods Have No Shadows," in *Cooking the World: Ritual Thought in*

Ancient India, the author observes that the common language of man is designed as a concealed language, falsified and obscure in comparison to the transparent, perfect, and truthful language of the Gods. The Gods, "loving the occult" (*paro'kṣakāma*), would have modified their perfect language in order to make it secret and not fully comprehensible to man. Unawares, men would thus be speaking jargon, an occult language: "In putting together their secret lexicon, the gods (and following them, men) acted in such a way that the manifest might give rise to the hidden. The hidden becoming common and familiar, also became immediate, while the clear, masked and protected by the hidden, became foreign and distant" (Malamoud 1996, 205).

5

Karma and *Bhāgya*

The Idea of Destiny in Astrological Consultations

Et Bhaga? Je ne perdrai pas notre temps à montrer que ce dieu "Part" s'occupe essentiellement de la richesse: la richesse est la matière essentielle des prières qu'on lui adresse, les mots qui la désignent (*rayí, raí, dhána, vásu, ápnas*) décorent les strophes où il apparaît.

—Georges Dumézil, *Les Dieux souverains des Indo-Européens*

Astrology and the Theory of Karma: Antagonism and Complementarity

The theory of karma has long been the focus of research by Sanskrit scholars and anthropologists interested in representations of human destiny in Brahmanical culture and Hindu society.[1] Two major edited volumes published in the 1980s—*Karma and Rebirth in Classical Indian Traditions* (O'Flaherty 1980) and *Karma: An Anthropological Inquiry* (Keyes and Daniel 1983)—illustrate the diversity of the formulations and uses of this theory, respectively, from a textual and ethnographic perspective.[2] By focusing on the variety of idioms of causality that are locally used, anthropologists made a fundamental contribution to relativizing the centrality and the preponderance of the theory of karma as an etiological discourse.[3] In most ethnographic works on destiny and misfortune, the theory of karma, as a Sanskritic, Brahmanical, and pan-Indian theory belonging to the "great tradition," is opposed to the diversity of vernacular and local idioms that explain destiny in terms of fatality, divine intervention, sorcery, or possession. According to these studies, the theory of karma is rarely mentioned to account for daily problems and is mainly used as a last resort or in exceptional circumstances, while "vernacular" idioms of causality are commonly used to explain the suffering and difficulties of daily life.

Despite the central position it occupies for a large number of Hindu families, and although it constitutes a particularly interesting idiom of causality, astrology is rarely mentioned in these works. As a Sanskritic, Brahmanical, and pan-Indian theory used to resolve difficulties and make everyday choices, astrology can shed new light on the question of etiological plurality and the articulation between different ways of expressing of causality. In this chapter we will focus on the relationship between astrological language and the theory of karma. The connection with other idioms of causality, like sorcery, possession, or the evil eye, will be mentioned occasionally here and further developed in chapter 7.

The theory of karma and astrology share some important common characteristics that differentiate them from other idioms of causality.[4] Not only are both theories strongly anchored in the Brahmanical tradition, sophisticatedly formulated in Sanskrit literature, and known in various regions of the Indian subcontinent, but they also share the same field of investigation. Both theories claim to *exhaustively* explain human destiny, accounting for all kinds of joys and misfortunes and, unlike other idioms of causality such as sorcery or possession, they attribute a crucial role to birth as a decisive moment in human destiny.[5] One could then say that they are "commensurate" and hence highly comparable. Amazingly, though, the relationship between these two "major" theories of human destiny has not provoked much interest in South Asian studies. The exceptions are the studies by François Chenet (1985) and Judy Pugh (1983a). The former, carried out by a philosopher and Sanskrit scholar, underscores the convergence between astrological theory and the doctrine of karma by showing, through a textual analysis, how astrology integrates the theory of karma into its own operatory process. The latter, written by an anthropologist, considers the ideas of karma and "fate" to be synonymous and analyzes the astrological representations of karma on the basis of her ethnographical survey conducted in Banaras.

While both studies seem to conflate astrology and karma into a single deterministic South Asian theory of destiny, I will adopt a different perspective here. Rather than showing the confluence and the convergences between the two theories of destiny, I will argue that astrology, because of its theoretical assumptions as well as its practical uses, constitutes an alternative ideology that is both antagonistic and complementary to the theory of karma. This complementarity is expressed, during astrological consultations, through the word *bhāgya*, "destiny," "fortune" (lit., entitled to a share [*bhāga*]) that is often opposed to *karm*, "act," "action," "ritual," "work." Through the analysis of the sematic field of the concept of *bhāgya*—related to ideas of "fortune," "share," or "wealth"—and its contemporary uses we will see how astrological discourse on destiny is made to match the expectations of urban middle- and upper-class families.

Before looking at the ethnographical material, it is important to clarify how the relationship between the theory of karma and astrology is approached in the classical treatises, thus examining a textual view that astrologers may sometimes refer to. As Chenet's (1985) and Pugh's (1983a) studies show, the doctrine of karma is explicitly mentioned in the Sanskrit texts on horoscopy. Essentially, from a theoretical viewpoint, the relationship between astrology and karma can be reduced to the assumption that the "invisible" (*adṛṣṭa*) fruits (*phala*) of acts carried out in previous lives become "visible" (*dṛṣṭa*) through the planetary configurations present at birth. Astrology would be like a "lamp" (*dīpa*) illuminating the fruits of previous lives' actions: "This science makes visible the maturation (*pakti*) [of the fruits] of good and bad acts accumulated in previous lives, just like a lamp (*dīpa*) [makes] objects [visible] in dark," writes Varāhamihira at the beginning of the *Laghujātaka* (LJ 1.3).[6]

Nonetheless, besides this statement that appears at the beginning of most treatises dealing with horoscopy (*jātaka*) and a few other isolated passages, the reference to karma plays no role in astrological theory. This is not surprising since the theory of karma and astrology are in fact based on a contrasting conceptual ground. While in the karma theory the moral behavior of a person determines his or her subsequent life conditions, according to astrological theory, destiny and human acts are regulated by natural and cosmic principles that are independent from human responsibility; bad and good behavior are thus seen as a necessary expression of the cosmic order and time.

Astrology seems to invalidate the theory of karma in several ways. Both doctrines deal with similar issues—the disparities in individual lives, the reasons behind suffering—yet they provide radically different explanations. This appears all the more clearly as both theories use the same word *phala* (fruit) to make sense of human destiny. According to the doctrine of karma, the "fruit" that affects human life is the product of good and bad actions done in past and present lives, while according to astrology this "fruit" emanates from the stars and especially planets (the very name "astrology," as a branch of *jyotiṣa*, is *phalita*, the science that studies the "fruits" of astral configurations).

Astrology elaborates a "cosmodicy" that is substantially different from that of karma.[7] Instead of blaming human responsibility, it envisages human destiny as being a part of the network of correspondences between the planets, the elements (air, fire, water, earth, and ether), colors, animals, the parts of the body, the humors (*doṣa*), social roles, castes, kinship relations, and so on. In addition to this cosmological network, in astrological theory, the nine planets (*navagraha*) are described as deities (or demons, such as Rāhu and Ketu) who bestow misfortune and happiness upon human beings (and can hence be pacified by *grahaśānti*, pacification rituals).

In light of these conceptual contrasts, I find it more convincing to consider the verse that presents astrology as a "lamp" that illuminates the karmic residue as an ingenious ideological construct intended to eschew potential antagonism between the two theories. In other words, the "lamp trick" aims at legitimizing astrology in relation to the theory of karma and transmigration, the latter being "fully established and almost universally accepted as a comprehensive world-view in classical and later Indian thought."[8] As Wilhelm Halbfass observes regarding other trends of thought in the Sanskrit tradition:[9]

> Concepts and theories which were initially used independently of and without reference to the karma theory, and which, in its earlier phases, appear side by side with it and as possible rivals, are reinterpreted in the light of the karma theory, are accommodated to or identified with it. (Halbfass 1980, 271)

In this respect, the case of astrology seems emblematic, as, historically, horoscopic theory was introduced to India as an exogenous science at the beginning of the present era, when Greco-Babylonian astrological theory was progressively integrated into Brahmanical culture (Pingree 1981). The "lamp trick" hence aims at reconciling two theories about human destiny that would otherwise be in contradiction: thanks to this, astrology's "natural" determinism, although devoid of any kind of moral reference, becomes compatible with the ethical approach and the idea of responsibility inherent to the karma theory.

The reconciliation of these two theories of human destiny occurs through an epistemological subordination of astrology to the theory of *karma*. Astral configurations can explain human destiny because they reveal the karmic residue, but in the last resort, the latter is the sole determining factor of human destiny. Astrology hence appears as a heuristic tool, a set of technical rules that allow one to more precisely measure the effects of the good and bad actions done in previous lives.

Nevertheless, while it serves to neutralize the potential rivalry between the two systems, astrology's (apparent) abdication before karmic causality does not erase the fundamental differences separating these two doctrines of human destiny. Astrology is supposed to explain a far wider field of phenomena than that covered by the theory of *karma*. While karma theory is only applicable to living beings, Hindu astrology is supposed to account for the "destiny" of all sorts of subjects that are a part of the cosmos: not only human beings, animals, and plants but also land, houses, nations, and so forth—as well as ritual acts, sacrifices, and rites of passage (*saṃskāra*), which, in order to be effective, must be performed under auspicious astral conjunctions.[10]

Despite their different assumptions, it would not make sense to emphasize the contradictions or incompatibilities between the two doctrines. In horoscope reading as practiced by astrologers, these two theories turn out to be deeply compatible, as their differences make them *complementary*. They offer Hindus two points of entry, two ways of seeing and explaining human destiny that complete each other in several ways.[11] In addition, the "cohabitation" of these two theories in the common field of the representation of human destiny seems to have marked them with a sort of common interpretative mechanism, for example, the extra-individual transmission of destiny (which we will deal with in depth in the following chapter).

However, to what extent, and in what manner, do the two systems differ and complement each other? This can only be evaluated by comparing specific texts or contexts and our study remains limited to an analysis of the work carried out by astrologers in Banaras.[12] We will hence start by seeing how human destiny is conceived and represented in astrological exegesis, before returning to the question of the intertwining of astrology and the theory of karma in the local etiological discourse.

The Allotted Share: The Semantics of *Bhāgya*

The word commonly used by astrologers and their clients to refer to destiny, as it is described in the horoscope, is not *karm* (Hindi for the Sanskrit *karman*), but *bhāgya*. During astrological consultations *karm* and *bhāgya* are often opposed to each other. The former designates human agency, effort, acts we do by will, while the latter refers to predetermined destiny, fortune, the fate written in the stars, and all the events that affect a person's existence independently of his or her will. The relationship between *bhāgya* and *karm* over the course of human existence can be summed up through the metaphor of the two wheels of a scooter, as expressed by a trader in precious stones who works with astrologers:

> *Bhāgya* and *karm* are like the two wheels of a scooter . . . if one has a puncture, one can still reach one's destination (*mañzīl*), but, as you can imagine, it's difficult to reach one's destination with a punctured tire . . . In life, one needs both; you need a good *karm* and a good *bhāgya* . . . For example, take a *rikshaw vālā* [rickshaw driver] and a politician . . . the former has a bad *bhāgya*, and however good his *karm*, he will never get very far; on the contrary, the latter has a good *bhāgya*, and if he is well behaved, he will obtain everything he wants in his life . . .[13]

Among the anthropologists who have worked on karma, the only one to my knowledge who has highlighted the importance of *bhāgya* as a category of destiny in popular Hinduism is Susan Wadley (1983b).[14] Examining the Hindi literature on the celebration of *vrat* (votive fasting), she observes:

> It is well known that the concept and term karma, however defined, is not prevalent or widely used in all Hindu communities. In the *vrat* literature, the most common term for destiny or fate is *bhāgya*. In these texts, karma quite clearly refers to actions, with specific attributions of human conditions due to actions. But *bhāgya* is destiny, or fate. (Wadley 1983b, 159–160)

Referring to *bhāgya* as a "counterpoint to the karma doctrine," she adds:

> It presents a potentiality of "luck" or chance or fate (understood as unrelated to past acts) that is not implied by either the classical concepts of karma nor the concept of karma found in the *vrat* literature. (Wadley 1983b, 161)

Unfortunately, Wadley does not go further in her analysis.[15] A brief review of the history and the meaning of the term will help us to better understand its uses in the context of contemporary astrological counseling.

The word *bhāgya* stems from the Sanskrit root *BHAJ-* (to share, to distribute, to divide, to allot) and is part of an illustrious lexical family—including words such as *bhagavat*, "the Prosperous one," "Lord" (*bhagvān* in Hindi), and *bhakti*, "devotion" (lit., distribution, share)[16]—whose first members are attested in Vedic literature. In the Ṛgveda, the word *bhaga* means good fortune, prosperity, and Bhaga, "The Dispenser," is a tutelary deity who distributes goods, wealth, and pleasure. The deity Bhaga is said to attribute "lots" of goods to men on the basis of a regular and predictable system of repartition without competition (Dumézil 1952). Nevertheless, interestingly, the generous and positive fortune-god of the hymns, Bhaga, in some later Vedic treatises—the Brāhmaṇas—has his eyes burned and becomes blind (Śatapata Brāhmaṇa I.7.4.6).[17] Bhaga's blindness may thus be seen as a dramatic representation of fortune's ambiguity: the one who allots prosperity and wealth does so according to an unsighted rule of distribution.

In classical Sanskrit as well as in contemporary Hindi, the semantic of the term *bhāgya* conveys a similar ambiguity. Derived from the noun *bhāga*, "share," "portion," "allotted share," "lot," "inheritance" (Monier-Williams 1994, 751), the word *bhāgya* is originally an adjective that indicates a person or a thing "entitled to a share." In its nominalized form, it goes on to become a noun meaning the "allotted share," the "share received," and by extension "fortune," "wealth," "fate," "destiny," "future" (Monier-Williams 1994, 752).[18]

In Hindi, the word *bhāgya* has two main meanings. In its broadest sense, *bhāgya* is the "the ineluctable rule of destiny according to which all human actions are predetermined" (*vah avaśyaṃbhāvī daivā vidhān jiske anusār manuṣya ke sab kārya pahle hī se niścit rahate hai*') (Varma 1971, 766) and means "fate," "destiny," "time."[19] This sense appears in common expressions such as "it is written in destiny" (*bhāgya mẽ likhā hai*) or "you can't get anything more than what fate has allotted to you" (*bhāgya se zyādā kuch nahī̃ miltā*). Thus, the word *bhāgya* may be accompanied by expressions like "whatever you must get, you will get it" (*jo miltā hogā, milegā*), "whatever has to be, it will be" (*jo honā hogā*). The word may also be used to refer to the moment decided by fate, as in the expression "nothing can happen before or after [the moment decided by] *bhāgya*" (*bhāgya ke pahle, bhāgya ke bād kuch nahī̃ hogā*). Here, it takes on the same meaning as the word *samay*, "time," also used to indicate the moment chosen by fate: "nothing can happen before its time" (*samay se pahle kuch nahī̃ miltā*). Thus, to explain to a client that one cannot change what is decided by *bhāgya* and one has to respect the times fixed by the planets, an astrologer used himself as an example:

> You shouldn't be impatient, we all have to make do with our own *bhāgya* (*ham ko apne bhāgya ke sahāre calnā paṛtā hai*, "we have to walk with our own *bhāgya*") . . . you see, I'm an astrologer, and yet, I cannot change my *bhāgya*: my son-in-law died a year after he married my daughter; I was almost killed by bandits on the train, and sometimes my jaw still hurts; I have a daughter who has just turned thirty and I haven't managed to get her married yet; sometimes I have a lot of money and sometimes I have none . . .

In this sense, *bhāgya* shows semantic affinities with *daiva* (from *deva*, "gods"), the impersonal and transcendent destiny described in epic and philosophical Sanskrit literature.[20] However, during astrological consultations, destiny is always referred to as *bhāgya*, and we never heard the word *daiva*. In our opinion, this is because *bhāgya* defines an idea of destiny "at hand"—the allotted "share" is what each person experiences during their existence, day after day. It is a sort of immanent, "embodied" destiny that evolves as the person goes through the different periods of his or her life. *Daiva*, by contrast, indicates a somewhat transcendent power, far removed from human beings and linked to a manifestation of divine power. In other words, *bhāgya*, like the horoscope, always has an "owner": it denotes not an absolute fate, but a fate that is intrinsically bound to a person "entitled to a share." This does not necessarily have to be a human being, thus: a piece of land, a house, an animal, a nation, and so on, are also said to have a *bhāgya*, a fate. Astrologers often employ expressions like *zamīn kā bhāgya*, "the fate of a land"; *makān kā bhāgya*, "the fate of a house," and so on.[21]

The second meaning of *bhāgya* is "fortune," "luck," "good chance," "prosperity," "wealth," "happiness." It appears in words such as the adjectives *bhāgyavān* (*bhāgyavatī* in the feminine form) or *bhāgyaśālī*, which literally mean "endowed with *bhāgya*" and are used to designate someone who is "lucky," "fortunate," "prosperous," "wealthy." Similarly, the adjective *bhāgyahīn*, "devoid of *bhāgya*," indicates an unhappy and unlucky person; the "giver of *bhāgya*" (*bhāgyadā*) is the lottery; *bhāgyoday*, the "rise (*uday*) of *bhāgya*," indicates the beginning of a favorable period. As we have seen, from the etymological point of view, this second meaning is the original one and still expresses the deepest sense of the concept of *bhāgya*. During astrological consultation, *bhāgya* is used to denote the "part," the "lot," the fortune that is attributed to everyone at birth. This "lot" may contain good and bad things but is viewed as an "asset" belonging to the person. Thus, the idea of *bhāgya* conveys a cosmology that contrasts not only with the idea of karma but also with the idea of "debt" (*ṛṇa*) at birth—debts to the sages, to the Gods, and to the ancestors—that characterizes Vedic and Hindu cosmology (Malamoud 1983). The following pages will show that a sort of ideology of "credit at birth" seems to prevail over any idea of debt, to characterize human destiny during astrological counseling. By birth, each person has a "credit," which is allocated to him or her over the course of his or her existence, independently of his or her acts and intentions.

The idea of *bhāgya* seems to be semantically close to the legal category of *dāyabhāga*, designating both "inheritance" and "partition" in traditional Hindu law.[22] *Dāyabhāga* is the share of wealth a member of a family owns by the very fact of his birth: "each member of the family acquires by his very birth an 'interest'—which, moreover, may vary—in the property, and it is this 'interest' which congeals and becomes materialised at the time of sharing" (Dumont 1983, 10).[23] Similarly, *bhāgya* designates a sort of "wealth" invested somewhere, which is ascribed at birth and its fluctuating interest "materializes" at certain moments of one's existence.

The lexical and semantic connection between the idea of *bhāgya*, fate, destiny, and the idea of *dāyabhāga*, lot, share of wealth, are explicitly expressed in the words of the client of an astrologer, whose elder brother had appropriated the whole family inheritance left by the widowed mother. The man, who owns a cycle repair and coal stall, attributed the unequal division of the family inheritance to the different *bhāgya* he and his brother enjoyed:

> Mother's wealth (*dhan*), mother's share (*hissā*), all the money (*paisā-rupaya*), and the family inheritance (*raqm-patāī*) . . . he took it all. He didn't even give me one rupee . . . So I said to him, "Brother, take all this wealth, it's in your *bhāgya*, it's not in my *bhāgya* (*tumhāre bhāgya mẽ hai, hamāre bhāgya mẽ nahī̃ hai*), if you want to give me a share, you'll give it to me . . . ," but he didn't give me anything . . .

According to this man, the family inheritance—the *dāyabhāga*—is part of the elder son's *bhāgya* and not in the younger son's: the younger son's access to the family wealth is hence optional and subject to the elder's will.

Finding Out the "Lot"

Through horoscope reading, astrologers can identify and calculate someone's *bhāgya*. The horoscope contains information about his or her *bhāgya* in both its acceptations: while the whole horoscope is supposed to describe the *bhāgya* in its more general sense of an ascribed fate, the ninth house of the horoscope, called *bhāgya bhāva* (house of *bhāgya*), indicates wealth, good luck, and prosperity. Similarly, in the case of palm reading, the totality of the characteristics of the hand reveal *bhāgya* as destiny, while *bhāgya* as prosperity can be examined through the line that starts at the wrist and runs toward the center of the palm, called the "line of *bhāgya* or ascent" (*bhāgya rekhā* ou *ūrdhva rekhā*).

Just like the lines of the hand, the twelve houses of the horoscope illustrate different kinds of *bhāgya*: the "*bhāgya* of money" (*dhan kā bhāgya*), the "*bhāgya* of marriage" (*śādī kā bhāgya*), or the "*bhāgya* of education" (*sikṣa kā bhāgya*), and so on. A person may, for example, have a very good *bhāgya* for financial wealth (second house, line of wealth) but a bad one for health (first house), or a bad one for marriage (seventh house) but a good one for career (tenth house). When consulting an astrologer, clients want to know the share, the portion, or the capital they are entitled to by birth in the different aspects of their life. They may thus ask questions such as: "Is there a house in our *bhāgya*?" "Is there a son in our *bhāgya*?"

"How many children we will have?" "Is there any land?" "Is there travel abroad?" "How many years (of life) have I been allotted in my *bhāgya*?"

Nevertheless, the allotment that people are entitled to according to the horoscope very often does not correspond to the share that they materially perceive and experience in their daily lives. Let us look, for example, at a consultation involving a couple that had come to see the astrologer because they were going through some financial troubles:

J: What is the matter?

♀: I would like to show you my hand.

J: What is your name?

♀: Candravati Devi

J: How old are you?

♀: About forty.

J: You have a lot of money! A lot of money, it's good, it will remain . . . [speaking to her husband] does she work a bit?

♂: No

J: Has she started any business (*vyavasāya*)?

♂: No, she stays at home.

♀: That's why we came. If the money is there, where is it (*paisā hai, to kahī̃ hai*)? We came for that, to know where we can get some money . . .

J: But you are much better off than others . . . The lines of your hand say there is no shortage (*kami*) of money . . .

♂: And *gurujī*, how is she in terms of her life span (*umar-vumar*)?

J: It's fine, she will live for seventy-seven years.

♂: No, a man told her she has a very short life, that she should have a *mṛtyunjay yajña* performed[24] . . .

J: She will live seventy-seven years . . . if you want to have a *mṛtyunjay yajña* performed, you can do that, it will be good for her health, but her health line (*svāsth rekhā*) is not bad, it's good. What the pandit told you, what made you worry that something would happen, that's over now, that was at the age of thirty-two to thirty-three, before the age of thirty-four to thirty-five, it was a physical problem, but it was five to six years ago, and she has come out of this period. Now her life will last till the age of seventy-seven, and even longer than that . . .

♂: So there's no danger (*khatarā*)? I won't have to marry again?

J: You won't have to marry again, that's out of the question. Do you have a hemorrhoids problem? Have you built your house?

♂: We have built a part of it, but at the moment . . .

J: Well, there's nothing to worry about . . .

♂: Actually *gurujī*, the house has not been completed, but now we would like to buy some land . . .

J: Land . . . according to her hand [= the wife's], there is a house (*makān hai*), there is land (*zamīn hai*), everything will happen (*sab kuch hogā*) . . . with regard to money, her fate (*dhan ka bhāgya*) is favorable (*acchā hai*), her life line (*āyu rekhā*) is good (*acchā hai*), everything in her hand is good, there's nothing to worry about (*koī cintā kī bāt nahī̃ hai*), you'll have no problems of any kind, no health problems, a long life, the kind of life one should have today . . .

♂: There's nothing to worry about then, *gurujī*?

J: No, everything is fine, her fate is good (*inkā bhāgya acchā hai*), she's a lucky woman (*bhāgyavatī mahilā hai*).

Through this dialogue with the astrologer, the couple tries to learn about the *bhāgya*, the "share" visible in the hand: How many years of life are there? Is land there? Is a house there? And if all these things are there for us, where are they?

Astrological consultations are structured around a confrontation between two levels of reality: the visible, objective, and incontestable "share" written in the horoscope (or in the hand) and the share perceived by the client. When referring to the horoscope, astrologers use the verb *honā*, "to be" (e.g., "the money *is* there"), while in describing people's experience, they use verbs like *lagnā*, "to look like," "to seem," or *mahsus honā*, "to feel like" (e.g., "you *feel like* you don't have any money"). The horoscope corresponds to the ontological level (where things *are*), while people's perceptions are put on a phenomenological level (where things *seem* to be). Through verbal interactions, practitioners and clients try to fill the gap that may arise between these, so that people may obtain things that they are entitled to and the truth of the horoscope may be preserved. In the aforementioned case, the astrologer stated that in the woman's *bhāgya* there *is* money, there *is* a house; therefore, he wants to know whether "in fact" the woman is involved in any commercial activity and if she has had her house built. As is often the case, the couple has astral "assets": *there is* money, even if the couple cannot see it; *there is* a house, even though it still has to be built; *there is* land, even if the land has yet to be bought; and *there are* still many years of life left. Both the astrologer and the client thus seek to establish the extent to which the allotted "share" matches the received "share."

According to astrologers, when one makes choices that do not correspond to what is written in the *bhāgya*, every attempt to succeed is futile: however hard one tries, one will never achieve the desired results. To explain this principle, an astrologer cited the example of a civil servant, whose milk farm was a failure, despite all his investments:

> This man has a farm with about eighty to eighty-five cows and buffalos, but every day an animal dies. Once, eight buffalos died in a single day . . . Yet, the farm is perfectly equipped: he has installed lights, fans, he even has an on-site veterinary doctor . . . the place is absolutely wonderful for cattle, and yet they continue to die. Imagine, over these last two years

> this man has invested and lost twenty to twenty-five *lakhs*[25] of rupees in this farm!
>
> Looking at his horoscope, I clearly saw this man did not have a *bhāgya* suitable for cattle farming. I told him "go into agriculture, it will be very fruitful (*phalit*). Sell all your heads of cattle, one after the other, progressively." The same cows that produced twelve liters of milk twice a day elsewhere, only produced two liters a day at his farm, and they eat far more than they ate in the place they were before. Obviously, the land is not suitable (*layak*) for cattle farming, but the real problem (*truṭi*) is that cattle farming does not suit this person.

According to astrological theory, the "share" concerning the profession (*jīvikā kā bhāgya*) can be discerned through the planetary situation in the tenth house of the horoscope—"house of profession" (*karm bhāva*)[26]—as well as through the position of the planet ruling the zodiacal sign found in the tenth house (*daśameśa*). In the aforementioned case, the tenth house of the civil servant's horoscope indicates a predisposition for agriculture (*kheti*) and not for cattle (*paśu*); despite all his efforts the man will never be able to achieve his goal of creating a milk farm.

The "share" each person is entitled to can be estimated with a high degree of precision. Thus, for example the same astrologer explained that with regard to the "agricultural lot" (*kheti kā bhāgya*), the horoscope tells you the type of crop that is suitable or "innate" (*sahaj*) to each person:

> According to what is written in the horoscope, I advise people to cultivate the category of product that will be profitable for them (*jo inko lābh milegā*): for example, for some it will be a pungent (*tītā*) product like *nīm*, for others a spicy (*tīkhā*) product like chilis, or a sweet (*miṭhā*) product like sugarcane, or a sour (*kaṭu*) product like tamarind . . . some people should cultivate legumes like lentils or peas, others grain like rice, wheat, or sorghum; others should cultivate vegetables and so on.

Just as the horoscope allows the astrologer to identify the agricultural products that are a part of a person's *bhāgya*, it also allows him to know each person's "share" in the field of studies. Families that can afford to invest in children's schooling consult the astrologer in order to make the right educational choices. The astrologer is asked to indicate the field of studies that suits their children, the subjects they will be better at, the type of profession in which they are likely to find their place and their fortune.

The astrologer's advice is supposed to ensure good results and prevent a "waste" (*barbād*) of time and money, which would be the consequence of an "adverse" (*pratikūl*, "against the flow") choice that is not conform to the *bhāgya*. Thus, a man whose son had just filled in the application forms for medical college went to see the astrologer Shree Kanth Shastri to know what his son's chances (*guñjāiś*) of succeeding in this field of studies were. Looking at the son's horoscope, the astrologer remarked that the harmful planet Rāhu was present in the *lagna* (ascendant or first house of the horoscope): this was a first negative sign as the *lagna* indicates everything concerning the body and health, and hence medicine. In addition, he noted that the planet Jupiter, which symbolizes studies and knowledge, was weak and was located in the eighth house (house of death). Nonetheless Saturn, the planet that represents government jobs, was in a strong position. He hence strongly dissuaded the father from encouraging his son to study medicine and advised him to direct the boy toward a government job instead:

> J: Medicine will not work out . . . he should study something ordinary (*sādhāran śikṣa*) . . . having him admitted to medical college is a waste of time (*samay barbād ho jāyegā*); he mustn't do that at all, he will never complete his studies.
>
> ♂: But he has just finished his BA . . . what should we get him to do now?
>
> J: Get him to follow another path (*dūsrā mārg*), orient him toward the Indian Administrative Service, the Public Civil Service, or the Railways . . . have him sit this type of exam. If he has obtained his BA, it's enough, he doesn't need to study further . . .
>
> ♂: But what kind of government job?
>
> J: He should get a job in an engineering institution.

♂: That's why I came to ask you, we have discussed it often over the last few days . . . we wanted to know the right thing to do (*sahī cīz*); suppose we make him do something else, we would end up wasting time and money . . .

Sometimes the "share," the wealth allotted at birth, can come from a person rather than from a specific profession, a piece of land, or a house. This was the case of a young man who had left for Bombay to try his luck in Bollywood. Looking at his horoscope, the astrologer Kameshwar Upadhyay noted that he did not have the "astral profile" to become a cinema star, as the harmful planet Rāhu located in his house of profession (*jīvikā sthān*) was "cutting off any luck" (*bhāgya ko kāṭnā*). Speaking to the mother, the astrologer observed that the young man's horoscope was negative from several points of view:

> His Rāhu is bad (*nīc*), his Saturn is bad, his Jupiter is bad . . . Your son will never be stable, he will keep changing jobs, he is going to give lots of troubles to his parents . . . he will never be successful as an actor. Please tell him to give up his career in the movie industry. He will never get a major role, he may just aspire, at best, to a marginal role . . . he's going to waste lots of money. Whatever he will earn, he will lose.

The mother confirmed the accuracy of the astrologer's remarks, adding that her son never listened to his parents. The astrologer went further in reading the horoscope and found that, despite his recurrent professional failures, the son would have a "rise of fortune" (*bhāgyoday*) because of his future wife:

> J: There is a very good thing in your son's life: your son will marry a great cinema heroine (*nāyikā*) . . . The marriage will be celebrated between July 2000 and June 2001.[27] His wife will be very beautiful, very nice and very rich . . . Your son will never listen to his parents, nor to his paternal uncles and aunties, but he will listen very carefully to his wife . . .
>
> ♀: Will he have a *love-marriage* or an *arranged marriage*?

J: He will certainly have a *love-marriage.*

♀: Oh my God!!!

J: He will choose the young lady whom he likes, he will win her heart and will marry her . . . and he does not like ordinary women, he has *very high standards* when it comes to women . . .

♀: Yes, he has *very high standards* . . .

J: When they meet, they will fall in love at first sight, he will have a *love-marriage* and his wife will be a millionaire . . . once he has married her, your son's fortune will rise (*bhāgyoday hogā*) . . .

So far, we have looked at *bhāgya* as an "inheritance" allotted to each person at the time of his or her birth. This is however supposed to fluctuate: there are phases or periods of life when the allotted share is important and others when, on the contrary, it is reduced to nothing. We will now look at how astrological theory and astrologers' discourses account for the variability of human destiny over the different periods of an existence.

Destiny's Fluctuations: *Daśā*s (Periods) and *Yog*s (Planetary Conjunctions)

Hindu astrology has developed a system subdividing human existence into planetary periods (*daśā*) that has no equivalent in Western astrology. Identifying the planetary period the owner of the horoscope is going through is one of the pivotal points of any astrological diagnosis.

There are several astrological methods used to calculate planetary periods. The method astrologers in Banaras normally refer to is called *viṃśottarī daśā*, based on an "ideal" life span of 120 years.[28] According to the *viṃśottarī daśā* system, human existence is divided into nine *mahādaśā*s (major planetary periods), each corresponding to a planet (see table 4).

Table 4. Duration of the *mahādaśā*s (major planetary periods)

Planet	**Duration of the *mahādaśā* (in years)**
Sun	6
Moon	10
Mars	7
Rāhu	18
Jupiter	16
Saturn	19
Mercury	17
Ketu	7
Venus	20

The Sun's *mahādaśā* lasts six years, the Moon's *mahādaśā* ten years, and so forth. The first *mahādaśā* one goes through is that of the planet that governs the *nakṣatra* (lunar mansion) in which the Moon is located at the time of birth: hence, if at the time of birth the Moon is located in Aśvinī, as Ketu is the lord of the Aśvinī *nakṣatra* the person will go through Ketu *mahādaśā* from birth to seven years of age, the Venus *mahādaśā* from seven to twenty-seven, the Sun's from twenty-seven to thirty-three, and so on. Each *mahādaśā* consists of nine "planetary sub-periods" called *antardaśā*s: each *antardaśā* is also ruled by a planet, and its duration varies depending on the planet.[29]

A person's *bhāgya* fluctuates according to the *mahādaśā* and the *antardaśā* he or she is going through. Indeed, when it comes to resolving a concrete problem, the astrologer pays particular attention to the planetary period the person is going through. According to astrological theory, depending on the benefic or malefic nature of the planet controlling the *daśā*, and its position in the horoscope, a *daśā* can be "abundant" (*saṃpurṇā*), "empty" (*riktā*), or "malefic" (*aniṣṭaphalā*) (*Bṛhajjātaka* 8.5). Using the *daśā* system, the astrologer identifies each person's allotted share during the different periods of his or her existence: a "full period" (*saṃpurṇā daśā*) means that the share allotted at birth will increase and fructify, while an "empty" (*riktā*) period indicates that it will be scarce, and a "malefic period" signifies that one will face sorrows and misfortunes. In this chapter I shall pay special attention to the contrast between "full" and "empty" periods, as the analysis of malefic periods is closely connected to the question of planetary influence, which will be examined in the seventh chapter. We will now see how astrologers use the *daśā* system to mark a contrast between periods of success, prosperity, and progress on the one hand, and failure, difficulties, and stagnation on the other.

The passage from one period to another can bring about a radical shift in life, as this astrologer explained to a couple of jewelers that were complaining about their financial situation:

J: [looking at the man's horoscope] What do you want to know?

♂: We have a lot of problems, *gurujī*.

J: What kind of shop do you work in?

♂: In a jewelry shop, but we have a lot of problems, lots of losses, the little we are able to earn, we lose it straight away. We cannot even tell you . . . our business is totally underwater . . . the debts keep increasing . . . as soon as we manage to pay back the money on one side, it has already gone out on the other . . . *Doctor Sāhab* (Mr. Doctor), people think we are hiding the money, that we are very rich, while in fact we have nothing at all. Please tell us, will these times change (*hamarā din phiregā ki nahī̃*)?

J: The bad period will last another year, it will take a year, but when you reach the age of forty, there will be an improvement (*unnatī*).

♂: We are totally lost; we've even thought of committing suicide . . .

♀: We got married sixteen or seventeen years ago and we have been through so many difficulties (*taklīf uṭhaye*), we can't even describe them . . . we want to see a change in our life . . . *Gurujī*, please tell us if something will happen, if there will be a change for the better . . . we're desperate. No one ever pays us the money they owe us and when we work up the courage to ask them, it's no use. The debts just keep piling up.

J: You must wait one more year, but after that your business will do very well . . .

♀: We've faced so many difficulties in life . . .

J: No, you won't have problems throughout your life, you just need to wait one more year, for another year you will still have problems, but in one year, an excellent period (*samay baṛhiyā*) will begin and your business will do very well.

To use the jeweler's words, "the times change" when one shifts from one period to another. When a person goes through an "empty" period, when his "share" is going to be small or miserable for a while, ritual precautions are taken to protect the person so that she will not lose the little she is entitled to.

During astrological counseling, empty and abundant planetary periods are used to define economic strategies of saving or investing. When going through an empty period, one should not try to obtain more than she has. If, on the contrary, the period is "full," if the person has a "good astral capital," she must invest in something in order for it to fructify. She must engage in some kind of personal enterprise. This economic philosophy of *bhāgya* is not purely metaphorical; it is explicitly formulated as an opposition that often recurs in astrological consultations, between a job (*naukrī*) and a business (*vyavasāy*). A person who is going through an "empty" period should aspire to a job (*naukrī*), while a person going through an "abundant" period should take advantage of it by investing in a personal business.

Let us look at a few examples of the contrast between *naukrī* (job) and *vyavasāy* (commerce, business) periods. This is the case of a man who was unemployed:

J [after drawing up the birth chart]: Ten months ago you entered an unfavorable (*pratikūl*) period filled with obstacles (*bādhā*) that will last another two to two and a half years. The situation (*paristhiti*) you have been in for the last ten months will not change at all till the month of September.

♂: This September?

> J: Yes, of the year 2000, then the very unfavorable (*bahut pratikūl*) influence (*asar*) will slowly, slowly start decreasing (*dhīre-dhīre kam honā śuru karegā*); but before things return to the way they were before, you will have to wait two to two and a half years. What are you doing at the moment?
>
> ♂: Absolutely nothing.
>
> J: Do not get involved in any business at the moment (*abhī bhī vyavasāy āp mat kijiyegā*), if you have any idea of doing business, don't do it now . . . Now, you should spend your time doing a job (*abhī naukrī karne hī āpkā samay gujarnā cāhiye*). Either you find a good job, or you don't find a good job, you must go through this period without doing any business. You need a job (*naukrī hī karnā āpko uccīt hai*). You will find a job before the 20th of May.
>
> ♂: But it's the 15–16th of February . . . It's a long time from the 16th February till the 20th of May!
>
> J: No, it's three months, three and a half months . . .

The astrologer strongly dissuades this man who is going through a negative period from getting involved in any kind of commercial activity. Here is a similar case of a thirty-year-old unemployed man who was unable to support his wife and his two children. The man went to see the astrologer with his wife:

> ♂: *Paṇḍitjī*, I want to know why I have not been able to begin a career (*kairiyar*) so far.
>
> J [examining the horoscope]: The career will begin after the age of thirty-two, it will be a wonderful career (*baṛhiyā hogā*). You will take some time to reach the age of thirty-two. I mean that for the next two to two and a half years, the situation will not change . . .

♀ [wife]: *Paṇḍitjī*, should he open a shop (*dukān karnā cāhiye*), or should he look for a job (*yā nokri karnā cāhiye*)? I mean, he is educated (*paṛhe-likhe hai*), what should he do?

J: For the time being, in my opinion, given the little he can do, it's better for him to get a job.

♀: It would be better if he got a job now?

J: Yes, it would be better for him to get a job now. After the age of thirty-two, he can do what he wants, open a shop or go into business, it will work.

♀: You mean that now, it's not in his fate (*inke bhāgya abhī nahī̃ hai*) . . .

J: If he opens a shop now, he will lose money, the money will be wasted. He needs regular employment now (*abhī naukrī karnā cāhiye*), in Central India, in the region between Jabalpur and Nagpur . . .

♀: He sits in his mother's shop doing nothing . . . You mean, *paṇḍitjī*, that if he does any kind of independent work, he will have problems (*yah apnā bhī koī kām karenge to nuksān ho jāyegā*).

J: Listen, it will not work, the shop will not work, what is the point of wasting time and effort (*bekār samay barbād karne kyā zarūrat hai?*) . . . In the period he's going through now, even if he has employment, he cannot do much, but at least he'll be able to fill his stomach (*apnā peṭ bharegā*). Whatever his level of education, it's more than enough to find a job.

"Astral capital" and financial capital seem to be managed according to similar principles and are somewhat transposed, the one onto the other, during astrological counseling. This appears even more clearly in the case of a landowning Ayurvedic doctor who consults an astrologer:

J: You're going to have a lot of money . . .

♂: Actually, I have no shortage of money . . .

J: Yes, but I mean to say that you will become *very* rich . . . In the planetary period that is coming (*daśā jo āpke pās ā rahā hai*) you're going to earn a lot of money (*dhan āp bahut acchā kamāyegā*) . . . You should absolutely do something else than medical practice in order to get this money . . . Think seriously about it . . .

♂: What can I do now? I'm old (*buṛhā*)!

J: But you're still so young!

♂: I'm forty-five to forty-six years old . . .

J: Nowadays, at forty-five, one is still young . . . sometimes people get married at the age of forty-five!

♂: Okay . . .

J: Stop talking of old age, nowadays men begin to enjoy (*jos*́) themselves after the age of sixty!!![30]

♂: I have some hope . . . I have willpower.

J: Try to increase your willpower (*icchā shakti*), because the coming twenty years are going to be exceptional (*baṛhiyā*) for you, particularly this year, 2002, will bring you something new . . . that's why you need to think about it . . . Do you have land?

♂: Yes, a bit . . .

J: Think of doing something else along with your work as a doctor, I cannot know, I don't know your village . . . Think of a business you can do in your village or in the area . . . you can make a huge profit from a small amount of money and you will see, with time, your business will grow and you will earn thousands of rupees . . .

So, the doctor must "prospect" (*ḍhūṃṛhnā*) for the wealth that the favorable twenty-year period (corresponding to Venus's *mahādaśā*) has assigned to him, although he feels old and despite the fact that he has no shortage of money. In an India where, since 2000, *Kaun Banegā krorepati?* (Who will become a millionaire?) is one of the most popular TV game show, hosted by the national movie stars Amitabh Bachchan and Shah Rukh Khan, it is not surprising to see that the language of fortune has entered the reading of horoscopes and that those who *can* become millionaires are encouraged to try their luck. Even if not everybody has "millions of rupees" in his or her *bhāgya*, the various cases presented here show that everybody is entitled to "profit" stocked somewhere and available at particular moments.

In addition to planetary periods, astrologers make extensive use of another key concept to explain to clients how to obtain the wealth that is due to them. The concept of *yog*, "astral conjunction," indicates the moment at which the good allotted to the person is available to him or her. By reading a person's horoscope, the astrologer may thus be able to say, for example, that "the *yog* for the house is there" (*makān yog hai*), "the *yog* for the land is there" (*zamīn yog hai*), "the *yog* for a car is there" (*kār kā yog hai*), "the *yog* for promotion (*promośan kā yog*) will arrive in six months," or "there is the *yog* of a son" (*ek laṛke kā yog hai*), "there is the *yog* of three daughters" (*tin laṛkiyõ kā yog hai*), and so on. The presence of a *yog* in the horoscope confirms the opportunity to see an event or a material asset take shape in the person's life—marriage, a promotion, a house, and so forth. Although the category of *yog* is most often used to indicate the presence of things people may wish to attain, astrologers may in some case refer to negative "lots," such as "an illness *yog*" (*rog kā yog*) or "the *yog* of a wound" (*coṭne kā yog*). In this case, some remedies may be prescribed to avoid the danger.

Most *yog*s indicate when a "lot" is temporarily stocked for the person. Thus astrologers use expressions like "the *yog* for marriage has come" (*vivāha yog ā gayā*), "the *yog* for marriage will come in five months" (*pāñc mahīne mẽ vivāha yog ā jāyegā*), or "the *yog* for marriage is going on" (*vivāha yog cālū hai*) to indicate the period when the arrangement of a marriage has more chances to succeed. Nevertheless, some *yog*s endure throughout one's life (*ajīvan yog*). Thus, if a person has a "permanent *yog* for going abroad" (*vides kā ajīvan yog*), she or he will keep traveling to different countries or will emigrate.

An astrologer's client provided a good representation of the idea of *yog*, comparing it to a "meeting": to have the *yog* of something, he explained, is like having an appointment. The thing is intended for you, it is waiting for you. In other words, *yog* indicates the presence of wealth one is entitled to, a deposited asset that one owns and that one can, or rather "must," lay claim to at a specific moment in one's existence—just as when an appointment is fixed, one must be present.

Let us look at the case of a woman from Ghazipur who brought the horoscopes of her daughter, her husband, and her son to know the astral situation of her loved ones:

> ♀: About my daughter Nitu, you looked at her horoscope last time and you wrote: "the *yog* for a job is now" (*naukrī kā yog abhī hai*). We would like to know in what field (*kṣetr*) she will find it, and when . . . Yesterday I took everybody's horoscope before leaving Ghazipur. Here is her horoscope . . .
>
> J: She will find a job in the commercial sector, for example in a bank, an LIC [life insurance company], something like that . . .
>
> ♀: She told me to ask you this because she wants to know where she should send a job application . . .
>
> J: In the commercial sector, yes . . . but be careful, because she has a lot of obstacles (*bādhā*) at the moment, there will be a delay . . .
>
> ♀: Should we perform something [a ritual remedy] for this?
>
> J: No, you should first think about settling her marriage. Actually, it's not the right time to think about the job. Now the *yog for marriage* has come.
>
> ♀: Really? So it has come?
>
> J: Yes, I had written last year that the *yog* for marriage would come in a year, and now one year is over . . . Within three or four months the marriage will be arranged . . . It will not be

celebrated, but it will be arranged. That's why I'm telling you to forget about the job for a while, right now is the time to think about marriage. Afterward, you will think again about the job . . .

♀: My daughter's father [= ♀'s husband] told me to ask you about his job . . . Here is his horoscope. He wants to know whether his promotion and his transfer will come through or not.

J: The *yog* for his transfer is about to come. It will come in August or September, in any case after June . . .

♀: Good! Will we have to move far away, or just in a close area?

J: You will not move very far. According to the horoscope, you will not go any farther than seventy-two miles.

♀: With the transfer, will his promotion come as well?

J: Yes.

♀: Please take a look at my son Sunil's horoscope, too. He lives and works in Delhi . . . I would like to know about his marriage . . . I only have these two children left to marry . . .

J: His *yog* has also come . . .

♀: Really? Good. In which directions should we look for his marriage? You know he is a *maṅgalā* . . . You told me you would perform something [a *pūjā*] at your place between the month of September and the month of January. Where will we find the right girl (*sahī laṛkī*)?

J: You will find a suitable match in the north direction from where you are. That is, if you live in Ghazipur, it will be in or around Gorakhpur, in that area . . .

As an "indicator" of wealth, a *yog* allows to know not only "whether" and "when" a certain good is available but also "where" it is located, where one needs to seek it to attain it. In this case, the girl should look for a job in the commercial sector, the husband's transfer will take place in a radius of seventy-two miles, and the family of the son's future wife is located to the north of Ghazipur. The astrologer's role consists not only in informing the clients of the "wealth" available to them at different moments of their existence, but also in showing them the path to follow in order to access the assets in question.

By studying a family's assets in terms of *yog*s, the astrologer can direct investment strategies. For example, if in the couple the woman has a "*yog* for three houses" (*tīn makān kā yog*), while the husband has no *yog* for a house, any family investment involving buying or building a house should be done in the woman's name. In the case of women, the existence of certain *yog*s in a horoscope can constitute a sort of "astral dowry." Clients may, for example, ask the astrologer to check whether the prospective daughter-in-law has a "*yog* for sons" (*laṛkõ kā yog*), the most valuable *yog* for a bride. If a housewife has a *yog* for a house or car, this is said to increase her husband's and her family-in-law's chances to get this kind of goods. The young girl's astral assets are hence considered an element of the wealth she possesses at the time of her wedding.

Just as the presence of a certain *yog* in the horoscope allows a person to attain something, the absence of this *yog* indicates difficulties or obstacles that prevent the person from obtaining this thing. For example, in January 2000 a young man went to see the astrologer B. P. Mehrotra to ask him about his sister's marriage. Looking at the horoscope, the astrologer realized that until the month of May of that year, the girl was going through a Venus *daśā*, during which Venus was unfavorable and would create many false illusions (*prapañc*) with regard to marriage. In addition, in this *daśā*, Saturn was the "husband's Lord" (*pati kā mālik*, ruler of the seventh house) and was in conjunction with Mars: the two malefic planets created further obstacles (*bādhā*) to the marriage. The astrologer hence concluded that until the end of the *daśā* in question, there was no point in arranging a marriage for the girl as she did not have a real *yog* for marriage:

> ♂: Please tell us something about her marriage . . .
>
> J: I have just told you . . . until the end of the Venus *daśā* she will not be married . . . there's no point in your trying to do it; until the month of May there will be no marriage (*vivāha nahī̃ hogā*) . . .

♂: But we received a proposal (*riśtā*) from Lucknow and one from Saharanpur.

J: What does the boy in Lucknow do?

♂: He works at a photo studio.

J: And the one in Saharanpur?

♂: We don't know.

J: In any case in the planetary period she's going through, there is no marriage *yog* (*is samay jo graha cal rahā hai, vivāha kā yog nahī̃ hai*) . . .

♂: But is there any *chance* [in English] that she will marry one of these two?

J: What do you mean by *chance*? *Chances are not astrology* [in English]. It is as if you were asking me if you are going to pass the exam and I replied "maybe." *That is not astrology*. From the 15th of June onward, this girl has a *temporary yog* for marriage, but it's a *yog* that only brings discussions (*bāte-bāt*). The real (*aslī*) *yog* for marriage will only begin in 2001, and this marriage will not be broken off (*na kaṭne vālā vivāha*). In the *yog* for marriage that occurs in the month of June, there will be a lot of discussions (*bātcīt*), you will meet people, you will have to offer them food, but apart from that, nothing will happen . . .

The strengths and weaknesses of a *yog* in a horoscope determine the extent to which the thing indicated by the *yog* can possibly exist in the person's life. The existence of a "temporary *yog*" indicates that the good can possibly exist, but it will be a precarious and deceitful possession. It is only the "real *yog*" (*aslī yog*) that will lead to a permanent achievement. Let us see another example. Looking at a woman's hand, the astrologer Kameshwar Upadhyay notices she has a "bad *yog*" (*duryog*) with regard to material possessions (generally represented by the fourth house in the horoscope):

> According to your hand, you will always have problems with a house, a piece of land, or a vehicle that belongs to you . . . if you have a house, things will constantly break inside the house; if you buy a piece of land, the land will be yours but you won't be able to use it. You have a *duryog* (bad *yog*) for material possessions like a house, a piece of land, a vehicle . . . if you have a car, it will always be being repaired . . . and if you buy clothes, they will get torn immediately . . . this is your *yog* . . .

So, if a "good *yog*" (*saṃyog*) shows the existence of something in the person's life, a "bad *yog*" (*duryog*) indicates its ontological fragility: clothes tear, the car will have to be repaired constantly, one cannot make use of the land, and so forth.

In some cases, the astrologer encourages the owner of the horoscope to make an effort to attain what "already exists," as its presence is confirmed by the *yog*. Thus, for example, an astrologer encouraged a man who had a government job with the railways, to make every effort to attain the promotion that had been in his *yog* for two years:

> ♂ [showing his horoscope and his hand]: Please have a look *gurujī*, when will my promotion happen? Will it happen or not?
>
> J: You have the *yog* for promotion (*promotion yog banā hai*, the *yog* for promotion is "ready"). It has been there for two years (*do sāl se promotion kā yog ā gayā hai*), but you need to make some effort (*prayās*). According to your horoscope, and your hand, you should wear an amethyst (*jāmuniyā*). The amethyst will help you; you will benefit from it (*āpko lābh milegā*). The *yog* for house has also come and your hand confirms that in a while you will have a house. If you find land somewhere, you should buy it . . .
>
> ♂: And the promotion, when will it happen? Will it happen or not?
>
> J: You will need to try a bit (*thoṛā sā kośiś karnā paṛegā*); if you don't try, it will not happen, *automatically* it won't happen,

> you will have to offer some bribes (*khilānā paṛegā*, you'll have to "feed" people) . . .
>
> ♂: But there is no one I can bribe, there's nothing, the situation is very bad . . .
>
> J: You must keep trying, you must keep trying . . .
>
> ♂: But I keep trying but I'm not getting anywhere; I'm in a situation where I cannot get a promotion, although I keep trying.
>
> J: No, it will happen, you must keep trying, if you don't keep trying, it won't happen (*binā kośiś karnā, nahī̃ hogā*). If it were to happen without your trying, it would already have happened. As the *yog* has been there for two years, you must try.

The man has the *yog* for promotion—"promotion is there"—but the *yog* is not strong enough for the promotion to occur necessarily. Personal effort, including bribes, is hence required to strengthen the *yog* so that the "lot" desired might be obtained.

Human Mistakes, Cosmic Flaws

We have seen so far that the concepts of *bhāgya*, *daśā*, and *yog* are used to define what is due or not to a person over the course of his existence. By establishing what a person is entitled to or not, astrologers determine what the person should or should not do, what he or she should or should not be. This brings us, in the last section of this chapter, to the issues of morality and responsibility and to the question of the relationship between astrology and the theory of karma presented at the beginning of this chapter.

Another example illustrates the contrast between what a person "is" and what he or she "should be" according to a horoscope reading. A thirty-eight-year-old employee working in the IT sector goes to the astrologer to know his professional future. Seeing that he was born in 1962, the astrologer explains to the man that he belongs to a category of exceptionally lucky *jātak-jātikā* (male and female "natives"), and that everyone belonging to this category enjoys great success in life:

> J: You were born in '62, that was the year when there was an *aṣṭa grahī yog* (astral conjunction of eight planets) . . . during this period (*samay*) many rituals (*havan-vavan*) were performed, I was in Bombay at the time[31] . . .
>
> ♂: Okay . . .
>
> J: Now you will go through an excellent period—do you have any business?
>
> ♂: No, I work for a computer company.
>
> J: Your horoscope shows there will be a lot of people working under you, your career will take you very far (*āge unnatī bahut zyādā hai*), a lot of people will work under you (*āpke anḍer bahut sāre ādmī kām karẽ*), you have this ability (*yogya*) written in your horoscope. But you have already reached the age of thirty-eight . . . you should have found something better (*āpko aur acchā milnā cāhiye thā*).
>
> ♂: Nothing has happened till now. In fact, I wanted to know if something will change, or if it will remain as it is (*isī tarah caltā rahegā*) . . .

Noting that the man is not aware of the excellent share that is his *bhāgya*, the astrologer insists, stating that the improvement is "inevitable" (*anivārya*), that it will necessarily happen:

> J: People who are born in your year (*is sāl mẽ gitne jātak-jātikā janme haĩ*) will all inevitably be successful (*sabko unnatī anivārya hai*) in their careers . . . so, as something excellent (*baṛhiyā*) has happened to everyone born in your year, something excellent will happen to you too (*āpko bhī baṛhiyā hogā*). My paternal cousin has the same horoscope as you, he was born in

the same year, he already owns about twenty cars, he supplies precious stones, he owns four or five stone quarries . . . The second thing that characterizes your horoscope is that a lot of men will work for you, and this is why I asked if you are a businessman. If you are not, you should still do some business in addition to your job . . . you will be successful (*unnatī hogā*), but you're facing a delay (*āpko* delay *ho rahā hai*), considering your age, you should have already achieved far more in your career (*bahut ādhik āpko unnatī ho jānā cāhiye thā*).

♂: My progress (*unnatī*) when does it begin?

J: *Actually* your progress began at the age of thirty-six. You are wasting the most precious time you have (*āpkā mahatvapūrṇ samay barbād ho rahā hai*). A wonderful opportunity will come your way, for people of your year it is certain (*niścit hai*) there will be an improvement. Two years too many have already passed and nothing has happened, but it will happen.

♂: For the time being, I have not seen any of this . . .

The Hindi verb *cāhiye*, "should," is used extensively to indicate how things *should* be: the man *should be* powerful and rich; he *should*, like all those born under the same planetary conjunction, have attained success and prosperity, but yet, he is a mere employee at a computer company. In the astrologer's discourse natural necessity—expressed by planetary conjunctions—becomes a moral necessity. Because everyone born in 1962 *must* achieve success—"it is inevitable" (*anivārya hai*), "it is certain" (*niścit hai*)—the employee *should* be successful. He *should* seek success by doing some business and he *should not* waste his time and wealth.

The astrologer incites the client to conform to the natural order established by the planets. As we saw in several examples, if, according to the horoscope, the person is entitled to a "small share," he should not ask for "more," he should not venture into undertakings to obtain what it is not due to him. Conversely, if the owner of the horoscope is entitled to a "large share," it is his duty to "demand" the share due to him by undertaking some kind of additional business, offering bribes, or in any event, by making an effort to obtain the allotted share. Astrologers define as "right," "correct," or "appropriate" behavior not that which conforms to moral values—like honesty, compassion, or wisdom—but rather what conforms to the order established by the planets.

This appears all the more evident when astrologers interpret and explain "bad behavior" (*duṣkarm*). Almost in the role of a defending lawyer, when he confronts a misbehaving client, the astrologer does not pass any kind of judgment: he seeks instead to understand which planetary configurations may explain his or her behavior, and he tries to identify the ritual remedies that can limit the damage created by the astral situation. The most common examples of "inevitable" bad behavior are adultery, religious negligence, and violence. Extramarital relations are supposed to be the product of a planetary conjunction in which Venus, the planet that symbolizes love and sexuality, and Mars, the planet of fire and ardor, are in a situation of *nīc rāśi*[32] under the *dṛṣṭi*[33] of Saturn, the most malefic planet.[34] Anyone who has this astral situation in their horoscope is said to be *kāmāndh* (blinded by desire) and will not be able to stop himself from having sexual relations with several partners. To better understand this, an astrologer claims to have done "fieldwork" in the prostitutes' area in Banaras (located near the airport), to study the palms of the women there and to try to understand whether it is the *kāmāndh yog* that makes women prostitutes. As a result of his survey, he states that three types of reasons could lead a woman to become a prostitute: either the *kāmāndh* astral conjunction, unfavorable economic conditions, or a lack of education. To explain the extent to which the *kāmāndh* astral conjunction deprives a person of any control over their actions, in addition to the prostitutes the astrologer cited the example of a colleague in Calcutta, who was afflicted by this astral configuration. Although she knew her own "weakness," the woman, an astrologer who was married, could not stop herself from having sexual relations with her own clients, to the extent that, to put a stop to this bad influence, she was forced to stop exercising her profession.

During consultations, numerous cases of adultery are evoked. Adulterous tendencies caused by planets are seen as a physical dependency and the English word "addiction" is sometimes employed in this context as something the person finds difficult to give up. Since the origin of this attitude is "innate," astrologers do not express moral judgments. Thus, when dealing with the case of a woman who had been betrayed by her husband, the astrologer explained that for this type of person "the need for extramarital relations is like an alcoholic's need for alcohol, or a smoker's need for a cigarette." The individuals are unable to change their own behavior, and it is up to their loved ones (and the astrologer) to try to help them get over it. In the same way, when dealing with young people "blinded by desire," who run away from home, or have premarital sex, astrologers do not pronounce a moral judgment upon them; they try instead to find concrete solutions to resolve these cases. They will try to find the girl or boy who has disappeared by calculating the *praśna*, they will prescribe remedies to reduce the influence of Mars—the planet responsible for the attraction (*moha, lagan*)—and to increase the Sun's influence so as to reinforce the person's *self-control*, and so on.

Another bad attitude that is often mentioned during consultations is devotional or ritual negligence. Some planetary conjunctions are thought to make the person reticent to any form of worship (*pūjā*) and prevent them from accomplishing meritorious actions (*puṇyas*). Those who have this astral profile are caught in a vicious circle since they will find it difficult to go to the temple and perform the rituals—oblations into the fire (*havans*), recitation of mantras (*japs*), among others—which could help them reduce the bad planetary influence. Furthermore, ritual negligence makes the person impure, and impurity only aggravates the planetary influence, which is supposed have a worse effect on impure people.

When confronted with a man afflicted by the malefic planet Rāhu, the astrologer Kameshwar Upadhyay recommended he have a *havan* (oblations into the fire) performed, although he was convinced his recommendation would not be followed:

> In your case, it is absolutely necessary to have a *havan* performed . . . but you are so oppressed by the planets (*grahõ se itnā pīṛit haĩ*) that I know you will not do it . . . when Rāhu is so bad, the person usually takes someone else up to the entrance to the temple and he says to him: "Take off your shoes and go and take the *darśan*: I'll stay outside to look after the shoes," so that they do not have to take the *darśan* and then they can go home . . . that's how bad Rāhu is!

We had been told of a similar case by a man whose brother-in-law was under the influence of the malefic planet Śani (Saturn). To help his brother-in-law escape the affliction of Saturn, the man used to take him to the temple dedicated to Hanumān, the God who is supposed to control Śani's influence. But his attempts were in vain:

> Every time we went to Saṅkaṭ mocan [the Hanumān temple] he stood outside, he waited outside. Once I said to him: "Come on, let's go in," but he said he didn't want to, that you shouldn't ever force yourself to do *pūjā* . . . We knew he was seized by Śani's anger (*prakop*) . . . but one Saturday, we went to the temple; I did the *pūjā* and he didn't. Then we went home by scooter, it was eleven at night, he dropped me at home and he had an accident on his way home. It was a small accident, but it was followed by a dispute that lasted the whole night, the police also came . . .

Another type of bad behavior explained in terms of planetary configurations is that of hoodlums (*badmāś*) or members of the mafia (*guṇḍā*s, *mafia vālā*s). Mars's bad influence, like Rāhu's and sometimes Ketu's, is supposed to provoke the desire to fight (*mārnā-pīṭnā*)—particularly among young people—to provoke fights (*hum-tām, jhagṛā-jhaṃjhaṭ, laṛāī*) and to create tension and arguments (*kalah, vivād, bātā-bāti*). For example, when the astrologer B. P. Mehrotra studied the horoscope of a man suspected of being involved in a homicide, he identified the planetary configuration (*yog*) that led to the use of explosive materials (*visphoṭak padārth*) and bullets for a gun (*golī-charrā bandūk*). He hence told the worried members of the family who had come to see him that the man's criminal behavior was in no way surprising, given the planetary situation. Thus the behavior of a thief (*cor*) or obtaining wealth by fraud (*nīc buddhi se dhan prāpt karnā*) is explained by the *nīc karm yog*—the astral configuration (*yog*) of bad (*nīc*) behavior (*karm*)—which occurs when two or several malefic planets (*pāp graha*s) are in the ascendant at the time of birth.[35]

Besides evil actions (*pāp*), planetary influence may also explain minor character defects such as impatience, laziness, greed, fickleness: thus the presence of a birthmark on the palm of the hand in the Ketu zone designates incorrigible greed, having Moon in the ascendant makes the person *cañcal* (unstable, fluctuating), and so on.

If this type of flaw is identified in the birth chart (or on the palm of the hand), it means that this is a character trait related to the person's "nature" (*svabhāv*) and is a "lifelong" (*jīvan bhar, ājīvan*) defect: in this case the astrologer diagnoses a "habitus" (*ādat*) that cannot be modified as it is not the result of a fault (*galtī*) on the person's part. Thus, for example, when looking at a young man's horoscope, the astrologer explained to the father that the son's lazy and "against the current" personality was an unalterable feature of his constitution:

> J: Because the Moon and Ketu are in the seventh house, these people do not want to do anything . . .
>
> ♂: How long will this last?
>
> J: The whole life . . . they are lazy (*ālsī*) people . . .
>
> ♂: Oh yes! He is so lazy! He's still asleep at seven o'clock . . .
>
> J: Yes, these people hate getting up in the morning . . . they are people who, if they start working, they work a lot, but if they're not in the mood to work, you cannot even ask them to fetch a glass of water, that is their nature . . . But for these people, getting up late is a habit (*ādat*), it's their nature (*svabhāv*) . . . what characterizes these people is getting up late, always being late, doing the opposite of what they are asked, that's how they live.

To explain the extent to which the son's behavior is in his nature, the astrologer continued the diagnosis comparing the young man to an anadromous fish:

> . . . *Candr* and *Ketu* are in the seventh house and this creates a lot of confusion (*baṛā gaṛbaṛ kar detā hai*) . . . he never finds his way; he wanders all over the place. Think of the *hilsā* fish . . . well, his *mentality* is a bit like that, like a *hilsā* fish . . . people like him always like to go against the flow. They like to follow their own path in the opposite direction, just like the *hilsā* fish . . .

Astrologically speaking, a person who is "good" is not someone virtuous, but someone who conforms to the cosmic order, who assumes the share assigned to him. Astrologers are not concerned by the moral quality of acts. An action is correct when it is "necessary" (*āvaśyak*), "inevitable" (*anivārya*), "established" (*niścit*), and corresponds to the person's "nature" (*svabhāv*) as written in the horoscope or in the hand. As we have seen, in astrological discourse, a person who behaves badly may also be treated as a "victim" of planetary influence, someone that should be helped, rather than condemned. Human existence is supposed to be the manifestation of an order—in the twofold sense, of a regular disposition and an injunction, a prescription—established by the cosmos.

Although he does not *condemn* moral faults, the astrologer obviously *sees* moral faults: adultery, violence, alcoholism, and so forth, are clearly recognized as immoral behavior. But it is precisely because the fault exists that an explanation is required (by the client) and a justification is provided (by the astrologer). Through horoscope reading, astrologers make sense of bad actions.

From what we have seen, it becomes clear that astrology provides an ideological complement to the karma theory. It explains why people do good and bad acts, while the karma theory takes the moral quality of action as a departure point. Although it happens rarely, astrologers may refer, during consultations, to past lives deeds and karmic retribution. As we will see, this happens when astrological theory does not seem to provide an exhaustive interpretative paradigm. Human responsibility is then evoked as an etiological supplement.

Most horoscopic treatises, as we have seen, mention the karma theory in a *śloka* placed at the beginning of the text, establishing that astrology is the science that makes visible the otherwise invisible fruits of acts accomplished in previous lives. Apart from this verse, astrological theory normally does not refer to the karma theory. Nonetheless, there are a few passages where the karma theory is mentioned in addition to the "lamp trick." In order to understand the type of events in human destiny for which astrology requires the inclusion of a "moral" etiology, it may be useful to briefly examine these passages in classical as well as contemporary publications.

Among the ninety-seven chapters of the *Bṛhatpārāśarahorāśāstra* (BPHŚ), a very popular horoscopy text among astrologers in Banaras, there is one, chapter 83, that refers to the theory of karma. This chapter is dedicated to elucidating (*dyotana*) curses (*śāpa*) uttered because of sins committed in past lives (*purvajanman*):[36] "what is the sin that makes a man unable to have a son?" (*aputraḥ kena pāpena bhavati*) is the question asked at the beginning of the chapter.[37] The text goes on to list the "planetary conjunctions for childlessness" (*santāna-hāni-yogs*) and particularly for the absence of a male son (*suta-kṣaya*, the "destruction" of the son). Depending on the astral situation at birth, one can know against whom the evil action was committed in the previous life—a snake, the father, the mother, the maternal uncle, a Brahmin, the wife, the ancestors—and hence who is responsible for the curse.

According to the *Jātakapārijāta*, another well-known classical treatise used in Banaras, the horoscope does not allow one to determine the life span of a child up to the age of twelve (JP 4.1a). This crypticness is due to the impact of sins committed by the parents in past and present lives:

> [Up to the age of twelve] because of the evil acts (*pāpakarma*) of the mother and the father, the child dies [seized] by the demons of childhood (*bālagraha*). If the child dies within the first four years, it is because of the mother's sins. If [he dies] in the middle four years, it is because of the accumulated sins of the father. If it comes in the last four years, it must be due to its own faults (*doṣa)* [in previous life]. (JP 4.1b–2)

Just as children's death is commonly attributed to karmic reasons, so are innate diseases and malformations at birth. According to *Jyotiṣ aur Rog* (Astrology and Diseases), a contemporary manual of medical astrology in Hindi, human diseases are divided into two categories: "congenital diseases" (*sahaj rog, janmjāt rog*) and "accidental diseases" (*āgantuk rog*). While the latter group of diseases is supposed to arise over the course of an existence because of all kinds of malefic influences (planets, evil eye, epidemics, wounds, etc.), the former is seen as the product of acts accomplished in previous lives: "The main cause (*mahattvapurṇ kāran*) of congenital diseases is acts (*karm*) done by the native (*jātaka*, "he who is born") in past lives (*purvajanm*). A second cause may be the acts done by the native's father and mother" (Sharma n.d., 53). The list of diseases classified under the category *sahaj rog* is as follows:

lūlāpan or *bāhuhīnatā*: arms abnormality or absence of arms
laṅgṛāpan or *paṅgutva*: lameness or absence of legs
kubṛāpan: back deformity, humpback
hināṅg: mutilation

kānatv or *kānā*: blindness or the loss of an eye
patnī kā kānatv: one's own wife's blindness or loss of an eye
gūṅgāpan: mutism
baharāpan: deafness
kam sunnā: weak hearing
kān kā kaṭnā or *phaṭnā*: having the ears cut off or torn
karn pīṛā: earache
napuṃsakatā: infertility
jāṛtā or *pāgalpan*: mental deficiency or madness (Sharma n.d., 55–64)

We can clearly see that, in this case, the term *rog* designates "abnormalities" or "malformations" rather than "diseases." Each of these malformations is supposed to be the result of acts the patient or his parents have done in previous lives and corresponds to certain astral configurations.

During the consultations we attended, karma theory was evoked to explain problems similar to those mentioned in the texts. This was the case of a couple that was unable to have children after twelve years of marriage, despite having tried several astrological remedies. According to the astrologer, this was due not only to the negative planetary influence but also to evil acts carried out by the man and the woman in their previous lives. Similarly, looking at the horoscope of a father who had just lost his one-and-a-half-year-old son, the astrologer explained that the bad position of the malefic planet Ketu in the father's horoscope had led to the son's death, and this was due to past life deeds. A third case we observed is that of a man suffering from leucoderma (*saphed dāg rog*, "white patch disease"), an incurable disease that astrologers see as congenital and caused by some sin committed in a previous life.

The question that arises is hence the following: Why, in the case of the death of children, infertility, malformations, or congenital diseases does astrological theory evoke human responsibility and resort to a "moral" theory of human destiny? And why, conversely, is human destiny explained in terms of a "natural" necessity when human faults and responsibilities could easily be designated—not only in cases of adultery, violence, or laziness but also in the cases of financial, educational, or professional failure that we looked at?

This is the paradox we are confronted with: astrologers in Banaras see events that involve human faults and responsibility as necessary and inevitable, while they attribute moral faults and responsibility to cases where the person has not only committed no obvious fault, but they seem rather to be the victim of an inevitable "natural" injustice. Human beings are seen as responsible for "fatalities" such as the birth of an abnormal child or the death of a child. In contrast, when guilty, they are discharged from any responsibility. In a sense, guilty people are seen as victims (of planetary situations), while victims (of fatalities or catastrophes) are seen as guilty.

To make sense of this paradox, one should not think that astrologers do not consider the fault of adultery as a fault, and they see the death of a newborn child as the result of a "intentional" fault on the part of the parents. On the contrary, astrologers share the client's view that betraying a spouse is bad behavior and the death of a son is a tragic event that descends upon a parent's destiny, despite himself. Nonetheless, the astrologer's task does not consist of confirming the evidence of shared perceptions, observing facts—in one case the fault, in the other misfortune—but it consists rather in explaining the facts by overturning the evidence so as to reveal an underlying cosmological order.

Some sections of this chapter were originally published in the journal *Social Analysis* (56/2) under the title "The Allotted Share: Managing Fortune in Astrological Counseling in Contemporary India" (Guenzi 2012).

6

Shared Destinies

Kinship Connections in Horoscope Reading

> Himācal, Pārvatī and Gaurī's father asks them: "Whose destiny (*bhāgya*) is each of you eating?" Parvatī says "I eat my own destiny." Gaurī says "I eat your destiny." Gaurī's answer is correct and Parvatī also admits she lives not only her own destiny, but her father's too.
>
> —*Bārahõ mahīne ke sampūrṇ hinduõ ke vrat tyauhār*,
> Hindi pamphlet dealing with votive fasts for the twelve months
> of the Hindu year, quoted by Susan Wadley,
> "Vrats: Transformers of Destiny"

According to horoscopic theory, the birth chart of the "native" (*jātaka*, "he who is born") not only concerns the individual for whom the horoscope is calculated but also affects all his relationships, particularly his family ties (*parivārik saṃbandh*). As stated in Sanskrit horoscopic treatises (*horāśāstras*) the mother, the father, the spouse, the children, the grandparents, the in-laws, the friends, the servants, and others, are also part of the native's personal destiny. By studying the planetary configurations at birth, astrologers are thus able to scrutinize the destiny not only of the owner of the horoscope (*jātaka*), but also of everyone the native is in a constant relationship with over the course of his or her existence. They can see, for example, the father's professional problems, the spouse's dark complexion and propensity for adultery, the mother-in-law's respiratory problems, the children's educational failures, a brother's scooter accident, the hostility of a colleague at work, and so on.

Through the analysis of astrologers' readings, as well as textual excerpts from horoscopic treatises, we will see in this chapter that the *destiny* of the native has multiple *destinations* since it may affect several people, well beyond the owner of the horoscope. The individual can thus be both the *recipient* and the *issuer* of a "share of destiny" (*bhāgya*). The "share" allotted to the native affects the destiny of those that are close to him or her, just as the "share" allotted to family members is a part of the native's "lot." Horoscope reading is based on the idea that every individual destiny is intrinsically made up of, and inseparable from, that of his entourage.[1]

By combining textual sources and ethnographic material, I will first look at the manner in which the destinies of family members are described as mutually linked. We will go on to see how this intertwining of destiny can be extended to include all kinds of professional and affective relationships and friendships. With regard to the texts we will refer to some Sanskrit treatises on horoscopy (*jātakaśāstra*) regularly used by astrologers in Banaras: the *Bṛhatpārāśarahorāśāstra* (BPHŚ) by Pārāśara, the *Sārāvalī* (SRV) by Kalyāṇavarman, and the *Sarvārthacintāmaṇi* (SC) by Vyaṅkaṭaśarman.[2] Textual excerpts are used here to illustrate the theory that informs astrologers' interpretations.

In horoscopic treatises, the destiny of the members of the family is dealt with from three angles: the "fatal signs" (*ariṣṭa*), the signification (*kārakatva*) of the planets (*graha*), and the twelve houses (*bhāva*). Let us start by examining the *ariṣṭa*s, the "disastrous conjunctions," which are likely to affect the parents and the child in particular.[3] The first person involved in the owner of the horoscope's destiny is the mother (*mātṛ*). Here are a few of the astral conjunctions that concern the mother and the child:[4]

> If Moon is aspected by three malefic planets, *mother's death will occur (*mātṛnāśa bhavet*)*. If Moon is aspected by favorable planets, *one can tell her happiness (*śubham vadet*)*. (BPHŚ 9.24)
>
> When Rāhu, Mercury, Venus, and Sun are situated in the house of wealth [= second house], *the death of the newborn's mother will happen (*tasya mātur bhavet mṛtyuḥ*)* and *the child will be born when the father is already dead (*mṛte pitari*)*. (BPHŚ 9.25)

> Moon with a malefic planet, aspected by strong malefic planets and situated in the seventh or eighth house [counting] from a malefic planet: *the newborn will be a "matricide" (*mātṛhan*).* (BPHŚ 9.26)

> Jupiter in the ascendant, Saturn in the house of wealth [= second house], and Rāhu in the third house: if this [astral configuration] is at the moment of birth, *the mother does not survive (*mātā na jīvati*).* (BPHŚ 9.31)

> When malefic planets are in *trikoṇa* houses [= first, fifth, or ninth], counted from the decreasing moon, without benefic planets, no doubt the *mother will abandon the child (*mātā parityajed bālam*) within six months.* (BPHŚ 9.32)

These verses describe the influence the son's horoscope can have on the mother: her death, her happiness, her actions depend on the destiny of the newborn. We note, interestingly, that the child, who is the owner of the horoscope, is not always the grammatical subject of the divinatory sentences. He may even be the direct object, as in the last sentence, where, instead of saying: "the child is abandoned by the mother," the texts say, "the mother abandons the child" (*mātā parityajed bālam*). The mother appears as a full agent in her son's horoscope.[5] Although she is a full *subject* in her son's destiny, she is also *subjected to* her son's destiny: she is obliged to abandon her son as her son's destiny forces her to. We find a similar divinatory sentence in the Sārāvalī:

> Malefic planets in the eighth, seventh, sixth, and twelfth houses: *the mother dies with her child (*mātā sutena sārdhaṃ mriyate*).* (SRV 10.55)

Here too the destinies are shared, they merge into each other. As a grammatical subject, the mother is the agent—she takes her son *with her* into death—but at the same time she is carried off by her son's destiny, she dies because of the latter's horoscope.

After examining the mother's fate, the chapters dealing with *ariṣṭa*s, the "fatal signs" at the birth of the child, go on to describe the influence of the newborn's horoscope on the father.[6]

> Saturn in the *lagna* [= ascendant], Mars in the house of passion (*mada*) [= seventh house] and Moon in the sixth house: if [this configuration] occurs at the moment of birth, *the child's father does not survive (*pitā tasya na jīvati*).* (BPHŚ 9.34)

> Jupiter in the *lagna* and Saturn, Sun, Mars, and Mercury sitting together in the house of wealth [= second house]: *the father dies at the moment of his son's marriage (*vivāhasamaye tasya bālasya mriyate pitā*).* (BPHŚ 9.35)

> Sun in the seventh house, Mars in the house of *karman* [= tenth house], and Rāhu in the house of losses [= twelfth house]: *the father lives with great difficulty (*pitā kaṣṭena jīvati*).* (BPHŚ 9.37)

> When Mars is in the tenth house, in the zodiacal sign of his enemy [= Mercury], *the father of the native will certainly die soon (*mriyate tasya jātasya pitā śīghram na saṃśayaḥ*).* (BPHŚ 9.38)

> Sun aspected by Saturn and in a Mars *navāṃśa* [= Aries or Scorpio]:[7] *the father leaves [the family] before the child's birth or is even already dead (*prāgjanmano nivṛttiḥ syān mṛtyurvā 'pi śiśoḥ pituḥ*).* (BPHŚ 9.40)

Similarly, in the Sārāvalī:

> . . . Sun in the *lagna* with Mars and Saturn, and without Mercury, Jupiter, and Venus: *this indicates (*kathayati*) father and grandfather's death.* (SRV 10.46)

> When the birth is diurnal and Sun is surrounded by malefic planets, or in conjunction with malefics: *no doubt the newborn "kills" (*hanyāt*) the father* (SRV 10.47)

> If at birth Sun is with malefic planets in a mobile (*cara*) sign, *this indicates (*kathayati*) [the father's] untimely death (*alpāyuṣa, *"short-lived") because of poison, of weapons, or water.* (SRV 10.49)

> When birth takes place at night, Saturn is with Mars in a mobile (*cara*) sign: this means *that the father will certainly die*

> *abroad (*paradeśa*).* Sun in conjunction with Mars and Saturn in any zodiacal sign: this *indicates the death of the father before the birth (*prāgjanman*) of the son* (SRV 10.53–54)

The father's death is described in greater detail than the mother's. Astral configurations provide information about the time of the father's death—when his son marries (BPHŚ 9.35), before his son's birth (BPHŚ 9.40; SRV 10.54)—the place—in a foreign land (SRV 10.53)—and the material cause—poison, weapons, or water (SRV 10.49). The circumstances—temporal, geographical, and so forth—of the father's death are relevant to the *jātaka*'s destiny, while for the mother, the only thing that matters is her death when the child is still young. Furthermore, several passages refer to the father's death "before the birth" (*prāgjanman*) of the child (BPHŚ 9.25 and 9.40; SRV 10.54): the destinies are so tightly connected that a son's influence on his father is endowed with a "retroactive" power.[8]

According to horoscopic theory, the Sun represents the father, and the Moon the mother. If the Sun or the Moon are aspected by malefic planets in the horoscope, this means that there will be an obstacle, a difficulty (suffering, diseases, etc.) in the father or the mother's life, respectively. Thus, in the BPHŚ we have:

> The Sun is the father and the Moon is the mother of all living beings. If Sun is aspected by a malefic planet or is surrounded by malefic planets: *definitively one should understand (*vijānīyāt*) a fatal danger for the father (*pitrariṣṭam*) of the newborn child.* Sun afflicted by malefic planets in the sixth or eighth house counting from Sun, or in the house of happiness [= fourth house]: *this also indicates (*vinirdiśet*) a fatal danger for the father (*pitrariṣṭam*).* If malefic planets are in these same positions counting from Moon: *mother's suffering (*mātur kaṣṭam*) is to be considered.* By analyzing the strenghth or the weakness [of planets], *one should predict whether there is suffering (*kaṣṭam*) or death (*mṛtyu*).* (BPHŚ 9.43–45)

Similarly, when Sun or Moon are in a favorable position, the parents will rejoice accordingly:

> [Moon or Sun] aspected by benefic planets: *happiness (*śubham*).* (SRV 9.49b)

> Shining Moon in its own zodiacal signs, or in exaltation (*svoccaga*), or in the fifth house, with Jupiter and Venus aspected by Mercury: *this gives extreme happiness (*atiśayaśubha*) to the mother; the same happens to the father as for the divine Sun.* (SRV 9.50)[9]

Planets may represent other members of the family within the horoscope. Thus, according to the BPHŚ, Mars indicates brothers and sisters, as well as the brother-in-law, while Mercury is the maternal family, including the maternal uncle. Jupiter is the paternal grandfather, Venus is the husband, and Saturn represents the children. Ketu is the wife, the parents, the parents-in-law, and the maternal grandfather (BPHŚ 32.19b–21).

The technical term used in horoscopic theory to designate the correspondence between the planets and the members of the family is *kārakatva*, usually translated by "signification." The planet that corresponds to a particular member of the family is called the *kāraka*, "indicator," "significator," of the relative in question: thus Mars is the *kāraka* of brothers, brothers-in-law, and the mother; Mercury is the *kāraka* of relatives on the maternal side; and so on.[10] By analyzing the position and the aspects (*dṛṣṭi*) of a planet, one should be able to identify the relative's personality and the events of his or her life. Thus the paternal grandfather's health, happiness, and personality can be deduced by examining the astrological configurations involving Jupiter in the *jātaka*'s horoscope, while the spouse will be studied on the basis of Venus, the children on the basis of Saturn, and so on.

The destinies of the members of the owner of the horoscope's family can also be studied through the houses (*bhāva*). According to the BPHŚ, the following houses represent the various members of the family:[11]

III = brothers and/or sisters (younger)
IV = mother, maternal grandparents
V = children
VI = maternal uncle
VII = spouse
IX = father
XI = brothers and/or sisters (older)

In order to know the situation of a family member, astrologers consider two things: the planets situated in the house corresponding to the relative in question; the planet that rules that house as a "lord" (*īśa, pati*). The "lord of the house" (*bhāveśa, bhāvapati*) is the planet ruling the sign located in the house in question.[12] Thus if the sign Virgo (*kanyā*) is in the fourth house (= house of the mother) of a horoscope, to know the problems that could possibly afflict the mother, in addition to looking at the planetary configuration present in the fourth house, one also has to examine the position of Mercury (the planet ruling the sign of Virgo) in the horoscope.[13]

To better understand the astrological theory of *parivārik saṃbandh*, family relationships, we will now focus on three crucial relationships that are examined in great detail in the texts and are frequently mentioned during consultations: brothers and sisters, parents and children, and husband and wife. We will then see how this theory can be extended to all kinds of family, professional, and affective relationships.

Brothers and Sisters

The third house—called *sahaja bhāva*, "house of those who are born together"—is the *kāraka*, "significator," of siblings (*sahaja, sodara*):[14]

> O Brahmin, according to the strength and the weakness of the planetary conjunctions (*yoga*) [in the third house] one can state the effects (*phala*) on the native's brothers (*bhrātṛ*) and sisters (*bhaginī*). (BPHŚ 14.15)

To scrutinize the destiny of the brothers and/or sisters of the *jātaka*, the astrologer will have to consider the situation of the planets that are in the third house and the situation of the lord of the third house. The following verses describe a brother or sister's death:

> The two planets [= the lord of the third house and Mars] are in conjunction with malefic planets or are situated in a sign ruled by a malefic: *after driving away brothers and sisters soon these two planets will destroy them, there is no doubt.* (BPHŚ 14.3)

> When situated in the third house, *Sun kills (*hanti*) the brother [or sister] born just before the native (*agre jāta*), Saturn [kills] the*

> *brother [or sister] born just after the native (*pṛṣṭe jāta*) and Mars kills both, elder and younger brother [or sister].* (BPHŚ 14.14)[15]

> The lord of the third house and Mars in the house of death [= eighth house] *are destroyers (*vināśaka*) of brothers and sisters*; Mars and the lord of the third house in *kendra* [= first, fourth, seventh, or tenth house], in *trikoṇa* [= first, fifth, or ninth house], in exaltation (*ucca*) or in a friendly division (*mitrasvavarga*): *[this] indicates happiness for brothers (*bhrātṛsaukhyam*).* (BPHŚ 14.5b–6)

The third house of the horoscope also indicates whether the native will have brothers or sisters and how many of them. According to the BPHŚ:

> The lord of the third house is a female planet (*strīgraha*) [= Moon, Venus], or a female planet is situated in the third house: *the native will have a [younger] sister*; similarly, if a male planet (*puṃgraha*) is the lord of the third house or is situated in it: *the native will have a brother*. If planets are "mixed" (*miśra*) [both male and female]: *the native may have both [brother and sister], and this should be told according to the strenghth and weakness [of the planets].* (BPHŚ 14. 4–5a)

> Mercury in the house of siblings, the lord of the third house in conjunction with Moon, the *kāraka* [= Mars, "significator" of siblings] with Saturn: *the native will have an elder sister, a younger brother, and afterward another brother who will die.* Those born after the third brother will die. The *kāraka* [= Mars] in conjunction with Rāhu, the lord of the third house, in a sign of debilitation (*nīca*): *one should predict that younger siblings will die, but the native will have three elder siblings.* The lord of the house of siblings in *kendra* [= first, fourth, seventh, or tenth house], Mars in *trikoṇa* [= first, fifth, or ninth house] counting from in exaltation with Jupiter, *twelve siblings are to be known. Among these, one should tell the death of two elder brothers of the native, as well as the third, the seventh, the ninth, and twelfth; the remaining six siblings will be long-lived (*dīrghajīvana*).* (BPHŚ 14.7–11)

> Mars in conjunction with the lord of the house of loss [= twelfth house] and with Jupiter, while Moon is in the house of brothers: *there will be seven siblings*. Moon in the third house aspected by male planets only, *one should understand that the native will have brothers*, while, if aspected by Venus, *it will be otherwise [the native will have sisters]*. (BPHŚ 14.12–13)

The gender of children to be born into a family has always been, and remains, a particularly delicate question in Indian society. To prevent female feticide, prenatal sex determination through ultrasound techniques has been banned in India since 1994. Astrological consultations may thus be used as a substitute for medical technologies in order to discern the sex of the child to be born. The astrologer Ram Naresh Tripathi describes, for instance, the case of a woman who had four daughters and desperately wanted a son:

> This woman came to me when she found out she was expecting a fifth child . . . she was very worried, she desperately wanted a son, but until then she had only had daughters. To understand the possible cause of the problem, I asked her to bring the horoscope of her last-born child, the youngest of her daughters. Looking at her horoscope, I saw that the girl would have a brother. I reassured the woman, telling her she would have a son. Then, according to the youngest daughter's horoscope, I prescribed the *pūjā* necessary to appease the negative planetary influences. Finally, the woman gave birth to a son.

The birth of a brother is a crucial event in the life of a girl. Describing her destiny, the horoscope cannot omit something like the presence of a brother in her life. But, similarly, the brother's destiny, his very existence, is decided by the sister's destiny: the brother cannot be born if his existence is not expected and hence "allowed" by the horoscope of the sister who precedes him.

I witnessed another case of astral influence between brothers at the astrologer Kameshwar Upadhyay's place. A man whose elder brother had just died in a road accident had come to show his horoscope. By analyzing the young man's horoscope, the astrologer saw that the planets Saturn and Ketu were having a harmful influence on his brother and stated that only the presence of a sister between the two brothers could have protected the elder brother. When I questioned him later about this case, the astrologer explained:

> I knew the young man's older brother very well; he had been my client for a long time. Nothing in his horoscope could have led one to think he would die a premature death, nothing at all. I hence understood that the indications of his death were, in fact, present in his brother's horoscope. Saturn and Ketu are so harmful in the younger brother's horoscope that even the mother is in danger. I have told her to be careful, to take precautions.

As we can see from this case, astrologically speaking, a person can have a decisive, fatal impact on the destiny of his or her close relatives. Indeed, when they are unable to identify the astrological cause of death (or of a serious illness) in someone's horoscope, astrologers may read the horoscopes of close relatives (parents, spouse, brothers, et al.) to see if their destiny is written elsewhere.

The most common procedure, nonetheless, consists of looking at the horoscope of the person directly affected by the problem. This provides the definitive key to the interpretation, and it is on this basis that the treatment is prescribed. In other words, if the presence of a difficulty can be identified through the horoscope of any member of the family, before intervening and pronouncing judgment the astrologer will ask to see the horoscope of the member of the family who is the most directly affected by the problem in question. Thus, when faced with a client whose horoscope showed signs of danger for the younger brother, Kameshwar Upadhyay explained:

> The *Rāhu mahādaśā* (planetary period) you are going through is not good for your younger brother. Because of your Rāhu, your brother will spend his whole life at a distance of at least six hundred kilometers from you. I am concerned about his health. You must show me his horoscope to see what effect your Rāhu will have on his life.

The influence of the native on his own brother's destiny is hence not considered absolute and must be evaluated through a combined reading of several horoscopes.

Parents and Children

As we saw, horoscopic treatises include a chapter dedicated to a study of the *ariṣṭas*, the "fatal signs" that indicate deadly astral configurations for the child's parents. More generally, the parent's destiny will be scrutinized through an analysis of the position of the "significators" (*kāraka*), as well as the houses that symbolize these kinship links. With regard to the mother, the astral situation of the fourth house should be examined along with that of the ruler of the fourth house and the planet Moon. Thus according to the BPHŚ and the SRV:

> A benefic planet in the fourth house (*mātuḥsthāna*, "house of the mother"), the lord of the fourth house in its sign of exaltation (*sva-ucca-rāśi*), and the *kāraka* ["significator" of the mother = Moon] endowed with strenghth: *this indicates the long life of the mother (*māturdīrghāyu*).* (BPHŚ 15.6)
>
> The lord of the fourth house in *kendra* [= first, fourth, seventh, or tenth house], Venus being in *kendra* as well, and Mercury in its own sign of exaltation: *one can predict full prosperity to the mother (*mātuḥ pūrṇaṃ sukham*).* (BPHŚ 15.7).
>
> Moon in the fourth or seventh house in conjunction with malefic planets: *suffering (*kleśa*) of the mother*; malefic planets in the seventh house counting from Moon, and Moon aspected by Mars: *death of the mother*; Sun in the tenth house counting from Moon in conjunction with malefic planets: *death of the mother*. (SRV 9. 34–36)

When listening to a client who was worried about his mother's health, but did not have the mother's horoscope, an astrologer explained:

> If your mother is ill, to know when she will recover, whether she will recover or not, I don't need your mother's horoscope, I can see it in your horoscope: by looking at the fourth house or the ruler of the fourth house. Then, certainly, if we want to know more, we need to look at her horoscope, also to see precisely how many more days of life she has left, how long she will have to suffer . . .

The case of a very agitated ten-year-old child, the only son of a couple that had been married for twelve years, is representative of the manner in which a child's horoscope is supposed to affect a mother's destiny. The concerned mother consulted the astrologer to understand why her son argued and fought with everybody, did not study at school—he had changed schools five times in five years—refused to eat, only talked about bombs and guns, and so on. The astrologer replied, explaining the son would do very well in life, he would become a senior civil servant in the Indian Administrative Service. The mother, who would suffer cardiac and psychological problems because of her son, represented the only critical point in his horoscope.

In horoscopic theory, the father's destiny is described in greater detail than the mother's. The ninth house reveals the destiny of the father as an individual (his health, his work, etc.), while the tenth house deals with heritage, the paternal family, funerary rituals dedicated to the father, and so on. The following verses are taken from the chapter on the ninth house and deal with the father's prosperity, poverty, longevity, reputation, and death:

> The lord of the house of fortune (*bhāgya*) [= ninth house] endowed with strenghth, Venus in the house of fortune, and Jupiter in *kendra* [= first, fourth, seventh, or tenth house]: *the father will be fortunate (*bhāgyasamanvita*).* (BPHŚ 20.3)

> Mars in the second or fourth house counting from the ninth, and the lord of the ninth house in a sign of debilitation: *the father is poor (*nirdhana*).* (BPHŚ 20.4)

> The lord of the ninth house in a position of high exaltation (*paramoccastha*), Jupiter in the *navāṃśa* of the ninth house, and Venus in *kendra* counting from the ascendant: *his father will be long-lived (*dīrghajīvana*).* (BPHŚ 20.5)

> The lord of the ninth house in *kendra* and aspected by Jupiter: *his father will be a king endowed with vehicles (*vāhanas*) or someone similar to a king.* (BPHŚ 20.6)

> The lord of the ninth house in the house of *karman* [= tenth house] and the lord of the tenth house in the ninth house

> aspected by a benefic planet: *his father will be very rich and famous.* (BPHŚ 20.7)

> The lord of the ascendant in the ninth house in conjunction with the lord of the sixth house: *this says that there will be hostility (*vaira*) between the two [= father and son]and the father will be despised (*kutsita*).* (BPHŚ 20.11)

> Sun in the sixth, eighth, or twelfth house, the lord of the eighth house in the ninth house, the lord of the twelfth house in the first house, and the lord of the sixth house in the fifth: *the death of the father occurs before the birth of the native.* (BPHŚ 20.13–14a)

> Sun in the eighth house, and the lord of the eighth house in the ninth house: *this indicates that the father will die within one year from the birth of the native.* (BPHŚ 20.14b–15a)

> The lord of the twelfth house in the ninth house and the lord of the ninth house in a division of debilitation (*nicāṃśa*): *the father will die during the third or the sixteenth year of life of the native.* (BPHŚ 20.15b–16a)

The BPHŚ also mentions the astral configurations that indicate the father's death when the son is of the following ages, presented in this order: two or twelve (20.16b–17a); sixteen or eighteen (20.17b–18a); seven or nineteen (20.18b–19a); forty-four (20.19b–20a); thirty-five or forty-one (20.20b–21a); fifty (20.21b–22a); six or twenty-five (20.22b–23a); thirty, twenty-one, or twenty-six (20.23b–24a); twenty-six or thirty (20.24b–25a).

A father may thus consult an astrologer to know the effects his son's horoscope will have on him. This was the case of a man, a reader at the Engineering Department at Banaras Hindu University, who consulted the astrologer Kameshwar Upadhyay to know why he was unable to obtain a promotion. Once he had shown his own horoscope, he admitted his suspicion that his son's horoscope had a bad influence on his life:

> ♂: The last time you told me my son was going through a bad Rāhu *daśā* (period) and so we had to perform fifty-one thousand *japs* (recitations of a mantra) . . .

J: Yes, it's true, your son has a problem with Rāhu . . . you must continue the *japs* because otherwise he may have an accident . . . you must repeat the treatment every six months . . .

♂: But there's nothing in my son's horoscope that seems dangerous (*khatarnāk*) for the father? The Rāhu *daśā* can create problems (*kaṣṭdāyī hai*) for the father . . . I have heard that the Rāhu *mahādaśā* (major period) can be fatal (*ghātak*, "deadly") for the father and for the ancestors (*pitṛ jana*) . . .

The astrologer allayed the father's suspicions, observing that as Rāhu was in the fourth house, it was the mother who was under threat from the bad Rāhu period the son was going through, but by doing the requisite *pūjā*, nothing would happen to either of the parents.

Let us now consider the opposite relationship, that is to say, the influence of the *jātaka*'s horoscope on his or her own children's destiny.

Children are represented by the fifth house:

O Brahmin, I'll tell you now the effects of the fifth house. The lord of the ascendant and the lord of the fifth house situated in the fifth house (*sutabhāva*, "house of children"), or in *kendra* or in *trikoṇa*: *one should predict complete happiness for the son (*pūrṇam putrasukhaṃ*)*. The lord of the fifth house in the sixth, eighth, or twelfth house: *there will be no son (*aputratā*)*. The lord of the fifth house is setting or is aspected by a malefic planet and is weak: *there will be no offspring or, if a son is born, it will die soon*. (BPHŚ 16.1–3).

The lord of the fifth house in the sixth house, and the lord of the ascendant in conjunction with Mars: *his first child will die and his wife will become sterile (*kākabandhyā*)*. (BPHŚ 16.4)

The passages quoted are followed by other verses (BPHŚ 16.6–32) concerning infertility, the adoption of children, the children's gender, illegitimate children, the children's bad behavior, the age at which the native becomes a father, the age when he has a child, the number of children, and so on. The parents' astral influence on their children is carefully examined during astrological consultations, and particularly when the children are young. To start with, astrologers consider that a single progenitor's horoscope does not provide sufficient information to explain the children's destiny, particularly at the time of birth. Thus, when talking to a woman who had just given birth to a daughter, the astrologer explained that if it was only dependent on her horoscope, she would have given birth to a son as she had the "*yog* of sons" (*laṛkõ kā yog*), but as her husband had the "*yog* of daughters" (*laṛkiyõ kā yog*), she had given birth to a daughter. In another case, when questioned by a man who wanted to know why his son had died just after his birth, the astrologer stated that the situation of his horoscope, particularly the position of Ketu, was not bad enough to explain the death of a child, and that the reason must hence lie in his wife's horoscope.

The influence of the parents' horoscopes is supposed to be extremely powerful during the first years of a child's life. Particularly in the event of a child's death, severe illness, or accident, astrologers consider that the parents' horoscopes must necessarily bear traces of these events. To quote an astrologer: "Such a great sorrow (*dukh*) is immediately visible in a father or mother's horoscope." Indeed, as we saw in the previous chapter, when a child dies, astrological theory integrates an interpretative *surplus* by invoking the karma theory.

In astrological terms a child's death appears in the form of *balāriṣṭa*s (fatal [*ariṣṭa*] astral conjunctions for the child [*bala*]), and in the parents' horoscopes one must specifically examine the fifth house and the position of the malefic planet Ketu, considered particularly dangerous for children. Questioned by a client who had just lost his only son, aged one and a half, after a close examination of the man's horoscope and the palm of his hand, the astrologer Kameshwar Upadhyay explained:

> Until the 31 August 2002 you are going through a Ketu *mahādaśā* (major period) and as Ketu is in the fifth house, this creates serious problems (*nuqsān*) for your children. In addition, the palm of your hand shows three lines that are cut, which indicates the loss of three children. As your wife also has Ketu in the fifth house of her horoscope, you should have taken precautions . . .[16]

Then the astrologer explained to us that Ketu's unfavorable position in the man's horoscope was an indicator of evil actions (*duṣkarm*) in past lives. In addition, according to the astrologer, the child's death had also been provoked by the sudden death of the child's grandfather eight months earlier: the grandfather's *ātmā* would have afflicted the grandson, thus causing his death.

The parents' horoscopes contain traces not only of serious events but also of less important problems that affect the children. Thus, for example, a couple had come to the astrologer Shree Kanth Shastri to learn whether their son was going to repeat his class at high school. But they had only brought their own horoscopes. After examining the parents' horoscopes, the astrologer reassured them, confirming there was no negative astral conjunction that could have led one to believe the child would fail educationally. In the same manner, a man had come to ask about his children's futures and, looking at his horoscope, the astrologer said to him:

> You really must take a lot of care of them; they will need a lot of *guardianship*. You have Rāhu in the fifth house, the ruler of the fifth house is the Moon, and it is in a bad position; there is a strong chance your children will be spoiled (*bigaṛne kā* chance *zyādā rahegā*). You will have to control them strictly . . . keep them at home with you, don't send them to stay in student hostels, and everything will be all right.

Through a close examination of the horoscope, the astrologer may distinguish the fate of each child. Shree Kanth Shastri thus explained:

> If, for example, someone comes to see me and asks about his or her children—one is not working, the other who is trying very hard but isn't successful, the third whose health is fragile . . . well, astrology contains a method to distinguish the fate of each child, the first, the second, the fourth, or the tenth. We can see all that from the father and mother's horoscopes. Of course, when there is a problematic child, you also have to examine his own horoscope.

The method used by this astrologer consists of studying the first child's destiny on the basis of the fifth house, the second child's destiny on the basis of the ninth house—that is to say, the fifth, counted from the fifth—the third child's destiny on the basis of the first house (*lagna*), which is the fifth counted from the ninth, and so on.

The merging of parents' and children's destinies not only concerns the diagnosis but also the treatment. I thus saw a case where the astrologer prescribed a ring with a pearl for a man to wear, to protect his son from the risk of catching a cold as the Moon was in an unfavorable position in the fifth house of the man's horoscope.[17] In another case, a woman who had Mars, the ruler of the fifth house, in a bad position was prescribed a ring with a coral stone in order to prevent an accident befalling her children.

Husband and Wife

The spouse's destiny is examined on the basis of the seventh house, the ruler of the seventh house, and the planet Venus. Nonetheless, one must note that, in this concern, astrological theory distinguishes between male and female horoscopes, as they are not symmetrical. Let us start by looking at the horoscope of a male native. The information about his wife is very detailed. According to the chapter of the BPHŚ dealing with the seventh house, the man's horoscope not only indicates what will happen in his wife's life—like her death, her health or sickness, and so on—but also her physical constitution and her personality. Let us look at some of the verses describing the native's wife:

> The lord of the seventh house situated in the twelfth, sixth, or eighth house, and not in its own sign or in his own sign of exaltation: *this makes the wife sickly (*rogiṇī*).* (BPHŚ 18.2)
>
> Venus in conjunction with a malefic planet, in any house: *there will be death of the wife (*strīmaraṇa*).* (BPHŚ 18.3b)
>
> The lord of the seventh house is strong, in conjunction with a benefic planet or aspected by him: *the native is wealthy, highly honored, happy, and fortunate*; the lord of the seventh house is in his sign of debilitation, or in his enemies' house, or is weak: *the wife of the native will be sickly and he will have several wives.* (BPHŚ 18.4)[18]

> Mars [in the seventh house]: *the wife has beautiful breasts (*sustanī*)*; Saturn: *she is sickly and weak*; Jupiter: *she has hard (*kaṭhina*) and elevated (*ūrdhva*) breasts*; Venus: *she has bulky and excellent breasts.* (BPHŚ 18.9b–10a)

> The lord of the seventh house in his sign of exaltation, a benefic planet in the seventh house, and the lord of the ascendant being strong in the seventh house: *the wife of the native is very virtuous, and she will raise children and great children.* (BPHŚ 18.14b–15)

> The lord of the seventh house in his sign of debilitation and Venus in the sixth or eighth house: *the wife will die when the native will have eighteen or thirty-three years*; the lord of the seventh house in the eight house, the lord of the twelfth house in the seventh house: *the death of the wife (*dāranāśa, *"destruction of wife") will occur when the native is nineteen*; Rāhu in the second house (house of progeny [*kuṭumba*]) and Mars in the seventh: *the death of the wife will occur three days after marriage because of a snake bite.* (BPHŚ 18.35–37)

The sixth chapter of the SC provides a detailed characterization of the *jātaka*'s wife. Depending on the different planetary configurations located in the seventh house, the wife is described as being: "religious" (*dharmaśīlā*), "devoted to her husband" (*pativratā, patibhaktiyuktā*), "swept away by sin" (*pāpaparāyanā*), "adulterous" (*kumārgacārī*), "inflexible" (*kaṭhināparādhā*), "virtuous" (*puṇyā*), "of good character" (*suśīlā*), "harsh toward her husband" (*patikarkaśā*), "murderous toward her husband" (*patighnī*), "destroyer of the family" (*kulanāśakārī*), "having a body purified by vows, fasting, and other ritual practices" (*vratopavāsādiviśuddhadehā*), "like a prostitute" (*veśyāsamānā*), "talkative" (*vācālikā*), "endowed with children" (*putravatī*), and so on (SC 6.44–58). Some stanzas also indicate the wife's social origins—"born in a low caste" (*nikṛṣṭajātā*), "born in a high caste" (*utkṛṣṭajātā*) (SC 6.68–69)—as well as her family's (*kula*) attitude toward the husband—friendship (*mitratā*) or dislike (*śatrutā*)—(SC 6.73); finally, there is a description of her breasts (SC 6.92–95) and genital organs (SC 6.96–104).

The *Sulabha-Jyautiṣa-Jñāna* (Khankhoje 1997), a manual of contemporary astrology, dedicates several paragraphs to the "knowledge of the wife through the husband's horoscope" (*pati ke kuṇḍalī se patnī sambandhī jñān*). After describing the variety of astral configurations concerning the wife of the owner of the horoscope, it concludes, stating that "through an analysis (*avalokan*) of the husband's horoscope, one can gain precise knowledge (*saṅkṣipt jñān*) of the wife's complexion (*raṅg*), appearance (*rūp*), qualities (*guṇ*), *dharm* (moral and religious attitude), and nature (*svabhāv*). It also provides a knowledge of her parents (*pitā-mātā*), her brothers (*bandhu*), her sisters (*bhaginī*), her children (*santān*), the diseases (*rog*), enemies (*ripu*), happiness (*sukh*) and misfortune (*duḥkh*) that she shares with her husband and her financial expenses (*dhanake vyaya*)."[19]

Similarly, the astrological text on medicine *Jyotiṣ aur Rog* (Astrology and Diseases) describes the astral conjunctions (*yog*) that enable knowledge of the diseases the wife will be afflicted by, based on the husband's horoscope (Sharma n.d., 152). For example, when in the husband's horoscope "Mars and Rāhu are in conjunction (*yuti ho*) in the seventh house, the blood (*rakt*) of the [wife's] menstrual flow (*mānsik srāv*) will be excessive" (Sharma n.d., 152); "when three or four malefic planets (*pāp graha*) are in conjunction in the sixth or seventh house, [the wife] will suffer from urinary diseases (*mūtrakṛcchra rog*)" (Sharma n.d., 152), and so on.

Nonetheless, in the man's horoscope, the seventh house indicates not only the spouse, but several spouses, as well as every woman with whom the *jātaka* may have a sexual relationship.[20] Thus, depending on the planets situated in the seventh house, the BPHŚ identifies the type of woman the *jātaka* will unite with sexually: sterile women, menstruating women, prostitutes, Brahmins, women of bad character, and so on (BPHŚ 18.7–9a).[21]

Unsurprisingly, in women's horoscope, the seventh house only admits a single husband. The asymmetry between the wife's and the husband's destiny, however, goes far beyond this difference. The disparity also exists at the conceptual level. Indeed, as we will see, the man's astral influence on the woman and the woman's on the man are studied through different methods.

Most horoscopic treatises devote an entire chapter to the study of *strījātaka* "women's horoscopy." As is the case for male horoscopes, the seventh house of a woman's horoscope indicates the personality and events of the spouse's life:

> Saturn [in the seventh house] and not aspected by a benefic planet: *the husband will be a coward (*kāpuruṣa*)*; a mobile sign [in the seventh house]: *he will be far from home*; Mercury and Saturn [in the seventh house]: *he will be impotent (*klīva*)*. (BPHŚ 80.17)

> The sign [of the seventh house] as well as the [seventh house of the] *navāṃśa* (ninth division) chart are ruled by Mars: *the husband will be fond of women (*strīlola*) and inclined to wrath (*krodhana*)*; by Mercury: *the husband is learned (*vidvas*), skillful (*nipuṇa*), and intelligent (*sudhī*)*; by Jupiter: *the husband will be endowed with all sorts of qualities (*sarvaguṇopeta*) and will control his senses (*jitendriya*)*; by Venus: *the husband will be fortunate, beautiful, and desired by women (*strījanavallabha*)*; the sign and the *navāṃśa* ruled by Saturn: *the husband will be old (*vṛddha*) and stupid (*mūrkha*)*. (BPHŚ 80.22–24a)

Let's see now how horoscopy dealing with women follows specific rules that differentiate it from male horoscopy. Thus, the BPHŚ illustrates the general rules governing women's horoscopes:

> The effect (*phala*) described up to here, O wise man, for males should be understood as similar for women. I'll tell you now what is specific to female horoscopy, in brief: through [the planetary situation] of the ascendant one should tell the effect on the body (*deha*) of the woman; through the fifth house, offspring (*prasava*); through the seventh, the fortune (*saubhāgya*) of the husband; through the eighth, widowhood (*vaidhavya*), O Brahmin; whatever effect is impossible for women should apply to her husband (*strīṇāmasambhavam yadyat tatphalam tatpatau vadet*). (BPHŚ 80.2b–4)

These verses establish two rules governing interpretation: the first is that while for men the death of the wife is dependent on the seventh house, for women the husband's death, or widowhood, should be deduced from the eighth house. Now, in all horoscopes, the eighth house is the one that indicates longevity and the death of the native. This rule hence presumes that for women, the death of the husband is equal to their own death. In other words, while the man survives the death of his wife, from an astrological viewpoint the wife does not survive the death of her husband. This type of asymmetrical relationship is a precise expression of the logic of the hierarchical relationship described by Louis Dumont.[22] The woman's destiny seems to be encompassed in the husband's:

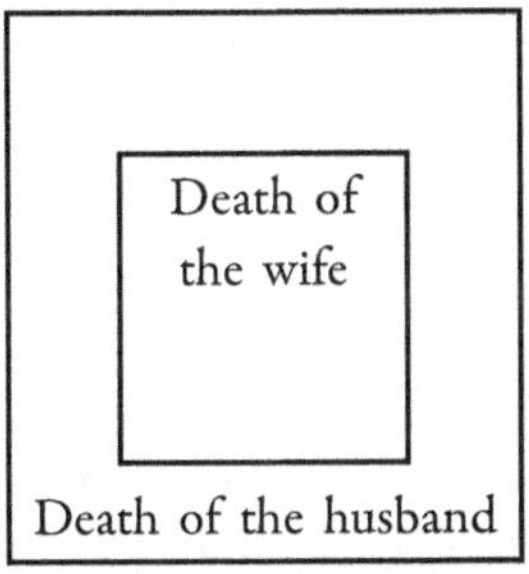

The second main rule of *strījātaka*, "women's horoscopy," stipulates that some of the astral configurations in the woman's horoscope are to be attributed to the husband. These are configurations whose effects cannot apply to the native. For example, in the case of a housewife whose horoscope indicates a business trip, the presence of this astral conjunction in the woman's horoscope indicates that it is the husband who will go on a business trip. In his commentary of the *Bṛhajjātaka*, V. Subrahamanya Shastry, clearly explains the scope of this rule:

> The effects may be divided into 3 classes, namely: (1) those that have to be applied to women, (2) those that concern men alone and (3) those that may be applied to both. Suppose for instance that there is Chandradhiyoga[23] in a woman's horoscope, while the same is absent from her husband. The native being a female, the effects described for the adhiyoga cannot be applied to her. In such a case, the effects of the yoga should be declared for her husband notwithstanding the absence of such yoga in his horoscope. (Qtd. in Santhanam 1984, 955)

In other words, women may be entitled to a share they cannot enjoy: the husband then becomes the beneficiary of the share of destiny that was allotted to the wife.

Once again, the reference to the hierarchical model allows us to understand how astrological theory perceives the relationship between spouses. The husband controls the destiny of his wife thanks to the *surplus* of—economic, professional, and political—capital attributed to him by society. But, like all hierarchical relationships, this encompassing relationship can be reversed. From an astrological viewpoint, indeed, the relationship is reversed: the woman is endowed with greater influence (*prabhāv*) over the husband than he has over her, as a large part of the wife's horoscope will have an impact on the husband's destiny.

The astrologer Shree Kanth Shastri describes the relationship of reciprocal encompassment between spouses as follows:

> Suppose a woman has a very good fate (*acchā bhāgya*), her horoscope shows she is a "giver of wealth" (*arth dāyini*). "Wealth giver" does not mean she will bring in money by working, but it means she will procure her husband's success as soon as she becomes part of her in-laws family (*śvaśurāl*). The husband's work will take a different path: if, for example, he had a business worth one rupee, after the marriage he will have a business worth ten rupees, this means ten times more money. Hence the man will be very successful thanks to his wife's good fortune.
>
> In the same manner, if the woman's horoscope indicates something bad for the husband, it does not mean the husband will treat her badly, but that he will have problems himself, and his problems will affect his wife . . . If, for example, the husband is sick, or if he has financial problems, these problems will affect his wife, right? This is why you will see that the woman's horoscope will indicate problems the husband will face.

The astrologer further explains how career, the family, and other aspects of the husband's life have a profound impact on the wife's destiny and will hence appear in the latter's horoscope:

> Suppose the husband is an engineer and he earns a lot of money, like fifty thousand rupees a month, but as he works a lot, his wife isn't happy. You will see that Mangal or Surya are present in the seventh house of the wife's horoscope, or you will see the influence (*prabhāv*) of some bad planets (*aśubh graha*) . . . you will see that there is an obstacle (*bādhā*) to

> happiness coming from the husband (*patisukh*). Similarly, if the husband works in the navy, suppose he is absent for two years and then returns, the wife will have to take care of the children on her own, while normally the responsibility for children is shared between the couple . . .
>
> Another example . . . suppose a young girl has barely enough to eat up to the age of twenty, her father and her brothers cannot take care of her . . . but her horoscope shows that at the age of twenty she will be married into a very important family (*bahut baṛe log*) and she will enjoy all kinds of happiness thanks to her husband (*patisukh*). At the age of twenty she finds herself belonging to a family of in-laws who have a high status (*bahut ūñce*), who can do whatever they want financially. As a result, she will get everything in terms of wealth (*dhan*). While before she could not even afford to take a rickshaw, after her marriage, she's sitting on her husband's motorcycle and they are wandering all over the place; she even goes to the market to do her shopping on the motorbike . . . through her husband she has found a motorcycle, a good job, kind parents-in-law. You can clearly see all of this in her horoscope . . .

According to astrologers, the principles of female horoscopy set out in classical treatises should be reinterpreted in light of the changes that have taken place in contemporary society. Many women today practice paid professions or occupy political positions and are not dependent on their husbands or parents. The good and bad effects of their horoscope should then be applied solely to them. Thus, in couples where the woman is a housewife—which constituted the majority of cases observed—her horoscope was taken into consideration to study the man's job and income, while in the rare cases where the woman exercised a paid activity, the effects, for example, of the tenth house (the house dealing with the profession, assets, etc.) were attributed to the woman herself.

Before we conclude this section on the relationship of reciprocal influence between the spouses, we must mention an astrological category that we did not find explicitly described in Sanskrit treatises, but which nonetheless plays a crucial role when it comes to marital relationships in contemporary India. This is the *maṅgalik* category: *maṅgalik*s—*maṅgalā* men and *maṅgalī* women—are people who are afflicted by the planet Mars (Maṅgala) in their horoscope. Because of this planetary influence, they are supposed to be potential murderers of their spouse, or at best, a permanent source of suffering and sorrow for their spouse. This category is constantly evoked during consultations, but we will discuss this matter in great detail in the next chapter.

Having analyzed the manner in which different family members are described within the horoscope, we will now conclude this chapter by attempting to highlight the general principles that govern the idea of a shared destiny in the theory of astrology. We will see that these principles are likely to be extended to every type of relationship the *jātaka* is involved in over the course of his or her existence.

Saṃbandhit Jyotiṣ, "Connected Astrology"

We have seen that the planets and the houses are "significators" (*kāraka*) for members of the family. Nonetheless, astrological theory goes much further than establishing a simple, unique correspondence between planets (or houses) and members of the family. Not only can the number of relationships in the horoscope be indefinitely extended, the wealth of information concerning the destiny of everyone "involved" in the *jātaka*'s horoscope can also be extended indefinitely.

To start with, let's look at a contemporary astrological manual in Hindi, the *Sulabha-Jyautiṣa-Jñāna* (Khankhoje 1997), where the native's network of connections is graphically represented (see figure 8). This chart

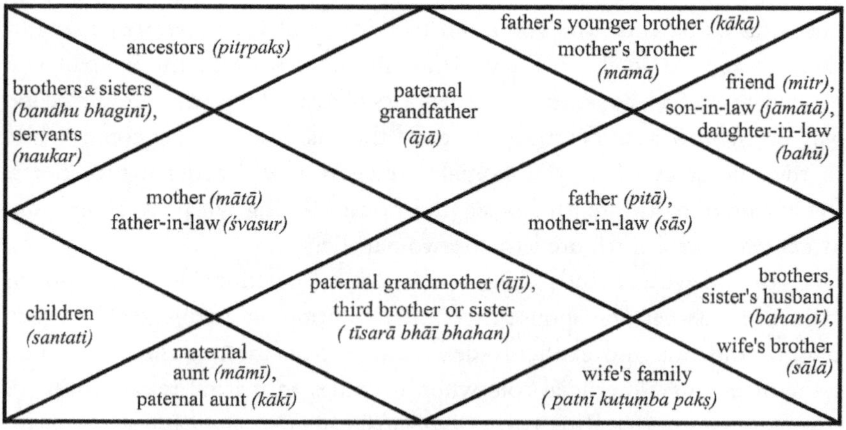

Figure 8. The native's connections in the horoscope, according to the *Sulabha-Jyautiṣa-Jñāna* (Khankhoje 1997, 91).

shows that not only kinship relations but other types of relationships, like those with servants and friends, are also relevant to the native's destiny. This corresponds to the astrologer Shree Kanth Shastri's explanation:

> By looking at the horoscope, through *saṃbandhit jyotiṣ*, "connected astrology," you may know what will happen to all those with whom the native (*jātaka*) has a connection (*saṃbandh*), be it of a family, professional, friendly, or neighborhood type.
>
> You can, for example, know the situation of the paternal aunt (*cācī*) of the native, wherever she is located, be it in America or England . . . you can know everything about the *jātaka*'s paternal uncle, his brothers, his sister-in-law, and so on. The horoscope not only tells you what will happen to the members of the family but also to the friends, colleagues, neighbors . . . you can even know what will happen to a thief who enters the native's house . . . Indeed, if a thief had entered his house and stolen something, you can know everything about him from the sixth house, the house of thieves and enemies . . .

For each kind of relationship being associated with a house, one has to study the situation of the house and of the planet ruling that house. Thus, to know about a colleague, we shall look at the tenth house, the professional house, and the ruler of the sign situated in the tenth house.

The destiny of a native's connections can be studied with surprisingly detailed precision. When inspecting a horoscope, astrologers follow a method that makes the "pivot point" of the horoscope vary so that it is possible to know anyone's personality and future in the smallest details.

To know about *ego*—the native—the "pivot," the starting point from which one reads the chart, is the *lagna*, the first house or the ascendant house. Now the same level of information that a horoscope provides for *ego* can be obtained for any other person connected to *ego* (parents, friends, neighbors, et al.). For this, one just has to read the horoscope using a different starting point. One can take the house that represents the relationship we are looking at as the "pivot" of the horoscope: the third for brothers, the fourth for the mother, the fifth for children, and so on. If, for *ego*, the fifth house indicates studies, to know *ego*'s brother's educational situation, one must look at the fifth house, counting from the third (i.e., the seventh house); to know about the brother's wife, one will look at the seventh house counting from the third (i.e., the ninth house), and so on. In other words, every individual horoscope potentially contains an infinite number of horoscopes, as many horoscopes as the *jātaka* has connections (family, professional, affective, etc.).[24]

This rule is summarized in the BPHŚ as follows:

> Just like the effects about the native are said [counting] from the *lagna* (the ascendant or first house), similarly all the effects about brothers and other connections are to be known [counting] from the third and other corresponding houses. (BPHŚ 23.7)

The astrologer Shree Kanth Shastri provides a more detailed explanation of this principle:

> Thanks to the "connected astrology" (*saṃbandhit jyotiṣ*), you can know, for example, what is going to happen to your husband: by analyzing the seventh house you can know what your husband will be like, by looking at the position of the ruler of the seventh house you can know what type of personality he will have; in the fifth house, counted from the seventh house, you can know how far he has studied; in the tenth house, counted from the seventh, you can discover his profession, whether he owns a factory, whether he is a worker, or works in an office. If, for example, Śani is present, you know he has a government job, as Śani always provides a government job . . . Depending on the different planets, you can see if he is going to work in a factory and what kind of factory it will be.
>
> Similarly, you can know about the children from the fifth house; according to the fifth house counted from the fifth house, that is to say the ninth house, you can know how they will do in their studies; according to the seventh house from the fifth house [= eleventh house], you can know about their husband or wife, so you can ask me about your daughter-in-law or son-in-law . . .

According to "connected astrology," every individual destiny is made up of a multitude of interwoven destinies. Before we conclude this chapter, it is interesting to compare our material with Karin Kapadia's (1995) observations based on a survey conducted in a village in Tamil Nadu that she called Aruloor.[25] To the best of our knowledge Kapadia's study is the only one that deals with the question of the relationship between personal horoscopes and the members of the family in Hindu astrology. Her monograph shows both striking differences and strong similarities with what we have described and will be useful to shed light on the distinctiveness of our material.

Kapadia's study focuses on the gender ideology of astrology and aims to show how, as a Brahmanical knowledge, astrology implicitly legitimizes women's submission. The author describes the "astrological life" of the women of Aruloor belonging to well-off families. Among these, she differentiates between Brahmin and non-Brahmin women.[26] For the former, the horoscope is calculated at birth, whereas for non-Brahmin women it is calculated at the time of the girl's first menstruation. In both cases, the woman's horoscope is considered potentially dangerous, although the range of relatives that may be affected varies:

> In the Brahmanical castes, those significant others who can be endangered [by a woman's horoscope] are solely the young woman's future affines: her future husband and her future father-in-law (and, to lesser degree, her future mother-in-law). In the Non-Brahmin castes, however, the range of affected kin is much wider. It includes her parents, her siblings, her Mother's Brothers and their families, *and* her future husband and parents-in-law.[27] (Kapadia 1995, 72)

Nonetheless, after marriage, women cease to have their own horoscopes and are generally subject to the husband's:

> In the upper castes and the socially aspiring castes, a startling change with regard to a woman's "astrological" life occurs at marriage. After marriage, a woman effectively ceases to possess a horoscope (either birth or menstrual) at all, because thereafter, her future is "read" by consulting the birth horoscope of her husband. This is vital for it implies, among other things, that she thereafter has no separate destiny. (Kapadia 1995, 81)

When a child is born, the husband also "abdicates" his astral power and the family's destiny is calculated on the basis of the newborn's horoscope: "above all, the birth of a child *portends*. The child spells the future destiny of the family it is born into because the moment of its birth is meaningful, imbued with good or bad portents" (Kapadia 1995, 78). This generally happens, Kapadia observes, particularly when it is a male child: especially in high-status families that follow the joint family residential model, the girls are in fact considered "temporary" presences, destined to become members of the affines' family. Hence their horoscopes are not taken as seriously as their brothers'. In addition, depending on the caste and the inherited wealth of the families, Kapadia remarks, in alternation the elder or the youngest son's horoscope is considered the family horoscope.

Not only is the son's horoscope consulted as the "family horoscope" but its influence extends to the maternal uncles' families too:

> A child's horoscope affects his Mother's Brothers and their families as well. So the fortunes of the Mother's Brothers are very prominent in his sister's son's horoscope. Pallar and Muthurajah informants claimed that a male child's horoscope would say even more about his *Mama*'s (Mother's Brother's) family than about his own. (Kapadia 1995, 81)

On this subject, Kapadia mentions the case of an informant who considered his own horoscope responsible for the repeated deaths that occurred in his maternal uncle's family.

Kapadia's study underscores the gender ideology transmitted by this alternative usage of horoscopes, as the woman's destiny is always subject to the control of the men who surround her:

> A woman's destiny after marriage, writ in the stars, is first read from her husband's horoscope and thereafter from her son's. This reflects the pattern in which control of a woman's life, in these wealthier classes, passes first from her father (whose horoscope ruled her youth) to her husband and finally, after the death of her husband, to her son, whose horoscope "rules" her life from the day he is born. In all this, the woman's own menstrual horoscope is of only temporary importance, despite its great significance to a large number of her kin. (Kapadia 1995, 82)

Although her analytical and interpretative approach differs from our own, Kapadia's observations enrich the considerations we have put forward so far. Kapadia describes a sort of "rotational" usage of the horoscope in the family cycle: depending on the period the family is going through, the destiny may be ruled by the girl who has her first menstruations, the husband, the newborn, or the father.

Although in Banaras we never observed the practice of using an individual horoscope as a "family horoscope" (nor did we find this practice described in classical treatises), we note that the principle of a shared destiny operates in both contexts. In Banaras no individual is seen as the sole ruler of the family destiny, but each member can affect his or her relatives' destiny. Let us mention the case of a family where the mother was to undergo an operation for her uterus and the children were to sit their exams. During the consultation, the astrologer explained that the results of the woman's operation and the children's examinations depended on the father's horoscope, in which several malefic planetary configurations were present. More generally, astrologers in Banaras believe that to understand the situation a family is facing it is necessary to take all the family members' horoscopes into consideration:

> When you want to know the situation a family is facing you must look at everyone's horoscope, the husband's, the wife's, and once they have children, you have to take the children's horoscopes into consideration, too. You have to take into consideration each one's destiny (*bhāgya*) . . . You have to take connected astrology (*saṃbandhit jyotiṣ*) into account . . . It is not appropriate to look at a single horoscope, as each *bhāgya* influences the others.

The working principle of "connected astrology" (*saṃbandhit jyotiṣ*) may recall the idea of the extra-individual transmission of karma that has been analyzed by Sanskrit scholars as well as anthropologists. Inspired by McKim Marriott and Ronald Inden's transactional theory (Marriott and Inden 1975 and 1977; Marriott 1976), some authors have shown that karma works as a "substance-code" transmitted down through generations between spouses or brothers.[28] From this perspective, a person's moral qualities, his or her sins and merits, are reified in a transferable substance—karma—that passes between those who exchange food or bodily substances, thus modifying their nature.

While it is true that, like karma, the destiny of "collective individuals" described in the horoscope "is a metaphor for the effects that human beings have upon one other" (O'Flaherty 1980, 29), in astrological language, as we saw in the previous chapter on the concept of *bhāgya*, the idea of sharing prevails over that of "transfer" or "exchange."[29] *Ego* shares his or her destiny with others and others are part of *ego*'s destiny. Relatives or close friends, and more generally others, too, do not appear as relations that would be external to the native but as a necessary and constitutive part of the individual's existence and future. They make an essential contribution to the construction of individual destiny.

Part III

Treatments

7

Astrology and Possession

Planetary Influence and Middle-Class Afflictions

In the two final chapters of this book, I shall investigate the way planetary influence (*graha prabhāv*) is described during consultations and dealt with through therapeutic and ritual procedures. Planetary influence, as an idea commonly expressed during verbal exchanges, takes a tangible form, is reified, and objectified in remedies prescribed by astrologers to control its effect. The analysis of planetary influence as a concept then, cannot be separated from the investigation of the treatments and ritual practices followed to limit its impact.

This chapter will focus on discourses and practices dealing with the influence of the four most "harmful" (*aśubh, pāp, krūr*) planets of Hindu astrology: Maṅgal (Mars), Śani (Saturn), Rāhu (ascending lunar node), and Ketu (descending lunar node). Although, according to astrologers, all the planets may have a positive or negative influence depending on their position in the horoscope, the negative influence of these four planets is the most feared. Verbal and visual representations concerning the planets focus most often on them, and most therapeutic and ritual practices prescribed during astrological consultations are directed toward them.[1] Called *krūr grahas* (cruel planets) or *pāp grahas* (evil planets), these planets are the focus of clients' concerns as well as astrologers' intellectual and material interests.

Idioms of Suffering

By studying planetary influence, I will show in this chapter that astrology constitutes an idiom of suffering well adapted to the values and expectations of many families hailing from the urban middle classes in twenty-first-century India. More precisely, I will argue that astrology fulfills the expectations of the middle class, not only because of its Sanskritized language and its mathematical formulations, but also because it is a way of expressing, through a rationalized and scripturally sanctioned idiom, ideas of misfortune found in popular Hinduism. Through a close examination of discourses and treatments dealing with planetary influence, I will show how astrology provides a formalized, objectified, and "scientific" language that is used to reformulate ideas such as divine possession, sorcery, or ghostly attacks. Generally, astrologers' clients regard the explanations of suffering and misfortune provided by lower-caste specialists such as *ojhā-sokhās* or *tāntriks* in Banaras, who intervene in the context of possession and sorcery, as "superstition" (*andhaviśvās*) or "deceit" (*ḍhoṅg*). In contrast, they appreciate horoscope reading due to its abstract, formalized, and objective language. In that it identifies the sources of the client's suffering through mathematical calculations, an astrological diagnosis corresponds to the rational ambitions of educated, urban clients. The complex structure of the horoscope that systematically distinguishes the different aspects of human existence through the working of houses (*bhāva*) satisfies the expectations of middle-class urban families, whose daily life is subject to a continual process of decision-making regarding education, marriage, career, health, and so on.

The material setting of astrological counseling also contributes to making this divinatory and therapeutic system particularly adapted to middle-class demands. Unlike other divinatory or medical sessions that can only be carried out in the presence of a specialist, astrological consultations can be conducted remotely. Physical proximity is not required to establish an astrological diagnosis or to carry out the treatment, as the person's date of birth or the time of the consultation are sufficient. In comparison to other divinatory or remedial practices where the body—either the specialist's, possessed by the deity, or the suffering patient's—is required for a diagnosis to be made, reading a horoscope does not require physical proximity and can be carried out anywhere. Nowadays, the relationship between an astrologer and his or her client can be maintained by email, telephone, or internet. Thus, consultations may happen with the astrologer never meeting his or her client. This could happen in the past (and happens today) when a relative, a neighbor, or friend went to the astrologer to ask for advice for someone who could not or did not want to travel there. Today, new technology has made astrologers in distant places increasingly accessible and, as we saw, astrologers in Banaras can maintain regular relationships with clients who live not only in other states in India but also as far away as the United States, Europe, or Australia. Telephone consultations are a common and regular practice. As it does not require spatial proximity, astrological counseling is well adapted to the requirements of families living in an increasingly globalized, mobile world, intersected by long-distance communication networks.

From the viewpoint of people who make use of these services, astrological diagnoses and explanations are radically different from those made by other ritual specialists—such as *ojhā-sokhā*s and *tāntrik*s—consulted by people belonging to the lower castes, and referring to possession or sorcery as etiological paradigms. However, my analysis will show that, despite the ideological affirmation of a "distinction," the terminology used to describe the influence of harmful planets is not in contradiction with ideas the middle classes consider superstitious. On the contrary, the language of planetary affliction shows substantial similarities with that of possession. In brief, we may say that astrology is the middle-class way of talking about possession and ghostly attacks.

The very word *graha*, planet, which literally means "seizer" (from *GRAH-*, "to seize") illustrates the continuum between these different etiological discourses—planetary affliction, ghostly attacks, divine curses. As has been amply demonstrated by Frederick Smith (2006), in Tantric and medical literature the word *graha* refers to demonical and invisible powerful beings that afflict human beings with all kinds of obstacles and sufferings. In astrological literature or contemporary devotional pamphlets, as well as during consultations, the Hindi words used to designate planetary afflictions also recall the vocabulary used to describe the action of powerful beings that possess or punish humans. The malefic planets are said to afflict humans with their "rage" (*prakop*), their "anger" (*krodh*), and their "gaze" (*dṛṣṭi*), and these terms are commonly employed in various Indian regions to describe the actions of harmful powerful beings that possess, curse, or cast an evil eye on their victims. Planetary influence is said to "get attached to" (*lagnā*) and the planets are said to "seize" (*pakaṛnā*) their prey. These two verbs are also commonly used to describe the way ghosts (*bhūt-pret*) attack their victims. Just like these latter, harmful planets are said to be responsible for all kinds of "problems" (*pareśānī*, *samasyā*), "obstacles" (*vighna*, *bādhā*), "adversities" (*vipatti*), "difficulties" or "sufferings" (*taqlīf*, *kaṣṭ, nuqsān, hāni, pīṛā*), "disorders" (*gaṛbaṛ*), or "delays" (*der*). Like the remedies used by specialists dealing with other types of harmful powerful beings, those prescribed by astrologers aim to "distance" (*dūr karnā*), "take down" (*utārnā*), "eliminate" (*nivāraṇ karnā*), "reduce" (*kam karnā*), "stop" (*stambhit karnā*), "pacify" (*śānti karnā*), or "make favorable" (*anukūl karnā*) the "bad influence" (*duṣprabhāv*) of cruel planets.

To show how ideas that are found in popular Hinduism are reformulated and translated into a "rational" and authoritative language that suits the values and requirements of the middle classes, in the following pages I shall examine three astrological concepts that are used to describe the harmful planetary influence of Maṅgal, Śani, Rāhu, and Ketu. Although these three "planetary syndromes"[2] are usually diagnosed through horoscope reading, they are well known in Banaras beyond the realm of astrological expertise (see table 5). They are part of the common language and representations shared by the inhabitants of the town.

These syndromes are also well known all over India, although their names and significations may vary from one region to another.[3] Curiously, however, despite their popularity and their large diffusion, these astral pathologies do not seem to be scripturally sanctioned in Sanskrit horoscope treatises.[4] They may hence have a non-Sanskritic origin as they share similarities with other types of afflictions—divine curses, ghostly attacks, the evil eye—described in ethnographies dealing with non-Brahmanical Hinduism.

While a philological and historical study of the origin of these astrological concepts is yet to be conducted, today we note that their

Table 5. Planetary Syndromes

Malefic Planets	Planetary Syndrome
Maṅgal (Mars)	*Maṅgal doṣ*, "Mars's flaw" (also known as *kuja doṣ* or *bhauma doṣ*, using other names for Mars)
Śani (Saturn)	*Śani sāṛhe sātī*, "Saturn's seven and a half years"
Rāhu and Ketu (lunar nodes)	*Kāl sarp yog* (or *kāl sarp doṣ*, or *naga doṣ*) "serpent's astral conjunction or flaw"

popularity is on the increase, particularly among the middle classes. Not only are they amply propagated by the media (newspapers, television, websites), they are also commodified on a global scale. For the last few years, for example, the national Times Music group has been selling CDs in its *Times Music Spiritual Collection* that are supposed to help the listener eliminate the harmful effects of "Mangal Dosh" and "Kal Sarp Yog." To promote the sales of CDs in the Delhi and Mumbai regions, as well as in the states of Gujarat, Rajasthan, Andhra Pradesh, Karnataka, Punjab, and Chandigarh, an advertisement appeared in the national daily newspaper, the *Times of India*, with the motto "Eradicate the hurdles of your life by chanting potent dosh nivaran mantras and experience the benefits of it."[5]

Innumerable websites sell diagnoses of, and advice and remedies for, these three types of afflictions, and most Hindu or Vedic astrology sites dedicate specialized sections to each of these syndromes. Astrological forums abound with questions on the effects of and treatment for these astral conjunctions. To cite an example, on the discussion forum of the site www.indiadivine.org, Welcome to the Sacred World of Hinduism, on May 18, 2008, a person with the pseudonym Manishg posted a message titled "Help me: Manglik Dosh, nivaran tips": [6]

> Hello all learned people,
>
> My name is manish, my birth details are 10 sep 1980, 10:06 am, jaipur (rajasthan) and the girls details are 15 march 1983, 9:20 pm, jalandhar (punjab) india.
>
> As per my kundali I am manglik and she is not.
>
> I am sure every lock in this world has a key, if there is a problem there is a solution.
>
> Please you all guys / gurus help me get some breakthrough.
>
> Thanks
>
> Manish[7]

On the site www.indiaparenting.com, dedicated to future or young parents, on March 18, 2009, the person calling herself Swati posted a message seeking advice on the seven and a half years of Saturn:

> my moon sign is cancer/karka rashi and am undergoing sade sathi. anyone else experiencing this phenomenon? how does it impact personal life/career/social life?
>
> have been married for 5 years with major stress/mental tension at all times. my inlaws came into the picture once my sade sati started and i feel that they are saturn/shani in my life.[8]

The three planetary syndromes we are going to discuss in these pages represent the most extreme and stereotyped forms of malefic influence. We will hence examine them in relation to the representation of each of these harmful planets.[9] Before proceeding, it is nonetheless important to recall that apart from the three planetary afflictions mentioned, there are other malefic planetary configurations that are a part of everyday language, such as, for instance, *mahādaśā*s (major periods). *Mahādaśā*s, just like the *sāṛhe sātī*, are "periods" that occur cyclically in each person's horoscope, while the *maṇgal doṣ* and the *kāl sarp yog*, as we will see, are "congenital" or "genetic" afflictions as they are with the person from birth till death—they are *ājīvan*, "lifelong."

Quarrels and Marriage: Mars and the *Maṅgal Doṣ*

While Śani (Saturn), Rāhu, and Ketu's effects are malefic in a generic manner, the definition of Maṅgal's influence is more clearly characterized. To start with, *Maṅgal prabhāv* (Mars's influence) is semantically related to strength, the color red, fire, ardor, as well as the *rajas guṇa* (quality of "passion" and "energy"). Consequently, from the viewpoint of physical afflictions, for example, Maṅgal is said to give rise to whatever has a violent impact on the human body, and which, in particular leads to a loss of blood: accidents (*durghaṭnā*), blows (*coṭ*), lesions (*vraṇ*), and so forth. Thus the text *Jyotiṣ aur Rog* (Astrology and Diseases) (Sharma n.d.), describe Maṅgal as the "main significator" (*pramukh kārak*) of all sorts of *ākasmik rog*s (sudden misfortunes), such as:

> afflictions (*pīṛā*) provoked by fire (*agni*), poison (*viṣ*) or weapons (*śastr*), accidents (*durghaṭnā*), explosions (*visphoṭ*), fights (*yuddh*), fear (*bhay*), eclipses (*grahaṇ*), demons (*rākṣas*)

and malefic planets (*krūr graha*), inimity (*śatrutā*), destructive vows (*vināśkārī saṅkalp*), fatal burns (*jāran-māraṇ*) . . . , blows (*coṭ*) from stones (*patthar*), weapons (*hathiyār*), wood (*lakṛī*), falling from a height (*ūñcāī girnā*) or the body being hit by a heavy object falling on it (*kisī bhārī vastu ke śarīr par gir jānā*). (Sharma n.d., 65)

In accordance with this, the astrologer Shree Kanth Shastri explained to a mother whose son was suffering from an eye disease that the position of Maṅgal in the child's horoscope clearly showed the inevitability of medical intervention:

♀: *Paṇḍitjī*, I don't want my son to have an operation and I want him to see again without undergoing an operation.

J: Hope is very less (*ummīd kam hai*) . . .

♀: I want him to be cured without an operation, just by the strength of the medicines (*davā ke jor se*) . . .

J: It's clear: he has to be operated on. Maṅgal and Ketu are in conjunction and, for one reason or another, in this position Maṅgal creates a loss of blood (*rakt kṣaraṇ karvātā hai*). He will have to have an operation.

According to this diagnosis, Maṅgal's *prabhāv* is stronger than the "strength" (*jor*) of the medicines and hence necessarily leads to a loss of blood.

Related to the semantic field of bleeding, blows, and wounds, we find disputes, quarrels, and angry behavior, which are also seen as the effects of Maṅgal's *prabhāv*. An example of the aggressivity and anger attributed to the influence of Maṅgal can be seen in the case of this woman, who went to consult the astrologer Kameshwar Upadhyay because she was continually arguing with her husband:

♀: He [the husband] keeps increasing the tension (*kalah*) at home . . . last night and this morning we fought so much that I have a headache (*itnā laṛāī-jhagṛā ekdam dimāg kharāb ho gayā hai, merā*) . . .

J: Your husband's horoscope is very good; he will never lack money in his life . . .

♀: Yes, but at the moment we don't have any money, and that's why there is so much tension (*kalah*) at home . . . is it my *bhāgya* or his that contains something bad?

J: Until November 8, 2001, he is going through Maṅgal *mahādaśā*, and, of course arguments, disputes, and discussions will take place (*hum-tām, jhagṛā-jhaṃjhaṭ, bātā-bāti to hogā hī*) . . .

♀: We've just spent five to six lakhs of rupees for our daughter's wedding, we've just repaired the shop that's falling to bits . . . and we've also just bought a piece of land . . . now, where is all this money going to come from???[10] You can't imagine how stressed (*pareśān*) he [my husband] is at the moment . . .

J: That's Maṅgal, isn't it? Anger (*krodh*), rage (*ugratā*) . . . your husband isn't saying so, but within, he's boiling with rage (*ubāl khā rahe haĩ*) . . .

♀: Indeed, he's boiling with rage, sometimes against his brother, sometimes against me; we can't bear it any longer . . .

A similar case is illustrated by the example of a young man, Sandip, who had not been able to marry the girl he was in love with, due to opposition from the families. Uninvited, he and some of his friends were planning to attend the wedding that had been arranged for the girl. As she was worried, Sandip's mother consulted the astrologer to find out what was going to happen at this wedding. The astrologer felt the question should be analyzed using the *praśn kuṇḍalī* (horary horoscope) and, opening the almanac, noted that at the time the mother asked the question, Maṅgal was exactly in the seventh house, the marriage house. He hence gave voice to his suspicions:

J: [Looking at the almanac] Is he by any chance preparing a plan to create a fight (*jhagṛā-jhañjhaṭ kī yojanā*) during the [girl's] wedding tomorrow?

♀: That's exactly what I fear . . . my son isn't a quarrelsome person (*jhagṛālū*), but his friends are teaching him how to become a thug (*badmāśī ke liye śikṣā de rahe haĩ*) . . .

J: The Maṅgal I see [in the almanac] is in the seventh house and it aspects Mercury . . .

♀: Please tell us the wedding will be performed peacefully tomorrow, that nothing is going to happen, he's not going to fight . . . if someone starts a fight tomorrow and the police come, everyone will know about it, our family's reputation will be ruined.

J: The position of Maṅgal could lead them to think up ways of creating a fight (*kalah kī yojanā banā sakte hai*) something like, "Let's go, let's fight (*mār-pīṭh kareṅge*), let's have an argument (*jhagṛā-laṛāī kareṅge*)"

In this case, as in the case of the child with an eye disease, the verbs employed to designate the influence of Maṅgal are causative: *karvānā*, the causative of "to do" (*karnā*), is used in the case of the operation on the child's eyes—Maṅgal makes a loss of blood occur; *banānā*, the causative of *bannā*—"become," "to be created," "to be formed"—is used to express the idea that Maṅgal's influence "creates," "gives shape," to something, in this case, plans to create a fight.

While Maṅgal's *prabhāv* is manifested in the form of fights, bleeding, anger, and so forth, the area of existence primarily affected by the influence of Mars is marriage. Maṅgal is supposed to create all kinds of difficulties in a person's matrimonial life by afflicting both the person for whom it is malefic as well as his spouse: delays in arranging the marriage, arguments between the husband and wife, divorce, as well as widowhood are attributed to Mars's influence (*prabhāv*). Thus, the young women of Banaras who have difficulty having their marriage arranged often wear coral in a ring or on a necklace, as this precious stone protects from Maṅgal. Apart from coral, to remove obstacles to the arrangement of a marriage, astrologers prescribe the performance of *japs* (repetitions of a mantra) for the pacification (*śānti*) of Maṅgal.[11]

When Maṅgal is in the first, fourth, seventh, eighth, or twelfth house of the birth chart, the person is said to have *maṅgal doṣ*, "Mars's flaw" (see figure 9). The term *doṣ* constitutes a very widespread polysemic category found in the different Indian languages and regions. It is used in a wide range of areas, from medicine to rituals and from law to divination. Depending on the context, it designates a moral fault, a defect, vice, physiological dysfunction, danger, divine malediction, misfortune, as well as other negative notions. In the case of *maṅgal doṣ* (and *kāl sarp doṣ*, which we will discuss later), the term *doṣ* designates a congenital defect, generally free of moral connotations (although sometimes associated with acts accomplished in previous lives), that "sticks" (*lagtā hai*) to the person from the time of his birth and has "to be removed" (*nivāraṇ karnā*) by ritual means.

A person who has *maṅgal doṣ* in his horoscope is supposed to cause all kinds of afflictions for his spouse as well as his in-laws: accidents, diseases, disputes, or suffering. In this position, as Maṅgal is endowed with *mārakatva*, the ability to inflict death (the "quality of killing"), it is supposed to provoke the spouse's premature death.[12] The term *maṅgalik*[13]—or *maṅgalā* for a man and *maṅgalī* for a woman—designates anyone who has *maṅgal doṣ* in his or her horoscope. The most famous Indian *maṅgalik* woman is undoubtedly the Bollywood star and Miss World, Aishwarya

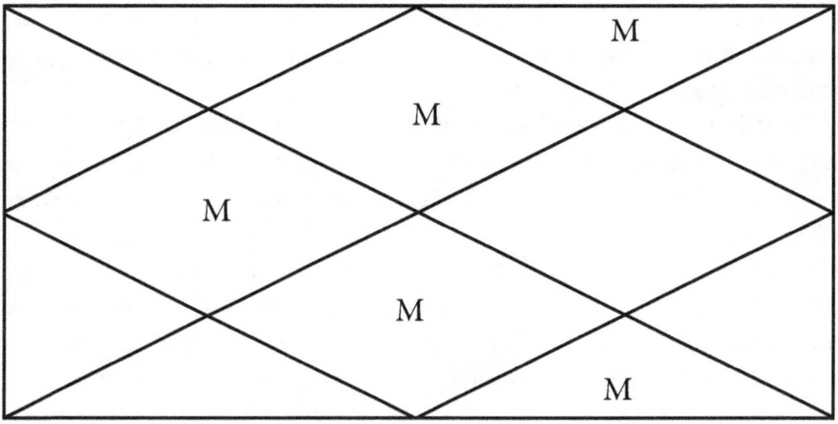

Figure 9. *Maṅgal doṣ* (Mars's flaw) in the birth chart (M = Mars).

Ray. At the time of her marriage to the actor Abhishek Bachchan, she was bombarded by the media with questions regarding her presumed astral defect and the rituals she is believed to have had performed to protect her husband and the whole Bachchan clan from misfortune.

One may note that since *maṅgal doṣ* is supposed to be harmful to anyone who has Mars in one of the five houses of the horoscope, almost half the population should be affected. There are hence several conditions that attenuate this astral flaw. To start with, astrologers emphatically state that all the astral configurations in the horoscope must be carefully examined, as some may cancel the effect of *maṅgal doṣ*.[14] Secondly, when two *maṅgalik* people marry, *maṅgal doṣ*'s destructive potential is supposed to be neutralized because of reciprocity. For this reason, the fact of being a *maṅgalik* or not may be a crucial factor in the choice of a matrimonial partner in Banaras and elsewhere in India. The importance of this category is attested, for example, by the matrimonial advertisements in the *Times of India*, specifying the "manglik" or "non-manglik"[15] identity of the marriage candidate (or the partner they are seeking). Following are a few examples.[16]

Section "Wanted brides":

> *Non-manglik* slim and really beautiful girl from high status family for Bansal 27/171 very well settled Tax Advocate belonging to a very renowned family of Advocates. Send biodata, photo, horoscope (must).

> Alliance invited from beautiful slim fair convented KK/SP[17] *manglik girl* of height not less than 5'22" for *Kanyakubj manglik* boy 27/171 BE (Hons) Roorkee currently doing MS in Comp Sc from USA coming India in June 1st week. Proposal for early marriage required with BHP must.[18]

> Alliance invited for tall 29/6'1" handsome, *shubh and lucky Manglik*, MBA only son v. high income. Own business at Delhi. Father Senior U.P. Govt. Office, tall cultured girl of middle class service background parents preferred. Send B/H.

Section "Wanted grooms":

> Suitable match for an educated *non-Manglik girl*, 23/165, from a very respectable and broad minded family of U.P. employed as Air Hostess with a foreign air lines based in Delhi. Boy to

be *non-Manglik* well educated and settled in service from a good family background. Write with BHP.

Match for Gaur Br. *Manglik* girl of status family fair b'ful talented MBA 26/163 Adhoc Lecturer in University decent marriage.

MD MS MDS BDS ENG MBA IAS Allied CA[19] match for *Manglik* Vaish BDS girl 26/166/50 tall beautiful smart fair belonging to status family of Doctors.

The advertisements in the *Times of India* "Matrimonials" supplement are divided into categories on the basis of caste ("Brahmin," "Rajput," "Yadav," etc.), profession ("Doctors," "Engineers," "IAS,"[20] etc.), regional belonging ("Punjabi," "Bengali," etc.), religion ("Muslim," "Sikh," "Christian," etc.), or other criteria ("Cosmopolitan," "NRI/Green card,"[21] "MBA," etc.). Most advertisements that mention "manglik" or "non-manglik" as one of the criteria for choosing the spouse appear in the "cosmopolitan," "Brahmin," "Agarwal," "Marwari,"[22] and "Rajput" categories.

Nonetheless, "manglik" also constitutes a separate category that gathers dozens of advertisements in the *Times of India* "Matrimonials": the families that choose to place their advertisement in this section consider that Mars's position in the horoscope is the main criteria for the choice of a matrimonial partner.[23] On this subject, it is interesting to specify that the "manglik" section is placed right after the category "disabled/handicapped" and just before "scheduled caste/scheduled tribe." The proximity with these two stigmatized social categories seems to confirm the perception of the *maṅgal doṣ* as a "genetic defect."

Another factor that may attenuate the impact of *maṅgal doṣ* is the couple's age. According to some astrologers, the destructive power of *maṅgal doṣ* is inversely proportional to the age of the spouses and late marriages are considered less dangerous. To quote the astrologer Dina Nath Tiwari:

If the woman is *maṅgalī* and the man is not, the man will have some kind of accident (*durghaṭnā*), and similarly, if the man is *maṅgalā* and the woman is not, the woman will have an accident . . . I have observed that this is true in ninety-nine percent of cases. But one must also know that this problem

> decreases with age: if the marriage takes place when both the spouses are very young, then it's very dangerous, later the danger decreases . . . As children have lots of energy, or vivacity (*phurtī*), and this same energy is still present in young people, but begins to diminish in adults, and is very weak in old people, in the same way, the *garam* (hot) influence of *maṅgal doṣ* becomes *naram* (sweet, tender).

To ward off the harmful effects of *maṅgal doṣ*, rituals may be performed. They consist of celebrating a "first marriage" (*prathama vivāha*) that serves to deflect all the *maṅgalik* person's influence onto a first nonhuman spouse. Thus, in Banaras, *maṅgalī* girls are either married to two clay jars (*kumbha*), which Varuna, the water God and protector of marriages, is invited to enter, or they are married to the *pīpal* (*ficus religiosa*) tree, an incarnation of the male god Vasudev.[24] *Maṅgalā* boys, on the other hand, can be married to a well (*kūāṃ*), as the well is the incarnation of the female deity Jaganmātā, Goddess Durgā.

These "first marriages" are performed particularly when the woman is a *maṅgalī*, because the premature death of the husband is generally considered more harmful than that of the wife.[25] Performing these "first marriages" is supposed to be *kanyāvaidhavyahara*, "destructive (*hara*) to the widowhood (*vaidhavya*) of the girl (*kanyā*)" and, as such, an astrologer explained, it is a way of "protecting society" (*samāj saṃrakṣan*). These first marriages are performed according to the rules and a girl who marries the clay jars must be dressed as if for an ordinary wedding. She applies the *sindūr* (vermilion) that would have been applied by the husband herself in this case. These marriages thus enable a transfer of the murderous potential of *maṅgal doṣ* to a first "divine" husband, making the "human" husband a "second husband" who would be safe from any danger.[26]

Performing these "shield" marriages does not however suffice to completely eradicate the mistrust toward *maṅgalī* girls. Let us look at the case of the wife of a professor at the Institute of Technology at Banaras Hindu University (BHU) who had consulted an astrologer from the Department of Jyotish to ask his advice on the choice of her future daughter-in-law. The woman told the astrologer she had selected five girls from the numerous replies to the advertisement published in the "Matrimonials" section of the *Times of India* for the marriage of her son, a researcher at the Biotechnology Department at BHU:

♀: I have brought you the horoscopes of the five girls we have selected . . . they are all of our caste [*kayasthā*] and they are all trained in the biotechnology sector. Please tell me how they match with my son's horoscope . . .

J: After doing the matching of the horoscopes (*kuṇḍalī milā karke*) I find the best result is Sheli, thirty *guṇ*s, then there is Dipti, with twenty-five *guṇs*[27] . . . But Sheli is *maṅgalī*, so in case you choose Sheli you should perform a *kumbha vivāha* (marriage to the clay jars) . . . My personal opinion is to choose Dipti; she has the *yog* for two sons and a daughter . . . her Jupiter is strong, so she has done well in her studies . . . Otherwise there's Nidhi, but she is also *maṅgalī* and because of Mars, she could have problems conceiving children . . .

♀: But why should I bring a *maṅgalī* woman into my home!!! We received over two thousand replies . . . and with all the women I could find for my son there's no reason to marry him to a *maṅgalī* . . .

Protective marriages aim to ward off the worst dangers, that is to say the death of the spouse, but they do not eliminate all the malefic effects associated with Maṅgal.[28] Over the course of several years of marriage, indeed, the non-*maṅgalik* spouse is supposed to be weakened by the partner's astral influence. To reduce the "daily" impact of Maṅgal on the spouse, astrologers prescribe coral (*muṅgā*), the precious stone associated with Mars, to be worn by the *maṅgalik* person.[29]

Thus, an astrologer explained to a man who had heart problems:

J [looking at the wife of ♂'s horoscope]: Your wife should wear coral, does she wear one?

♂: No, she doesn't.

J: She has to wear coral (*inko ek muṅgā kā zarurat hai*), it's for you (*āpke liye hai*), she is a bit *maṅgalī* (*kuch maṅgalī hai*) . . .

♂: Please help me . . .

J: Let me explain a bit better . . . the coral she should wear, she should wear it for you, to protect your health (*āpko svasth rakhne ke liye*) . . . She is a little *maṅgalī* (*thoṛī maṅgalī*), she is clearly *maṅgalī* (*kaṛī Maṅgalī*), and you are not at all *maṅgalā*, this is also why you have health problems.

♂: She is very short-tempered (*krodhī*), *gurujī*.

J: Obviously, she must be short-tempered . . . she has Maṅgal in the seventh house, she has Śani (Saturn) in the ascendant sign . . . of course she is short-tempered!

Maṅgal's influence, as we have seen, is often associated with excess, violent strength that ultimately weakens the spouse. Let us mention the case of a Bengali businessman whose wife had run away from home. This man, a rich importer of chemical products, had gone to consult the astrologer Shree Kanth Shastri, in order to locate his wife who had left home five months before, and of whom he had not had any news for the last twenty-two days.[30] The astrologer calculated the *praśn kuṇḍalī* (horary horoscope) to establish where his wife was, and when she would return home, but to understand why she had left home he studied the man's horoscope and hand:[31]

♂: Since she left, everything is upside down, I am depressed, I feel like committing suicide . . . I have looked everywhere, in Swami Vivekananda's ashrams, in Mother Teresa's ashrams, and Tagore's ashram in Santiniketan. I even went looking for her in Kerala, but I have had no news at all . . .

J: Don't worry, she will return soon, according to the *praśn kuṇḍalī* she could even come back today . . . The problem is in your horoscope . . . your Maṅgal is very strong and it is located in the seventh house [house of marriage]: this gives you success, a reputation in society, it gives you power over people . . . but it affects your married life and this is why your wife ran away from home . . . You see, if your wife's Maṅgal had also been strong, you would have had a very happy married life, but as this isn't the case, both of you are suffering . . .

The astrologer later explained to us that this woman had been traumatized at the age of six, as she had seen her parents assassinated by gangsters before her eyes. After this event, the woman had been housed at the police station for several months, then entrusted to a paternal uncle. At the age of fourteen she had been forced to marry this man, who was eighteen and went on to become an influential businessman. While the influence of Maṅgal made the man rich and powerful, it weakened this woman whose astrological vulnerability seems to express the wounds life had inflicted upon her.

We saw that while Maṅgal's *prabhāv* is malefic, it is nonetheless associated with strength, excessive strength that is likely to turn into aggressivity, disputes, and direct or indirect attacks against others.[32] We will now see that the harmful influence of Śani, Rāhu, and Ketu is, on the contrary, more closely associated with a person's weakness and fragility.

Sāṛhe Sātī and Saturnian Business

While, as we saw, Maṅgal is associated with the *rajas guṇa*—strength, ardor, the color red, the *kṣatriya varṇa*, and so on—Śani (Saturn) represents the *tamas guṇa*—ugliness, spitefulness, indolence, the color black, the *śūdra varṇa*, and so forth. This planet is seen as the most intimidating, responsible for all kinds of sorrows, pain, and human misery. Unlike other planets, Saturn also enjoys the status of a full-fledged God among Hindus: *Śanidev*, *Śani bhagvān*, *Śani mahārāj*, or *Śani bābā* are the names by which the devotees address Saturn as a God. It is honored by a personal cult in numerous temples in North and South India. In Banaras, the devotion to this planetary God is visible at several places: not only the two Śani shrines located near the *Viśvanāth Mandir* in the sacred center of the town but also countless *pīpal* trees (*ficus religiosa*) everywhere in town, near the homes of devotees. On Saturday mornings oil lamps (*dīp*) are lit and placed around the foot of the tree to pay homage to the planetary God.[33] The importance of Śani is visible as well in Hanumān temples and shrines, where oil lamps are lit to place Śani under the control of the Monkey God.

Śani's malefic reputation today is clearly illustrated by the first page of the introduction to the book *Śani kā Prakop: Usse Bacāv* (Saturn's Wrath: How to Keep Safe; Shrivastava 2001):

> The power (*prabhāv*) of Śani's cruel gaze (*krūr dṛṣṭi*) is well known to all. The afflicted person (*ākrānt jātak*) is bound by a chain of curses (*abhiśāpõ kī śṛṅkhalā se ābaddh ho jātā hai*). Due to Śani's influence, we see the occurrence of physical suffering (*śārīrik kaṣṭ*), financial difficulties (*arthahāni*), dishonor (*sammān-kṣaya*), obstacles at work (*kāryāvarodh*), fleeing (*palāyan*), exile (*niṣkāsan*), imprisonment (*kārāvās*), poverty (*daridratā*), wandering (*vibhram*), fear of enemies (*śatrubhaya*), and many other situations that give rise to sorrow (*duḥkhad*). If Śani is truly angry with someone (*pūrṇatayā kupit ho jāye*), no one is capable of stopping its destructive action (*sarvanāś*). Indeed, the person afflicted (*pīṛit vyakti*) by Śani could be called "an incurable patient (*asādhya rogī*) of misfortune (*durbhāgya*)." (Shrivastava 2001, 7)

In his *Epics, Myths and Legends of India*, Paul Thomas had already noticed the danger associated with Śani and had described the fear this planet provokes among the Hindus:

> Śani is a "malefic among malefics" and Hindus dread his influence above everything else. All misfortunes and calamities are traced to him. A person born under Śani will be slandered, his riches will be dissipated and his son, wife and friends destroyed; he will live at variance with others and endure many sufferings. (Thomas 1958, 122)

Similarly, the *Navagraha Anukūlan Tantra*, a text that describes the characteristics of each of the nine planets and the remedies to pacify them, describes the effects of Śani in the following manner:[34]

> Śani's bad influence (*duṣprabhāv*) creates a situation where the person will have to suffer all kinds of sorrow (*nānā prakār ke kleś bhogne kī sthiti mẽ pahuñcā detā*). People seized by Śani (*Śani-grast log*) lose their peace of mind (*mānsik śānti naṣṭ ho jātī hai*); they encounter adversity (*avarodh*) and obstacles (*vighn*) in the realization (*saphaltā*) of their actions; the door to progress (*pragati*) is closed to them while the path of regression (*avanati*, "descent") is open to them. (Shukla 1993, 122)

It is interesting to note that, particularly in the case of Śani but also of other planets, the same terms apply equally to the action of the planet and of the personified deity. Thus the term *prabhāv* designates both planetary influence and the power exercised by the deity; similarly *dṛṣṭi* designates both the planetary aspect (the influence planets exert on each other depending on the angular configuration in which they are located in relation to the earth) as well as the "gaze" of the planet as a divine and anthropomorphic agent.

The concern provoked merely by mentioning the planet Śani marks most astrological consultations. Clients sometimes go to see an astrologer driven only by the fear of being under Śani's control. For example, one had read in the newspaper that Śani was passing through the zodiacal sign of his own *lagna* (ascendant) or his own *rāśi* (lunar sign), another had had his hand read by a friend or a street practitioner who had detected a *Śani sāṛhe sati* in it, yet another is going through a difficult period and self-diagnosed a period of affliction by Saturn. In these cases, astrologers normally reassure the clients by explaining that these vague discoveries are negligible as Śani's impact on a person can only be evaluated through a detailed analysis of the horoscope. Nonetheless, it may also happen that Śani is not mentioned during a consultation and, once the client has left, the astrologer tells us that he did not want to upset the client's peace of mind (*mānsik śānti*) and thus concealed the fact he was going through a bad Saturnian period. Indeed, while Śani himself is supposed to destroy a person's peace of mind, the fact of being aware one is going through a bad Saturnian period would only, according to some astrologers, create a sort of vicious circle of anxiety.

The representation of Saturn's malefic and destructive power reaches its paroxysm with Śani's *sāṛhe sati*—Saturn's "seven and a half years," a period seen as particularly dangerous. The fear of being struck by *sāṛhe sātī* haunts the thoughts of most clients who consult astrologers. In the words of a client who was going through this negative period:

> Śani's anger (*prakop*) [during this period] is such that even if you are convinced you are doing everything properly, things will end up going badly. For example, even if you are very attentive while driving your car, you will have an accident. Even if you are very careful while walking, you will end up stumbling. A physical injury (*sarīrik kṣati*) will occur violently (*zabardasti*),

> so you even risk death or mutilation . . . And this sort of thing happens mainly on a Saturday. There are all kinds of problems (*dikkat*) on Saturdays . . . you will find that out of twenty-five accidents, twenty-three occur on a Saturday . . .

From the viewpoint of astrological theory, the *sāṛhe sātī* period is calculated on the basis of the lunar birth sign called *rāśi*. The *sāṛhe sātī* begins when Śani is in the twelfth house counting from the *rāśi*, and it continues while Śani passes through the two houses following the twelfth, that is to say, the house of the *rāśi* itself, and the second house in relation to the *rāśi*. Given that Śani takes about two and a half years to travel from one house to another, *sāṛhe sātī* lasts seven and a half years.[35] This harmful period occurs about every thirty years in a person's life, and one may hence go through *sāṛhe sātī* three times in a lifetime.[36] Thus, for example, if someone goes through their first *sāṛhe sātī* between the age of seven and fourteen and a half, he will go through the second between the ages of thirty-seven to forty-four and a half, and the third between sixty-seven and seventy-four and a half. Hence the common belief is that a person loses his grandparents during the first *sāṛhe sātī*, his parents during the second, and he dies during the third. The *sāṛhe sātī* is divided into three periods of two and a half years, known as *ḍhāīya* (period of two and a half years) or *caraṇ* (period). Each *ḍhāīya* brings different types of sorrows: the first mainly gives rise to economic problems (*ārthik kaṣṭ*), the second to health problems (*śāririk kaṣṭ*), and the third to problems with the family (*parivārik kaṣṭ*).

As Mridula Trivedi wisely observes in her astrological study on Śani, "Śani's *sāṛhe sātī* (period of seven and a half years) is a *kāmadhenu* for many astrologers."[37] *Kāmadhenu*, the cow that fulfills desires, is mentioned here to suggest that astrologers grow wealthy thanks to the malefic reputation surrounding this astral period. While it is true that numerous specialists draw financial benefits from the fear the Saturnian period provokes, consultations are not the only means by which Śani's reputation is commercially exploited. Several astrological books on Śani are sold in bookshops in the towns of North India. Thus, among the publications, one finds *Śani Śaman* (Appeasing Saturn; Trivedi 1996), *Śani Graha Pīṛā Nivāraṇ Vidhi* (Instructions for Eliminating the Suffering Provoked by the Planet Saturn; Vatsa 1996), and *Śani kā Prakop: Usse Bacāv* (Saturn's Wrath: How to Keep Safe; Shrivastava 2001). Over the last years the astrologers Trivedi and Trivedi, based in Delhi, who had anticipated Saturn's growing popularity not only in India but also abroad, translated and republished *Śani Śaman* in English (*Shani Shaman: Wooing Saturn*, 2 vols., 2002). In 2010 they published two other works on the subject of Saturn, currently available in the United States and online: *Secrets of Saturn* and *Saturn the King Maker*.[38]

Mass media, new technologies, and the tourist industry are constantly broadening the scope for business related to the planetary God. Innumerable websites sell online consultations as well as remedies to pacify the Saturnian influence, particularly during the seven-and-a-half-year period: necklaces, rings, precious stones, rituals, *yantra*s, products for *pūjā*, and so on. Śani temples that are particularly famous in India—such as the one at Shingnapur in Maharashtra or the one in Thirunallar in the Pondicherry region—are included in tourist circuits organized by travel agencies, and are now surrounded by hotels and stalls selling all kinds of goods. Cell phone service providers are also among the beneficiaries of the fear associated with Saturn's influence. They send regular text messages to inform their clients of Saturn's passage through the various signs of the zodiac and offer personalized consultations. Thus, during my staying in Tamil Nadu and Pondicherry between 2006 and 2008, I regularly received messages like the following on my cell phone:

> Sani peyarchi.[39] To know how Sani's movement from kataga [Cancer, *karkaṭa* in Sanskrit] to simha Rasi [zodiacal sign of Leo] will impact ur rasi [zodiacal sign], and get pariharam [ritual remedies], sms SANI to 5455. sms MENU for services. Rs.3/sms

> The impact Saneeswaran [Saturn] has on your rasi [zodiacal sign] can be moderated by doing pariharam [ritual remedies] and pooja. To know the pariharam for ur rasi, type SANIPAR sms to 5455. Rs. 3/sms

The new Śani temple, Śanidhām, the "abode of Saturn," recently built in an affluent suburb of New Delhi, confirms the vitality of the planetary God in contemporary India.[40] It was erected in the 2000s by the multimedia guru-astrologer Daati Maharaj, who presents the daily television program on astrology, *Dātī Gurumantra*, on several channels. This guru astrologer encourages spectators to visit his grand and gleaming temple that holds "the largest Śani statue in the world." The credits of his television program marked by the motto: "Śani is not the enemy, he's a friend" (*Śani śatru nahī̃, mitra hai*), refer the viewer to the website www.shanidham.in. Not only does this site provide information on Saturn, Daati Maharaj, and the functioning of the Shanidham temple, it also sells horoscopes, books, and booklets on Saturn, as well as devotional objects related to him and the other planetary deities. A weekly Hindi magazine, *Śani neśans ṭaims* (*Shani Nations Times*), is distributed electronically and in print form. Śani's media popularity is also illustrated by the series *Mahima Śani Dev ki*, broadcast every week on the NDTV imagine television channel since July 2008. Although these forms of media coverage are yet to be studied, their existence and popularity are testimony to the fruitful encounter between astrological concepts, new technologies, and the media (Udupa 2016).

Of Snakes and Demons: The *Kāl Sarp Doṣ*

According to the epic and Purāṇic traditions, Rāhu and Ketu are two demons: Rāhu is the demon of the eclipse[41] and Ketu is the personification of comets. In the astrological tradition, the two demons Rāhu and Ketu are seen as two planets that belong to the group of the *navagraha*s, the "nine planetary deities."[42] Although they are seen as planets, from an astronomical viewpoint Rāhu and Ketu have no physical existence and are mere mathematical points. They, in fact, indicate the points at which the Moon's orbit meets the ecliptic. In astrology these points are called the "Moon's ascending node" or "Dragon's Head" (Rāhu) and the "Moon's descending node" or "Dragon's Tail" (Ketu). As these are the points where the lunar and solar eclipses occur, Rāhu and Ketu are also called *chāyā-graha*s, "shadow-planets."

As planets, Rāhu and Ketu retain the demoniacal nature attributed to them by mythological traditions and are seen as cruel (*krūr*), mean (*duṣṭ, ugr*) planets that provoke suffering (*pīṛādāyak, kaṣṭaprad*), give rise to misfortune (*amaṅgalajanak*), and create obstacles (*vighnakārī*).[43] In particular, these planets are supposed to project a "shadow" (*chāyā*) over a person's life and they are associated with depression, suicide, sorcery attacks, drug dependency, possession by ghosts, and generally all sorts of harmful occult powers.

Rāhu is described as a malefic demon seizing the different parts of the body: depending on its position in the horoscope, Rāhu is said to be located "in the head" (*sir mẽ*), "in the stomach" (*peṭ mẽ*), or "in the legs" (*pair mẽ*) of the person. When Rāhu is located "in the head" the person is anxious, unstable, depressed, or may, for example, suffer epileptic fits; when Rāhu is located "in the stomach" it provokes all kinds of problems like dysentery, constipation, flatulence, and so forth; when it is located "in the legs" Rāhu prevents the person from resting. It forces them to move around all the time and provokes changes in the job or the place of residence.

Rāhu and Ketu's *mahādaśā*s (major periods) create widespread fear among the clients of the astrologers in Banaras, to the extent that these periods are supposed to penetrate a person with harmful influence even outside their effective duration, like a shadow projecting the body beyond its physical limits. One example is provided by the case of a twenty-five-year-old man who worked for the navy in Pune and who had broken his leg during an exercise. His mother had gone to the astrologer Kameshwar Upadhyay to learn whether this accident was a sign that working for the National Defence Service did not suit her son, something a friend had suggested looking at the young man's palm. The astrologer explained to the woman that although Rāhu's *mahādaśā* had ended in 1998, the accident that occurred in December 1999 was only a posthumous effect, "a sequel" to the recently ended Rāhu *mahādaśā* that affected his legs:

> Since 1998 your son has been going through a favorable Jupiter (*Bṛhaspati*) *mahādaśā* that will bring him lots of money and happiness, but he should not forget that he is coming out of eighteen years of Rāhu's *mahādaśā* . . . this is the reason he broke his leg, there are still some residual effects of Rāhu's *mahādaśā* . . .

To reduce the harmful effects of Rāhu and Ketu's *mahādaśā*, clients wear precious stones, particularly *gomed* (hessonite) for Rāhu and *lahsuniyā* (chrysoberyl) for Ketu. They can also recite prayers (*jap*)—or have them recited by ritual specialists. They can make offerings (*Rāhu-dān*, *Ketu-dān*) to Brahmins: dark-colored cloth or clothing, plates, grain, lentils, mustard oil, money, or other types of goods.

One specific type of offering made during the Rāhu and Ketu *mahādaśā* is the *chāyā-dān*, the "gift of the shadow."[44] The harmful planetary influence is seen as a "black shadow" (*kālī chāyā*) that envelops (the verb used is *maṇḍarānā*, "to fly around," "to surround") the person and weakens them. To repel (*khiñcnā*), cleanse (*jhāṛnā*, "sweep away"), this "black shadow," the person must look at his own face reflected in a recipient (*kaṭorī*, *pātr*) containing oil and then offer the oil to a poor Brahmin in the street.[45] This process should be repeated every Saturday for several weeks (a minimum of four and a maximum of sixteen) and the size of the recipient and the quantity of oil used must be proportional to the size of the person's face (while for a child, 250 ml. should be sufficient; for an adult, at least 1.5 liters of oil are required).[46] By doing this, the person is supposed to get relief from the harmful influence of the "shadow-planets" (*chāyā-graha*).

Outside the *mahādaśā*, Rāhu and Ketu's malefic effects are supposed to affect the person suffering from *kāl sarp yog*, "the planetary conjunction of the snake" (also called *kāl sarp doṣ* or, sometimes, *nāga doṣ*).[47] The name of this planetary conjunction is certainly linked to the fact that in Hindu iconography, Rāhu and Ketu are often represented as being, respectively, the head and the tail of a snake. Although this iconography is probably influenced by Greek astrology[48] and hence does not seem to be indigenous, its transplantation to India has given rise to interesting combinations of celestial demons and other serpentine deities, such as the Nāgas. Thus, in her analysis of astrological representations in a village in Tamil Nadu, Karin Kapadia mentions the "Naga dosham" as a planetary conjunction that the lower castes associate with the cobra deities Nagappa and Nagamma.[49] Similarly, in Banaras as elsewhere in India, to repel *kāl sarp yog* certain astrologers prescribe rituals that are to be performed on *nāga pañcamī* (the fifth day of the bright fortnight of the month of Śrāvaṇa). From a textual viewpoint though, this festival has nothing to do with the two demons Rāhu and Ketu but is rather connected to the terrestrial Nāga deities. Still due to an iconographic rather than a conceptual affinity, the demons Rāhu and Ketu are also associated with Śiva, as this god has a privileged relationship with snakes. As we will see later, in Banaras the rituals that seek to repel the ill effects of this astral conjunction are often performed in Shaivite temples.

From an astrological viewpoint, *kāl sarp yog* occurs when, in the birth chart, all the planets are located on the same hemicycle of the ecliptic with respect to the lunar nodes (the latter are always located at 180° in relation to each other). In other words, in the birth chart with the twelve houses, this means that all the planets are located in the six houses between those occupied, respectively, by Rāhu and Ketu. In a horoscope that shows this astral conjunction, Rāhu and Ketu are said to "eat" (*khānā*) the other planets. The two demons are said to hold the favorable planets and their positive influence hostage, and because of that, despite all his or her efforts, the person is not able to obtain what he or she desires. This was the case of a thirty-year-old woman who had several planets in a favorable position in her horoscope and who, according to the astrologer Chattopadhyay, should at her age have had a university degree in hard science, a secure job as an engineer, and a husband. However, the astrologer explains:

> This woman is already thirty and she is not married, nor has she become an engineer, nor has she studied science. She is a very mediocre student and everything she does is mediocre. Why is this?
>
> It is because she has *kāl sarp doṣ*. All the planets [in her horoscope] are situated on the left side. She has a "complete" (*pūrṇ rūp se*) *kāl sarp doṣ*. If at least one planet had been on the right, it would have been lighter, but her *kāl sarp doṣ* is very strong. Even if you have an excellent horoscope, you will obtain nothing in your life, neither a job, nor marriage, as Rāhu and Ketu devour (*khā lete haĩ*) the other planets. They put obstacles (*avarodh kar detā hai*) to any progress (*agragati*).

The clients afflicted by this planetary flaw also describe its influence in terms of frustration. According to a forty-year-old man, a technician at a public health institution in Banaras, *kāl sarp yog* has the following effects:

> I have had *kāl sarp yog* since the time I was born and this is very oppressive (*taṅg kartā hai bahut zyādā*) . . . it means that, for example, even if you behave well (*āp sahī rahate huye bhī*) people accuse you of being wrong (*galat kaheṅge*), you will always suffer because of enemies (*śatruõ se hameśā pīṛit raheṅge*) . . . the mouthful comes so close to the mouth, and then disappears (*muṃh tak nivālā āyegā aur calā jāyegā*), it's

> always like that . . . and you go through suffering (*kleṣ*) in the family, you argue with your wife all the time (*kackac hotā rahatā hai*) . . . so all these problems . . . Whatever effort I make, I still remain "zero" (*sab kuch karte huye bhī mẽ ziro hū̃*), but there is no remedy for this . . .

The same fears seem to preoccupy those who consult online astrologers today. On the website hindijyotish.com, the article "Even *Kāl Sarp Yog* Can Bear Positive Fruit" (*kāl sarp yog bhī śubh phal detā hai*) provoked a reaction from 181 internet users, who for the majority were worried and wanted to know what impact the snake conjunction would have on their lives and the remedies to follow to limit the harmful effects. Most of them were young graduates born in the 1980s: they were wondering what their professional future and their marriage would bring, in a language that is a combination of English and Romanized Hindi. On May 24, 2009, the pseudonymous "Ravi sagar" expressed his fears in the comments section of the site in the following manner:

> Dear sir, i m MCA [Master of Computer Applications] qualified person now working but not got the job according to my profile, i always work hard but result got either very late or negative i think it is of *Kaal sarp yog* in my *kundali* [horoscope]. please tell me when will i get a good job and *mera bhagya kab Uday hoga* [when my luck will rise] and *meri shadi kab aur kaisi hogi* [when and how my marriage will take place]? my dob [date of birth]:-23-08-82,11:30pm, place Moradabad (U.P)

Nonetheless, while in certain cases it prevents any kind of success, in others this planetary conjunction is supposed to make the person extremely powerful. In the discourses of clients and astrologers, people with *kāl sarp yog* either have no control, or complete control, over the events surrounding them. Astrologers often quote the examples of Nehru and Mussolini in this respect, as personalities who acted under the influence of the conjunction of the snake and whose lives were marked by a shift from absolute power to extreme sorrow on their deaths. In order to represent the effects of *kāl sarp yog*, the astrologer Kameshwar Upadhyay explained that this planetary conjunction gives a person's life the form of a snake, the sinusoidal form of the reptilian indicating the "ups" and "downs" of life. *Kāl sarp yog* would "raise the person up very high" (*bahut upar uṭhāte hai*) and "bring them very low" (*nīc nīc utārte hai*) over the course of his or her existence. Powerful and successful periods are followed by periods of weakness and disgrace.[50]

Among the remedies prescribed to reduce the ill effects of *kāl sarp yog* one finds a silver or gold ring in the shape of a snake set with stones to protect from the influence of Rāhu and Ketu. Another remedy consists of having a *kāl sarp pūjā* performed, the *pūjā* to the planetary snake (*kāl sarp*). The procedure followed during a *kāl sarp pūjā* is as follows: after measuring his own finger, the person afflicted by *kāl sarp yog* must have a snake made of silver nine times longer than the length of his own finger, and he must place this on Śiva's head on *ekādaśmī* (the eleventh day of a lunar fortnight). After he has performed *Rudrābhiṣekam*[51] with twenty-five liters of milk, he must make an offering of the snake (at a Śiva temple, or in the Ganges). By doing this the person will be released (*mukt rahanā*) from the harmful influence of *kāl sarp yog* for two or three years.

Just as devotion to the God Hanumān is supposed to reduce Śani's harmful influence, worship of Śiva is supposed to enable control over *kāl sarp yog*'s bad influence. Particularly when it involves Rāhu and Ketu, Śiva is worshiped in the form of Kāl Bhairav or Baṭuk Bhairav. People afflicted by Rāhu and Ketu often go to temples dedicated to these two Gods.[52] At the entrance to the Kāl Bhairav temple, on the right there is a sanctuary dedicated to the *navagraha*s, the "nine planetary deities." After circumambulating the sanctuary dedicated to the *navagraha*s, the afflicted person takes the *darśana*, the "vision," of Kāl Bhairav. When he leaves, in order to eliminate any residual planetary influence the person must "rotate" (*ghumānā*) edible substances around his own head—for example, chick peas, balls of jaggery, cream, sweetmeats, and so forth—and then offer them to the dogs around the temple to eat, as the dog is Kāl Bhairav's vehicle.[53]

In this chapter we examined the expressions used to describe harmful planetary influence and some ritual practices followed to get rid of it. As we saw, planets "seize" their victims in a manner that is very similar to that of ghosts (*bhūt-pret*) or other demonic beings possessing or taking over the person (Smith 2006).[54] What fundamentally differentiates the characterization of the harmful influence of the planets from the rage (*kop*) attributed to Gods or demonic beings is the fact that the impact of the planets can be calculated, measured, and evaluated in an objective manner. Furthermore, astrological diagnosis can be carried out through new technologies—computer, cell phone, iPhone, and so on—and spread through mass media—newspapers, radio, television, internet, among others. These tools can either be integrated into the consultation or become the very site of the consultation between the specialist (or pseudo-specialist) and the client. Scripturally sanctioned and deeply rooted in Brahmanical culture, astrology has very easily been grafted onto "modernity," thus becoming a language of destiny that, in contemporary India, is adapted to the requirements of the lifestyle of the urban middle classes.

8

More or Less Effective

Remedies and Efficacy

Since Malinowski's work on magic in the Trobriand Islands, the question of the efficacy of so-called "ritual" or "magical" practices continues to be debated within the discipline of anthropology. Do these practices have an effect on the actors involved? And if so, what type of effect? How? Most studies dealing with ritual efficacy attempt to show that magical or ritual acts do indeed have an effect on the actors who accomplish them, even if this effect does not correspond to the participants' explanations or expectations. Despite the diversity of approaches, anthropologists seem to share the idea that the efficacy of ritual action does not necessarily consist in a transformation of external reality (provoking rainfall, an abundant harvest, etc.), but it brings about a transformation of the social group or the individuals involved in the action. Depending on the type of transformation induced, the efficacy has been explained in functional, structural-functional, symbolic, performative, or phenomenological terms.[1]

Among the authors who have dealt with ritual efficacy, some have looked specifically at the question of the intentions (or beliefs) of the actors involved in the ritual or therapeutic processes (Ahern 1979; Tambiah 1979; Humphrey and Laidlaw 1994; Endres 2008). Although they emphasize the need to take the point of view of the actors into consideration to understand the efficacy of the acts accomplished, these studies nonetheless give little weight to the reflexive dimension of efficacy, how efficacy itself—as a quality of things, acts, and persons—is perceived, evaluated and analyzed by those performing the ritual. Rather than examining the impact of the ritual or therapeutic process on the actors, in this chapter we focus on ideas and theories that are used to describe and explain the manner in which the prescribed treatments function and do or do not produce a desired effect. In other words, the idea of efficacy will not be dealt with here as an analytical category, but as a concept mobilized by astrologers and their clients to classify and evaluate different therapeutic treatments.

We will hence see that during astrological consultations the efficaciousness of a treatment is not designed as an "all or nothing" quality. It is rather a graded attribute, a more or less feature whose graduation can be measured and calculated using certain parameters, such as its cost, its duration, and its weight. Rather than opposing efficacy to inefficacy, the discourse on the therapeutic value of a substance or an act is structured around the continuum between "more efficacious" and "less efficacious." Despite this quantitative dimension though, efficacy is not merely perceived as an objective quality, inherent to the substance or the therapeutic act. The efficacy of a treatment is also a subjective quality, linked to the identity of the patient involved, and cannot be evaluated separately. Thus, the same remedy can be efficacious for a poor client and inefficacious for a rich landowner. Following a reasoning that recalls that of sacrifice, the greater or lower efficacy of a treatment depends not only on its therapeutic properties, but also on the effort the patient makes to achieve the desired outcome.

To solve their clients' problems, astrologers in Banaras draw from an eclectic and varied universe of "remedies" (*ilāj*, *upāy*, *upacār*). They combine techniques drawn from different Indian religious and intellectual traditions, such as Brahmanical and tantric rituals, devotional practices, and gemology (*ratnaśāstra*). As Sanskrit astrological treatises contain very little information about the remedies to control planetary influence (the exception being the *graha-śānti*, rituals for pacifying the planets), most therapeutic methods employed by astrologers are elaborated on the basis of family and local traditions, apprenticeship with a guru, and personal experience.[2] Although astrological therapy is not as codified as astrological theory, we nonetheless observed that astrologers in Banaras share a common "pharmacopeia" that mainly consists of three types of treatments. To start with, worship (*pūjā-pāṭh*) of the main deities of the Hindu pantheon. This may consist in vegetal oblations offered into the fire (*havan*, *hom*, or *yajña*), a murmured repetition of sacred formulae using a rosary (*jap*), reading prayers aloud (*pāṭh*), as well as other forms of devotion like *darśana* (vision). The second category of remedies is gemstones (*ratna*) to be worn in rings or necklaces; third, astrologers use so-called "tantric" remedies, including amulets (*jantar*) and practices of purification from harmful influences (*jhāṛnā-phūknā*).

Astrologers generally describe harmful planetary influence as a shortage of power in the afflicted person. Planets may give rise to obstacles (*bādhā*), difficulties (*taklīf*), and suffering (*duḥkh*) that affect a person's ability to control their own destiny and thus prevent the realization of desire and projects. As the introduction to a brochure of prayers dedicated to Saturn, the *Śani Cālīsā*,[3] clearly states: "When despite all your earnest efforts in life you are unable to accomplish something, this is the time to worry about your planetary situation."[4]

In order to find a solution to their clients' problems, astrologers resort to objects, substances, or beings—like precious stones, tantric amulets, the Gods, the astrologer himself, and so on—who are considered "powerful" (*prabhāvśālī, śaktiśālī*). These objects or beings are not, however, all endowed with the same type of power. Following is a glossary of categories commonly employed during consultations to define the influence of certain objects or beings on human destiny, in order to elucidate the different types of power involved in astrological therapy:

> *Prabhāv*: the category of *prabhāv* (from the verb *pra-BHŪ-*, "to rule over," "to be master of," "to control") is used to designate the influence of the planets over human destiny and, depending on the context, can be translated either as "influence" or "hold." Indeed, the semantic field of the word *prabhāv* includes both influence as a natural action and as control exerted by a personified subject on someone else. This word hence explains the ambiguous status of the planets that are seen as being both physical bodies that emit "rays" and "vibrations," and anthropomorphic Gods endowed with intentionality. While the influence of the planets as divine beings is controlled by the deities of the Hindu pantheon, the natural influence of the planets as astral bodies is controlled by precious stones. The word *prabhāv* is also used to indicate the therapeutic power of a treatment, a "powerful" remedy is said to be *prabhāvśālī*, "endowed with *prabhāv*."
>
> *Śakti*: this word designates both spiritual and physical "power,"

"strength," "energy," particularly that which the gods are endowed with (Wadley 1975), but which can also be possessed by human beings, substances, and things.[5] Astrological therapy generally seeks to reinforce the *śakti* of the person afflicted by the planets, by using the Gods' *śakti* and by giving *śakti* to tantric remedies and precious stones.

Siddhi: from the Sanskrit root *SIDH-*, "to be accomplished," "to be fulfilled," "to succeed," *siddhi* designates the supernatural powers acquired through tantric practices of "accomplishment" (*sādhana*). Most astrologers in Banaras claim to possess *siddhi*s and to use them to make tantric remedies for their clients effective.

Bal: in astrological language, a planet's power is defined in terms of *bal* (strength). Depending on its position in the horoscope, a planet can be *prabal*, "very powerful," or *durbal* "weak."[6] Just like *prabhāv*, the word *bal* is also used to indicate both the "strength" of planets as things that have a physical impact on the life of human beings, and the "strength" planets possess as divine beings endowed with intentionality.[7] Nonetheless, the "strength" of the planets is controlled by the Gods, who are considered more "powerful" (*balvān*) than the planets.

Manobal, *ātmabal*: *manobal* (mental strength) or *ātmabal* (spiritual strength), as well as "willpower" (the English term is used), refer to the determination to carry out one's decisions or wishes and the confidence in one's own skills. A weakening (*kamzor*) of *manobal*, *ātmabal*, or willpower is considered one of the most common effects of harmful planetary influence. Astrological remedies hence seek to restore the person's self-confidence and conviction that she or he is capable of deciding his or her own destiny.

Power: the English word "power" is commonly used in Hindi to designate electric power. In the astrological context, the term "power" is used to indicate the efficacy of precious stones in capturing planetary rays. In more technical terms, this word indicates the efficacy of precious stones in terms of carats (just as the word power is used to indicate the corrective strength of a pair of glasses). When asked how much "power" one needs for a stone, the answer is provided in carats.

Adhikār: authority (*adhikār*) is the category through which the supremacy of the Gods in relation to the planets is defined. The relationship between Gods and planets is indeed often compared to that between the king and his ministers, as the authority of the planets is subordinate to that of the Gods.

In astrological therapy, the power of a remedy is used to oppose the *graha prabhāv*, the planetary power seen as responsible for a client's problems. Each type of remedy nonetheless "works" (the verb used in this context is *kām karnā*) differently, by mobilizing a specific type of power. Thus, the efficacy of tantric remedies (*tāntrik upāy*, *tāntrik prayog*) is said to be due to the astrologer's *siddhi*s, while the worship of the gods (*pūjā-pāṭh*) appeals to divine *śakti*. Precious stones are considered powerful in themselves, by virtue of a "physical" and "natural" strength invoking "scientific" principles and categories. As we will see, these distinctions are not however clear-cut, and the same remedy is sometimes said to combine several "active ingredients."

Before we go on to examine the efficacy associated with each category of treatment, let us look at the hierarchies of efficacy established between the different remedies.

Price and Efficacy

When talking about the therapeutic power of different types of remedies, astrologers not only make qualitative distinctions but also refer to quantitative, measurable, and objectifiable criteria. Thus, money, the monetary value of a treatment, is a common idiom through which the therapeutic power of a remedy is objectified and quantified. In general, a direct proportionality is established between the cost of a treatment and its efficacy: the more expensive the remedy, the more effective it is supposed to be. The cost of the remedies prescribed by astrologers in Banaras can range from a few rupees to several tens of thousands of rupees. Generally, the most onerous treatments are those involving the performance of *pūjā* by pandits (ritual officiants) or the purchase of precious stones. The price of these two types of treatments can range from a few hundred to several thousand rupees, depending on the nature of the *pūjā* or the type of stone prescribed. Conversely, tantric remedies are fairly cheap, including amulets (*jantar*) that only cost a few dozen rupees and treatments the astrologer carries out directly on the person's body. Thus, for *jhāṛnā-phūṅknā* (or *jhāṛ-phūk*), "sweeping and blowing away" bad influences afflicting the person, the client leaves a few rupees as a token of appreciation.

The cost of a remedy is seen as proportional to its long-lasting effects. From what astrologers say, *pūjā* and precious stones are long-term treatments—their power lasts several years or sometimes forever; whereas the power of *jantar*s and other tantric remedies is said to be limited—it runs out after several days or months, and then the remedies need to be replaced. *Pūjā* and precious stones are said to act on the cause, attacking the root of the problem and, hence, providing permanent relief. *Jantar*s and other tantric remedies, by contrast, only act at the level of the symptoms and are hence considered incapable of eliminating the true cause of the problem (harmful planetary influence in particular). Just like a sticking plaster, tantric remedies mainly provide momentary protection, but they do not ensure that the problem will not recur. Thus, *pūjā* and precious stones are said to have a *bhaviṣya-kālik* effect "that lasts into the future," while tantric remedies are said to have a *tātkālik*, "momentary," effect.

While everyone can afford tantric remedies, only well-off clients can opt for a *pūjā* and precious stones. As the astrologer D. N. Tiwari said, "Just as there are people who go to public hospitals and others who can afford to be treated at luxurious private clinics, for us [astrologers] there are people who can only afford tantric remedies, while others can buy precious stones and have large-scale *pūjā* performed." One nonetheless notes that there are few tantric remedies that are supposed to be extraordinarily efficacious and work unfailingly. In this case their cost, which is normally about ten rupees, can be as high as several thousands of rupees. Thus, for example, a teacher at the *jyotiṣa* department at Banaras Hindu University says he has a very effective *jantar*, "100% *sure*," which for the sum of five thousand rupees (an amount the practitioner claims he donates in its entirety to a Kālī temple) guarantees that a pregnant woman who has already had several girls will give birth to a son.

The proportionality between price and therapeutic efficacy also apply to different options the client can choose for each remedy. Thus, with regard to having a *pūjā* performed, astrologers differentiate between three hierarchically organized modalities: "ordinary" (*sādharan* or *sāmānya*), "average" (*madhyam*), and "superior" (*ucc*). The *pūjā* performed according to the "superior" method is considered far more efficacious than the *pūjā* performed according to the "ordinary" method, but it is also far more expensive (it can cost up to several tens of thousands of rupees). The "ordinary" *pūjā*, however is more economical but does not guarantee lasting results, and finally, the "average" *pūjā* is a compromise between "quality and price"; it guarantees good results, while remaining affordable.[8] Thus, when it comes to prescribing a *pūjā*, astrologers have to take two factors into account: the client's financial situation (*ārthik sthiti*) and the gravity of the problem. If the client is rich and the problem is very serious, the astrologer has no hesitation prescribing a *pūjā* of the "superior" type; if the problem is serious but the client cannot spend several thousands of rupees on a "superior" *pūjā*, he prescribes an "average" or "ordinary" *pūjā* depending on the client's financial capabilities. If, on the contrary, the problem is not serious, even if the client is affluent, an "ordinary" *pūjā* or less costly remedies are considered sufficient.

The price of a *pūjā* is essentially determined by the quantity of work carried out by the Brahmin officiants, called pandits, who perform the ritual and the cost of the materials. In the case of a *havan* (offering of oblations into the fire), in addition to the pandits' remunerations the price of the *pūjā* includes the cost of the wood, the cereals, dry fruit, ghee, or other substances that are thrown into the fire. With regard to the ritual work, the cost of a *pūjā* is calculated on the basis of the number of pandits hired and the number of days the *pūjā* takes. A pandit's salary for a day's work is about two hundred rupees. Hence for a *pūjā* that takes eleven days to complete, and is performed by four pandits, the cost will be 8,800 rupees. On this subject it is important to specify that the efficacy of a *pūjā* performed over eleven days by a single pandit is supposed to be exactly the same as a one-day *pūjā* performed by eleven pandits: the efficacy depends solely on the "quantity" of ritual work carried out. Some astrologers have a fixed team of pandits who work for them. Hence depending on the number of pandits available, the number of days over which the *pūjā* is performed varies, while other astrologers appoint pandits on a daily basis and call upon the number required for the quantity of work the *pūjā* demands.

The "quantity" of work required to perform a specific *pūjā* is defined by the number of *jap*s (murmured repetitions of the mantra) or sacred readings (*pāṭh*) repeated by the ritual specialists. Let us look at the case of the Mahāmṛtyuñjay *jap*, a *jap* dedicated to Śiva (in the form of Mṛtyuñjay), which is very commonly prescribed to treat serious illnesses, to protect from death, or to ward off the harmful effects in case of the untimely death (*akāl mṛtyu*) of a member of the family. Depending on the gravity of the problem, and the scope of the effect one seeks to obtain, astrologers prescribe the repetition of this *jap* various numbers of times. Thus, the astrologer Neelkanth Shastri explained:

> There is no fixed duration for the Mahāmṛtyuñjay *jap*, there is never a fixed duration for a *pūjā*. It all depends on the planet's wrath (*prakop*). If the planet is very angry, you have to recite a lot of *jap* . . . suppose someone is ill, we will have one hundred thousand *jap*s recited; if he is very ill, we will have four hundred thousand *jap*s recited; if he is about to die, it will be four million *jap*s, and so on . . . it depends on the planets. For one person it can last five days, for another a month and a half, or for yet another, three months.

The devotional pamphlet containing the ritual instructions for performing the Mahāmṛtyuñjay *jap* indicates the number of times this *jap* must be repeated depending on the type of result desired:

> If a country is in danger and is under attack from enemies, if there is an epidemic in a country, in these cases, one should have ten million Mahāmṛtyuñjay *jap*s recited.
>
> If you're sick, if you see ill omens in your dreams, for good results you should have 125,000 Mahāmṛtyuñjay *jap*s recited.
>
> In case of untimely death (*akāl mṛtyu*), because of fire, drowning, or a snake bite, to remove [the possibility of being afflicted by the dead person's ghost] you should have ten thousand Mahāmṛtyuñjay *jap*s recited.
>
> If you have bad news that concerns you or someone in your family, or one of your friends, if you are going on a journey, you must have one thousand Mahāmṛtyuñjay *jap*s recited.

Clearly, the number of *jap*s is proportional to the gravity of the problem and the scope of the effect one seeks to obtain—fighting an epidemic, curing a sick person, warding off the ill effects of a premature death, and so forth. This determines the amount of work to be carried out by the ritual specialists, and consequently the cost of the *pūjā*.[9]

With regard to stones, the price is also seen as proportional to the efficacy: "the price (*qimat*) varies according to the *rays*, the more the number of *rays*, the higher the price (*iskī rays jitnī baṛhegī utnī qimat bhī baṛhegī*) . . . ," the astrologer B. P. Mehrotra explained to a client.

To start with, the price of a stone varies according to the number of carats (*ratti*). In astrologers' prescriptions, the number of carats reflects the gravity of the client's planetary situation: a higher number of carats is said to increase the number of planetary rays the stone can absorb, which gives it its therapeutic efficacy. The cost of a stone also varies depending on its authenticity, transparency, and luminosity. Just like the number of carats, these qualities are supposed to increase the stone's ability to absorb planetary rays and hence enhance its therapeutic power. Stones are divided into two categories: *ratna*s, precious stones, more expensive, and *uparatna*s, semi-precious stones, which are cheaper. For each gem—for example, the ruby (*māṇikya*), the gemstone that represents the Sun and costs several thousand rupees—there exists a cheaper semi-precious substitute, in this case *saugandhik* ("fragrant," spinel), *tāmṛā* ("coppery," grenat), or the *maisūrī māṇikya* ("Mysore ruby," or "star ruby" in English), and so on, that only costs a few hundred rupees. To explain the difference between an "authentic precious stone" (*aslī ratna*) and a "semi-precious stone" (*uparatna*) an astrologer compared the two types of stone to natural sunlight and artificial light, respectively: "Wearing a semi-precious stone instead of a precious stone is like walking in the dark lighting the path with an electric torch, instead of walking in daylight in the sunshine." Semi-precious stones are thus helpful, but this assistance is much weaker than that provided by precious stones. Clients hence seek strategies to obtain maximum results for their spending capacity. One of the astrologer B. G. Bhaduri's clients explained that as he could only afford a "crumb" of a diamond (Venus's stone), one millimeter in diameter, the ring he had made held the tiny diamond, and next to it a large American diamond (semi-precious substitute for a diamond) "to increase the power" of the fragment of authentic diamond.

From the prescriptions written by astrologers one notes that the cheapest precious stones are always prescribed for a limited period, whereas the more "precious" (*kīmatī, mūlyavān*) stones are prescribed without a specific therapeutic duration. Thus, stones like the amethyst (for Saturn), the Zircon (for Rāhu), and the chrysoberyl (for Ketu) that each cost a few hundred rupees are prescribed for a few years at most, after which they must be replaced. In contrast, stones like the diamond (for Venus), the ruby (for the Sun), the sapphire (for Saturn), the emerald (for Mercury), and the yellow topaz (for Jupiter) that cost between several thousand and several tens of thousands of rupees, are stones that are supposed to never lose their efficacy and are hence generally prescribed "lifelong" (*ājīvan*).[10]

Astrologers we worked with only prescribe the stones and they are not concerned with where the client gets them, just as a doctor is not involved in the choice of pharmacy where the patient chooses to buy medicine. Normally, after receiving the prescription for a specific stone from the astrologer, the client goes to any jewelry shop (the one his family frequents, or a neighborhood one).[11] Once he has bought the stone, he goes back to the astrologer to check the authenticity of the stone, whether the price he paid corresponds to the quality, and to know if it has any defects (*doṣ*).[12]

While the cost of a remedy is generally an indicator of its therapeutic power, there are nonetheless remedies prescribed by astrologers that are not evaluated in monetary terms, as they are the fruit of the client's devotional efforts. For these remedies, the quantitative evaluation of their efficacy is not expressed in terms of money but in terms of time: the more time the person dedicates to the devotional effort, the greater the benefits. Thus, when an astrologer prescribes to take *darśan* (vision) of a God on a particular day of the week, for example, Hanumān on Saturday, or Bhairav on Sunday, he specifies the regimen length according to the benefits the client seeks to obtain. The efficacy of *darśan* may become apparent only after several months. After this "running-in" period (that varies depending on the God and the astrologer's opinion) the benefits of the treatment increase with time: thus two or three years of weekly *darśan* guarantees far better results than eight to ten months (in both cases, the *darśan* must not be interrupted, otherwise the person has to start again from the beginning). This is also the case of ritual fasting (*vrat*), the power of which is supposed to vary according to the period of observance.

The money/time equation is explicitly expressed in the case of the repetition of prayers (*jap*, *pāṭh*): the astrologer's client can choose to spend money and have the prayers recited by ritual specialists, or "spend" time and recite them himself. In both cases the efficacy is said to be the same—what counts is the number of times the prayer is repeated.[13] In one case the client sacrifices his money, while in the other he sacrifices hours and days of his own time. From what the astrologers say, few clients today are ready to invest in a prolonged devotional effort. They are increasingly rushed and prefer to spend money rather than their time.

By creating a relationship of proportionality between monetary value, the duration of the devotional act, and efficacy, astrologers make therapeutic power into an objective and quantifiable quality. By using several quantitative parameters, such as the number of *japs*, the number of carats, the number of pandits employed, or the number of hours, astrologers "calculate" the power of a remedy and prescribe a dosage that corresponds to the client's economic situation and the gravity of the problem to be addressed. The "objective" measurement of therapeutic power hence allows astrologers to adapt remedies to the "subjectivity" of individual cases. The remedy must be appropriate for the clients and accessible to them, it must take into account their wealth, poverty, difficulties, or availability. On this subject, we have shown elsewhere (Guenzi 2005) that some ritual treatments carried out to relieve a person from harmful planetary influences are explicitly based on a practice of measurement where the "dose" of the treatment is defined so as to correspond to the bodily constitution of the person. This is the case, for example, in the "gift of the balance" (*tulā dān*), where the amount of gifts offered is equivalent to the person's weight. In the same manner in the "gift of the shadow" (*chāyā dān*) the quantity of oil offered must be proportional to the size of the face.

After shedding light on the "quantitative" aspect of therapeutic efficacy, as it appears in astrologers' discourses and practices, let us now consider the question of the qualitative characterization of efficacy.

Gods and Planets

In Banaras, to control planetary influence, worshiping the gods is seen as far more effective than any form of devotion addressed directly to the planets. A power hierarchy marks the relationship between the Gods and the planets. According to astrologers, just as a minister is subordinate to a king, an officer to the army chief, a secretary to a president, or a son to a father, the planets are subordinate to the gods. For this reason they prescribe worshiping the major Gods of the Hindu pantheon rather than the planetary deities: "If you are a mere soldier and you are beaten by four or five officers," explained the astrologer Neelkanth Shastri, referring to a person afflicted by four or five planets, "you can try to fight the officers, but it is better for you to go directly to the army chief to ask for his help."

The performance of rituals aimed at pacifying the planets is thus rarely prescribed. Rather than *grahaśāntis*, rituals to appease planets that are described in great detail in medieval texts,[14] or planetary offerings (*grahadān*), astrologers prescribe the worship of gods like Śiva, Viṣṇu, Durgā, Hanumān, Bhairav, and others, whose power (*śakti*), authority (*adhikār*), and strength (*bal*) are supposed to be very effective in controlling planetary influence. Planetary worship is not only considered less effective and less powerful but often also less auspicious (*śubh*) than a ritual dedicated to the "satisfaction" (*prasannatā*) of a God. Nonetheless, in this regard, we should clearly distinguish between the *navagraha*s, the "nine planetary deities" as a group, and the planets taken individually. As a group, the *navagraha*s are beneficial and auspicious deities, and invoking them is supposed to repel the obstacles and adversities that could prevent the successful outcome of a ritual. For this reason, to perform most domestic or life-cycle rituals (*upanayana, vivāha*, etc.) and when offering oblations into the fire (*yajña, havan*), the *navagraha*s are generally invoked at the beginning, straight after paying homage to Gaṇeśa.[15] In addition, some astrologers occasionally prescribe *yajña* or *havan* dedicated to this group of deities to support the client's success in a particular area. As indicated in the *Yājñavalkyasmṛti*, "one desirous of prosperity, to remove evil and calamities, of rainfall (for crops), long life, bodily health and one desirous of performing magic rites against enemies and others should perform a sacrifice (*yajña*) to the nine planetary deities."[16] Hence the *navagraha*s are not seen as planets whose malefic influence has to be pacified, but auspicious deities who remove obstacles and help the person accomplish his or her desires. Nevertheless, they play a somewhat marginal role in astrological discourse and we will not pay too much attention to them.

The status of the harmful planets we dealt with in the previous chapter—Saturn, Mars, Rāhu, and Ketu—is quite different: these inauspicious planets are not worshiped through the offering of oblations into the fire (*yajña*), and many precautions are taken when carrying out any form of direct appeasement. In particular, they should not be worshiped inside the house and astrologers strongly discourage this type of practice that may lead to dangerous and inauspicious effects.

Astrologers' "prescriptions" generally recommend performing three types of *pūjā*: offering of oblations into the fire (*havan*, *yajña*), murmured repetition of sacred formulae with the help of a rosary (*jap*), and reading prayers aloud (*pāṭh*). While the first type of ritual—*havan*, *yajña*—always requires the assistance of Brahmin professional ritualists (*paṇḍit*), *jap*s and *pāṭh*s can be recited either by pandits, or individually by the devotees themselves. In addition, other devotional practices like regular *darśan* (vision) of a certain God, or observing a ritual fast (*vrat*), can be prescribed for a certain number of months.

But what relationship do astrologers establish between a problem caused by a planet and worshiping a particular God or Goddess? How do they decide which of them to honor for the different planetary afflictions the client suffers? When questioned on the relationship between the various planets and the multiplicity of gods in the Hindu pantheon, some astrologers quote a classification described in canonical Sanskrit treatises that identifies a "supervisory deity" (*adhiṣṭhātrī devatā*) of Vedic origin for each planet:

Sūrya (Sun) = Agni
Candramā (Moon) = Varuṇa
Maṅgal (Mars) = Skanda
Budh (Mercury) = Viṣṇu
Bṛhaspati (Jupiter) = Brahma
Śukr (Venus) = Indrāṇī[17]
Śani (Saturn) = Yama
Rāhu and Ketu = Rudra

This classification, which establishes semantic affinities between the planets and the Vedic deities, is nonetheless completely irrelevant when astrologers have to make a pragmatic decision regarding which deity to worship for a particular planetary problem. From our observations, the astrologer's choice of the *pūjā* to be performed is generally based on the type of problem the client has and the areas of intervention attributed to each God. Thus, for example, when the problem is related to marriage, particularly for unmarried girls, the *pūjā* recommended is generally the one to Viṣṇu, often accompanied by a *pūjā* to Durgā *aparājitā* (the unvanquished); in the case of health problems, danger of death, or to obtain a male descendant, it is the *pūjā* to Mahāmṛtyuñjay; to resolve any kind of conflict, win legal cases, for professional difficulties, or any kind of difficulty that one attributes to an act by an "enemy," the *pūjā* to Baglāmukhī (a form of the Goddess) is prescribed; for mental disorders, one goes to Narasiṃha;[18] and so on. The appropriate *pūjā* is hence chosen depending on the client's problem and in accordance with the specific powers attributed to the different gods, rather than on the basis of the planetary configuration.

According to the astrologer Neelkanth Shastri, it is not always possible to attribute responsibility for a problem to "one" or "two" planets, sometimes because it is provoked by a complex astral combination, sometimes because a large number of clients do not have a complete or correct horoscope. For this reason, performing *pūjā* according to the type of problem is a means of "eliminating (*kāṭnā*) obstacles (*vighn*) created by all kinds of 'unidentified planets' (*anirṇīt graha*)." However, if the malefic influence of a specific planet seems particularly patent to the astrologer, the *pūjā* to the God or Goddess is followed by the repetition of a *jap* dedicated to the planet in question (*Maṅgal-jap*, *Rāhu-jap*, etc.).

Besides the aforementioned forms of *pūjā*, astrologers may prescribe devotional forms of worship resting on a crucial connection between the Gods and the planets. In Banaras, as elsewhere in India, a privileged relationship links Hanumān to Śani, and Kāl Bhairav to Rāhu and Ketu. Hanumān, the God of physical power (*bal*, *śakti*), and Bhairav, the Kotwal ("policeman-magistrate")—respectively Viṣṇu's (in the form of Rām) and Śiva's assistants—are the Gods the Hindus in Banaras invoke in order to "physically" force the malefic planets to submit to the divine order.[19] Hanumān and Bhairav—the latter particularly in the forms of Kāl Bhairav and Baṭuk Bhairav—are supposed to "destroy" (*naṣṭ karnā*), "cut" (*kaṭnā*), and "paralyze" (*stambhit karnā*) the malefic planetary hold. Hence to reduce Śani, Rāhu, and Ketu's harmful influence, astrologers advise clients to go for *darśan* (vision) to the temples dedicated to these gods for a certain number of months, or to recite *pāṭh*s (sacred readings)—such as the *Hanumān cālīsā* or *Bajraṅg bān pāṭh* for Hanumān or the "1,008 names of Bhairav" for Bhairav—a certain number of times.

While these devotional practices and the *pūjā* performed by the ritual specialists address the God's *śakti*, in tantric types of treatment it is the astrologer's powers that are mobilized.

Tantric Remedies and the Astrologer's *Siddhi*

Tantric treatments are based on the idea that the astrologer is endowed with special powers (*siddhi*) obtained as a result of an initiation (*dīkṣā*) from a guru and after accomplishing a series of tantric "realization" (*sādhana*) practices.[20] Because of his *siddhi*s, the astrologer is able to prepare "powerful" (*śaktiśālī, prabhāvśālī*) remedies, or to heal people afflicted by planetary influence through therapeutic gestures.

The most common tantric remedy is the *jantar*, made of *Betula utilis* birch leaf (*bhojpātr*) or, more frequently today, a piece of paper on which the astrologer draws a ritual diagram (*yantra*, hence the name *jantar*) or a sacred formula (*mantra*).[21]

To write a mantra or draw a *yantra* the astrologer uses a special ink (*syāhī*) made of a mixture of ingredients: saffron (*kesar*), musk (*kastūrī*), *kuṃkum* (red powder made of curcuma and lime), lac dye (*alatā*), *goracanā* (lit., "cow's pigment": a yellow powder made from cow's bile), sandalwood (*candan*), and *aṣṭhagandh* (a mixture of eight perfumed dyes). This mixture can vary from one astrologer to another, as can the wood used for the pen—pomegranate (*ānār*), sandalwood (*candan*), *tulsī* (Indian basil), or jasmine (*jūhī*).

Each *jantar* is dedicated to a deity who is geometrically represented by a *yantra* and phonically represented by a mantra: each *jantar* is hence supposed to contain the *śakti* of the deity it is dedicated to, in a condensed form. There are also *jantar*s dedicated to the planets but just as astrologers prefer to prescribe *pūjā* to the Gods rather than the planets, they rarely prescribe *jantar*s for the planets.

To prepare a *jantar* the astrologer draws a ritual diagram or writes a mantra on a piece of paper or a birch leaf, as he softly murmurs (or mentally recites) the *bīj* mantra ("seed mantra," concise mantra) corresponding to the ritual diagram (or the mantra) that is outlined (or written).[22] Reciting the mantra orally (or mentally) is supposed to infuse the written diagram or mantra with "vital breath" and it is called the "installation of life-breath" (*prāṇa pratiṣṭhā*) or "purification" (*śodhan*).

Astrologers emphasize that this apparently simple gesture is the result of countless hours of work, during which each *yantra* (or mantra) has been written tens of thousands of times, and every mantra recited millions of times, before it can be effectively employed as a *jantar*. This work has to be performed anew for every type of *jantar* (some astrologers say they possess the *siddhi* to create at least about a hundred different types of *jantar*s). Repeatedly reciting mantras aloud (*jap*) and the written transcription of mantras and *yantra*s is said to endow the astrologer with that particular *jantar*'s *siddhi* (*jantar kī siddhi*). By doing this, the astrologer is supposed to "awaken" (*jāgānā*) a certain mantra or *yantra*, which thus acts efficaciously on the person who wears it.

As we saw for the other remedies, in the case of *jantar*s, too, efficacy is measured in quantitative terms: the *jantar*'s power is proportional to the number of times the astrologer has transcribed the *yantra* or mantra, and the number of times he has recited the mantra. Thus, a *yantra* drawn 122,000 times is more effective than a yantra drawn "only" 10,000 times; a mantra recited 2,400,000 is more effective than a mantra recited 100,000 times. For this reason a client justified his mistrust of *jantar*s, stating, "It is impossible to know 'how much' *siddhi* it contains, how much effort (*mehanat*) went into it . . . if the astrologer has spent a lot of time on it, the *jantar* will work (*phāydā degā*), but otherwise . . . how does one know how much *siddhi* a *jantar* contains?"

*Jantar*s are supposed to be effective through physical contact and can be used in several manners: they can be worn as an amulet, burned, ingested, or inserted into an object. The way in which the *jantar* is used depends on its purpose: thus "amulets to be worn" (*pahanne vālā jantar*) are generally used to make the person stronger (physically, psychologically or financially); *jantar*s "to be burned" (*jalāne vālā*) are meant to ward off bad influences (ghostly attacks, evil eye, etc.); although they are rarely used by astrologers, *jantar*s "to be drunk" (*pine vālā*) are prescribed as medicines for health problems;[23] *jantar*s "to be inserted" (*dabāne vālā*)—into clothes, under a cushion, and so forth, are used to manipulate a person, without him or her realizing it. For example, to stop someone from drinking, to bring a premarital or extra-conjugal relationship to an end, to bring someone who has run away back home, and so on.

The most common type of *jantar* is the one to be worn on the body, inside an amulet. Amulets are small "protective boxes" (*kavac, varm*, "armor") made of copper containing a *jantar* that people wear around their necks, their arms (right for men, left for women), or waist (particularly for children). By metonymy, amulets are also called *jantar* even if sometimes, particularly in cases of health problems, instead of a *jantar* they contain a root (*mūl*) or herb (*jaṛī*). An amulet is supposed to protect (*rakṣā karnā*) the person who wears it from any harmful influence by reinforcing his *śakti* (energy) and his willpower (*ātmabal, manobal*).

In addition to *jantar*s, astrologers use other tantric therapeutic techniques, such as "sweeping-blowing away" (*jhāṛnā-phūknā*, casting out), a treatment that often accompanies the prescription of a *jantar*. The *jhāṛnā-phūknā* can be carried out in two ways: by running a peacock feather duster around the person's body, or by massaging his forehead, holding his wrist in the hands. In both cases, while he is carrying out the treatment the astrologer recites a mantra for which he possesses the *siddhi*. In the first case, the duster is supposed to "sweep away" (*jhāṛnā*) any harmful influence; in the second, the pressure of the astrologer's hands on the person's body is supposed to "instill/breathe" (*phūknā*) the power of the mantra into the body, thus reinforcing the person's *śakti* and willpower.

While the use of *jantar*s and the performance of *jhāṛnā-phūknā* are very common among astrologers, there are also tantric "specialties" that vary from one astrologer to another, and are used for different purposes: a copper tray onto which a mantra has been "blown" is applied to the back of a person who has been bitten by a dog, in order to absorb any poison that may have been injected into his body; a clay jar bearing the inscription of a *yantra* on the outside and a mantra on the inside is used to draw people who have run away back to their homes; a mixture of *sindūr* and fish bile thus helps a woman recover her husband who has run off with a mistress; a block of salt mixed with cumin is used to resolve family disputes, and so forth. Each astrologer thus has his own "tantric recipes."

"Vedic" and "Tantric" Methods

When faced with a client who, for example, is worried about the outcome of a legal procedure he is involved in, the astrologer can choose to have a *baglāmukhī pūjā* performed by ritual specialists, or to give him a *baglāmukhī jantar*. Both these treatments resort to Baglāmukhī's *śakti*. This Goddess is a form of Durgā invoked to resolve conflicts and defeat enemies; similarly, for a client who has to undergo an operation the astrologer may prescribe a *pūjā* dedicated to Mahāmṛtyuñjay or give him a *mahāmṛtyuñjay jantar*, and so on. These two ways of proceeding are seen as the expression of two different "ritual methods" (*ṛti, paddhati*): respectively, the "Vedic method" (*vaidik ṛti, vaidik paddhati*) and the "tantric method" (*tāntrik ṛti, tāntrik paddhati*).[24] The "Vedic method" consists of having *havan*s, *jap*s, and *pāṭh*s performed by Brahmin ritual officiants, while the "tantric method" consists in having *jantar*s and other tantric remedies prepared by the astrologer. Both ritual methods are employed to satisfy clients' wishes, but they have very different qualities and are used in different contexts.

To start with, as we saw, the "Vedic method" is expensive and hence limited to a well-off clientele, whereas the "tantric method" is more economical and accessible to everyone. Thus, for example, an "ordinary" *pūjā* for Baglāmukhī costs five thousand rupees (twelve days of work for two ritual specialists), while a *baglāmukhī jantar* only costs about ten rupees.

According to astrologers the effects of a long and laborious "Vedic" treatment are visible in the long term and bring permanent benefits, while treatments prepared following the tantric method provide immediate relief and work effectively at the level of symptoms. On this subject, the astrologer Shree Kanth Shastri used to say that tantric remedies are better suited than *pūjā* to the demands of modern life as the people of today are always in a hurry and want remedies that are immediately accessible and demand no effort.[25]

Another feature that differentiates the "Vedic method" from the "tantric method" is that the former is always used for beneficial purposes, while the latter can also be used for harmful and malefic purposes. In general, the "Vedic method" is used to create well-being, to protect a person's health, ensure longevity, enhance professional success, or promote the success of a marriage. Tantric remedies, on the other hand, also have a destructive potential: they are used for beneficial purposes when they serve to support a person or eliminate obstacles and conflicts, but they can also be used for the opposite reasons when their aim is, for example, to undermine a family's happiness, weaken a person's health, or alter the way a girl thinks.

The astrologers we worked with say they follow only the "virtuous path" (*sātvik mārg*) of tantra, never employing their *siddhi* for malefic purposes. In this respect they seek to differentiate themselves from practitioners called *tantr-mantr*s, who, on the contrary, are believed to abuse their tantric powers to bewitch victims with no moral concerns. Indeed, from everything we observed, astrologers use tantric treatments either for therapeutic reasons, or to correct *adharmik*, "unrighteous," behavior: thus, when a man betrays his wife, the astrologer may give her a *jantar* to be placed under her husband's cushion to make him break off the relationship with his mistress; when a daughter runs away from home with a boy, the astrologer gives the parents a *jantar* to make her return, and so on.

The "tantric method" is supposed to work by physical contact, independently of the will or consent of the person who receives the treatment: the person in question just has to be in contact with the tantric remedy, by one means or another, to feel its effects. Rituals performed according to the "Vedic method," on the contrary, do not require physical proximity—the person for whom the ritual is performed may be in America or Australia; the only condition is that the *saṅkalp*, or "declaration of purpose," must be in his name[26]—but in this case, the person for whom the ritual is performed has to be spiritually involved in terms of his or her *śrāddh*, "faith."

The third category of remedies we are going to look at, precious stones, is also supposed to work by physical contact. Planetary gems, like tantric remedies, have a "local" impact by contact with the person's body, while *pūjā* functions at a macrocosmic and global level. Nonetheless, from another viewpoint, the therapeutic power of stones resembles that of a *pūjā* (performed by ritual specialists), in that they are said to have a "long-term" effect and only a well-off clientele can afford them. As we shall see, the therapeutic distinctiveness of precious stones lies in their supposed "natural" power associated with their biochemical and magnetic properties.

The Power of Stones: Rays and Radiations

While tantric treatments or *pūjā* can be prescribed by ritual specialists other than astrologers, "gem therapy" (*ratna cikitsā*) is a field of competence specific to astrologers. Each planet is associated with a gemstone, as shown in table 6.[27] In Banaras, and more generally in India, precious stones are rarely worn as mere items of jewelry for purely decorative and aesthetic reasons. Gemstones are supposed to have an impact on the body and, just as one does not take a medicine randomly without knowing what effects it has, one does not wear a gemstone without knowing its therapeutic functions.[28]

Table 6. Correlation between Planets and Gemstones

Planet	**Gemstone**
Sun	Ruby (*māṇikya*)
Moon	Pearl (*motī*)
Mars	Coral (*mūṅgā*)
Mercury	Emerald (*pannā*)
Jupiter	Topaz (*pukharāj*)
Venus	Diamond (*hīrā*)
Saturn	Sapphire (*nīlam*) Amethyst (*jāmuniyā*)
Rāhu	Garnet hessonite (*gomed*)
Ketu	Cat's eye (*lahasuniyā*)

Nonetheless, unlike medicines and just like all jewelry, wearing one or several gemstone rings is a clear sign of distinction in the Bourdieusian sense of the term. It symbolizes the person's belonging to the well-off section of the population that regularly consults astrologers and the possession of sufficient means to buy gemstones set in silver or gold rings. Gemstone rings are an investment of hundreds, thousands, or even tens of thousands of rupees and hence differentiate the middle and upper classes of Banaras society from the lower classes who do not wear this type of remedy-ornament.

In Banaras one notes that it is mainly men, between the ages of twenty-five and fifty to sixty, who wear this type of ring. According to the Brahmanical tradition this period of life corresponds to the existential phase (*āśrama*) of *gṛhastha*, "householder," when men are supposed to fulfill major responsibilities toward society and the family. The gemstone rings that glitter on the fingers of Banaras's businessmen, politicians, civil servants, academics, entrepreneurs, lawyers, or doctors are a means to display professional and family responsibilities.

The topaz is highly indicative of this. By intensifying Jupiter's beneficial influence, this gemstone is said to "increase decision-making abilities" (*nirṇay lene kī kṣamatā baṛhānā*) and is generally prescribed to adult men who have professional and family responsibilities. Topaz is said to promote success in business, progress in a person's career, to reinforce intellectual potential and control over childrens' education, goals toward which the "modern" *gṛhastha* of Banaras's upper middle and upper class aspires. However, this gemstone is so costly that, more than a means of attaining professional success, the topaz is a symbol of having attained it. This transpires in the words the astrologer Shree Kanth Shastri addressed to a young married man who has two children. As long as he was unemployed this "householder" could not display a topaz, the symbol of social success:

> You need a white topaz (*saphed pukharāj*) for your situation to improve, but as you're unemployed for the moment, it doesn't make any sense to tell you about the white topaz . . . you won't be able to buy it, as it will cost you 4,000–5,000 rupees.[29] So for the time being, forget about it. Start by wearing an amethyst [gemstone for Saturn] that will cost you 225–250 rupees and it will be very beneficial (*bahut lābh milegā*) . . . then, in two and a half years, when your favorable period begins, you will be able to do business, you will have money, and at that time you will have the means to buy yourself a white topaz.

When worn by women, stones have a different connotation, particularly when the women are not employed, as is often the case in Banaras. Gemstone rings on the hand of a woman are generally not seen as an indication of responsibilities or a mark of distinction. On the contrary they can be seen as the sign of a "problem" the woman is facing: for example, difficulty with her marriage, children, or an illness. As this type of problem is often interpreted as a "defect/flaw" (*doṣ*) in the woman, not only do women wear fewer gemstones than men but above all they do not tend to display them.[30] Women wear them more often as a necklace beneath clothes, rather than as rings, so they can benefit from the positive effects of the stones without revealing to others the problems they may be experiencing.[31]

Whether for a man, an adult woman, or a child, the astrologer indicates the "dosage" in his prescription for gemstones. This includes the number of carats, the *muhūrta* (appropriate time) when the stone should be worn for the first time, and where it should be worn on the body. "Sapphire, ten carats, Saturday, right hand, middle finger," for example.

The power is defined depending on the person's planetary situation, the *muhūrta* is established depending on the day of the week that corresponds to the planet for which the gemstone is prescribed: Monday for pearls (Moon), Tuesday for coral (Mars), and so on.[32] The position, on the finger, at the neck, at the waist, or on the arm, generally depends on the person's preference; but concerning the hand or the arm, it is always the right for men and the left for women.

Before the person wears a gemstone for the first time, one should perform *prāṇa pratiṣṭhā* ("installation of life-breath" or consecration). This ritual, traditionally performed for divine images, serves to call upon the deity to enter into the image (*mūrti*) so that the image becomes the deity itself.[33] In this case, the gemstone is a sort of "mini-*mūrti*" (a *mūrti* made, in fact, of "stone") into which the vital principle must be invited in order to make it effective. To perform a gemstone's *prāṇa pratiṣṭhā*, the astrologer Neelkanth Shastri immerses the gemstone in a liquid called *pañcāmṛta* (mixture of five nectars) that consists of Ganges water, milk, curd, honey, and ghee (clarified butter), to which he adds sandalwood powder and flowers. Touching the gemstone with a finger, he mentally recites the *bīj* mantra ("seed-mantra," or concise mantra) that corresponds to the planet for which the gemstone is to be worn, and he utters the following words: "I am going to have this person . . . [stating the person's name] wear this ring: may her desires (*abhiṣṭhī*) be pure (*śuddh*) and may the purpose of wearing this ring be accomplished." Otherwise, the person who is to wear the gemstone ring can perform a purification (*śodhan*) ritual himself: before wearing the gemstone, the person must immerse it in Ganges water mixed with milk and recite the *bīj* mantra of the planet that corresponds to the gemstone. The astrologer's prescriptions regarding the time and appropriate place to wear a gemstone and the performance of *prāṇa pratiṣṭhā* are supposed to increase the gemstone's efficacy.

The gemstone's power does not only affect the person who wears it but may also have an impact on his entourage. In the chapter "Shared Destinies," we saw that the planetary configurations in a person's horoscope can affect all those close to him. For this reason, an astrologer may, for example, prescribe a coral to protect a man from the harmful influence of Mars emanating from his wife's horoscope. And just as the effect of a horoscope's planetary configurations is supposed to spread within a family, similarly, the effect of a gemstone worn by one person may be felt by all those close to him. Astrologers can hence prescribe a gemstone for a person so that her spouse, son, or brother can benefit from its effects. Thus, a woman can wear a gemstone to increase her husband's income. This was the case of a woman wearing a cat's eye (*lahasuniyā*), Ketu's gemstone, around her neck. She described its effects to the astrologer in the following manner:

> When I started wearing this cat's eye, I noticed that his [her husband's] income was fairly stable: we had enough to live and slowly we were able to save some money. But now, with the children's problems, all the money has been spent and we have nothing left, we've even had to borrow money. So, at the beginning *lahasuniyā* was very effective (*usse bahut lābh milā*), but I've been wearing it for a few years now . . .[34]

As mentioned earlier, topaz, often worn by men, is supposed to reinforce the father's authority over his children. Thus, a scientist at Banaras Hindu University was wearing a ring with a topaz to improve his son's educational performance:

> Until class seven, my son was a brilliant student; he was always among the top four students of his class . . . But when he went into class eight, the first term was okay, but in the second term, the situation began to deteriorate, he didn't want to study . . . so I started wearing the topaz.
>
> A few years earlier, I had shown his horoscope to an astrologer who had told me he would have problems studying when he reached the age of twelve . . . I thought this phase was approaching, that it was a little earlier than what the horoscope said, but the phase was approaching . . . So, I decided to wear the topaz. According to the fifth house of my horoscope [the house of children], you can see that I have very little influence over my son, I have no control over him . . . but since I started wearing the topaz, his studies are better and improving, he has progressed a lot, and there is a *mental feeling* between us . . .

Hence the topaz supports this man in his role as a father, which has repercussions on his son's studies. When asked about the reasons why he had decided to wear a gemstone himself, rather than having his son wear it for his studies, he explained:

> According to astrology, your own horoscope can tell you the problems experienced by your ancestors, your father, your mother, your brothers and sisters, your friends . . . so if one of them is affected by a problem, it is also your problem to some extent. So, you can wonder whether making an effort yourself won't help the others too. If we reinforce ourselves, we can resolve other people's problems too. This is how my son's studies improved—I was too weak at that time, and the topaz made me stronger.

The gemstones are divided into two categories, according to their action: those that protect from the influence of malefic planets and those that strengthen the influence of benefic planets. Thus, when he looks at a horoscope, an astrologer has the choice of two strategies: "Either you enhance what is already good" (*baṛhiyā ko aur baṛhiyā kar do*), explained an astrologer, "or you set properly what is bad" (*kharāb ko ṭhīk kar do*). In the first case the emphasis is on "strengthening" the person internally—the English word *empowerment* is often used in this context—in the second case, the focus is on "protection" from external influences. These approaches are not mutually exclusive though, as any kind of external protection implies strengthening the person, just as strengthening the person provides protection from external influences. For clients who can afford it astrologers use both strategies simultaneously: they prescribe a basic "strengthening" gemstone (often to be worn lifelong) depending on the benefic planet located in the first house (*lagna*) of the horoscope at the time of birth and, in addition, they have the person wear one or several other "protective" gemstones that help them live through unfavorable planetary periods. These have to be changed once the planetary period ends; for example, a garnet should be removed once Rāhu *mahādaśā* ends, or a cat's eye once Ketu's *antardaśā* ends.

"Stones increase the benefic aspects by absorbing rays of the planets and flowing them into the human body." This sentence in English is quoted in the printed computer-calculated horoscope the astrologer Praveen Issar distributes to her clients under the name "Shubham Computer Astrologers" in Banaras. Stones for the malefic planets are said to "reduce" (*ghaṭānā*) the quantity of planetary rays the person absorbs, while stones for the benefic planets are supposed to "increase" (*baṛhānā*) the quantity of rays.

In both cases, the gemstones "set" the quantity of rays the body needs, by expelling the excess and absorbing those that are lacking.

To transmit the rays to the person's body the stones must touch the body: the finger, the neck, the arm, the waist, depending on where one wears the stone. Gemstones worn in rings are considered the most effective as they are directly exposed to "planetary light," while gemstones worn on necklaces, tied to the arm or the waist, are supposed to be less effective as they are covered by clothing. For this reason, some astrologers prescribe a higher number of carats when the person wears the stone beneath his clothing. Thus, as an example, nine carats if the stone is worn set in a ring, twelve if it is tied around the arm.

The stone must remain whole. In a pearl necklace, for example, the hole through which the string passes is said to disperse the planetary rays. When stones are set in rings, they are cone shaped with the tip touching the finger. Astrologers explain that the upper, almost flat surface serves to capture a maximum number of planetary rays, while the tip of the cone, in contact with the finger, transmits the quantity of rays the person needs in small doses, like "drops." As the stone rubs against the pores of the skin, the body absorbs the rays; blood circulation is then supposed to ensure the distribution of the rays to the different parts of the body. Some astrologers relate this explanation to the Ayurvedic medical system, claiming that the planetary rays the stones transmit to the body help recreate the balance between the three humors (*tridoṣa*)—wind, bile, and phlegm—when their harmony is perturbed by the planets. To describe the principle behind the gemstone's efficacy, other astrologers use categories like "magnetic fields" created by the planets and captured by the stones, "electrochemical reactions" between the stone and the body, the metabolism of planetary radiations, and so forth. Yet others explain the efficacy of stones by natural metaphors, comparing them with a magnifying glass: as the rays of the sun are concentrated through a magnifying glass and can create a fire, planetary rays passing through gemstones can have surprising effects on the human body.

These kinds of "physical" explanations provided by astrologers regarding the healing power of gemstones are shared not only by most of their clients but also by many academics from the science departments at Banaras Hindu University, who themselves wear gemstones on their fingers. We interviewed a number of researchers and professors at the Geophysics

Department at Banaras Hindu University, to understand how they explained the power of precious stones. A reader at the aforementioned department explained the efficacy of the topaz (*pukharāj*) he wears on his finger in the following manner (in English):

> We wear this [*pukharāj*] because whatever radiation we are getting from Jupiter, that radiation will get absorbed by the body and the *pukharāj* will enhance it. We want to increase the absorption of this radiation—that's why we wear it. Radiations govern the whole metabolic system and circulation of the body. For example, when a child is born, whatever radiation it gets exposed to, his body will absorb that radiation, but for instance if someone has gone to the other side of the celestial globe, it would not get exposed and the body will not get enough that particular radiation. If we want to enhance that particular radiation, there are numbers of stones that have been made for this and by wearing this it really helps to improve this radiation.

Similarly, a colleague from the same department explains:

> Look, I am also wearing topaz for Bṛhaspati (Jupiter) that is our Guru[35] . . . when Guru is weak then it is said that you should wear this. Bṛhaspati controls your whole brain. If your Guru is good, then you will progress a lot and if your Guru is not very good then it will affect your progress and your progress will be very slow. In order to make it better or stronger there is the *ratna cikitsā* (gemstones therapy) . . . it helps for the improvement . . . This stone absorbs the rays from Bṛhaspati and supplies it to your body . . . The influence on the human body of the magnetic, electromagnetic and gravitational field is up to a greater extent, because ¾ part of our body is liquid . . . that's why the planetary radiations affect our body to a greater extent and that's why we use stones . . .

The natural power of stones is normally designated by the English term *power* (commonly used in Hindi to designate electricity). When referring to a gemstone, people may say, "It should have more *power*" (*aur power cahiye*), thus meaning that it should have a higher number of carats. In Banaras astrologers rarely prescribe a gemstone with a number of carats lower than seven, as stones beneath this carat threshold are said to have too little *power* to capture planetary rays.[36] Nonetheless, a high number of carats, or more *power*, does not necessarily means higher efficacy. Too many carats, or excessive *power*, can in fact be superfluous in certain cases, or even harm the person wearing the gemstone. Hence, the power of a stone must be chosen in relation to the person's planetary situation and the "quantity of rays" he needs. On this subject, a researcher at the History Department at Kāśī Vidyāpīṭh, a college in Banaras, recounted his experience with a gemstone that was too powerful:

> It was the first day I was wearing this stone. It was a cat's eye. That day, my wife lost a sari at the drycleaners, and I had a violent argument with my colleagues at the Kāśī Vidyāpīṭh History Department.[37] Once I got home in the evening, I tried to understand why I had reacted so badly and why my day had been so awful. That was when I realized the stone I was wearing was too strong for me, it was a forty-carat stone!

The researcher then decided to give it to a friend who was having problems:

> For him, the stone worked very effectively, since he had health problems and other family problems, but it was too powerful for me. It's like when we eat too much, it can harm you, you must only eat as much as you need.

While the number of carats allows one to identify the *power* of the stone using a quantitative criterion, there are also other qualitative parameters that need to be taken into account to evaluate a stone's *power*. It's transparency, for example, is supposed to enhance the absorption of planetary rays. Astrologers nonetheless consider that a gemstone's clarity can sometimes be erroneous, as is the case today of synthetic stones, which are more transparent than real gemstones. According to them, while the presence of a minor flaw, a "stain" (*dāg*), a "filament" (*reśā*), or "net-like" (*jālā*) formations, can be sometimes considered a "defect" in the gemstone, it is essentially a guarantee of its authenticity. Let us look at the case of a woman who went to an astrologer to know whether she should change the amethyst (*jāmuniyā*, a gemstone that protects from Saturn) she had been wearing for several years, and replace it with a new, more powerful one:

> ♀: Listen, should we add more *power*? I mean, do I need a stone with more carats?
>
> J: Nowadays you can't find stones of this color. The stones you find today lose their color in two or three days. Look, this stone is so old, but it is still so colorful.
>
> ♀: I've had it for five or six years now . . .[38]
>
> J: Five or six years later, it is still like a *jāmun* fruit [fruit of the rose-apple tree, from which the amethyst gets its name, *jāmuniyā*] . . . in stones you buy today the color is added, it's artificial, they color the stone and then they sell it. You can recognize real stones because they are irregular, they have some kind of stain in them, while today's stones are like glass, they're all the same inside. If you want you can change the stone, but you won't find one like this, this color will last another ten to twelve years.
>
> ♀: Okay, I'll keep this stone then.

Astrologers complain about the synthetic gemstones now available on the market. Clients buy them as they are cheaper, although they may have doubts about their efficacy. The *power* of precious stones is seen as a "natural" property and is described as the result of thousands of years over the course of which they have absorbed planetary rays. For this reason, the astrologer Siddhartha recommend his clients buy authentic gemstones:

> Of course a stone with blemishes is less effective. But what really counts is that it is authentic (*sahī*), that is the real question, the stone must be authentic. This is why I always tell my clients it's better to spend a bit more, but to be sure they're getting an authentic gemstone . . . before gemstones used to spread their color like a chandelier (*jhāṛphānūs*), yellow, red,

black . . . nowadays, eighty percent of stones are artificial. For example lapis lazuli is not very expensive and you can easily find it in the market, you can find lapis lazuli for fifteen to twenty rupees a carat, but the lapis lazuli you find today is often mixed with cement. It's like the medicines a doctor gives you—if they are real, they have an effect (*asar hogā*), but if they aren't real, people think the doctor is incompetent: he prescribed a medicine, you bought the medicine, but it has no effect.

Gemstones of inferior quality are however not devoid of power. The astrologer Shree Kanth Shastri reassured his clients, who were worried as they were unable to buy a stone of excellent quality, with these words:

♂: We wanted to buy a good quality stone, but we had to buy a cheap one (*thoṛā baṛhiyā vālā kharidnā cāhte the lekin ham saste vālā le liye*) . . .

J: No, no, for the time being it doesn't need to be an excellent stone . . . what you need at the moment is to increase your self-confidence, the stone you have bought is fine for that . . .

♀: It's not going to create problems for us (*nuksān koi nahī̃ hai*)?

J: No, this stone cannot be harmful (*nuksān to degā nahī̃*), on the contrary . . . for the time being it will increase your self-confidence (*manobal baṛhāyegā*) . . . it won't help you earn more money (*paisa-vaisa nahī̃ degā*), your business will not improve (*vyavasāy mẽ koi pragatī nahī̃ hogā*), but you will find mental peace (*mānsik śānti āpko milegā*) and you won't encounter frustration (*frustrations nahī̃ hogā*), that is to say, the stone will be useful for this (*yah kām karegā āpko*) . . .

Reinforcing self-confidence and willpower (*ātmabal, manobal*) is one of the main therapeutic qualities of gemstones. Their effectiveness on the mind is attributed to the biochemical and metabolic mechanism of the planetary rays. This is the astrologer Siddhartha's explanation:

> Stones serve to reinforce self-confidence (*ātmabal*). When people are going through a bad period (*burā samay*) their willpower is weakened, people fall into a depression . . . stones work in such a way that, depending on the planet for which you are wearing a stone—for example, a *nīlam* stone for Śani—the stone catches the rays of the planet and once it has absorbed them, it diverts them toward your mind so that you think "this planet cannot do anything to me" . . . The stone absorbs the rays and gives you mental power.

Willpower and self-confidence, reinforced by the gemstone, while reducing stress favorize better success in work, studies, relationships, and so forth. The healing power of a stone is not always felt immediately though: the rays stones transmit to the body have to be "metabolized" by the organism before the person is able to appreciate their benefic effects. Thus describing the treatment he had prescribed for an engineer who had had appendicitis and other health problems, an astrologer compared the immediate efficacy of a *jantar* with the slower effects of precious stones:

> He told me everything that had happened. To provide immediate relief (*turant arām*) I gave him a *jantar* straightaway: he was in bed, he did not even have the strength to walk. Inside the *jantar* I gave him, there was a *bel* [*aegle Marmelos*, wood apple] root. Once the *śodhan* ["purification" of the *jantar*] was done in his name, I gave him a *jantar* to be worn the first time on a Sunday . . . I gave him the *jantar* last Sunday and this Sunday they came to see me as he is already so much better. Along with the *jantar* I also gave him some stones: a ruby, a white topaz, and a cat's eye. The cat's eye is for hemorrhoids, the white topaz for Jupiter, and the ruby is for the Sun, for his overall health. But he still hasn't felt the benefits of these stones. The *jantar* I gave him worked immediately but he will have to wait a bit as it takes longer for the stones to act.

According to astrologers and clients, while it takes time to feel the benefic outcomes of a stone, harmful effects are immediately perceived. Some stones are supposed to provoke a negative reaction in the person who wears them, and this reaction can be felt within the first twenty-four to forty-eight hours of the person wearing the stone. For this reason, astrologers usually advise people to "test" a gemstone for twenty-four to forty-eight hours: if a negative event occurs, if the person feels uneasy or have a nightmare during this time, it means the stone does not suit him or her. A flaw (*doṣ*) in the stone—for example, a lack of luster (*camak*) or the presence of a stain (*dāg*) or a filament (*jāl*) inside it—or the stone's excessive power may be seen as responsible for the incompatibility between the gem and the person. Furthermore, according to some astrologers, people born under certain signs (ascendant, *lagna*, and lunar, *rāśi*) are incompatible with certain stones. For example, someone born under the sign of Aquarius should not wear rubies, just as Aries or Scorpios should not wear diamonds, and so forth.

A "bad stone" (*doṣī ratna*, "defective stone") or a stone that does not suit the person (*galat ratna*, "wrong stone") is considered potentially harmful, not only for the person wearing it but also for those close to him, and they must be exchanged by the lapidary. Thus, for example, the book *Navagraha upāsnā* (Worship of the Nine Planetary Deities) (Shastri n.d.) describes the negative effects of a defective ruby:

1. Misfortune (*dukh*) strikes the brother when the ruby lacks luster (*camak*).
2. Death of cattle (*paśunāś*) occurs when the ruby is the color of milk.
3. Misfortune (*dukh*) strikes the person's father or the person himself if the ruby is bicolored.
4. A ruby with a mark (*cihn*) or a filament (*jāl*) breeds disputes.
5. A crack (*cīr*) in the ruby provokes a wound from a weapon.
6. An earth-colored (*maṭamailā*) ruby provokes obstacles (*bādhā*) in the procreation of children.

In Banaras people believe that if a "bad stone" is not exchanged, its long-term effect will be contrary to the desired therapeutic result. Thus, if a pearl (*motī*) is usually worn to protect from the risk of colds and to reinforce mental stability, a "bad pearl" is supposed to increase the risk of mental instability and catching a cold.

Nonetheless, three gemstones are more "dangerous" (*khatarnāk*) than the others: coral (for Mars), diamond (for Venus), and sapphire (for Saturn). Coral in particular is supposed to increase aggressivity and give rise to disputes between a husband and wife. This is how an astrologer describes the potential harmful effects provoked by an incompatibility between coral and certain zodiacal signs:

> If someone having Libra as ascendant (*lagna*) or lunar sign (*rāśi*) wears a red coral, you will see that within twenty-four hours there will be a dispute in the family (*parivār mẽ jhagṛā ho jāyegā*), the person will have a problem with his life partner and there may even be a divorce. The same thing can occur when the ascendant is Taurus, Capricorn, or Aquarius, there will be no peace in the family (*parivār mẽ aśānti ho jāyegā*).

A reader from the Geophysics Department at BHU described the effect of coral on his adolescent son in the following manner:

> The astrologer who was interpreting his horoscope said that he should wear *prabāl,* one kind of gemstone.[39] So I got that one made, but he [the astrologer] also said that the stone may make his attitude more aggressive, and that's what happened . . . now he is more aggressive, two years after wearing that. From the past six months I am watching, gradually he has become more aggressive.

The diamond, Venus's gemstone, normally supposed to encourage beauty, sexuality, and procreation, can, as a side effect, provoke uncontrolled sexual behavior, a lack of modesty (*caritr hīnatā*, "lack of character"), and even lead to extramarital relationships.

Nevertheless, the gemstone with the most malefic effects is unsurprisingly the sapphire (*nīlam*), Saturn's gemstone. When a sapphire does not suit the person wearing it, it is supposed to provoke unhappiness and all kinds of accidents. According to the astrologer Siddhartha, a person whose ascendant sign is Cancer or Leo who wears a sapphire may become a murderer of his or her spouse:

> Even if he is going through *Śani sāṛhe sātī* (the seven and a half years of Saturn) a person with Cancer or Leo as their ascendant

> should never wear a sapphire as it signifies that Saturn is the master of the seventh [house of the spouse] and the eighth house [house of death]. In these cases wearing a sapphire can immediately place the person's wife in a situation of *markeś* (danger of death), either by being the victim of an accident or by falling ill with arthritis, for example . . .

Sapphire's malefic potential is such that astrologers advise people to test it on a day when they are not planning to leave the house, so there is no risk of an accident, or even more prudently to test it without wearing it, just by placing it under the pillow one sleeps on in the night, and then to analyze the quality of the sleep. One type of sapphire considered particularly dangerous is the *khunī nīlam*, "blood sapphire," that has a red mark (*chinṭ*) in the blue of the stone. This sapphire is a very powerful remedy but may provoke physical accidents (*śārīrik doṣ*) and should be tested more carefully than the others. If it is not appropriate, it is believed that an accident is likely to occur within twenty-four hours of wearing it.

Like other stones the sapphire is supposed to have a very strong effect on the wearer's mind (*buddhi*): just as an appropriate sapphire will reinforce self-confidence and willpower, a bad one diverts, makes thoughts "wander" (*bhramit karnā*). Thus, from experience, a client described the effect a sapphire had on his thoughts: "When a sapphire is not suitable (*suit nahī̃ kartā hai*), the person mistakes a snake for a rope (*sāṃp ko rassī samajh baiṭhe*) and a rope for a snake (*rassī ko sāṃp samajh baiṭhe*).[40] Thoughts take these kinds of turns (*pher*) . . . you see metal and think it's paper."

The malefic potential of the sapphire can however be neutralized by topaz, the gemstone of Jupiter, the planet that controls the mind. For this reason, according to some astrologers, when a person wears a topaz next to a sapphire its harmful effects are neutralized. Hence jewelers always place a topaz in the drawers where sapphires are stored: "If a single sapphire can kill a person, imagine the harmful effects a hundred sapphires together can have . . . for this reason, we always place a topaz alongside them," a lapidary explained to me.

If some stones are more likely than others to provoke unexpected and unwelcome effects, any change observed in a stone is seen as suspicious. When a stone moves (*hiltā hai*), is being worn down (*ghistā jā rahā hai*), or breaks (*ṭūṭ jatā hai*), or when it is lost, the client usually goes to an astrologer to know what to do and how to interpret the change. A crack in the stone is seen as a sign that the stone has protected the person from a harmful event and has hence exhausted its power: the stone must be replaced as soon as possible.[41] Sometimes, even the smell of the stone can provoke suspicion. Thus, a businessman from Bombay had gone to see the astrologer Kameshwar Upadhyay because the *gomed* (Rāhu's stone) he was wearing "had an unpleasant smell":

> ♂: You prescribed this *gomed* stone for me, but it stinks so badly that I was not able to wear it, even for a week! It stinks only on me, not on anyone else who tried it on! On others it didn't smell. It smells so bad that no one wants to sit next to me! and I can't even eat with this hand!
>
> J: Do you smell bad when you sweat?
>
> ♂: No, I don't smell bad when I sweat. I can wear the same pair of socks for a month and they don't smell.
>
> J: The *gomed* stone protects against all kinds of harmful external influences (*uparibādhā*: lit., "obstacles coming from above"), it protects against *ṭonā-ṭoṭkā* (sorcery), *kālā-jādu* (black magic) . . . it would be better to change it: wear an amethyst.

The bad smell of the stone is interpreted as the sign that the stone has protected the person from harmful external influences, particularly sorcery attacks.

The loss of a stone is often seen with concern, as a bad omen, the sign of a negative event that the person will not be able to avoid. The malefic influence of the planet is supposed to be so strong that it removes all means of protection. This is the case recounted by Dr. Agarwal, an abdominal surgeon and the owner of a large private clinic in the Sigra neighborhood. This surgeon wears four stones—a coral for Mars, an emerald for Mercury, a sapphire for Saturn, and a *gomed* for Rāhu—set in rings that he only removes during operations. When he operates, Dr. Agarwal slips the four rings onto his watchstrap and places all these items in his shirt pocket, so that the stones remain in contact with his body. He believes the stones, particularly the *gomed*, protect him from any kind of professional accident. Before he started wearing them, the doctor had

had problems with his patients—"suppose some patient died, or started screaming, fighting, or some nuisance . . . ," as he puts it himself—but as soon as he began to wear the rings he never had an accident during an operation. Nonetheless, he was personally the victim of an accident when he lost his coral ring. This is how he recounts what happened next:

> I was at my niece's wedding and I lost the coral ring. The next day I called the jeweler to order another one immediately, but that very day I had a heart attack. People say it's a bad sign when you lose a stone . . . my *purohit* (priest) says, my astrologer says that when you lose a stone, it means something bad is going to happen and you must replace the stone as soon as possible.
>
> Just after the heart attack, at ten in the night, I called the jeweler to tell him to bring the coral I needed immediately. An hour later he arrived with the stone and I asked him to tie it to my arm with some tape. After that, the pain stopped, whereas before, despite the medication, I was in severe pain.

The renewed contact between the coral and the surgeon's body calmed the pain, as the stone provided the surgeon with the "dose" of planetary rays he needed.[42]

In this chapter we have seen that in Banaras, the efficacy of remedies is evaluated and dealt with through elaborate discourses and practices. Both astrologers and their clients constantly question the methods to be followed to guarantee, increase, and prolong the benefic effects of a treatment. The material presented shows that the question of efficacy is conceived more in terms of degree and duration than in terms of success or failure. The power of a treatment is a quantifiable property that can be measured on the basis of several criteria: the number of carats for the gemstones, the number of days and specialists necessary for the rituals, the number of mantras recited for the amulets, and so on.

The concept of efficacy, as it is expressed during astrological consultations, is complex and multifaceted. It combines several principles of causality. Following the "sacrificial" model of efficacy, the power of a remedy depends on the effort—be it physical, intellectual, or financial—invested by the client in order to attain his or her goal (health, promotion, marriage, etc.). The "financial" model of efficacy establishes a direct proportionality between the monetary value of a treatment and its therapeutic value: the more expensive the better. Efficacy is also subject to an "analogical" principle—in the Descolian sense—of compatibility between the chosen remedy and the person, since every treatment needs to be adapted to suit the age, the gender, the zodiacal sign, and the planetary situation of the person. A "theological" type of efficacy is evoked when rituals that call upon divine intervention are performed for therapeutic purposes. Astrologers also recognize the "psychological" efficacy of remedies that increase their clients' self-confidence. A "karmic" model (in the sense of *karman*, "action") of efficacy is mentioned when one attributes the power of healing to the merits (*puṇya*) acquired through the performance of ritual acts. Finally, a "scientific," or "biomedical," model of causality is invoked to explain precious stones' efficacy in terms of absorption and transmission of planetary rays. The diversity of these idioms of causality shows that astrological discourse and practice are constantly adapting to an ever-changing urban society, where the values of sacrifice and devotion coexist with those of money and science. Rather than mutually eliding each other, the different languages of causality combine in ever-evolving configurations.

Conclusion

Astrology has a somewhat paradoxical and ambivalent place within Brahmanism. On the one hand *jyotiṣa*, the astral discipline, is recognized as a constitutive part of Brahmanical orthodoxy. From the Vedic period up until today, sacrifices and other ritual activities such as marriage or laying the foundation to a house must be performed according to the *muhūrta*s, the auspicious times calculated by astrologers. Astrological expertise is hence a necessary requisite for any Brahmin priest.

On the other hand, astrology is based on an atypical, alternative, or even "revolutionary" ideology with respect to Brahmanism. The caste system, the opposition between purity and impurity, hierarchy, the four stages of existence (*āśrama*), and other structuring principles found in Brahmanical thought, do not have a normative value for the human existence as described in astrological literature. The doctrine established in the Sanskrit horoscopic treatises (*jātakaśāstra*) and used today by astrologers offers an alternative model of human destiny. To start with, the "native" (*jātaka*) as an individual is more important than the birth group (*jāti*), as the stars can turn a tramp into a king and a king into a tramp, as the popular saying goes. As human behavior is ruled by planetary influence, moral responsibility as described in the theory of karma as well as the observance of *svadharma*, or "one's own duty," or the duty attached to the group one belongs to, becomes secondary. Finally, we observe that during his or her existence, rather than four stages of a linear progression—the *āśrama*s of student, householder, anchorite, and renouncer—the person goes through planetary periods (*daśā*) of varying durations and fortunes, which can help the person to both progress and regress, but which are not marked by moral ideals.

Similarly, the relationship between astrology and devotional Hinduism is also somewhat marked by ambivalence. On the one hand, astrological doctrine describes a system of cosmological correlations between the planets, the zodiacal signs, the directions, colors, the parts of the body, plants, regions, and other elements that very exhaustively explain how things are organized and how the world in which we live functions. In this system, the gods do not have a necessary or privileged role, but like other elements they fit into the networks of cosmic correlations. It is the planets that play a determining role. Their position in relation to the twelve houses, and the twelve zodiacal signs, allows the astrologer to explain what is happening, what is going to happen, and how to intervene in order to modify the situation. In this sense, astrological doctrine could easily "get rid" of devotional Hinduism.

On the other hand, though, the nine planetary deities (*navagraha*) described in astrological literature are an integral part of the Hindu pantheon and are represented as anthropomorphic Gods in numerous Hindu temples. Purāṇic literature abounds with iconographic details, ritual prescriptions, and mythological tales concerning the worship of the planetary deities. These astrolatric practices, established in texts and still observed today, show that astrology is perfectly integrated into the devotional rationales of popular Hinduism. In addition, the rituals to control planetary influences regularly prescribed by astrologers during consultations are clear proof of the interpenetration of horoscope theory and devotional practices. In this context, the planets have a subordinate status in relation to the major divinities of the pantheon and are hence subject to their power.

While from a theoretical viewpoint it is possible to identify conceptual contradictions and cleavages between Brahmanical or devotional Hinduism and astrology, all the material presented in this study shows that what prevails in the texts and observed practices is a process of adaptation and adjustment. Thus, we have seen that astrology and the karma doctrine are two theories of human destiny that function according to contrasting principles of causality, one deterministic and the other based on the moral quality of acts. How does one recognize the legitimacy of one without invalidating the other? This is the question astrologers of the past must have pondered and those of today continue to ask. The answer can be found in a short passage quoted at the beginning of horoscopic treatises, where the planets are said to make "visible" (*dṛṣṭa*) the "invisible" (*adṛṣṭa*) fruits of actions accomplished over past lives. This passage formally attributes epistemological priority to the karma theory, whose legitimacy is little questioned in Brahmanical circles. In practice nonetheless, it allows astrologers to continue to read human destiny in heaven without this being seen as a subversive practice. Despite their being substantially contradictory, these two theories are used as two complementary ways of saying the same thing.

From the colonial period to date, the relationship between astrology and another paradigm of thought that became progressively dominant in India—modern science—is also marked by continual processes of adaptation and adjustment. In this case, too, we are faced with an ambivalent relationship, marked both by claims of foreignness and attempts at reconciliation. This is particularly evident at the level of governmental educational policies, although it takes radically different forms for the British administrators of the colonial period and the Hindu nationalists who have recently promoted the creation of Vedic astrology departments at Indian universities. Between the end of the eighteenth century and the middle of the nineteenth century, British administrators involved in founding educational institutions in India recommended the teaching of the astral discipline (*jyotiṣa*) as they considered that the *siddhānta*s (Sanskrit treatises on astronomy) were driven by a rationality compatible with modern European science, although at a less advanced level. However, they condemned the teaching of the astrological and divinatory (*phalita* and *saṃhitā*) branches of *jyotiṣa*, which they saw as the worst superstitions. Hence, during the colonial period, due to its different constitutive branches, the astral discipline was seen as the most "scientific" knowledge developed in India on the one hand, and the most absurd and irrational on the other. It represented both the emblem of universal rationality, shared by the colonizers and the colonized, and the sign of an irremediable otherness, radically separating the civilized from the "savages."

Although formulated differently to fulfill other objectives, at the turn of the twenty-first century this ambivalent relationship to modern science is also visible in the postcolonial context in the Hindu nationalist party's enthusiasm to create Vedic astrology or "astral science" (*jyotir vigyan* or *jyotirvijñān*) departments at Indian universities. In this framework, astrology is said to be both "scientific"—that is, knowledge going through processes of empirical verification and aiming at universal validity—and "Vedic"—that is, knowledge produced by divine revelation and intrinsically Hindu and

Indian. A similar ideology runs through the projects conducted over the last decades by researchers at the Banaras Hindu University Department of Jyotish and funded by the government. These projects aim to show that the principles behind the ancient Sanskrit horoscopic treatises, taken in combination with statistical and experimental studies, can be used to predict, diagnose, and treat illnesses of biomedical nosology such as cancer, cardiovascular diseases, or diabetes.[1] Astrology, in these researches, is thus characterized both as a science compatible with the biomedical paradigm and as an autonomous and exclusively Indian science drawing inspiration from Brahmanical sources.

While in the case of the dominant paradigms of thought, such as the theory of karma, modern science, or Brahmanical Hinduism, we see processes of rapprochement, there are other contexts in which astrologers seem to be adopting distancing strategies. This is true of another paradigm of causality widespread in South Asia but generally associated with the lower castes and the illiterate: possession. As we have seen, as etiological systems dealing with misfortune, astrology and possession share important similarities. Planets are described as "seizers" (*graha*) and their modus operandi can be compared to that of demonic beings (*bhūta*, *preta*, as well as *graha*) that possess humans. Expressions used during astrological consultations to refer to planetary influence are very similar, if not identical, to those used by specialists of possession in relation to attacks by ghosts and other harmful beings. Similarly, the ritual and therapeutic procedures followed by astrologers aim to "eliminate" (*nivāraṇ karnā*) the planetary influence physically present in the victim's body. Nonetheless, as astrologers and their clients generally see possession by demonic beings as a form of superstition followed by the lower castes, and devoid of any rationality, astrologers and clients are keen to distinguish between these two ways of explaining misfortune.

The Future of Astrologers

As we have just seen, astrological theory was, and continues to be, adapted and repositioned in relation to other locally existing theories of causality. These processes of adjustment are more evident than ever in contemporary India, where the profession of astrologer seems to enjoy unprecedented vitality.[2] This popularity can at least be partially explained by astrologers' ability to adapt their profession to the values and lifestyles of the urban middle and upper classes. As we have seen, in Banaras, astrologers continually "update" their professional identity, their divinatory and therapeutic idioms, as well as the technology used in consultations. In the professional identity of today's astrologers we see the coexistence of two types of qualification: on the one hand, belonging by birth to the Brahmin caste and being a male, along with an apprenticeship to a teacher (often the father), on the other hand, academic degrees that are (at least in principle) open to all and objectively certify the acquisition of skills. In the same way, when it comes to practicing the profession, we note that certain astrologers wear traditional pandit's clothes, receive their clients at home, hold collective consultations without an appointment, have no fixed timings or rates, and perform rituals for their clients. Others emulate the liberal professions: they have an office, secretaries, waiting rooms, wear Western clothes, follow a system of fixed appointments to see their clients, and prescribe their remedies on letterhead. The "modernity" of these astrologers does not lie in privileging one model over another, but in combining both. The best-reputed and most popular astrologers in Banaras are, in fact, those who combine the status of Brahmin with university degrees, ritual skills with professionalism, and who have offices to ensure confidentiality but also sometimes open the doors of their homes.

More subtle and less obvious processes of adaptation than those involving professional identity can be perceived by reading between the lines of a semantic analysis of the dialogues between practitioners and clients during consultations. Human life is described as an asset, a "share" (*bhāgya*), a wealth—in terms of health, goods, reproduction, career, and so forth—attributed to us at birth, and which can increase or decrease depending on the astral periods we go through over the course of an existence. The astrologer's role consists of guiding the client along this path, helping him or her make the right investments at the right times to maximize the benefits and minimalize the risks, thanks to remedies and ritual protections. Even if it is not explicitly mentioned, the capitalistic—or "stock market"—metaphor seems to be a subtext that allows one to decipher the hazards, the ups and downs, of human destiny. The exegesis of the horoscope seems to translate into symbolic terms the expectations of success and the acquisition of material comfort that drive many middle-class families in Banaras.

The individualism behind horoscope theory, where statutory hierarchies established on the basis of the birth group do not constitute an analytical criterion of human destiny, is another of the astrology's strengths in an urban society aspiring to the values of modernity. By reading the horoscope, the astrologer is able to provide detailed answers to questions about schools, higher studies, marriage, the search for a job, health, and other areas where clients have to make personal decisions. However, as we have seen, far from propagating an individualistic ideology, horoscope theory also represents the family as a unit of analysis. The spouse, children, parents, brothers, and sisters are all carefully described in each person's horoscope and the astrologer can reconstruct the destiny of a whole family on the basis of a single horoscope. Hence the destiny of the owner of the horoscope cannot be considered separately from that of the people close to him. In this sense, astrology seems to reconcile individualistic and family values, which corresponds to the viewpoint of the clients, whose individual choices can never be made without taking the family context into account.

Because they are based on mathematical calculations and empirical observations, astrological diagnoses also seem to satisfy the scientific and rational ambitions of middle-class families who have had a higher education. The explanations of planetary influence in terms of electromagnetic fields, wavelengths, and radiations are commonplace among specialists as well as clients. The desire to conform to the biomedical model also appears in treatment procedures, as the dosage of the remedies is carefully established on the basis of quantitative criteria and efficacy is often evaluated in terms of mechanical causality. However, it is not so much the scientific approach per se that makes astrology particularly well suited to the clients' demands, but rather the rational framing of Hindu ritual and devotional practices. Using "objective" criteria, the astrologer establishes *which* ritual a particular person should perform in order to attain a specific goal, as well as *when*, *how*, and for *how long* it should be done.

Thanks to the use of computers, software programs, and other technological tools during consultations, astrology appears as a modern and innovative type of knowledge, despite its ancient roots. Furthermore, the massive use of cell phones and the web has a major impact on the way contemporary astrology is practiced. This is due to a pragmatic specificity of astrological consultations. Unlike medical diagnosis or the diagnosis of possession, where the practitioner necessarily has to meet the client, look at, examine, and listen to him or her, horoscopic diagnosis does not require any kind of sensorial perception or spatial proximity between astrologer and client. It can be conducted regardless of each party's geographical location. Thus, even in the distant past, messengers (*dūta*) in the form of a relative, a friend, or a neighbor could carry out a consultation in someone else's name. Today cell phones and the internet allow a client to consult his or her astrologer from anywhere in the world. The astrologer only requires the client's birth details. In the globalized world we inhabit, marked by increasingly frequent travel, astrologers can accompany their clients everywhere and be present at every moment.

Given the popularity of astrology in France of the 1970s, a group of French sociologists supervised by Edgar Morin conducted a collective study, published as *La croyance astrologique moderne* (1981). They noted that astrology cannot be seen as an "archaic residue, the remnants of a superstition that would have inexplicably resisted the broom of reason" as "*there is a specifically modern trend of astrology*, a development taking place not *despite* the modernization of society, but in *response* to it" (*il y a un cours proprement moderne de l'astrologie*, un développement qui s'opère non pas *en dépit* de la modernisation de la société, mais en *réponse* à elle) (Fischler in Morin et al. 1981, 14). These remarks can doubtless be applied to contemporary Indian society where, rather than being weakened, astrology seems to gain popularity thanks to the increasing technologization and globalization of urban society.

It would nonetheless be inappropriate to reduce the work astrologers in Banaras do to the role of Mother Shipton, and the popularity of astrology to a mass media phenomenon. As we have seen, the astrologer's social role in Indian society cannot be compared to that of his counterparts in France or in other Western countries. It should be understood in light of the social, historical, religious, and regional context, as we have tried to highlight throughout this work. Far from exhaustive, this study seeks to reveal the wealth of interrogations the study of astrological practices in Banaras raises. There are nonetheless questions that remain unanswered, which we hope will be elucidated and studied in greater depth in future studies. The favor today's astrologers enjoy could indeed be examined, for example, from the perspective of the decline of the priesthood. Following the disappearance of kingdoms in India, the Brahmin priest (*purohit*) lost his main patron, the king, and was forced to reinvent new means of subsistence. This is true of certain Brahmins described in this study, who "converted" to the profession of astrologer after several generations during which priesthood had been the family's main occupation. Charging for consultations and the wide variety of treatments on offer makes the profession of astrologer far more profitable. Moreover, it does not involve giving up the ritual function: on the contrary, it provides an ideological framework that legitimizes the need to perform rituals. The astrologer can hence continue to be a priest, as was the case in earlier times, and even today in villages, where the priest also officiated as an astrologer. It remains to be understood whether this shift from the occupation of "priest cum astrologer" to the profession of "astrologer cum priest" is limited to specific cases, or whether it is a general trend that can be observed in other regional contexts.

Annex

Bachelor's and Master's Syllabi in *Jyotiṣa* at Banaras Hindu University (BHU)

Bachelor's (*Śāstrī Parīkṣa*) in *Jyotiṣa*

TEACHING PROGRAM (*PĀṬHYAKRAMA*)[1]

First Year (*Prathamavarṣa)*

Gaṇita
(Mathematics and Astronomy)

Exam (*patra*)	**Subject**	**Credits**
I, II, III	Hindi, history of ancient India, and a subject chosen among the following: grammar, literature, or philosophy	300
IV	Trigonometry of arcs (*cāpīya-trikoṇam-iti*)	100
V	Study of the *Dīrghavṛttalakṣaṇa* (Characteristics of Ellipses)	60
	Study of the *Rekhāgaṇita* ("Mathematics of Lines" [Sanskrit translation of Euclid's *Elements of Geometry*]), chapters 11 and 12	40
VI	Study of planetary movement (*gati-vijñāna*)	50
	Practical exercise (*prayogika*): knowledge of instruments (*yantra-paricaya*)	50

continued on next page

Gaṇita
(Mathematics and Astronomy)

Continued

Exam (*patra*)	Subject	Credits
VII	Study of the *Calanakalana* ("Differential Calculus"), chapters 1–2[b]	50
	Study of the first part (*tantra*) of the *Tājikanīlakaṇṭhī* (treatise on the *tājika* horoscopy)	50

[a]Sanskrit manual of astronomy composed by Sudhākara Dvivedī (1855–1910) and edited by Krishna Chandra Dvivedi (Laghugranthamālā 33, Varanasi: Sampurnanand Sanskrit Viswavidyalay, 1981).

[b]Treatise on differential calculus composed by Sudhākara Dvivedī and edited by his son Padmakara Dvivedi (Varanasi: Master Khelarilal & Sons, 1941).

Phalita
(Astrology and Divination)

Exam	Subject	Credits
IV	Study of the *Bṛhajjātaka* (treatise of natal horoscopy)	100
V	Study of the *Samarasāra* (treatise on divination / reading of omens)	50
	Study of the *Vāsturatnākara* (treatise on topomancy)	50
VI	Study of the celestial spheres (*gola*) and the treatise *Laghupārāśarī* (treatise on natal horoscopy)	50
	Practical exercise (*prayogika*): about the celestial sphere (*khagola*)	50
VII	Study of the second part (*tantra*) of the *Tājikanīlakaṇṭhī*	80
	Study of the Malayalam treatise *Praśnasaṃgraha* (treatise on interrogations)	20

Second Year (*Dvitīyavarṣa)*

Gaṇita
(Mathematics and Astronomy)

Exam	Subject	Credits
I, II, III	Hindi, history of ancient India, and a subject chosen among the following: grammar, literature, or philosophy	300
IV	Study of the *Siddhāntaśiromaṇi*: the first part of the treatise dedicated to the foundations of mathematics (*gaṇita*), up to the passage dealing with the calculation of the true (*spaṣṭa*) longitude of the planets, chapters 1–2	100
V	Study of *Sūryasiddhānta*	100
VI	Study of the *Siddhāntaśiromaṇi*: the section from the chapter on the "three questions" (*tripraśna*), chapter 3, up to the chapter on lunar eclipses (*candragrahaṇa*), chapter 5	50
	Practical exercise (*prayogika*): planetary mathematics to calculate the almanac (*pañcāṅga-graha-gaṇita*) and knowledge of the instruments (*yantra-paricaya*)	50
VII	Study of the *Calanakalana*, chapters 3–4	
	Ordinary knowledge of the length of an eclipse (*sthiti-vijñānasya sāmānya-paricaya*)	50

Phalita
(Astrology and Divination)

Exam	Subject	Credits
IV	Study of the *Sūryasiddhānta*: from the beginning up to the section dealing with solar eclipses (*sūrya-grahaṇa*), chapter 5	100
V	Study of the *Jātakapaddhati* (manual illustrating the mathematical calculations required to prepare horoscopes)	50
	Study of the *Pañcasvarā* (treatise on divination)	50
VI	Study of the *Bhāvakutūhala* and the *Jātakālaṅkara* (treatises on natal horoscopy)	50
	Practical exercise (*prayogika*): knowledge of the almanac (*pañcāṅga*) and instruments (*yantra*)	50
VII	Study of the *Bṛhatpārāśarahorāśāstra* (treatise on natal horoscopy)	100

Master's (*Ācārya Parīkṣa*) in *Jyotiṣa*

Teaching Program (*Pāṭhyakrama*)

First Year (*Prathamavarṣa)*

Gaṇita
(Mathematics and Astronomy)

Exam (*patra*)	**Subject**	**Credits**
I	Study of the *Siddhāntatattvaviveka*: from the section on shadows (*chāyā*) to the section on lunar eclipses (*candra-grahaṇa*)	100
II	Study of the *Siddhāntatattvaviveka*: from the section on solar eclipses (*sūrya-grahaṇa*) to the end of the treatise	100
III	Study of the *Ketakīgrahagaṇita*: up to the section dealing with the true (*spaṣṭa*) longitude of planets	50
	Explanation (*upapatti*) of the *Grahalāghava*, up to the section dealing with the "three questions" (*tripraśna*), chapter 4]	50
IV	Study of the section of the *Ketakīgrahagaṇita* dealing with the "three questions" (*tripraśna*)	50
	Practical exercise (*prayogika*): experience (*prayoga*) with ancient instruments (*prācīna-yantra*)	50
V	Study of the *Pratibhābodhaka*[c]	70
	Study of the *Bhābhramarekhānirūpaṇa*[d]	30

[c]"Teaching light" is a treatise composed by Sudhākara Dvivedī and edited by Krishna Chandra Dvivedi (Laghugranthamālā 37, Varanasi: Sampurnanand Sanskrit Viswavidyalay, 1985).

[d]Sanskrit treatise on the "Analysis (*rūpaṇa*) of the lines of rotation of the celestial bodies (*bhābhramarekha*)" composed by Sudhākara Dvivedī and edited by Krishna Chandra Dvivedi (Laghugranthamālā 34, Varanasi: Sampurnanand Sanskrit Viswavidyalay, 1981).

Phalita
(Astrology and Divination)

Exam	Subject	Credits
I	Study of the *Narapatijayacaryā* (treatise on divination)	100
II	Study of the *Jātakapārijāta* (treatise on natal horoscopy), from chapter 11 to the end	100
III	Study of the *Jyotirvidābharaṇa* (astrological treatise dealing with auspicious times or *muhūrta*), from chapter 12 to the end	100
IV	The second half of the *Sūryasiddhānta*	50
	Practical exercise (*prayogika*): experience (*prayoga*) and introduction to (*paricaya*) Indian instruments (*bhāratīya-yantra*)	50
V	Study of the first half of the *Bṛhatsaṃhitā* (treatise on divination)	100

Second Year (*Dvitīyavarṣa*)

Gaṇita
(Mathematics and Astronomy)

Exam	Subject	Credits
I	Study of the *Āryabhaṭīya*	100
II	Study of the *Pañcasiddhānta*	100
III	a) Study of the *Vāstavacandraśṛṅgonnati*[e]	50
	b) Examination of Western astronomy (*pāścātya-jyotiṣa-siddhānta-samīkṣa*)	50
IV	Conception and writing of a dissertation (*svaśāstrīyo nibandhaḥ vyutpatti*)	50
	Practical exercise (*prayogika*): knowledge (*paricaya*) of modern instruments (*ādhunikayantra*)	50
V	Oral examination (*vāk parīkṣā*)	100

[e] "About the progression (*unnati*) of the phases of the moon (*candra-śṛṅga*; lit., "horns of the moon," that is, crescent moon or eclipsed moon)." The *Vāstavacandraśṛṅgonnatisādhana* is a treatise composed by Sudhākara Dvivedī and edited by Krishna Chandra Dvivedi (Laghugranthamālā 36, Varanasi: Sampurnanand Sanskrit Viswavidyalay, 1981).

Phalita
(Astrology and Divination)

Exam	Subject	Credits
I	Analysis (*samīkṣā*) of ancient Western astrology (*prācya-pāścātya-phalita-jyotiṣa*)	50
	Study of the *Jātakakroḍa* (treatise on natal horoscopy)	50
II	Study of the second half of the *Bṛhatsaṃhitā* (treatise on divination)	100
III	Study of the *Phaladīpikā* (treatise on natal horoscopy), chapters 1–16	
IV	Conception and writing of a dissertation (*svaśāstrīyo nibandhaḥ vyutpatti*)	50
	Practical exercise (*prayogika*): observation (*vedha*) of the planets (*graha*)	50
V	Oral examination (*vāk parīkṣā*)	100

Glossary

This glossary presents the meaning of the terms as they are used in the context of astrological consultations.

aṅgavidyā: physiognomy, "knowledge of the parts of the body"

antardaśā: planetary subperiod

ariṣṭa: evil astral configurations, particularly for young children (*bālāriṣṭa*) and their parents

bādhā: obstacle, difficulty

bhāgya: destiny, fortune, lot (from *bhāga*, "share")

bhāva: house (one of the twelve houses of the horoscope)

bhūt-pret (Sk. *bhūta, preta*): malevolent ghosts

bṛhaspati: the planet Jupiter

budha: the planet Mercury

cakr (Sk. *cakra*): horoscope (lit., "circle")

dakṣiṇā: fee paid for astrological or ritual services

dān (Sk. *dāna*): ritual gift

darśan (Sk. *darśana*): auspicious sight, meeting of the devotee's and the deity's eyes

daśā: planetary period

dīp (Sk. *dīpa*): oil lamp made of clay (used to worship the planet Saturn, especially on Saturday) *dṛṣṭi*: a) planetary "aspect" (the angular relationship between planets in the horoscope); b) "gaze" of a planetary deity

gaṇita: the mathematical branch of astral knowledge

ghumānā: ritual act consisting in having things such as lemons or chili revolving around the head to remove bad influence

gomed: hessonite (gemstone for the planet Rāhu)

graha: a) planet; b) planetary deity; c) demon

grahadān (Sk. *grahadāna*): gift offered to the planets

grahaṇa: eclipse

kāl sarp doṣ: harmful astral configuration where all the planets are hemmed between the two lunar nodes Rāhu and Ketu

kaṣṭ: suffering, difficulty

kendra: in the horoscope, the first, fourth, seventh, and tenth houses (the "central" ones)

kuṇḍalī: horoscope

havan (Sk. *havana*): ritual that consists in making an oblation to the gods by pouring ghee and other vegetal substances into the sacrificial fire (syn. *yajña*)

hastarekhāśāstra: chiromancy

horā: astrology as a branch of astral science (*jyotiṣa*)

janm kuṇḍalī (Sk. *janma kuṇḍalī*): horoscope, natal chart

jantar: amulet

jap (Sk. *japa*): murmured repetition of mantras

jātaka: a) natal horoscopy, one of the three branches that compose astrology (along with *praśna* and *muhūrta*); b) the "native," the owner of the horoscope

jhāṛnā-phūṅknā (or *jhāṛ-phūk*): ritual treatment to cast out bad influences afflicting a person (lit., "sweeping and blowing away") *jyotiṣ* (Sk. *jyotiṣa*): astral science composed of three branches: astronomy (*siddhānta*), astrology (*phalita* or *horā*), and divination (*saṃhitā*)

jyotiṣī: astrologer

kāraka: "significator" (lit., "doer"), a planet that represents a particular aspect or person in the horoscope

ketu: descending lunar node, one of the nine planets of Hindu astrology

lagn (Sk. *lagna*): ascendant or first house of the horoscope

lahasuniyā: cat's eyes (gemstone for Ketu)

lakṣaṇ (Sk. *lakṣaṇa*): symptom, sign, mark, characteristic, omen

mahādaśā: planetary period

maṅgala: the planet Mars

maṅgal doṣ: "Mars's flaw," harmful astral configuration that may cause injury to the spouse

maṅgalik (f. *maṅgalī*, m. *maṅgalā*): person suffering from *maṅgal doṣ*

māṇikya: ruby (gemstone for the Sun)

manobal: mental strength

motī: pearl (gemstone for the Moon)

muhūrta: a) auspicious moment to undertake an activity; b) branch of astrology dealing with auspicious moment

mūṅgā: coral (gemstone for Mars)

nakṣatra: a) constellation; b) one of the twenty-seven lunar mansions, corresponding to an angular section of 13°20' on the ecliptic; c) astral divinities, that is, the twenty-seven wives of the Moon

navāṃśa: division corresponding to one-ninth of a zodiacal sign

nīlam: sapphire (gemstone for Saturn)

ojhā-sokhā: exorcist, possessed oracle

pañcāṅg (Sk. *pañcāṅga*): almanac

pareśanī: problem, difficulty

phalit (Sk. *phalita*): astrology

pukharāj: topaz (gemstone for Jupiter)

prabhāv: influence, hold (referring to the impact of planets on human life)

prāna pratiṣṭhā: "installation of life-breath," ritual performed to increase gemstones' efficacy

praśna: lit., "interrogation"; branch of astrology that calculates a horoscope according to the moment of the consultation

pūjā: worship

rāśi: zodiacal sign

ratna: precious stones

rāhu: ascending lunar node, one of the nine planets of Hindu astrology

saṃbandhit jyotiṣ: "connected astrology," horoscope reading focusing on the "native's" family and entourage

saṃhitā: divination, reading of omens

saṃkrānti: entry of the Sun into a new zodiacal sign

saṃskāra: ceremonies of "perfection" or rites of passage of the Hindu life cycle

sāmudrikaśāstra: physiognomy

saṅkalp (Sk. *saṅkalpa*): "declaration of purpose" made before starting a ritual performance

śani: the planet Saturn

śānti: appeasement, ritual to pacify a deity (especially planets)

sāṛhe sātī: period of seven and a half years during which the influence of the planet Saturn is supposed to be very harmful

siddhānta: astronomy

siddhi: extraordinary powers acquired through ritual initiation

svabhāva: one's own nature

śubh (Sk. *śubha*): auspicious

śukra: the planet Venus

sūrya: Sun

tājika: Perso-Arabic astrology in Sanskrit, a branch of horoscopy dealing mainly with annual predictions

tithi: lunar day

ṭonā-ṭoṭkā: sorcery

trikoṇa: first, fifth, and ninth house of the horoscope

yajña: ritual that consist in making an oblation to the gods by pouring ghee and other vegetal substances into the sacrificial fire (syn. *havan*)

yog (Sk. *yoga*): astral configuration having special effects

vāstuśāstra: science of sites and buildings, topomancy

Notes

Introduction

1. Iyengar (2007).

2. Independence is seen as a (new) birth, so the Indian nation has a horoscope that astrologers consult regularly to make predictions regarding the country's future. About horoscopes calculated for territories, land, as well as for other nonhuman subjects, see Guenzi and Singh (2009).

3. Emphasis added. For the complete speech Nehru pronounced on the declaration of India's independence, see McArthur (1992, 234–237). The text is also available online at http://www.fordham.edu/halsall/mod/1947nehru1.html (Internet Modern History Sourcebook).

4. Brahmanand Colony is notably home to a large number of professors as it is close to the Banaras Hindu University campus.

5. During my fieldwork, a thousand rupees was more or less equivalent to sixteen to seventeen US dollars. This is the price Gyanvati's father had fixed for foreign clients. For an Indian client, the same horoscope cost 550 rupees.

6. English transcription of *sāhityācārya* (master's degree in Sanskrit literature) and *jyotiṣācārya* (master's in astrology).

7. D/o (daughter of): Murlidhar Pandey, deceased.

8. For an ethnographic study of this Brahmin community specializing in astrology and Ayurveda, see Guenzi (1997). Stietencron carried out a textual study of the history and mythology of the Śākadvīpīya Brahmans (also known as Maga or Bhojaka Brahmans), analyzing the passages of the Sāmba Purāṇa and the Bhaviṣya Purāṇa in which this caste of Sun priests is mentioned (Stietencron 1966 and 2005). On the social history of Magas as Brahmins of foreign origin, see Bronkhorst (2016, 121–132).

9. The Hindi word *banārsī* means "from Banaras." I will use the adjective "Banarsi" to designate everything "from Banaras."

10. Unfortunately, Gyanvati will not be mentioned often in the chapters of this book, because in the years following our meeting her activity as an astrologer and, moreover, her consultations with clients were drastically reduced. Following her marriage in 1997, Gyanvati left to live with her in-laws, in the north of Banaras, an hour and a half away by auto-rickshaw from her family home. Despite her husband's seeming approval of her continuing to practice her profession, the housework, the two children, and the change of residence made it difficult for her to continue her consultations with clients. In order not to completely cease her activity and to ensure the family tradition is not interrupted, Gyanvati collaborated with her brother Manesh for some time. Manesh was seeing clients for consultations, interpreting horoscopes, and prescribing remedies at their father's place, while Gyanvati was doing the preliminary work of calculating and writing the horoscopes, a job she could do at home, on her own time.

11. Vernant (1991, 304).

12. Regarding this latter point, astrology as a discipline that successfully reconciles pragmatic requirements and transcendent truths, see Mandelbaum (1964 and 1966). This author makes a distinction between religion's "pragmatic complex" and "transcendent complex" and attributes to astrology the role of a "bridge" between the two complexes: "Astrology, in India as in Ceylon, provides a much-used bridge between the two complexes. It postulates a cosmic process that is impersonal, abstract, transcendent, immutable. At the same time, it offers means by which each person can adapt to the universal movement so as to advance his welfare" (Mandelbaum 1964, 13).

13. Several major studies have been dedicated to the conflicts and debates that inflamed discussions about the legitimacy of astrology in Europe between the twelfth and seventeenth centuries and led to the epistemological break between religion, astrology, and science that characterizes modern thought. Among these studies I refer the reader particularly to Boudet's (2006) remarkable work on the medieval period. For later periods, see Garin (1983), Simon (1992), Kassel (2005), Drévillon (1996), Curry (1987 and 1989), and Thomas (1971). From a methodological viewpoint, among these works I would particularly like to mention Simon's monograph on Kepler's thinking. The historian shows, from an anthropological perspective, that the "rationality" and "structure of thought" that presides over Kepler's work is fundamentally different to ours. Although he is considered one of the founding fathers of modern science, Kepler makes no distinction between "scientific theories" (dealing with the formulation of optical or astronomical laws) and "astrological theories" (dealing, for example, with speculations on the souls of the planets), as all of them make a fundamental contribution to the investigation of the laws of nature. According to Simon the need to make a qualitative distinction between "scientific theories" and "astrological belief" is nothing more than one of twentieth-century man's "retrospective anachronisms."

14. Here, the categories "paradigm of thought" and "intellectual paradigm" refer to the idea of "scientific paradigm" formulated by Kuhn (1962), but in a wider sense that includes the human and social sciences.

15. *The Humanist*, September/October 1975 (text available online at http://www.astrologer.com/tests/objections.html).

16. In general, despite being considered an "irrational belief" (or an "apparently irrational belief," to put it in Dan Sperber's words), astrology has not provoked the interest other beliefs or practices like magic, sorcery, or inspired divination, also qualified as "irrational," have engendered in the field of anthropological studies. These constitute subjects of study around which vast anthropological debates have taken shape. This is probably due to the erudite, technical, and mathematical aspects of astrological knowledge, which do not allow this discipline to be classified among popular beliefs, magical practices, or even religious representations.

17. With regard to this, one only needs to mention the scandal provoked by the doctoral dissertation defended at the École des hautes études en sciences sociales in Paris by the astrologer Élizabeth Teissier.

18. The difficulty of translating the unified nature of astral knowledge into our epistemological categories arises, for example, in the manual of Indian studies *L'Inde classique* (2 vols.) by Renou and Filliozat (1985 and 1996). Here the different subjects of *jyotiṣa* are scattered across several thematic sections: astronomy is classified among the "sciences" (1996, 177–194); astrology and divination are included in "magical practices" (1985, 615–620); and the planets are dealt with in the section dedicated to "major deities" (1985, 489–492). The structure of the calendar is described in the appendix, along with notions of chronology (1996, 721–738).

19. To mention just a few of the numerous "Indian," "Hindu," or "Vedic" astrology manuals (the epithets vary depending on the authors) to be found in Indian, European, or American bookshops, see: Bhat (1967), Defouw and Svoboda (1996), Dreyer (1990 and 1997), Frawley (1990), Raman (1992), V. D. Sharma (1973), and Stone (1981). For a synthetic, scholarly, and accurate summary of the technical aspects of the different branches of Indian astrology, see Chenet (1998a).

20. Among the monographs on Indian astronomy produced by Orientalists and European historiographers, we can mention those by Bailly (1787), Delambre (1817), Bentley (1825), Guérin (1847), Biot (1862), Müller (1862), Burgess (1893), Thibaut (1899), and Kaye (1924). For a discussion of some of these works in the context of the French Enlightenment, see Raina (1999, 2000, 2001, and 2003). For a history of astronomy during the colonial period, see Sen (2014).

21. On this subject, see Sarma (1995), Bayly (1996), Dodson (2007), and Sen (2014).

22. To mention just a few reference works on the history of Indian astronomy and mathematics, see Dikshit (1969), Billard (1971), Pingree (1978b), Sen

and Shukla (1985), Subbarayappa and Chattopadhyaya (2008), Plofker (2009), and Sen (2014).

23. Among the scholars who, before the twentieth century, made a combined study of the astronomical and astrological branches of *jyotiṣa*, one should certainly mention the polymathic, eleventh-century Arab traveler Al-Biruni, who describes Sanskrit works on astronomy and astrology in his *India* (Sachau 2000 [1910]).

24. To mention just a few of his works in this field, see Pingree (1970–1994, 1976, 1978a, 1981, and 1997a). An argument supporting the need to consider the history of astrological and divinatory literature an integral part of the history of science is presented in the pamphlet article "Hellenophilia versus the History of Science" (Pingree 1992). Here the author states, "Astrology and certain 'learned' forms of divination, magic, alchemy, and so on are 'sciences'" (Pingree 1992, 559). Despite this declaration of intent and his invaluable contribution to the study of the history of astrology, Pingree's work nonetheless shows a predilection for scientific and technical, rather than cultural, data. We can see the works by the historian of science Michio Yano as a continuation of Pingree's lineage since they also reveal a certain interest in astrology and divination (Yano 2003, 2004, and 2005). Bill Mak's groundbreaking research takes a critical stance on some of Pingree's assertions and while arguing for a probably autochthonous origin of many Indian concepts, he invites further investigation on the intellectual exchanges between the Greeks and the Indians in the early centuries of the Common Era (Mak 2013, 2014, 2018, 2019a, and 2019b). Outside India, Francesca Rochberg's (2004) work on Mesopotamian culture is an exemplary illustration of the fecundity of an approach including horoscopy and divination in the study of the history of science.

25. Pingree's works (1981, chap. 9, and 2001) open a path toward a survey in this area, and Minkowski's research (2001, 2002, 2004, 2010, and 2014; O'Hanlon and Minkowski 2008) fruitfully investigates astronomers' intellectual networks during the early modern period. In what more specifically concerns the profession of astrologer and his role at royal courts, see the studies by Inden (1985 and 1992), Friedman (1986 and 1989), Sircar (1952), and, most recently, Geslani (2011, 2016, and 2018), as well as Beinorius (2015).

26. See, for example, Banerjea (1948), Mallmann (1963), Mitra (1965), Pal and Bhattacharya (1969), Sivapriyananda (1990), and mainly Markel (1995).

27. Kemper (1979 and 1980), Pugh (1981, 1983b, and 1984) and Perinbanayagam (1981 and 1982).

28. Kapadia (1995, chap. 4) and Tarabout (2007, 2012, and 2015). A pioneering study, dealing with astrology from an ethnographic perspective, as a system for explaining misfortune in Tamil Nadu, is the work by the missionary Diehl (1956). About *nāḍī* astrology in Tamil Nadu, see Gansten's (2003) textual study. On practices related to astrological knowledge, see also Guenzi (2008) and

Guenzi and Singh (2009). Chanda's (2002) monograph about Bengali astrologers contains interesting information but is unfortunately weak in terms of analysis. I refer to Gerke (2012) for an in-depth ethnography of the concepts and practices related to Tibetan astrology in India, in the Darjeeling region. For an original portrait of an artist astrologer in Mumbai, see Grimaud (2014).

29. To mention just a few of the studies on the structure of the calendar: Freed and Freed (1964), Fuller (1980), Gaborieau (1982), Merrey (1982), Nicholas (2003), Pugh (1983c), Tarabout (2002b), and Wadley (1983a). The question of the calendar and the identification of appropriate times are also dealt with in Kane (1968–1977, 5: 463–510).

30. Avdeeff's PhD dissertation (2014) on Valluvar astrologers in Tamil Nadu is a promising contribution developing this approach.

31. The most varied aspects of the town of Banaras have been studied and described by historians, geographers, Sanskrit scholars, anthropologists, sociologists, linguists, historians of religion, and all kinds of writers. Given the immense wealth of this literature, in this context, rather than providing a brief description of the town, I prefer to refer to the bibliography mentioned in Singh (1993, 319–341), where monographs in Western languages are mentioned along with the Sanskrit and Hindi sources that focus on the town of Banaras. An exhaustive, updated bibliography, compiled by Jörg Gengnagel and Axel Michaels, is also available online at http://www.sai.uni-heidelberg.de/abt/IND/publikation/bibbanaras/bibbanaras.php.

32. The fieldwork took place February to March 1999, September 1999 to March 2000, December 2001 to May 2002, October 2005 to January 2006, as well as July to August 2008.

33. The primary textual sources used in this study were chosen according to certain methodological criteria. In what concerns the contemporary astrological literature in Hindi, most of the works and articles we cite are written by astrologers from Banaras (generally academics). Regarding the classical Sanskrit treatises, where possible, we also consulted editions published in Banaras and/or edited and commented by local astrologers. This is the case, for example, of the *Bṛhatsaṃhitā* (Dvivedi 1996; Pandey 2002–2005; and Jha 2011), the *Bṛhajjātaka* (Jha 1974; Pathak 2013), the *Laghujātaka* (Mishra 1993), the *Muhūrtacintāmaṇi* (Joshi 1992; Pandey 1992), or the *Bṛhatpārāśarahorāśāstra* (Pathak 1972). We generally preferred the locally distributed and published literature on astrology and planetary worship. Most of the astrological treatises cited in this work are not only used by the astrologers we worked with but are also included in the university courses for students following a bachelor's or master's degree program in astrology (see the annex at the end of this volume).

34. The questionnaire dealt with family identity (geographical origin; the caste the person belonged to; occupation of the father, grandfather, and forefathers,

etc.), studies and professional training, the place where the person exercised his or her profession and the office hours, divinatory techniques employed, price of a consultation (or other means of payment), the clientele's socioeconomic background, remedies prescribed, and divinatory or therapeutic specializations where relevant. The places where these astrologers practice their profession are marked on the map of the town (fig. 1).

35. Neelkanth Shastri, Shree Kanth Shastri, Dina Nath Tiwari, Kameshwar Upadhyay, Paras Nath Ojha, Chandra Mawli Upadhyay, Ram Chandra Pandey, Deoki Nandan Shastri, Svami Charan Chaturvedi, B. P. Mehrotra, Nagendra Pandey, and Ram Shankar Ray. Our study focused mainly on the first four of these astrologers, whom we followed very closely and regularly.

36. From what we were able to observe in Banaras, in certain cases, exorcists and sorcerers may hold "planets" (*graha*)—"the seizers" (from the root *GRAH-*, "to seize")—responsible for their clients' problems. Nevertheless, in these cases, planets are seen not as astral bodies endowed with an individual identity and situated in a particular planetary configuration but rather as generic evil powers that afflict the person just like other ghosts.

37. Pugh (1981, 32) confirms that the Muslim specialists are not known as "astrologers," even if they sometimes use astrology. According to this author, astrology is far more present in the Sunni community than among the Shias.

38. In what concerns the divinatory and astrological techniques practiced among Banaras's Muslim community, we refer to Pugh (1983a and 1988); for a wider view of Muslim esoteric practices in the Indo-Pakistani subcontinent, see Gaborieau (1992). For a general view of divination and astrology in the Islamic tradition, see Fahd (1987 and 1992) and Saliba (1992).

Chapter 1. The Many Branches of a Tree

1. According to Pingree (1981, 118), in India and elsewhere, there are about one hundred thousand manuscripts dealing with different aspects of *jyotiḥśāstra*. As Plofker notes: "It has been estimated that perhaps one-tenth of all extant Sanskrit manuscripts deal with *jyotiṣa* or some other aspect of Indian exact sciences" (2012, 173).

2. For a discussion of the Sanskrit terminology that designates different types of science and knowledge during the early modern period, see Pollock (2011).

3. Regarding the concept of discipline, see Boutier, Passeron, and Revel (2006).

4. About concepts "traveling" from one discipline to another see the "nomadic concepts" examined by Stengers (1987).

5. See especially Pingree (1963, 1989, and 1997a).

6. On the relationship between astrology and medicine, see also Yano (2005) and Beinorius (2008); for an ethnographic approach, see Guenzi (2008). On the relationship between astrology and ritual, see Geslani (2011, 2016, and 2018).

7. The passages cited here refer to the two principal recensions of the JV known as *Ṛk* and *Yajus*: the *Ārcajyotiṣa* or *Ṛgvedavedāṅgajyotiṣa* (RJV), in thirty-six verses, which is part of the Ṛgveda and is attributed to Lagadha (or Śuci quoting Lagadha); and the *Yājuṣajyotiṣa* or *Yajurvedavedāṅgajyotiṣa* (YJV), in forty-four verses, probably a later work that is part of the *Yajurveda*. On the *Jyotiṣavedāṅga*, its dating and its various editions, see Kuppanna Sastry and Sarma (1985), as well as Pingree (1981, 9–10), Plofker (2009, 35–40), and Ōhashi (2015).

8. The term "auxiliary" seems particularly suited to a characterization of *jyotiṣa*, not only because it designates a subsidiary and accessory type of knowledge but also because its etymology is connected to the semantic field of divination. According to Benveniste (1969, 148–151), the Indo-European root *AUG-* designating strength, power (particularly of divine origin), would have given rise to the Latin verb *augere*, "increase" (power), from which both *auxilium* (help, support) and *augur* (augur, predict) are derived. Both these concepts convey the idea of an increase in power (of human action) that corresponds well to the idea of *jyotiṣa* as an auxiliary discipline specializing in augural (reading of planetary omens) and inaugural (celebration of beginnings) activities.

9. From an astronomical viewpoint, the five-year *yuga* corresponds to the time the Sun and the Moon take to be in conjunction in the same *nakṣatra* (Kuppanna Sastry and Sarma 1985). Nonetheless, according to Achar (1997), rather than corresponding to astronomical criteria, the five-year lunisolar cycle is an attempt to adapt the calendar to the fivefold structure of Vedic sacrifice. Achar's interpretation facilitates an understanding of the coherence of this treatise that is problematic from an astronomical viewpoint, something that has been underscored by numerous authors.

10. The YJV (v. 36) identifies certain *nakṣatra*s as fierce (*ugra*) and others as cruel (*krūra*).

11. The name of the deity that rules over the *nakṣatra* should replace that of the sacrificer during the *saṅkalpa*, the "declaration of intent" that precedes the performance of a ritual.

12. On celestial phenomena in the Vedic corpus, see Bergaigne (1963 [1878–1897]) and Oldenberg (1903).

13. In Vedic literature, the *nakṣatra*s are generally seen as "constellations" rather than as regular divisions of the ecliptic. In the twenty-eight-*nakṣatra* system that is found in Vedic literature, Abhijit is inserted between Uttarāṣāḍhā and Śravaṇa and the distance between constellations is variable, while in the twenty-seven-*nakṣatra* system, each one occupies a fixed space of 13°20' (Yano 2003, 378).

14. According to the *Śatapatha Brāhmaṇa* (II, 1.2), for example, the appropriate *nakṣatras* for performing *agnyādhāna* are Kṛttikā, Rohiṇī, Mṛgaśīrṣa, Pūrvā Phalgunī, Uttara Phalgunī, Hasta, and Citrā (Kane 1968–1977, 5, I: 506).

15. Similarly, according to a passage of the *Taittirīya Brāhmaṇa* (1.5.2), a man who wants to ensure his daughter will be loved by her husband and will not be sent back to her parents' home must marry her when the Moon is in Niṣṭyā (Kane 1968–1977, 5, I: 497 and 527). As the names of the *nakṣatras* have evolved over time in the literature, Aghā is later known as Maghā, Arjunī becomes Pūrvā (or Uttarā) phalgunī, and Niṣṭyā Svātī.

16. Kane (1968–1977, 5, I: 524).

17. About appropriate timings in Ayurvedic medical doctrine, see Zimmermann (1980), Ciurtin (2004), Yano (2005), and Beinorius (2008).

18. In his philological study of the *Yavanajātaka*, Mak (2013, 2014, and 2019a) contests Pingree's assumption of the Greek origin of the treatise, as well as the precision of his dating. According to the evidence he collects, although the *Yavanajātaka* incorporates elements of the Greek theory, it is not, as stated by Pingree, the translation of a lost Greek astrological treatise. In his view, the *Yavanajātaka* "was most likely an original attempt by the Indianized Greeks to amalgamate Greek astral science with the Indian one based on a preexistent tradition in India" (Mak 2014, 40). The date of composition of the treatise still has to be ascertained and would be at some point after 22 CE and before the early seventh century, most probably in the late sixth century (Mak 2019a, 22).

19. In astrological theory, these two demons of Hindu mythology come to represent the ascending and descending lunar nodes that correspond to the points of intersection between the Moon's orbit and the ecliptic circle.

20. In this article, the author contrasts the Vedic principle of *nidāna* with the Buddhist principle of *karman*, the former designating a relationship of connection and the latter a causal relationship.

21. On the concept of "resemblance," see Foucault (1970 [1966]).

22. While most of the treatises composed after the fifth century are dedicated to a specific branch of *jyotiṣa*, a few eclectic treatises appear from the thirteenth century onward, particularly in texts with an encyclopedic vocation like the *Jyotirnibandha* by Śūramahāṭha Śivadāsa (second half of the fifteenth century) (Katre 1942) and the *Jyautiṣasaukhya* by Nīlakaṇṭha (second half of the sixteenth century) (Pingree 1981, 115–117).

23. On Varāhamihira's origins, see Biswas (1949). On the Maga Brahmins or Śākadvīpīya, see Stietencron (1966) and Bronkhorst (2016). In Banaras, the Śākadvīpīya Brahmins still occupy pride of place among the town's astrologers.

24. "The Greeks (*yavana*) are indeed barbarians (*mleccha*), but they have brought this science to perfection. If even they are honored as sages, then why

would an astrologer (*daivavid*, "knower of destiny") who is a Brahmin (*dvija*) [not be] even more [honorable]?" (BS 2.30).

25. According to Bhaṭṭotpala, the famous commentator of Varāhamihira's works, this verse is taken from Garga and other authors. In his gloss, referring to verse 1.9 of the BS, he quotes the following verse by Garga: "The outstanding Brahmin (*dvijapuṅgava*) who knows mathematics (*gaṇita*), natal horoscopy (*jātaka*), and divination (*śākhā*), expert in the three branches (*skandha*), is said to be a *saṃhitāpāraga* (great expert in *saṃhitā*)." About Garga as an author, see Geslani et al. (2017).

26. BS 2.36, for instance, provides an enumeration of the three branches *gaṇita*, *horā*, and *saṃhitā*.

27. The *Paitāmahasiddhānta*, described by Varāhamihira in the *Pañcasiddhāntikā* composed in the year 80 of our era, should not be confused with the *Paitāmahasiddhānta* mentioned earlier, which is a part of the *Viṣṇudharmottara Purāṇa*.

28. On the mnemotechnical systems used in the oral transmission of the exact sciences, see Yano (2006).

29. Each *pakṣa* claims affiliation to a founding treatise: thus, for example, the *Brāhma-pakṣa* refers to the *Paitāmahasiddhānta* (beginning of the fifth century), the *Āryapakṣa* to the *Āryabhaṭīya* (around 500), the *Saurapakṣa* to the *Sūryasiddhānta* (around 800, based on an older treatise). The differences between the schools, in terms of the units used to measure time, can be significant: thus, if according to the *Brāhmapakṣa* a *kalpa* (cosmic cycle) contains one thousand *mahāyuga* (cycles of 4,320,000 years), according to the *Ārya-pakṣa* it contains 1,008 and the *kalpa* is hence 4,354,560,000 years long instead of 4,320,000,000. In addition, according to the first school, Kaliyuga (the age we are living in now) corresponds to a tenth of a *mahāyuga*, while according to the second it corresponds to a quarter. For further details, see Pingree (1981, 13–31) and Plofker (2009, 70–72).

30. On *nābhasayoga*, see Pingree (1978, 330–334).

31. In some treatises such as, for example, the *Muhūrtacintāmaṇi*, the study of the *muhūrtas* is considered part of the *saṃhitā* branch of astral literature rather than of the customary *horā* or *phalita* branch. The study of the *muhūrtas* can, in fact, be considered both a "reading of omens" and a type of "horoscopy." In figure 3, the *muhūrta* section could also have been connected to the divinatory branch (*saṃhitā*).

32. For these two subdivisions, Varāhamihira composes the *Ṭikanikayātrā* (Pandit 1951), the *Yogayātrā*, and the *Bṛhadyātrā*, as well as the *Vivāhapaṭala* (Pingree 1981, 107–109).

33. The *Arthaśāstra* (1.9.9 and 10.3.44) shows the astrologer's importance as adviser to the king, although this treatise also warns against the potential dangers of paying excessive attention to the astrologer's opinion (9.4.26) (on the king's

ambiguous attitude toward magical and divinatory devices in the *Arthaśāstra*, see Malamoud 1997).

34. As described in the *Arthaśāstra*, the elements of the sixfold strategy are: peace pact (*saṃdhi*), initiating hostilities (*vigraha*), remaining stationary (*āsana*), marching into battle (*yāna*), seeking refuge (*saṃśraya*), and double stratagem (*dvaidhībhāva*) (*Arthaśāstra* 7.1.1–19); the four methods are conciliation (*sāma*), gifts (*dāna*), dissention (*bheda*), and military force (*daṇḍa*) (2.10.47) (Olivelle 2013, 49–50).

35. Here we use the "three culture" concept to show the epistemologically eclectic nature of *jyotiṣa* in comparison to the disciplinary divisions familiar to the European tradition. In Lepenies's (1990) work, however, the "three cultures" are the humanities, the natural sciences, and the social sciences.

36. According to the example provided by Varāhamihira, if one chooses four substances out of sixteen, it is possible to create 1,820 combinations of perfumes (BS 76. 20, 22).

37. On magic squares, see also Roşu (1989), Kusuba (1993), and Minkowski (2008).

38. There are also technical terms that have vastly different meanings in the different branches of *jyotiṣa*, with no apparent semantic continuity. The concept of *varga*, for example, in the *siddhānta*s designates the "square" (both numerically and geometrically) while in horoscopy treatises it indicates the divisions of the zodiacal signs used in a predictive manner.

39. Among the authors whose work deals with several branches of the astral discipline, apart from Varāhamihira, Pingree mentions Lalla (between the eighth and ninth centuries), Śripati (eleventh century), Bhojarāja (eleventh century), Parameśvara (ca. 1360–1450), as well as certain authors of encyclopedic treatises like Sūramāṭha Śrinivāsa (fifteenth century) and Nīlakaṇṭa (sixteenth century) (Pingree 1981).

40. Although politicians still consult astrologers today, they do so to have their career or family future predicted rather than that of the country they are leading.

41. Among the Indian universities that offer courses in *vāstuśāstra*, we can mention Lal Bahadur Shastri Rashtriya Sanskrit Vidyapeetha (Delhi), Potti Sreeramulu Telugu University (Hyderabad), as well as Banaras Hindu University (Varanasi).

42. The *tājika* technique that is applied both to natal horoscopy (*jātaka*) and to horary astrology (*praśna*) is today seen as an integral part of *jyotiṣa* and is used by astrologers in different regions of India, particularly to interpret "yearly forecasts" (*varṣaphala*). In Banaras, the university course in *jyotiṣa* includes the study of the *Tājikanīlakaṇṭhī*, a treatise on *tājika* composed by Nīlakaṇṭha in Banaras in 1587.

43. The Kerala school is specifically known for the progress made in the field of infinitesimal calculus for $\pi/4$. Traditionally known as the "Leibniz series," after the European mathematician who discovered it about three centuries after his colleague from Kerala, these series have recently been renamed the "Mādhava–Leibniz series." The fourteenth-century *jyotiṣī* also discovered Newton's sine and cosine series that are today known as the "Mādhava–Newton series." While Mādhava's texts expounding these discoveries have been lost, his work came down to us thanks to his disciples, particularly Nīlkaṇṭha Somāyajin (1444–1545) and Jyeṣṭhadeva (sixteenth century).

44. Today, the appropriate horoscope is identified by means of the right thumbprint, but the antiquity of this technique remains unconfirmed (Gansten 2003).

45. Even today, the *Grahalāghava* is one of the works studied in the first year of a master's degree in *jyotiṣa* at Banaras Hindu University (cf. annex).

46. On this subject, see the genealogies established by Pingree (1981, 125–127).

Chapter 2. Professors and Prophecies

1. Some of the universities these researchers are associated with are Allahabad University, Lal Bahadur Shastri Sanskrit University (Delhi), Lucknow University, J. R. Rajasthan Sanskrit University (Jaipur), K. S. Darbhanga Sanskrit University, Ranchi University, Jiwaji University (Gwalior), and others.

2. I am very grateful to Professor Chandrama Pandey for offering me a copy of the book. The conference and the edited volume are dedicated to the memory of Professor Rajmohan Upadhyay, director of the Faculty of Sanskrit Studies and of the Department of Jyotish at BHU from 1960 to 1984. The volume, published by the Department of Jyotish in 2008, is called "Commemorative volume (*smārikā*) for Pr Rajmohan Upadhyay. Conference on ancient Indian astrology (*akhil bhāratīya jyotiṣ sammelan*)" and contains ninety-seven contributions on cancer and astrology.

3. In the Sanskrit education system, these degrees correspond to *śāstrī* (BA), *ācārya* (MA), and *vidyāvāridhi* (PhD).

4. Besides the Department of Jyotish, the Faculty of Sanskrit Studies at BHU includes the departments of *veda*, *vyākaraṇa*, *sāhitya*, *vaidik darśana*, *Jaina bauddha darśana*, *dharmaśāstra*, and *mīmāṃsā*, as well as *dharmāgama*. The Faculty of "Veda and Vedāṅga" at SSU consists of the *veda*, *dharmaśāstra*, *jyotiṣa*, and *vyākaraṇa* departments.

5. Although the town's reputation is corroborated in the early modern period, and amply described in Purāṇic literature, the British government's educational

policies make a fundamental contribution to enhancing and amplifying Banaras's Brahmanical prestige (Dalmia 1997).

6. For a detailed history of Benares Sanskrit College (that becomes the Sanskrit University in the twentieth century), see the studies by Dalmia (1996, 1997) and especially by Dodson (2002, 2007); on Banaras Hindu University, see Dar and Somaskandan (1966) and Renold (2005).

7. Nicholls (1907, 1).

8. On this subject, the pedagogical experiment conducted by the colonial officer Wilkinson at Sehore (Maharashtra) is well known. In his school, founded in 1839, the *siddhāntas* (astronomical treatises) were taught as propaedeutic resources to prepare the students to learn the concepts and methods of modern science (Wilkinson 1834). On this subject, see Sarma (1995), Bayly (1996), Prakash (1999), Minkowski (2001), Dodson (2007), and Sen (2014); for a study of the notion of "useful knowledge" in the educational projects conducted by the British in India, see Dodson (2002).

9. Harrison's fascinating study, "From Medical Astrology to Medical Astronomy: Sol-Lunar and Planetary Theories of Disease in British medicine, *c.* 1700–1850" (2000), shows that the attitude of the British toward astrology has not always been one of outright condemnation. On the contrary, in the eighteenth century, the British doctors settled in India were deeply interested in medical astrology. They conducted empirical and statistical studies, in the framework of Newtonian mechanistic physics, in order to prove the influence of heavenly bodies, particularly the Sun and the Moon, on human health. On the changing attitudes of the British colonial administrators toward the teaching of astrology in Banaras, see Guenzi (forthcoming).

10. The text that was long considered the "manifesto" of the reforms carried out by the British from the1830s onward is the famous "Minute on Indian Education" (1835) by T. B. Macaulay. It marks the victory of "Anglicist" policies that aimed to replace the usage of the vernacular languages, Sanskrit, Persian, and Arabic in Indian schools with English (Macaulay 1935).

11. We were unable to find historical data that allowed us to establish whether astrology (*phalita*) was reintroduced into the teaching program at the Sanskrit College before the latter was transformed into a university in 1958. Further research needs to be carried out in this area. In 1958 the university was called Vārānaseya Saṃskṛta Viśvavidyālaya, and it was renamed Sampūrnānanda Saṃskṛta Viśvavidyālaya in 1973, under the U.P. University Act.

12. Dar and Somaskandan (1966). Vaidik College was the initial name given to what was later to become the College of Theology. Despite Pandit Malaviya's efforts, the observatory was never built.

13. Probably discouraged by the lack of career opportunities for this degree, students preferred Sanskrit studies courses, or diplomas in the modern sciences, available at other departments in the university (Renold 2005).

14. The text of the "Guidelines for Setting Up Departments of Vedic Astrology in Universities under the Purview of the University Grants Commission" was published on the Government of India, Ministry of Education, website (http://education.nic.in/circulars/astrologycurriculum.htm) and was accessible there for more than ten years. The document can still be consulted today at http://sci.astrology.hindu.narkive.com/xZXLxXas/guidelines-for-setting-up-departments-of-vedic-astrology-in-universities.

15. The person promoting the campaign was Minister for the Development of Human Resources (1998–2004) Murli Manohar Joshi. In this context, one may note that the name "Joshi" is not an ordinary surname. In the past, Brahmans of this name were associated with the profession of astrologer (*jyotiṣī*). Nonetheless, before becoming a minister, Mr. Joshi was a university professor of physics.

16. Excluding the staff's salaries (about twenty thousand rupees a month for a professor, fifteen thousand for a reader, and ten thousand for a lecturer), the UGC allocated four hundred thousand rupees for the library (about ten thousand euros at the time), six hundred thousand rupees for the observatory, and five hundred thousand rupees for the computer laboratory and "Horoscope bank."

17. Emphasis added in this and the following quotes.

18. This is the list of universities selected by the UGC: B. R. Ambedkar, Agra, Birla Institute of Technology and Science, Himachal Pradesh, Jammu, Jiwaji, Lucknow, Madurai Kamraj, Mysore, Punjab, Ranchi, Rajasthan, Rashtriya Sanskrit Vidyapeeth, Saurashtra, Shri Jagannath Sanskrit, Shanmuga Arts, Science, Technology & Research Academy, Vikram, Gurukul Kangri Vishwavidyalaya, Kurukshetra, and Osmania. As certain universities (Saurashtra, Kurukshetra, Madurai Kamraj, Gurukul Kangri, Birla Institute of Technology, and Osmania) did not have the capacity to set up the department, they returned the funds they had received for this purpose in the year 2003–2004. Moreover, over the year 2003–2004, additional funding, amounting to 234,000 rupees was allocated to Shanmugha Arts, Science, Technology and Research Academy (University Grants Commission 2004, 101).

19. About the saffronization of education see, among others, Guichard (2010). M. M. Joshi, the minister who promoted this finance law, is known to be a member of the Rashtriya Swayamsevak Sangh (RSS), "National volunteer organization," an extremist fringe of the Hindu nationalist party.

20. Here we present some of the arguments quoted in articles that appeared in *Frontline* magazine as well as in the daily newspapers *The Hindu* and the *Asia Times*, between May and September 2001. For an analysis of the arguments for and against this bill, see Sundar (2002).

21. Supreme Court of India 2004.

22. The mobilization of academic astrologers from Banaras is described in an article published in the *Times of India* on September 18, 2001 (at a time when the rest of the world seemed busy with other issues). The following are

a few excerpts from the article entitled: "Vedic Scholars Defend Astrology": "Scholars of Vedic Astrology have joined hands to convey to people, especially those who are opposing the introduction of astrology in the University curriculum, that astrology is the basis of modern sciences. Prof. Ram Chandra Pandey, head of the Department of Astrology, Banaras Hindu University, Prof. Uma Shankar Shukla, head of the Department of Astrology, Sampurnanand Sanskrit University, Dr. Kunj Bihari Sharma, former head of the Department of Astrology, Sampurnanand Sanskrit University, Dr. Vyas Mishra, head of the Department of Veda, Banaras Hindu University and Dr. Paras Nath Ojha, head of Jyotirveda Vigyan Sansthan have come on a single platform to justify the introduction of the ancient subject in university curriculum. "The fact is that astrology provides the very base to modern sciences," they said, adding that it was a matter of great concern that 'jyotish,' the oldest science of the world, was being described as an unscientific subject without any proof" (http://articles.timesofindia.indiatimes.com/2001-09-18/lucknow/27256282_1_astrology-vedic-university-curriculum).

23. The Arya Samaj, founded in 1870, is a reformist religious movement that was highly influential in North India. It saw the Vedic texts as the founding scriptures of the Hindu religion, endowing them with an authority similar to that of the Bible for Christians and the Koran for Muslims. The reform this movement proposed was essentially to free Hinduism of all its "corruptions" posterior to the Vedic religion, such as the adoration of divine images, the caste system, or child marriage.

24. On contemporary reformulations of the Arya Samaj's "scientific literalism," see Malamoud's (1993) study of the celebration of a Vedic sacrifice in Kerala in 1990, where the organizing committee had commissioned a group of international scientific experts to analyze and measure the biochemical effects produced by ritual performance on the human and natural environment.

25. In the Arya Samaj's founding text, the *Satyārthaprakāśa*, astrology is described as a harmful and vulgar superstition (*jhūṭh*), not to be taught in educational institutions (Dayananda Saraswati 2008 [1875], 64). In his writings, Dayananda Saraswati aims to liberate the Hindus from the dependency on astrologers, who are likely to take advantage of peoples' ignorance by attributing the cause of misfortune to presumed planetary influences. He thus writes that the "horoscope" (*janampatra*) should rather be called a "sorrowscope" (*śokapatra*), and that astrologers are evil planets themselves (*graharūpa jyotirvidābhāsa*) (Dayananda Saraswati 2008 [1875], 35–36).

26. There are currently countless books available on the market that use the appellation "Vedic Astrology." To mention only a few of the most popular in chronological order of publication: B. Behari, *Myths and Symbols of Vedic Astrology*, Passage Press (1990); D. Frawley, *The Astrology of the Seers: A Comprehensive Guide to Vedic Astrology*, Motilal Banarsidass (1990); R. G. Dreyer, *Vedic Astrology: A Guide*

to the Fundamentals of Jyotish, Weiser Books (1997) (it is interesting to note that this author changed the title of her first work, *Indian Astrology: A Western Approach to the Ancient Hindu Art*, published in 1990, replacing the adjective "Indian" with "Vedic" in the revised edition); K. S. Charak, *Elements of Vedic Astrology*, Uma Publications & Motilal Banarsidass (1996); K. Sutton, *Vedic Astrology*, Collins & Brown (2000); N. Rao, *Vedic Astrology: An Integrated Approach*, Sagar (2001).

27. In the following chapter we will see that astrologers in Banaras are also directly affected by the international business of astrology.

28. According to the data published by the University Grants Commission, for the year 2003–2004, SSU had twenty-three students registered for their BA degree course, forty for the master's degree, and eighteen for the PhD. According to the data provided by the BHU administration, the number of students registered at their university for the *jyotiṣa* course was similar.

29. During fieldwork conducted in 2005 and 2008, there were no women preparing degrees in *jyotiṣa* among the students or teachers at this department, at either of the two universities. We nonetheless met two women in Banaras who had obtained master's degrees in *jyotiṣa* from BHU in the 1990s. According to the teachers at the Department of Jyotish, very rarely—every five or six years—would a woman register for this type of degree. More commonly women attend the *jyotiṣa* classes to pursue a personal interest, but generally without registering for the course. They may also attend diploma courses that use Hindi as a medium instead of Sanskrit and are much shorter (one or two years).

30. The question of the astrologer's reputation will be discussed in the following chapter.

31. Generally, students visit the home of their adviser more frequently, but they may also go to other teachers' homes.

32. Religious teachers perform rituals for the families of members of the armed forces and they assist the sick. The army recruits them as junior commissioned officers (JCO), and this is a highly sought-after status as it provides access to major privileges in terms of salary, residence, and first-class travel. There are several categories of religious teachers in the army depending on the faith they represent: the Hindu teacher is called "pandit," the Sikh "granthi," the Muslim "maulvi," the Buddhist "bodh monk," and the Christian "padre." There are more "pandit" positions than the others and they are reserved for Sanskrit graduates. Although a qualification in *jyotiṣa* is not specifically required, it is appreciated, as it is a preparation for both ritual as well as therapeutic functions.

33. When there is a doubt or a discussion about a specific *muhūrta*, the department's researchers organize a "pandit's meeting" (*paṇḍit sabhā*) that gathers not only *jyotiṣīs* but also Brahmins specializing in the *dharmaśāstra*. The identification of *muhūrta*s is based not only on astronomical data but also on ritual rules established by the different Hindu communities.

34. The Sudhākar Dvivedī observatory was meant to revive the Mān Singh observatory in Banaras. The latter, built in the eighteenth century on the banks of the Ganges under the patronage of Sawāī Jai Singh II, is today reduced to a heritage building managed by the Archaeological Survey of India and devoid of any scientific function (about the construction of this observatory, as well as the uses of the Sawāī Jai Singh II observatories in contemporary India, see the PhD thesis by Susan Johnson-Roehr [2011]). The construction of a new observatory on the site of the Sanskrit University is part of a much larger project to rehabilitate the ancient *jantar-mantars* of Sawāī Jai Singh's time. The promoter of this project, Kalyanadatta Sharma, an astrologer and researcher (Singh and Sharma 1978; Sharma 1992), had observatories built in stone from the 1980s onward in Haridwar, Delhi, and Ayodha, as well as on the hills around Jaipur. (I thank Christopher Minkowski and Sreeramula Rajeswara Sarma for having shared this information on the other observatories built by Kalyanadatta Sharma with me.)

35. Among the classical treatises edited and published by professors of the departments of BHU and SSU, there are, for example, the *Bṛhatsaṃhitā*, the *Laghujātaka*, the *Muhūrtacintāmaṇi*, the *Jātakālaṅkāra*.

36. On this subject, an astrologer explained that the reason the divorce rate was far lower in India than in Western countries could be precisely because families were having the horoscopes of the partners analyzed before the marriage.

37. See, for example, the proceedings of the seminar organized by the Department of Jyotish in March 2007 (Pandey and Mishra 2008), and the works by Pandey (2003), Jha (2003), Jha (2006), Shastri (2006), and Tiwari (2006). In popular literature, see, for example, Chaturvedi (2007), Sharma (n.d.), Bhasin (1981), and Charak (1997).

38. To my knowledge, the only treatise dealing with medical astrology as a separate field of research is the *Vīrasiṃhāvaloka*. Composed in North India in 1383 (Meulenbeld 1999–2002, IIA: 229–230), one disease at a time, this interesting treatise compares the etiologies and therapies established, respectively, by astrological, Ayurvedic, and karmic (*karmavipāka*) theories.

39. In the expression *rogayoga*, the term *roga*, generally translated as "disease" designates any kind of physical affliction, "rupture" (*roga* is derived from the root *RUJ-*, to break), and hence indicates diseases, accidents, dangers, or poisoning.

40. See, for example, Pandey (2003), Tiwari (2006), and Upadhyay (2008).

41. For an analysis of the discourses aiming to biomedicalize Ayurvedic theory at universities or among contemporary practitioners, see Langford (2002). For a brilliant historical study on the conceptual transformations of Ayurveda during colonial times due to the introduction of small technologies and medical devices, see Mukharji (2016).

42. In a private interview, the director of the Department of Jyotish at BHU explained to me that the thirty horoscopes of the women suffering from breast

cancer had been sent to the department's researchers by doctors at the Mumbai Tata Medical Institute. I was unable to crosscheck this information.

43. When consulting the home page of BHU's Faculty of Sanskrit Studies in 2011 (http://www.bhu.ac.in/svdv/index.html), a text running along a red banner stated: "Data collection notice for the major project at Jyotish Dept." (*sic*).

44. According to an article published in the *Hindustan Times* on September 6, 2009, this medical astrology project has received 32 lakh rupees of funding from the University Grants Commission, the highest government body regulating university policy (Mohapatra 2008). The author of this article states that not only astrologers but doctors from AIIMS (All India Institute of Medical Science), Guru Teg Bahadur, and Moolchand hospitals in Delhi were involved in this project. This aspect of the study deserves further attention, but the involvement of medical staff in this research project should not surprise the reader. We indeed note that one of the professional distinctions the director of the University College of Medical Science in Delhi, Dr. S. Dwivedi, received for the year 2007 was "Invited speaker in National Symposium on Medical Astrology organized by Sri Lal Bahadur Shastri Kendriya Sanskrit Vidyapeeth (Deemed University) on 'Diabetes—Etiopathogenesis, Symptoms and Prevention,' 3–4 Nov 2007" (http://www.ucms.ac.in/d_medicine.htm). In addition, the most successful author of popular books on medical astrology, Dr. K. S. Charak, is a surgeon at the Indian Spinal Injuries Center, New Delhi.

45. The desire to assert a continuity between Brahmanical knowledge and scientific knowledge is nonetheless not a prerogative of researchers in astrology but is shared by a number of academic scientists. In Banaras, not only do scientists regularly visit astrologers, they are themselves often providing astrological advice. On efforts to legitimize astrology as a science, see also Yongjia (2008).

Chapter 3. Sacred Specialists, Modern Professionals

1. Based on a survey I conducted, as well as the estimations provided by Pugh (1983b, 283), there would be three hundred to four hundred astrologers in Banaras. Nonetheless, this estimate does not take into account the high number of amateurs who occasionally provide astrological counseling, though earning their living by other means (e.g., civil servants, engineers, employees, etc.).

2. According to Parry (1994, 33), almost a fifth of the population in Banaras belongs to a Brahmin caste.

3. Orthopraxy is particularly important since the efficacy of Hindu rituals is supposed to be dependent on the formal and technical precision with which they are conducted, rather than on the moral and spiritual qualities of the specialists who perform them.

4. Ghats are the flights of steps that run along the river Ganges.

5. For a discussion of astrological predictions in television programs in India, and in particular in Bangalore, see Udupa (2016).

6. Aishwarya Rai's horoscope is supposed to contain the *maṅgal doṣ* (Mars's flaw), an astral configuration held as particularly harmful for marriage, for the spouse of the owner of the horoscope, as well as for his or her in-laws. We will look at this astrological concept in chapter 7.

7. On this subject, see among others, the article published in the *Times of India* on November 28, 2006: "Were Rituals Aimed at Removing Hurdles?," http://timesofindia.indiatimes.com/articleshow/msid-618856,prtpage-1.cms, as well as the one in the *New York Times* on January 18, 2007, "Letter from India: Aishwarya Rai and Abhishek Bachchan—Star-Crossed Stars and a Ravenous Press," http://www.nytimes.com/2007/01/18/world/asia/18iht-letter.4254883.html. Despite the media frenzy regarding Aishwarya's astral problems, the Bachchan's family astrologer in Banaras, whom we met several times, denies having performed rituals of planetary purification for the future spouse. We are unable to know whether the astrologer's assertions were an attempt to protect his privileged relationship with the Bachchan family or whether the media shared false information.

8. For ethnographic examples describing the decline, at the community and family levels, associated with the acceptance of planetary gifts, see Van Der Veer (1988) on the Bhareriyas, Raheja (1988) on the Dakauts, and Guenzi (2005) on the Bhrigu and the Giri. The fallen status of these communities is also evident in inscriptions, as Gupta (1983) shows in the case of the Shakadvipi. During our field research we did not meet any Joshi or Shakadvipi Brahmans who still accept gifts for the planets. We also noted that the increasingly rare people who accept this type of offering in Banaras are not astrologers but merely poor Brahmans who are ready to accept this type of inauspicious offering as a means of survival.

9. Astrologers belonging to castes that in the past specialized in the acceptance of offerings to the planets do not seem to suffer any particular kind of discrimination today: on the contrary, they occupy prestigious positions, particularly within the university, and are highly respected.

10. Even today in villages, it is often the *purohit*, or household priest, who possesses ritual and astrological skills, and there is no professional figure specializing exclusively in astrology. With regard to North India, see, for example, Raheja (1988) and Berti (2001).

11. These astrologers are Siddhartha, B. P. Mehrotra, and Kunji Bihari: the former belongs to a family that claims to be Kshatriya (the *varṇa* below Brahmins in the caste hierarchy), while the two others are, respectively, from Khatri (from Punjab) and Agrawal communities, two *jāti*s (caste, birth group) specializing in trade.

12. Gyanvati Pandey, whom we mentioned in the introduction, and Praveen Issar, a young graduate in astrology from Banaras Hindu University specializing in computer horoscope preparation.

13. For a study of the pandit category viewed in terms of its historic evolutions as well as its contemporary form, see Michaels (2001). While referring specifically to the current context of Banaras, the definition of the title pandit we have provided here corresponds to the one suggested by Michaels in his introduction to the aforementioned volume. However, we should state that in Banaras the word "pandit" generally has two meanings. On the one hand it is used as an honorific title attributed to "learned" Brahmans and "custodians of wisdom," but on the other it is also commonly employed to designate any Brahmin who knows a few Sanskrit texts by heart and it does not necessarily imply an honorific recognition of his knowledge. Ritual officiants are called pandits, but far from being seen as learned or wise, on the contrary they have a reputation for being "technicians of Sanskrit" often of questionable morality.

14. When astrologers have other university qualifications, lower than the doctorate, these degrees are mentioned on the visiting card after the name: thus "Pdt. Kashi Nath Chakrabarty, M. A. Jyotish Shastri," "Pd. Ghanshyam Mishra, jyotishastra acharya," and so on (for the equivalences between British university degrees and Sanskrit titles, see note 3, chapter 2).

15. In the context of Banaras, the higher status claimed by practitioners who only *accept* payment, over those who *ask* to be paid, is also mentioned by Clémentin-Ojha (2000, 322) in reference to the distinction between *karmakāṇḍī*s and *paṇḍa*s.

16. It is however important to note that this "discourse" that seeks to proclaim superior status may in some cases be contradicted by practice. When I returned to the field in 2005, for example, an astrologer teaching at BHU had resigned from his academic post despite his young age, which was about forty, to become a full-time "professional" practitioner. It was the money he earned from his consultations, rather than his teacher's salary, that had permitted him to build a large house in a residential area of Banaras, with an attached temple made of marble, to perform *pūjā* for his clients. His lifestyle was constantly improving, and he had no regrets at having left his job at the university.

17. According to our survey, the only exception to this rule is a Khatri family from Punjab, where the profession of astrologer was passed down from father to son.

18. On the essential and constitutive value of the *dakṣiṇā*, the ritual fee paid to the officiants who perform a sacrificial act, see Heesterman (1959) and Malamoud (1976).

19. Kashi (Kāśī, "The Luminous"), one of the names for the city of Banaras, is used in particular to emphasize the sacred nature of the town.

20. When an astrologer is paid, whether it be a "spontaneous" payment or a fixed rate, the client normally leaves one extra rupee above the round number: for a fee of fifty rupees, he will leave fifty-one; for a fee of one hundred rupees, he will leave one hundred and one. This is supposed to make the payment auspicious (*śubh*).

21. These rates correspond to years 2000–2005. They may be twice, three or four times more expensive nowadays since the cost of living is much higher today in Indian urban cities.

22. Hence both astrologers use the title "Shastri" instead of the family surname Chattopadhyay.

23. Among his gurus, like Jayachandra Chakravarti and Danda Swami, Shree Kanth Shastri also mentions a Muslim guru, Haji Abdul Sayad, with whom he would have learned several therapeutic methods specific to the Muslim rituals (*musalmān ṛti*).

24. As specified in note 13 of this chapter, it is necessary to distinguish between the honorary title of "pandit," attributed to scholars, and the substantive "pandit" that designates a Brahmin ritual officiant.

25. When I returned to Banaras in 2008, Neelkanth Shastri had gone to his natal village a few months earlier for health reasons: "Even though Bābā thought he would never fall ill, the planets don't spare anyone" (*graha kisī ko nahī̃ choṛtā hai*), stated his elder son. According to his family, Bābā was in fact suffering the effects of the negative period of Ketu (*ketu mahādaśā*) that had begun in November 2007. In their father's absence, the three sons had not waited long to take over his role of astrologer and were thus able to take advantage of his well-established clientele. The eldest son had moved into the room that had been Bābā's office, and a print of his portrait, along with his father's, surrounded by the rays of the sun, was displayed on the door to the consultation room. The central hall had been transformed into a space for *pūjā*. The second son had started a practice in the village, while the third had set up his office in a room in the building where Bābā used to do *pūjā*. From what they said, Bābā had given them permission to practice (lit., to "sit," *baiṭhnā*) in his place but had prohibited them from reading hands, as this required further study. Nonetheless, according to the local inhabitants and the clients who regretted Bābā's prolonged absence, his illness had been brought on by family disputes and he was saddened by the rivalry between his two children who now shared his clientele and his fame at two ends of the same street.

26. This separation between home and office recalls Gaston Bachelard's reflections in *The Formation of the Scientific Mind*, when he compares the scientist working in a laboratory with the alchemist who makes no difference between his home and his laboratory: "Nowadays, it seems that those who work in laboratories can detach themselves more easily from their work. Their emotional lives are

no longer mixed up with their scientific lives. Their laboratory is no longer at home, in attic or cellar. They leave it in the evening just as one leaves an office, and they go home to their families, to other cares and joys" (2002 [1938], 57).

27. The astrologer's new dog that was far better treated than its predecessor wore a collar studded with precious stones around its neck, and amulets with therapeutic and apotropaic properties.

28. Even in terms of the methods of payment, despite the board displaying a rate of two hundred rupees for the consultation, we observed that people continue to pay whatever they want and according to their means.

29. For example, in 2000 the astrologer had been actively involved in the protest movement against the shooting of Deepa Mehta's film *Water* in Banaras. This film, dealing with the institution of child widowhood, was seen as an attack on the image of Hinduism that should be banned. As the leader of the protest movement, the astrologer was interviewed several times by the press and local television stations. The protest movement mobilized a large section of the population and led to general strikes, making it impossible to shoot the film in Banaras. In 2005 the astrologer also took an active part in the protests against the construction of the Ganges dam at Tehri, as he saw it as an international conspiracy by foreign multinationals to kill the Goddess Ganga. This politicized practitioner has no hesitation in making astrological consultations a tribune for publicizing his ideas and positions.

30. This privileged network of clients developed as a result of the friendship between the astrologer and the politician Amar Singh that developed in 1992, before the latter became a well-known leader of the Samajwadi Party. Apparently thanks to Amar Singh the astrologer met "the Big B" (Amitabh Bachchan), Mulayam Singh Yadav, as well as a whole network of Bollywood stars and multimillionaire businessmen. We were unable to verify the accuracy of the list of celebrities the astrologer says are part of his clientele, but the articles in the local press, and some photographs, confirm he works for some of them. As the astrologer wanted to preserve "professional confidentiality" with regard to the services he has provided to these media personalities, we were unable to obtain much information on the type of consultations provided. The importance of these relationships should however be relativized, as the consultations generally take place over the telephone, and the relationship can be occasional. According to the same astrologer, unlike ordinary clients who develop an exclusive relationship of trust with an astrologer, celebrities often consult several specialists in order to later check the validity of the prognostics (and hence the astrologer's reliability).

31. Today, an increasing number of astrologers work for companies and hotels, are employed by telephone service providers, or work at call centers (for portraits of these "new astrologers," see Wadhwa [2004]).

32. The interpenetration between astrology and commercial practices is even more visible in Calcutta, where a high percentage of practitioners exercise their profession at jewelry shops (Chanda 2002).

33. As we will see in chapter 8, these shops not only sell the "classics" of Indian astral prophylaxis—like gemstones and amulets—they also deal in objects classified under the "feng shui" (*pheṅg śuī*) or *vāstu* category, most of them imported from China.

34. As examples of the type of description the astrologer receives from his American associates: "John Davis, born on 29 July 1959, in Toronto. John will have soon a small surgery for his hernia. Please can you prescribe yajna [ritual] for his upcoming hernia surgery"; "Susan Kieler, born on 20 May 1977 in Austin. Susan is an actress who wants to become a movie star. Please perform a yajna [ritual] so that she will become famous."

35. On the relationship between the person's planetary situation and the type of *pūjā* to be performed, see chapter 8 in this volume.

36. This information dates from 2008. In 2017 Jitendra Narayan Pandey still works for Cyber Astro as senior vice president, but has moved to the headquarters of the company in Gurgaon.

Chapter 4. Horoscopes and Truth

1. For a discussion of the connection between knowledge and technical skills, in the context of South Asian studies and anthropology, see the introduction to Mahias (2011).

2. According to philologists, the term *horā* is a transcription of the Greek ὥra, but according to Indian astrologers seeking to claim the autochthonous nature of Indian astrology, it is a word of Sanskrit origin, formed out of the elision of the initial *a* and the final *tri* of the term *ahorātri*, literally, "day (*ahar*) and night (*rātri*)" (the first time this etymology is mentioned is in Varāhamihira's *Bṛhajjātaka* [BJ 1.3]). The term *phalita*, more commonly used than *horā* by today's astrologers, comes from *phala*, "fruit," and hence indicates the science that studies the "fruits" or "effects" of the movement of the stars.

3. The discipline that includes both chiromancy and physiognomy is called *sāmudrikaśāstra*.

4. This divinatory technique is explained in the *Śivasvarodaya*, a text that became popular in France following Daniélou's translation (1982). On this text, see also Pellissero (1991) and Chenet (1998b).

5. With regard to oneirology in the Sanskrit literary tradition, see Esnoul et al. (1959), O'Flaherty (1984), and Upadhyay (1996). For an ethnographic study, see Khare (1967).

6. While the term used to designate an astrologer reputed for his horoscope readings is *vidvān*, "scholar," the term generally used for a specialist excelling in other techniques is *pāraṅgat*, "expert." The latter term emphasizes the practical aspects of knowledge.

7. We prefer to describe this approach as "deductive" rather than "predictive" as the latter term implies a relationship of temporal anteriority of the utterance to the event, which is not necessarily the case, for example, when the astrologer "divines" the number of brothers or children a person has.

8. This category generally designates everything related to sorcery (*ṭonā-ṭoṭkā*), the evil eye (*nazār*), the spirits of the dead (*bhūt-pret*), and so forth.

9. Although the two words *cakr* and *kuṇḍalī* are often employed as synonyms, *cakr* is most often used to refer to a simplified horoscope in the form of a single diagram, while *kuṇḍalī* indicates a connected series of diagrams, as they are presented in the *janm kuṇḍalī*.

10. Nonetheless, many astrologers consider that the nation's future should be calculated on the basis of the date India was declared a republic (January 26, 1950).

11. Our goal here is not to enter into the technical details of the theory of Hindu horoscopy. For this, the reader may consult handbooks of Hindu astrology written by both Indian and Western authors, which provide detailed explanations of the subject (see note 19, Introduction).

12. The traditional horoscopes we saw are decorated along both sides of the length of the seven-meter-long scroll. On the left there are representations of the twelve zodiacal signs, while on the right there are anthropomorphic figures of the nine planetary deities and the three Gods, Varuṇa, Prajāpati, and Yama. The choice of adding "three" Gods to the nine planets meets the need for symmetry with the twelve zodiacal signs that run along the left side of the horoscope, but we cannot explain why it is specifically these three Gods of Vedic origin.

13. Computerized horoscopes are considered more reliable, from a descriptive viewpoint, in terms of the calculation of the positions of the stars, but their interpretative and therapeutic sections are little appreciated. For this reason, most people who consult astrologers prefer horoscopes that are handwritten by astrologers and their assistants.

14. The diagram reproduced here is the one generally used in North India and hence in Banaras. In South India and in Bengal, the twelve houses are also inscribed within a quadrangle but are disposed differently.

15. The list of the twelve houses presented here uses the names provided in the *Bṛhajjātaka* (BJ 1.15) and the *Lāghujātaka* (LJ 1.18) by Varāhamihira, in the *Bṛhatpārāsarahorāśāstra* (BPHŚ 11.2–13) by Pārāśara, and in the *Jātakapārijāta* (JP 1.49–52) by Vaidyanātha.

16. We will discuss the representation of the individual in the horoscope in chapter 6.

17. When filling in the horoscope, the ascendant sign (*lagna*) is placed in the first house and the following signs are placed, in zodiacal order, in a counterclockwise direction: if, for example, the ascendant is Libra, this zodiacal sign is attributed to the first house, Scorpio to the second, Sagittarius to the third, and so on. The planets are then placed according to their position in relation to the signs. Astrologers generally pay little attention to lunar mansions when interpreting horoscopes. Because of this, we will deal with *nakṣatra*s in the paragraph concerning the study of *muhurta*s, auspicious moments for undertaking activities, where they play a fundamental role.

18. For a discussion of this system of cosmological correspondences, see Guenzi (2008).

19. The potato harvest takes place in February and October. At the time of the harvest the farmer may decide to sell the potatoes immediately or store them in government warehouses to sell them at a higher price when the season is over.

20. As Tarabout's (2002a) study shows, the theory of *praśna* formulated in the texts attributes great divinatory value to the person who asks the question: the first initial of his name, the constellation (*nakṣatra*) under which he is born, the direction his body faces, the direction in which he looks, his posture, his clothing, his mood, the parts of his body or the objects he touches while asking the question, and so on, play a major role, as *signs* in the formulation of the diagnosis (on this subject, see also chap. 51 of the *Bṛhatsaṃhitā*). Nonetheless, according to our survey of astrologers in Banaras these indications involving the questioner himself are rarely taken into account, and the diagnosis of the *praśna* is mainly based on astrological data, that is to say, on the horoscope calculated at the time the question is asked.

21. In the case of a *praśna* regarding the temple in Kerala described by Tarabout (2002a), the questioner's "neutrality" toward the question asked seems to be an asset, when one uses a child as an "innocent" messenger of the divine for the ritual of the "eight auspicious objects" (*aṣṭamaṅgala*).

22. Title of respect the client uses to address the astrologer.

23. About regional differences in Hindu calendars, see Merrey (1982).

24. Pugh's analysis is based on four Hindi almanacs that are widely circulated in the Banaras region: the *Hṛṣīkeś Pañcāṅg* (or *Kāśīviśvanāth Pañcāṅg*), the *Viśva Pañcāṅg*, the *Paṇḍit Gaṇeś Āpajī Pañcāṅg*, and the *Paṇḍit Gaṇeś Dutta Pañcāṅg*. Her study mainly focuses on *muhūrta*s for the life cycle rites, for foundation laying ceremonies and for beginning agricultural work. For an analysis of the contemporary uses of the concept of *muhūrta* in Maharashtra, see Leutgeb (2000).

25. *Uttarāyaṇa*, the "northern path," indicates the term that runs from the winter solstice to the summer solstice and *dakṣiṇāyana*, the "southern path," indicates the six months between the summer solstice and the winter solstice.

26. The *nakṣatra māsa*s last about thirteen days and are defined by the Sun's passage through each of the twenty-seven *nakṣatra*s along the ecliptic.

27. *Śuklapakṣā* designates the "luminous" fortnight that runs from the new moon to the full moon; *kṛṣnapakṣa* designates the "dark" fortnight that runs from the full moon to the new moon.

28. Some of the astrologers in Banaras are themselves publishers and authors of almanacs.

29. The *Kāśīviśvanātha Pañcāṅga* (or *Hṛṣīkeśa Pañcāṅga*) is known as one of the most authoritative almanacs in Banaras. It is published in two versions, one in Sanskrit and the other in Hindi. Here we are referring to the Sanskrit version as it is more complete and contains more details on the subject of *muhūrta*. Some terms appear in Hindi because they are presented in this manner in the Sanskrit version of the almanac.

30. *Caitra* is the first month in the Hindu calendar and runs more or less (depending on the years) from the middle of the month of March, till the middle of the month of April.

31. For a description of Hindu *saṃskāra*s, see Pandey (1994).

32. The present participle of the verb to be (*AS-*), *sant-* (*in initio compositi*, *sat-*), designates the "appropriate," "right," "correct" nature of a certain moment.

33. The *mūla nakṣatra*s are six *nakṣatra*s—Aśleṣā, Maghā, Jyeṣṭhā, Mūlā, Revatī, and Aśvinī—ill-omened for a birth: if, at the time of the child's birth, the Moon is in one of these six *nakṣatra*s, the parents need to perform a pacification ritual known as *mūl śānti* (pacifying the *mūl*).

34. This is in no way a unique case. Astrologers often see clients who want to know the best time for a delivery; the option of having a caesarean makes it far easier to manipulate destiny. This enthusiasm for a "surgically created horoscope" has also become a lucrative business on the internet. Several sites specializing in Hindu or Vedic astrology sell services in this field. Thus, for "only" $99, the "Himalayan Ashram of Vedic astrologers" (http://www.soothsayers-india.com) provides a service called "Pre Determining the Birth Time of Your Child" that allows people to identify the most auspicious time for a child to be born by caesarean.

35. The three types of divinatory knowledge we have described so far—*jātaka*, *praśna*, and *muhūrta*—belong to the branch of *jyotiṣa* known as *horā* and this term indicates the time-related aspect of divination.

36. On the author of this treatise, Kālikāprasadā Śarman, "royal astrologer" (*rāja-jyautiṣī*) in Banaras in the twentieth century, see Pingree (1970–1994, 2: 32).

37. The "ideal lifespan" of a human being's life is the same as that of horoscopic theory: 120 years.

38. In Hari Krishna Dikshit's opinion, each planet is supposed to govern a part of the face, about the size of a 25 paise coin (a coin earlier in use that was worth a quarter of a rupee).

39. For an in-depth textual and historical analysis of physiognomy in India, see the detailed and systematic study recently published by Zysk (2016).

40. Chapters 68 and 70 examine the different parts of men and women's bodies. Chapter 69 identifies a man's physical typology depending on the dominant planetary influences. Chapters 50 and 51 also deal with physiognomy, but according to Bhaṭṭotpala's commentary (tenth century of our era) these are later additions that should not be attributed to Varāhamihira. Chapter 50 deals with the different parts of the body the *praśna* questioner touches, and chapter 51 with the significance of pimples (*piṭaka*), wounds (*vraṇa*), and marks on the body (*tilaka*).

41. Although, as we saw, Hindu horoscopy is not anthropocentric, physiognomy is even less so: the body of human beings is studied no differently to that of other animals. The chapters of the *Bṛhatsaṃhitā* dedicated to a study of the "signs" (*lakṣaṇa*) of the human body, in fact follow the chapters dealing with the *lakṣaṇas* of cows, dogs, cockerels, tortoises, goats, horses, and elephants.

42. The consultation took place on January 11, 2000.

43. Horoscopes can in fact be manipulated to convince matrimonial partners of the woman's youth, as horoscopes are always exchanged before a marriage is arranged.

44. This planetary conjunction occurs when the three planets are in an exalted position in the horoscope.

45. In this case too, there is an allusion to the idea that the child may have been swapped at the hospital.

46. The consultation took place on November 23, 1999.

47. Here again empirical evidence is questioned through the astrological diagnosis: as the mother has difficulty accepting the daughter's educational failure given the astrologer's statement that she "should have" passed the exams, she prefers to think the failure is not "real" but the result of a trick.

48. The fact that the young girl does not even have long hair, which is generally the case in India, is the "coup de grace" that puts an end to the astrological diagnosis.

49. We will deal with this subject in detail in chapter 6.

50. On this subject, astrologers can consult either the horoscope of the person or the horoscope of the *praśna*. In both cases, they generally look at the position of the malefic planets (*pāp graha*) in relation to the houses VI, VIII, or XII, which, respectively, represent diseases and enemies (VI), death (VII), and losses (XII). On this subject Sharma's text *Jyotiṣ aur Rog* (Astrology and Diseases), provides a list of the planetary configurations (*grahayog*) that serve to identify the disorders caused by evil spirits (*piśāc*), charms (*abhicār*), curses (*sāp*), and bewitchment (*mohan*) (Sharma n.d., 89–90).

51. For details of the astrological configurations that allow one to test the questioner's truthfulness, see, for example, Bhat (1992, 29).

52. The consultation took place on November 14, 1999.

53. Leucodermia is a disease greatly feared by people in India; it results in the progressive loss of "patches" (*dāg*) of pigmentation,and a loss of skin sensitivity.

54. The consultation took place in February 2000.

55. About the rules and principles to calculate horoscope matching according to astrological theory, see Kemper (1980).

56. In the text *Jyotiṣ aur Rog* (Astrology and Diseases) the *gupt rog*s include the following diseases: gonorrhea (*prameh*), pain during urination (*mūtrakṛcchra*), syphilis (*upadaṃśa*), vaginal discharge (*pradar*), and sterility (*napuṃsakatā*) (Sharma n.d., 92).

57. According to the astrologer, the man did not even want to cross-check the astrological information with medical tests as he had such faith in the truth of the horoscope. One can of course wonder if this "astrological revelation" was the only and real reason why the marriage was canceled, as the astrologer proudly claimed, or whether the horoscope was merely used as a pretext. We have no means of checking this. In any event, this example illustrates how horoscopes may be used to justify a choice. Seen from this angle, this case is in no way exceptional, as we will see in chapter 7, where we deal with weddings between *maṅgalā* and *maṅgalī* couples.

Chapter 5. Karma and *Bhāgya*

1. The Sanskrit word *karman*, "act," is known as "karma" in English and most of the anthropological and Indologist literature hence refers to the "theory (or doctrine) of karma." We will follow this convention. Nonetheless, when we refer to the Sanskrit term itself (and not to the theory) we will use the uninflected form *karman* and, in the same manner, when referring to a recorded interview in the field, we will use the term in the Hindi form of *karm*.

2. A third book on the theme, also published in the United States and edited by Neufeldt (1986), deals with postclassical developments in the theory of karma. However, this work adopts a more philosophical approach, unlike the anthropological perspective that marks the first two volumes.

3. On this subject, see also Kolenda (1964), Obeyesekere (1968), Sharma (1973), Nuckolls (1981), Wadley and Derr (1989), Berti (1992), Nichter (1992), as well as Nichter and Nichter (2010).

4. Despite the diverse forms it takes in the different textual traditions, the theory of karma will be mentioned here in its most minimal form, as a doctrine that postulates a relationship of causality between the moral quality of acts and their fruit in this life, as well as past and future lives. For a discussion about general definitions of the karma theory, see O'Flaherty (1980, xi).

5. As stated in Patañjali's *Yogasūtra*, when entering a new body, the karmic residue determines three things: *jāti* (birth, the genus into which one is born),

āyus (life span), and *bhoga* (the experience of pleasure and suffering) (Potter, 1980, 244). These three aspects of human existence are also, and precisely, the core of horoscope theory.

6. Chenet quotes similar passages from other astrological treatises: "[the astronomical cosmos, the Zodiac] completely reveals the portion arrived at maturity [able to produce their fruits] of good and bad actions performed during previous existence" (*Bṛhajjātaka* 1.3); "The results of previous actions that Creator and Destiny have proclaimed by registering them on [lines of] the forehead, this science elucidates them, just as a lamp reveals objects in the midst of thick shadow" (*Vṛddhayavanajātaka* 1.3) (Chenet 1985, 111). In the *Bṛhatpārāśarahorāśāstra* planets are defined as *karmaphalada* (bearing the fruit of *karman*) (BPHŚ 2.3).

7. On the interpretation of the doctrine of karma as a theodicy, based on Max Weber's reflection and on her ethnography in a village of Himachal Pradesh, see Sharma (1973). Here we will prefer the term "cosmodicy" to "theodicy," since the "cosmos," rather than God, is concerned.

8. Halbfass (1980, 269). The author mentions certain materialistic and fatalistic trends in Indian thought as being the only exceptions.

9. Halbfass (1980) deals, in particular, with the idea of *apūrva* in the Mīmāṃsā and the idea of *adṛṣṭa* in the Vaiśeṣika.

10. In other words, even if we admit that the "lamp trick" makes it possible to formally reconcile natal horoscopy with the karma doctrine, the difficulty arises when we attempt to apply it to other astrological methods, such as *praśna*, *muhūrta*, and *saṃhitā*. For example, how can karmic residue explain the fact that the same person obtains different results depending on the astral configuration present at the time he undertakes an activity, as set out in the branch of astrology dedicated to *muhūrta*s? This impasse, and others, are examined in Krishan's (1983) study, the only author, to my knowledge, who emphasizes the difficulty in connecting the two theories of human destiny.

11. With some reservations, we could suggest the hypothesis that the limited "impact" of the theory of karma on popular Hinduism may also be due to the importance of astrology as an alternative theory of human destiny. In fact, astrology seems to be much better adapted than the karma theory to explaining human destiny as it is experienced on a daily basis with its everyday issues.

12. The relationship between astrology and karma theory could be fruitfully studied from a textual perspective, through an analysis of the literary genre of *karmavipāka* (maturation [of the fruits] of actions done in previous lives). As Pingree (1997b) shows in his seminal work, which as far as I know was never followed up, treatises on *karmavipāka* approach the study of diseases by combining astrological and karmic approaches. Among them, Rājavīrasiṃhatomara's *Vīrasiṃhāvaloka*, composed in North India in 1383, for example, is a nosological treatise that compares astrological, Ayurvedic, and karmic approaches to the study

and treatment of each disease (see also Meulenbeld 1999–2002, IIA: 229–230). Another later treatise, the *Jñānabhāskara*, composed in the fifteenth century, studies diseases as being caused, respectively, by astrological and karmic forces. The suggested therapies are different: diseases caused by planetary influences are treated through the performance of rituals of pacification (*śānti*), while karmic effects are neutralized though rituals of expiation (*prāyaścitta*) (Pingree 1997b). For an ethnographic study of the rituals described in the *karmavipāka*, see Nichter and Nichter (2010).

13. In the image of the two wheels of the scooter, we can clearly identify a "modernized" version of the well-known metaphor of the two wheels of the chariot found in the *Yājñyavalkyasmṛti*, where the two wheels are those of destiny (*daiva*) and human effort (*puruṣakāra*): "Just like the movement of a chariot is not possible only by a single wheel, destiny (*daiva*) cannot succeed without human effort (*puruṣakāra*)" (*yathā hyekena cakreṇa rathasya na gatirbhavet/ evaṃ puruṣakāreṇa vinā daivaṃ na sidhyati*) (*Yājñyavalkyasmṛti* I.350–351). Nonetheless, the categories employed are different (*daiva/puruṣakāra* vs. *bhāgya/karm*) and we will return to these differences later.

14. From a textual viewpoint, Long (1980) mentions *bhāgya* as one of the names used in the Mahābhārata to refer to destiny, but then, when he analyzes the idea of destiny in the epic, he only takes the terms *daiva* and *diṣṭa* into consideration.

15. Although in his conclusion to the edited volume *Karma: An Anthropological Inquiry*, Daniel emphasizes that the opposition between karma and *bhāgya* "is a distinction worth pursuing further" (1983, 292), the question does not seem to have aroused the interest of anthropologists since. However, in her study on narratives about destiny, duty, and devotion among female Hindu *sādhu* in Rajasthan, DeNapoli refers to the combined themes of karma and *bhāgya* as narrative strategies with which women negotiate their own ambiguous public position as ascetics (2009, 91).

16. According to Van Buitenen, the word *bhakti* that originally signified "distribution," "sharing," progressively came to mean "accepting or adopting something as one's allotted share" (1981, 24). The etymology of the word *bhāgya* and the semantic differentiations originating from the root *BHAJ-* in the history of Hindu religious traditions, would, in my opinion, deserve further investigation. Sharma (1977) elaborates some stimulating remarks about Sanskrit and vernacular terms stemming from the root *BHAJ*-related to food distribution.

17. On the basis of this blindness, Dumézil (1956) asserts an explicit parallel between the Vedic deity Bhaga—corresponding to the Avestan Baga, "God," and the Phrygian Bagaios "Lord"—and the Roman Goddess Fortuna.

18. Sanskrit is not the only language to recognize an etymological relationship between the idea of "share" and destiny. Balaudé (1997) examines, for example, the

relationship in Greek between the verbs that signify "to share" (*meiromei*, *daiō*) and the nouns that express the idea of destiny (*moira*, *heimarmanè*, and *daímōn*).

19. The *Mānak hindī koś* provides the following definition of *bhāgya*: "the divine rule or rule of destiny according to which all events occurring during the existence of living beings, and especially human beings, are seen as predetermined and ineluctable; as effects of this, human beings experience all kinds of happiness and sorrow and their life goes on" (*vah īśvarīya yā daivī vidhān jiske sambandh mẽ yah mānā jātā hai ki prāṇiyõ, viśeṣataḥ manuṣyõ ke jīvan mẽ jo ghaṭnāẽ ghaṭtī hai, ve pūrv-niścit aur avaśyaṃbhāvī hotī hai aur unhī̃ ke phalasvarūp manuṣyõ ko sab prakār ke sukh duḥkh prāpt hote haĩ aur unke jīvan kā kram caltā hai*) (Varma 1965, 4: 209).

20. On the opposition between *daiva* (or *diṣṭa*) and human effort (*puruṣakāra*), see Woods (2001), Nayak (1997), Long (1980), and Weiss (1980).

21. Guenzi and Singh (2009).

22. On this subject, see Kane (1968–1977, 3: 543–661). The word *dāy-abhāga* literally means "the share of *dāya*," with *dāya* meaning the "given share," wealth, or inheritance (Kane 1968–1977, 3: 543).

23. This passage by Dumont refers to the question of inheritance rights as defined by the Mitākṣarā legal school that was predominant all over India, except Bengal (where the Dāyabhāga school is followed). Concerning the debate between the two schools, see Kane (1968–1977, 3: 552ff.) and Dumont (1983, 9–13).

24. Sacrificial ritual that is usually performed in case a life is in danger.

25. 1 *lakh* = 100,000 rupees.

26. *Karma bhāva* signifies "house of *karman*," with the word *karman* meaning, in this context, "profession," "career," and "leadership."

27. This case was observed on November 22, 1999.

28. *Viṃśottarī daśā* is the most widespread system in North India, while in the South, the *aṣṭottarī daśā* (based on a life span of 108 years) system is usually followed. On the system of *daśā*s it is interesting to note that this is a purely conventional predictive system, that is to say, it does not use any astronomical data. The duration of the *daśā* does not correspond to the duration of planetary orbits and the series of planets that control the successive periods does not obey the respective ranking in the solar system. The principle that governs this system is hence not of an astronomical nature but is used to establish alternating good and bad periods over the course of an existence.

29. The planet that rules the first *antardaśā* of any *mahādaśā* is the same as the one that rules the *mahādaśā* itself. The duration of every *antardaśā* is equivalent to the number of years the *mahādaśā* in question lasts, multiplied by the the number of years of the planet's *mahādaśā* divided by 120. Thus, Jupiter's *antardaśā* would be the first *antardaśā* of Jupiter's *mahādaśā* and will last for a period of 16 years × 16/120 (or 0.13) = 2 years, 1 month, and 18 days; Saturn's

antardaśā will be the second *antardaśā* of Jupiter's *mahādaśā* and will last 16 years × 19/120 (or 0.1583) = 2 years, 6 months, 12 days, and so on.

30. The astrologer is sixty years old.

31. According to the astrologer, at that time, people feared that this unusual planetary conjunction could have an inauspicious influence. For this reason many rituals were performed in order to avoid negative effects. Some historic testimonies of worries and rituals celebrated in 1962 because of *ashta grahi yog* can be found on the internet.

32. When a planet is located in a zodiacal sign (*rāśi*) governed by an enemy planet, it is said to be in *nīc* (lower, inferior) *rāśi*.

33. *Dṛṣṭi*, "gaze," or "aspect" in astrological language.

34. Sometimes, in this conjunction, instead of Mars it could be the Moon, which is believed to provoke a largely "mental" obsession with sex. When Saturn is in the zodiacal sign of Taurus (*vṛṣa*) the person is supposed to have incestuous relations or adulterous relations within the family. In addition, we must note that when Venus and the Moon are together in the fourth house, and are aspected by Saturn or Rāhu, the *kāmāndh* conjunction is supposed to affect the mother of the owner of the horoscope, who would hence be of a "loose character."

35. On the astrological details of this *yog*, see Khankhoje (1997, 75).

36. The chapter is called *Purvajanmaśāpadyotanādhyāya*.

37. BPHŚ (83.2).

Chapter 6. Shared Destinies

1. The profusion of details a horoscope can provide about the native's entourage can be illustrated by the fact that classical treatises describe in great detail the women who will attend the birth of the native. Thus, according to astral conjunctions, one can state the type of ornaments they will be wearing, their physical features, and their behavioral attitudes (SRV 9.21–23), the caste they belong to (SC 2.61–64), and whether they are widows (SC 2.65).

2. As the philological history and the dating of these texts is complex and controversial, we refer to Pingree (1981, chap. 5) and to Kane (1968–1977, V, part I, section II). In what concerns the editions, for the BPHŚ and the SRV, we refer to the editions by Santhanam (1984 and 1996); for the SC, we follow Bhasin's (1997) edition. The translations from Sanskrit are mine.

3. The word *ariṣṭa*, from the root *RIṢ*-, "to be hurt or injured," "to perish," "to hurt," "to destroy," is also used in medical literature, where it designates the "symptoms of death."

4. We refer here to the *athāriṣṭādhyāya*, "chapter dealing with the *ariṣṭas*," which corresponds to the ninth chapter of the BPHŚ and to the tenth chapter of

the SRV. When quoting Sanskrit verses, to make the reading of divinatory sentences easier, we distinguish between the "protasis" (the clause expressing the condition that precedes the independent phrase and states the astrological conditions) and the "apodosis" (the main clause of a conditional sentence that states the effects of the astral configurations) by putting apodoses in italics.

5. As we will see later in this chapter, horoscope treatises mainly refer to male natives, as a female's destiny is treated in a separate chapter about "female horoscopy" (*strī-jātaka*).

6. In the second verse of the BPHŚ (9.25) mentioned earlier, the father had already been mentioned.

7. The *navāṃśa* is one of the "seven systems of divisions" (*saptavarga*) of the zodiacal signs used by Hindu horoscopy. It refers to the division of zodiacal signs into "nine (*nava*) parts (*aṃśa*s)." Each fraction of 3° and 20' corresponds to a zodiacal sign, which makes it possible to multiply the possible interpretations of astral charts.

8. On this subject, we should note that in the first of these three verses (BPHŚ 9.25) death is expressed by a past participle (*mṛta*) in the locative absolute form (*mṛte pitari*): this expression hence states that at the birth of the child, the event of the father's death has already occurred. In the second *śloka* (BPHŚ 9.40), however, it is the optative *syāt* of the verb "to be" (*AS-*) that designates the event of the death. The optative—based on the present theme—means that at the time of the child's birth, the death of the father that has already taken place will occur. This expression seems to us to be particularly striking, as it would be based on the principle according to which an earlier event can be determined by a later event. But is it precisely in this violation of the principle of *consecutio temporis* that the idea of embedded family destinies is most powerful.

9. On this subject, according to the Sārāvalī, Sun as the indicator of the father is replaced by Saturn in the case of nocturnal births.

10. The *kāraka*s can however change depending on the texts and the different astrological traditions.

11. As for the planets, the association between the houses and the members of the family can also vary according to the texts and the astrological traditions. We will limit ourselves to the BPHŚ here, in order to reduce the technical complexities as far as possible, and to facilitate an understanding of the fundamental principle.

12. Each zodiacal sign is ruled by a planet: the ruler of Aries is Mars, the ruler of Taurus is Venus, and so forth.

13. One will hence examine whether Mercury is in a completely exalted or debilitated position, if it is aspected by benefic or malefic planets, and so on.

14. The words *sahaja* (from *saha*, "with," and *ja*, "born") and *sodara* (from *sa-udara*, "co-uterine") mean "those who are born together" and thus do not make a gender distinction between brothers and sisters. To distinguish between brothers and sisters, the terms *bhrātṛ* (brother) and *bhaginī* (sister) are used.

15. Other astral configurations indicating the *sodaranāśa*, the destruction of brothers and sisters, can be found in the SC (4.2–14).

16. The astrologer is referring to the performance of rituals or the act of wearing precious stones.

17. The Moon is supposed to create physical problems connected to cold and humidity, like colds in the example cited.

18. One cannot help noting the misogynist nature of this verse: while the beneficial effects of the planetary configuration mentioned are attributed to the man, the malefic effects of the same configuration are attributed to women.

19. Khankhoje (1997, 277).

20. On the number of wives, see BPHŚ (18.19–21) and specifically SC (6.15–36) where the number of wives is evaluated up to one hundred, two hundred, or even three hundred.

21. Similarly, among the native sexual partners, the SC includes a sterile woman, a menstruating woman, a pregnant woman, a dark-skinned hunchbacked woman, as well as a four-legged animal (SC 6.80–83, 85).

22. See the postface to the Tel edition of *Homo hierarchicus* (Dumont 1979).

23. *Candrādhiyoga*, that is to say, *adhiyoga* based on Candra (Moon), is an astral configuration that appears when benefic planets are in the sixth, seventh, and eighth house from the Moon. Depending on the strength of the planets involved, the *jātaka* will become a king, a minister, or an army chief (see, i.e., BPHŚ 37.5). The effects of this conjunction are hence considered "impossible for women" (*strīnām asambhava*).

24. To gain an idea of the thoroughness of the information a horoscope can provide on *ego*'s entourage, one may quote the manual of medical astrology, *Jyotiṣ aur Rog* (Astrology and Diseases). It provides very detailed descriptions of the astral configurations responsible for pimples and skin infections (*phoṛā-phuṃsī, vraṇ*) that affect the father, the mother, the children, the brothers, and other members of the owner of the birth chart's family (Sharma n.d., 76).

25. See in particular chapter 4, "Blood Across the Stars: Astrology and the Construction of Gender" (Kapadia 1995, 68–92).

26. The use of horoscopes, Kapadia observes, is in fact limited to the well-off families in the village, as the poor families cannot afford to have a detailed horoscope drawn up.

27. The author explains that the unmarried daughter's horoscope is supposed to have a specific influence on the maternal uncle's family, as the girl is normally married into this family.

28. See, in particular, O'Flaherty (1976 and 1980), V. E. Daniel (1983), and S. Daniel (1983).

29. The concept of the "collective individual" is developed by Descombes (2001). Although devoid in this context of its philosophical meanings, this expression perfectly describes the status of the person within the horoscope. The

individual, "he who is born" (*jātaka*), the owner of the horoscope, consists of a set of social and family relationships.

Chapter 7. Astrology and Possession

1. About the representations of the nine planetary deities (*navagraha*), see Markel (1995). About the *navagrahas* as a group in Sanskrit literature and in contemporary practices, see Guenzi (2008). On devotional narratives, iconographic representations, and ritual practices addressed to Saturn, see Guenzi (2005).

2. Here, we choose to employ the term "syndrome" (which etymologically signifies "running together, concurrence [of symptoms]") as it refers to a complex group of symptoms that characterize a pathology, and this closely corresponds to the types of planetary afflictions we are dealing with here.

3. In Tamil Nadu, for example, *maṅgal doṣ* is more commonly called Sevvay dosham (*cevvāy tōṣam*, from *cevvāy*, "red," the Tamil name for Mars); similarly *kāl sarp yog* is sometimes known as Naga dosh (in Tamil, *nāga tōṣam*), in certain regions of India. This also signifies the "the serpent's flaw." For an analysis of these categories in the Tamil context, see Kapadia (1995, 82–89) and Allocco (2009 and 2014).

4. From our research, although the classical horoscopy treatises do not mention these categories, some of them, like the *Bṛhatparāśarahorāśāstra* (BPHŚ) or the *Sarvārthacintāmaṇi*, nonetheless contain passages that could be related, even if not necessarily genealogically, to these astrological categories. For example, in the chapter on women's horoscopy (*strījātaka*), the BPHŚ describes the astral conjunctions that lead to widowhood (*vaidhavya*) (BPHŚ 82.47, 48, and 49) that recall certain aspects of *maṅgal doṣ*. The *Muhūrtacintāmaṇi* mentions marriage with the jar (*kumbha vivāha*) in the section dealing with the astral conjunctions (*yoga*) of widowhood (*vaidhavya*) (Joshi 1992, 305–308). In what concerns the origin of the *śani sāṛhe sātī*, it is mentioned in a medieval treatise, the *Dharmasindhu*, which contains the instructions for a pacification (*śānti*) rite for an "affliction that lasts seven and a half years" (*sārdhasaptavarṣikapīḍā*) caused by Saturn (Kane 1968–1977, 5: 2nd part, 756). On the *kāl sarp yog*, see note 47, this chapter.

5. The advertisement, as it appeared in the *Times of India* of September 25, 2008, indicates cell phone numbers to call for each state and town, in case the client wants to order the CD by phone.

6. "Help me: advice on eliminating *maṅgal doṣ*."

7. http://www.indiadivine.org/audarya/vedic-astrology-jyotisha/446962-help-me-manglik-dosh-nivaran-tips.html.

8. http://www.indiaparenting.com/boards/showmessage.cgi?messageid=47&table_name=dis_zodiac_signs.

9. Representations related to Mars's influence will be examined here in greater detail than those related to the other planets. We have dealt extensively with Saturn in a previous publication based on a case study (Guenzi 2005).

10. The couple owns a sari shop in the north of Banaras.

11. On this subject, it is interesting to note that certain Muslim ritual officiants, specializing in the treatment of victims of sorcery, also establish a relationship between Maṅgal and the difficulties young girls have in getting married. We observed several of their consultations and treatments. These officiants spoke of *Mahāmaṅgal*, "the great Maṅgal," as a malefic demon that prevents young girls from getting married, and for which one must wear coral and observe a fast on eleven Tuesdays. According to these officiants, to celebrate the end of the fast, Hindu girls should go to the *Maṅgalā Gaurī* temple in Banaras, and Muslim girls should throw yellow offerings (yellow rice, yellow flowers, yellow sweetmeats) into the Ganges. All the girls who have completed the ritual fast must wear a yellow thread (*tāgā*) on their arm.

12. For a literary account of the life of a young Bengali girl suffering from *maṅgal doṣ*, see Sharma's tale "Rites of Passage" (Sharma 1995).

13. A person is said to be *prabal maṅgalik*, "very strongly *maṅgalik*," when Maṅgal is located in the houses mentioned, counted not only from the ascendant (or first house) but also from the sign in which the Moon is located at the time of birth. The strength of *maṅgal doṣ* is, however, mitigated when Maṅgal is found in a house occupied by a sign it rules over, that is to say, Aries and Scorpio.

14. *Maṅgal doṣ*, "Mars's flaw" is neutralized, for example, if the *lagna* (or first house) is occupied by Aries, if the fourth house is occupied by Scorpio, if the seventh house is occupied by Capricorn, if the eighth house is occupied by Cancer, and so forth. For a list of the astral conjunctions that cancel or reduce the *maṅgal doṣ*, see Khankhoje (1997, 272–273).

15. "Manglik" is the Indian English transcription of *Maṅgalik*.

16. The advertisements quoted are taken from the *Sunday Times*, "Matrimonials" (May 15, 2002). Emphasis added.

17. KK and SP indicate the two Brahmin subcastes Kanya-Kubja and Sarjupari.

18. BHP is an acronym for biodata, horoscope, and photo.

19. These acronyms, respectively, stand for: Medical Doctor (MD), Master of Surgery (MS), Master of Dental Science (MDS), Bachelor of Dental Science (BDS), Engineer (ENG), Master of Business Administration (MBA), Indian Administrative Service (IAS), and Charted Accountant (CA).

20. Indian Administrative Service employees.

21. Non-Resident Indians, or Indians living abroad, most often in the United States, United Kingdom, or the Gulf countries.

22. Agarwals and Marwaris are castes traditionally associated with trading activities.

23. We were unable to carry out an in-depth study of this subject, but according to our survey the categories that are mostly concerned with the "manglik" or "non-manglik" identity seem to be those involved in liberal professions (lawyers, engineers, doctors, etc.), business activities, information technology, as well as civil servants and academics.

24. The Hindi almanacs can contain instructions on the procedure and the formulae to be recited at a *kumbha-vivāha*, "marriage with a clay jar." See, for example, the *Hṛṣīkeś Upādhyāy Hindī Pañcāṅg*, the Hindi edition of the *Kāśīviśvanātha Pañcāṅga* (Department of Jyotish 1999–2000, 6).

25. According to the astrologers Mridula and Prakash Trivedi, authors of the work *Foretelling Widowhood* (2008), entirely dedicated to identifying astral conjunctions responsible for widowhood, the most fortunate Indian women are those whose horoscope shows the *akhaṇḍa saubhāgya yoga* astral configuration (astral conjunction of uninterrupted conjugal happiness). This "conjugal happiness" configuration means that the wife dies before her husband: "The conjunction of *akhaṇḍa saubhāgya yoga* in the horoscope of women is most fortunate for them. Almost one hundred per cent of married women have an inner desire to die before their husbands but only a few are fortunate to have their desire fulfilled" (Trivedi and Trivedi 2008, 277).

26. An astrologer recounts that in earlier times, *maṅgalī* girls were married to a God in a temple and they were forced to spend three years at the temple before they could be married to a "human" husband. Nonetheless, according to him, as during these three years the girls were often the victims of sexual abuse by the priests, the tradition gradually became obsolete.

27. The number of *guṇ*s, "qualities," shows the degree of compatibility of a couple using the *kuṇḍalī milānā* method, the matching of the horoscopes. The mathematical calculations for this method are described in the sixth chapter of the *Muhūrtacintāmaṇi*, in a section called *guṇa-gaṇana* (calculation of qualities) and describing the eight criteria (*aṣṭakūṭa*, "eight peaks") that give the final score. About its applications in Sri Lanka, see Kemper (1979).

28. In other words, protective marriages serve to terminate the *mārakatv*, the deathly potential attributed to Maṅgal's *prabhāv*.

29. Nonetheless, in certain cases, astrologers prescribe coral for the non-*maṅgalik* member of the couple, as a direct protection against the harmful influence of Maṅgal transmitted by the *maṅgalik* spouse.

30. After four months during which she had taken refuge with her daughter in a church, the woman returned home for a few days to return the daughter to her father, and then she left again.

31. As this consultation took place in Bengali, we only have the English translation without the transcription.

32. It is because of this excessive strength that being *maṅgalik* is considered more dangerous and undesirable in a woman than a man.

33. For a study on the iconography, the myths, and the astrological characterization of Śani, as well as on Śani's shrines, priests, and devotional practices in Banaras, see Guenzi (2005).

34. "Tantras to Gain Favor with the Nine Planets" by Shukla (1993).

35. For someone born, for example, with the Moon in Aries, *śani sāṛhe sātī* occurs when Śani passes through the signs of Pisces (twelfth in relation to Aries), Aries itself, and Taurus (second in relation to Aries).

36. Remaining for two and a half years in each house of the horoscope, Śani indeed takes thirty years to pass through all twelve houses. At the end of thirty years, Śani hence returns to the twelfth house in relation to *rāśi*. In other words, every recurrence of *sāṛhe sātī* begins twenty-two years and six months after the end of the preceding *sāṛhe sātī*.

37. "*Śani kī sāṛhesātī anek jyotirvidõ ke liye kāmadhenu hai*" (Trivedi 1996, xi).

38. With regard to the works mainly intended for an American audience, we should also mention Svoboda's text, *The Greatness of Saturn: A Therapeutic Myth* (1998), a translation of the Gujarati version of the *Śani mahātmya* by Pranjivan Harihar Shastri. The author, an American from Texas who studied Ayurvedic medicine and *jyotiṣa* in India for several years, writes in the preface that he was inspired to write a book by the end of his seven and a half years of Saturnian affliction. He thus explains the motivations that drove him to write: "My motives are both selfish, for I hope to make Saturn happy by this action, and altruistic, for I hope that others can similarly use it to make their own lives happy by pleasing Saturn" (Svoboda 1998, 21). The books aims to serve as a *kathā*, a devotional tale that, when read aloud, is beneficial to the reader.

39. Tamil word designating the entry of a planet into a zodiacal sign; it corresponds to the Sanskrit term *saṃkrānti*.

40. The temple is situated in South Delhi, near the posh areas of Hauz Khas and Greater Kailash. About Śani's shrines and their *pujārī*s in modern Delhi, see Bellamy (2014).

41. The Mahābhārata (1.17.4–8) narrates that during the churning of the Ocean of Milk, Rāhu drank the nectar of immortality reserved for the Gods and was decapitated by Vishnu after the Moon and the Sun had denounced him. For this reason, Rāhu's head, which became immortal thanks to the nectar, takes its revenge by devouring the Moon and the Sun at the time of the eclipses.

42. With regard to the separate origin of the demons Rāhu and Ketu and their progressive inclusion (Rāhu to start with and then Ketu), in the group of the *navagraha*s, the "nine planetary deities," see Gail (1980), Duchesne-Guillemin (1990), and Markel (1990 and 1995).

43. For this characterization of Rāhu and Ketu, see Shukla (1993).

44. The same kind of offering can also, at times, be made to Śani. Raheja mentions the *chāyā kā dān* among the "disarticulative substances" used to remove inauspiciousness from the body (Raheja 1988, 91).

45. Like the *tulā dān* (the "gift of the balance," offering of one's body-weight of gifts), the *chāyā dān* also seems to have initially been prescribed to protect the king and the kingdom's well-being. In a study based essentially on the *Viṣṇudharmottara Purāṇa*, Inden (1985) mentions the practice that involves the king looking at his own face reflected in a plate of ghee every morning. The priest then had to examine the plate and the qualities of the ghee, to read the omens they represented: "If the ghee was clear and sweet-smelling, there would be victory (*vijaya*), if it smelled bad or slipped in the dish, it foreboded danger (*bhaya*), and if his face was distorted (*vikṛta*) in it, he would obtain death; if radiantly handsome (*suprabha*), well-being (*śubha*)" (Inden 1985, 31).

46. This treatment is prescribed particularly for jaundice, as it is supposed to remove the bad color from the person's face.

47. Despite its current popularity, we find no trace of the *kāl sarp yog* in the classical horoscopic treatises and the origin of this astrological concept remains obscure. The reference to snakes nonetheless exists in certain classical works. Quoting the sage Parāśara, in the *Bṛhajjātaka* (BJ 12.2b) Varāhamihira mentions a "sarpa yoga," although Rāhu and Ketu are not evoked in this respect. The BPHŚ (chap. 85) describes astral configurations provoked by the "serpents curse" (*sarpaśāpa*) that cause sterility. These planetary configurations deal particularly with the fifth house (house of children) and Rāhu plays a major role. To eliminate their ill effects, the BPHŚ prescribes performing a *nāga-pūjā* (a ritual to propitiate snakes) with a golden idol in the shape of a snake, which corresponds to the contemporary practices that aim to eliminate the *kāl sarp yog*. Even if these are two different astral conjunctions, most contemporary astrologers seem to conflate *kāl sarp yog* (planetary conjunction where all the planets are on the same side, in relation to the two lunar nodes) and the *nāga doṣ* (planetary configuration described in the classical treatises, concerning the fifth house of the horoscope).

48. On this topic see Gail (1980) and Markel (1995).

49. Kapadia (1995, 86–89). See also Allocco (2009 and 2014).

50. The areas of life affected by the *kāl sarp yog* are supposed to vary depending on where Rāhu and Ketu are located at the time of birth: for example, if Rāhu and Ketu are, respectively, located in the fifth and the eleventh houses, the effects of the *kāl sarp yog* will mainly be felt in the areas of studies and children (fifth house) and money, profit (eleventh house).

51. Consecration (*abhiṣekam*) of Śiva in the form of Rudra.

52. On the Bhairava cult in Banaras, see Chalier-Visuvalingam (1986).

53. The dog is an appropriate receptacle for this type of substance loaded with negativity, not only as Kāl Bhairav's vehicle but also as an animal deeply scorned by the Hindus. In fact, while doing the *ghumānā* (rotating the substances around the head) it is prohibited to give this type of substance to a domestic animal (*pāltū jānvar*), cows in particular, as after having eaten it sixteen times, they could fall ill or even die. This type of substance should be given to stray animals in the street like dogs, which, in Banaras, are rarely kept as pets.

54. Hence the Hindi expression *x par graha ā gayā*, which literally means "the planets have come on x," is used to designate a sort of malefic possession by the planets.

Chapter 8. More or Less Effective

1. These approaches characterize theories of ritual efficacy originally developed, respectively, by Malinowski, Evans-Pritchard, Lévi-Strauss, Tambiah, and Csordas. For a review of the different ways of envisaging ritual efficacy in anthropology, see Podemann Sørensen (2006) and Hüsken (2007). On the question of ritual efficacy, see Sax, Quack, and Weinhold (2009), as well as the special issue of the *Journal of Ritual Studies*, "The Efficacy of Rituals" (Quack and Sax 2010).

2. Unlike Sanskrit astral treatises (*jyotiḥśāstra*), popular works in Hindi found in bookshops and at bookstalls in Banaras are filled with ritual and therapeutic instructions to be followed to free oneself from planetary influence (see, e.g., Gaur 1997; Shastri n.d.; and Shukla 1993). We have nonetheless noted that the remedies prescribed by astrologers generally differ to those indicated in this type of literature.

3. *Cālīsā* designates an "aggregate of forty," in this case the forty verses that make up this prayer to Śani (along the lines of the most famous *cālīsā* dedicated to Hanumān).

4. "Jab jīvan mẽ, kaṭhin pariśram ke bād bhī, kām pūrā nahī̃ ho pātā, tab ham graha nakṣatrõ kī sthiti kī cintā karte hai."

5. According to Wadley, *śakti* "carries the concepts of strength, energy, and vigor; but the strength is based on spiritual force, not physical force" (1975, 55). Nevertheless, this contrast between "physical" and "spiritual" does not make sense for our research. In his study of the wrestlers of Banaras, Alter observes that "wrestlers use the term *śakti* to refer to their strength. They do this because for them strength is never something which is simply physical. . . . *Śakti* refers unambiguously to the size of a wrestler's neck and thighs, the gleam in his eye, his appetite, and the radiance of his oiled body, and also his devout, passive, and self-controlled disposition" (1998, 139). But the examples quoted by Wadley are

even more convincing of the dual nature, both physical and spiritual, of *śakti*. The author observes that everything that exerts control over the human condition is considered *śakti-sampann*, "endowed with *śakti*": thus, the grain of wheat is "endowed with *śakti*" because if it does not grow, people will not be able to eat; the plow is "endowed with *śakti*" because if it does not work properly, there is no sugarcane; a young married couple is "endowed with *śakti*" due to their potential for fertility and prosperity; a snake is "endowed with *śakti*" because it can kill humans with its poison (Wadley 1975, 56). These examples clearly show that all physical strength involves a spiritual power, just as all spiritual power involves physical strength, and both dimensions are constitutive of the idea of *śakti*.

6. A planet's astrological "strength" is defined in relation to six types of *bal*: *sthānbal* (*bal* that varies depending on the position [*sthān*] of the planet, that is, the house and the zodiacal sign), *digbal* (*bal* that varies depending on the directions, *diś*), *kālbal* (*bal* that varies according to the time [*kāl*], day or night, the month and year), *ceṣṭābal* (*bal* that varies according to the type of movement [*ceṣṭā*], retrograde or not), *dṛgbal* (*bal* that varies according to planetary "aspects," *dṛṣṭi*), and *naisargik bal* (*bal* that varies according to the "natural force," *svābhāvik bal*, of the planet: thus, the Sun is considered the most powerful of the planets, followed, in order, by the Moon, Venus, Jupiter, Mercury, Mars, and Saturn).

7. Another word that confirms the dual connotation of the planetary status is *dṛṣṭi*. The word *dṛṣṭi* designates both a planet's "gaze" as a divine anthropomorphic being, its intervention, and the astrological aspect, that is to say, the mutual influence the planets exert over each other when they are in certain angular configurations in relation to the earth.

8. The relative prices of these three methods of performing *pūjā* vary depending on the astrologer and the type of *pūjā* to be performed.

9. On the importance of numbers and enumerations concerning ritual, for the Vedic period see the chapter by Malamoud, "Exegesis of Rites, Exegesis of Texts" (1996, 247–258). The connection between ritual efficacy and enumeration is clearly established by White (1996) who, on the subject of tantric ritual, remarks: "This Vedic fascination [with numbers] becomes a veritable obsession in tantrism, in which we witness nothing less than an explosion of numbers, categories and numbers as categories. In the tantric case, the hallucinating proliferation of number-based homologies—between microcosm, mesocosm and macrocosm—appears, in the final analysis, to reassure the tantric practitioner of the efficacity of his ritual acts" (1996, 16).

10. Two stones represent Saturn: the sapphire—which can cost as much as twenty thousand rupees—and the amethyst that costs a few hundred rupees. Thus, the amethyst has to be replaced regularly, while the sapphire is supposed to retain its efficacy for an unlimited period. According to the astrologer Kameshwar Upadhyay, the amethyst has a maximum life span (*kul āyu*) of ten months, after which it loses all its efficacy.

11. Nonetheless, there are cases where the clients insist that the astrologer procure the stone, as they place greater trust in the astrologer than in the lapidary; in these cases, the astrologer procures a precious stone for the client. Nonetheless, on several occasions I noticed the astrologers' reluctance to procure the stone themselves; they emphasize they are not involved in the gem business, and it is not their profession to buy or sell precious stones.

12. In the event that the astrologer is not satisfied with the stone the client has bought, he suggests the client exchange it for a better one. Thus, the operation can be repeated several times.

13. Efficacy is the same provided that the devotee recites the prayers "according to the rules" (*vidhivat*) and pronounces the words correctly.

14. In what concerns the methods of celebrating the *grahaśānti*, the rituals for pacifying the planets, according to medieval literature, see Kane (1968–1977, 5: part 2, 749–756), Mishra (1973, 120–123), Dange (1986, 1105–1120), Vogel (2007). About astrology and *śānti* rituals, see Geslani (2011 and 2016).

15. The representation of the *navagraha*s at the entrance to temples is an expression of the same principle, according to which the *navagraha*s are apotropaic deities who should be honored before paying homage to a major God (Markel 1995).

16. *Yājñavalkyasmṛti* 1.294 (quoted in Kane 1930–1962, 5: 749).

17. Indra's wife.

18. The "Lion-man," the fourth avatar of Viṣṇu.

19. About Hanumān as a symbol of physical strength, see Alter's (1992) study of the wrestlers (*pahalvān*) of Banaras; about his temple in Banaras, see and Claveyrolas (2003); on Bhairava as Kotwāl of Banaras, see Chalier-Visuvalingam (1986).

20. For ethnographic examples of *sādhana* accomplished to obtain supernatural powers for healing purposes, see Kakar (1982).

21. On mantras and ritual diagrams in Hinduism, see the edited volume by Padoux (1986). See, in particular, Padoux's introduction for an explanation of the continuity between the sound of the mantra and the spatial representation of ritual diagrams; for a specific description of the idea of *yantra* (particularly in contrast to the *maṇḍala*), see the contribution of Brunner (1986). With regard to mantras and *yantra*s as used in medicine and in Indian alchemy, see Roşu (1986).

22. More precisely, it is the ritual diagram (or written mantra) that corresponds to the phonic mantra, rather than the opposite. As Padoux observes in the introduction to the edited volume *Mantras et diagrammes rituels dans l'hindouisme*, diagrams are only a sort of "spatial medium" for the phonic element, which is the mantra, and "no Hindu ritual diagram exists without its corresponding mantra: mantras bring the diagrams 'to life'; through them, the Gods are settled (using *nyāsa*); through them rites are performed" (1986, 1).

23. These *jantar*s are written with soluble ink that dissolves in water. The *jantar* is placed in water, and the person drinks it.

24. Toffin (1989) identifies a similar opposition between a "Vedic pole" and a "tantric pole" of priesthood among the Rājopādhyāya Brahmans of Nepal.

25. Precious stones are also seen as belonging to this second category of remedies, which are immediately accessible and hence suit the demands of modern life.

26. Indeed, we have seen that most of the clients for whom the astrologer Paras Nath Ojha performs *havan*s, *jap*s, and *pāṭh*s are foreigners. These types of rituals can also be ordered by internet and are available at a number of sites that sell diagnostic and therapeutic services in the field of Hindu or Vedic astrology.

27. Some horoscopy treatises like the *Jātakapārijāta* (JP 2.21) mention the stones associated with each planet. The names of the stones used in astrology are, respectively, in Sanskrit (S) and Hindi (H): *māṇikya* (S and H) for ruby; *muktā* (S) or *motī* (H) for pearl; *pravāla* (S) or *mūṅgā* (H) for coral; *gārutmata* (S) or *pannā* (H) for emerald; *pūṣparāga* (S) or *pukharāj* (H) for topaz; *vajra* (S), *hīra* (S), or *hīrā* (H) for diamond; *indranīla* (S) and *nīlam* (H) for sapphire; *gomeda* (S and H) for garnet hessonite (or zircon); and *vaiḍūrya* (S) or *lahasuniyā* (H) for cat's eye (or beryl).

28. Sometimes, as one can take one's own medication without seeking a prescription from a doctor, some people wear stones without consulting an astrologer, as the beneficial effects of certain stones are well known even among laymen. Not surprisingly, the owner of a large precious stone shop in the town center defined himself as a "pharmacist" in an interview: "Just as a pharmacist gives you a *Crocin* [common painkiller] if you have a headache," he explained, "I know the appropriate stones for all kinds of symptoms . . ."

29. Topaz is cheaper than many other very expensive stones like diamonds, rubies, sapphires, and emeralds, but is more expensive than amethyst, zircon, or chrysoberyl. The price of a topaz, between the most expensive stones and the cheapest, means that it can be used as a sign of distinction or economic privilege, while being accessible to a fairly wide-ranging clientele.

30. Thus, for example, as we saw in the previous chapter, people may think that a woman wearing coral, Mars's stone, has a *doṣ* (defect/flaw) related to marriage.

31. Apart from women, children and teens also normally wear stones concealed beneath their clothing, either for practical reasons (playing or practicing a sport), or because they do not want to show their friends they are wearing a stone. For children, just as for women, stones are not considered a symbol of power but rather a sign of weakness.

32. In theory, the *muhūrta* (appropriate moment) to wear a stone for the first time should be defined in relation to the *nakṣatra* (lunar mansion) rather than the days of the week, but for practical reasons, astrologers prefer to refer to

the days of the week. In addition, one should choose the right *muhūrta* not only when wearing a stone but also when purchasing the stone and at other crucial moments. Thus the manual *Sampūrṇa Ratna Vijñān* (The Complete Science of Precious Stones; Joshi n.d.) indicates the appropriate *nakṣatras* and their "sections" (*caraṇa*) for buying the stone, for setting (*jaṛvānā*) it in a ring, for performing the *prāṇa pratiṣṭhā* (installation of life-breath) ritual or the purification (*śodhan*) ritual and, finally, for wearing (*dhāran karnā*) it the first time (Joshi n.d., 193–204).

33. On the *prāṇa pratiṣṭhā* performed for divine images, see Courtright (1985), Clémentin-Ojha (1990), Einoo and Takashima (2005), Colas (2012), and Keul (2017).

34. The woman is referring to the exhaustion of power that occurs after several years of wearing fairly cheap stones such as cat's eye.

35. Guru, "teacher," is another name for Jupiter, the planet that governs mind (*buddhi*).

36. A man who sold precious stones and who had worked in several regions of India told us in an interview that only astrologers in Banaras prescribe such a high number of carats. According to this salesman, in Madhya Pradesh, Gujarat, and Maharashtra, the minimum number of carats is much lower (about two carats).

37. This confirms the idea that stones have an effect not only on the person who wears them but also on those close to them: the researcher's wife lost a sari because of the stone her husband was wearing.

38. As we saw, the power of an amethyst is supposed to wear out after a certain time, for this reason, after five or six years, the client is concerned and wants to know if the stone is still effective.

39. *Prabāl* is another name for coral.

40. On the popularity of the snake-rope metaphor, found in several Upaniṣads to explain the illusions created by *māyā* and widely used "among all strata of Hindu laity," see Bharati (1961, 212–213).

41. These concerns regarding changes in the stone seen as signs of a loss of power recall attitudes toward divine *mūrtis*, which are believed to no longer be inhabited by the deity when they are broken, burned, removed from their pedestal, and so forth (cf. Clémentin-Ojha 1990, 118–119).

42. Tarabout (1999, 134–135) describes a similar case in Trivandrum, Kerala, involving a psychiatrist who says he was saved from a heart attack by a ring set with a sapphire.

Conclusion

1. Parallels can be established between the reading of the horoscope in order to identify potential predispositions to diseases and the genome sequencing

offered by some American companies, which both serve the same purpose. On the return to "divination" as a perverse effect of biomedical research, see Lock (2005) and Palmié (2007).

2. The vitality of astrology as a business in contemporary India is something the Indian press is well aware of. On this subject see, for example, the reports that appeared in *Outlook India* (Wadhwa 2004) and the *Telegraph* (Banerjee and Banerjee 2007). According to Wadhwa, the turnover of the business of astrology in India would be something like four hundred billion rupees and it would be the second sector in terms of rate of expansion, after the insurance sector.

Annex

1. This is the program published by the Department of Jyotish at Banaras Hindu University for the academic year 2000–2001. I would like to thank Setsuro Ikeyama, Agathe Keller, and Mahesh K. for their clarifications regarding the content of the *gaṇita* texts. I am nonetheless responsible for any mistakes. In what concerns the recently composed treatises (nineteenth and twentieth centuries), I have provided supplementary information in the notes. For the texts that do not deal with astronomy, I refer to the astrological branch dealt with in parenthesis.

Bibliography

Abbreviations of the Sanskrit texts cited and the editions cited:

BJ = *Bṛhajjātaka* of Varāhamihira (Jha 1974)
BPHŚ = *Bṛhatpārāśarahorāśāstra* of Pārāśara (Santhanam 1984)
BS = *Bṛhatsaṃhitā* of Varāhamihira (Jha 2011)
JP = *Jātakapārijāta* of Vaidyanātha (Chaudhary 1953)
JV = *Jyotiṣavedāṅga* of Lagadha (Kuppanna Sastry and Sarma 1985)
LJ = *Laghujātaka* of Varāhamihira (Mishra 1993)
MC = *Muhūrtacintāmaṇi* of Rāma (Joshi 1992)
RJV = *Ṛgjyotiṣavedāṅga* (Kuppanna Sastry and Sarma 1985)
SC = *Sarvārthacintāmaṇi* of Vyaṅkaṭaśarman (Bhasin 1986)
SR = *Sāmudrikarahasya* of Kālikāprasadā Śarman (Sharma and Mishra 1999)
SRV = *Sārāvalī* of Kalyāṇavarman (Santhanam 1996)
YJV = *Yājuṣajyotiṣavedāṅga* (Kuppanna Sastry and Sarma 1985)

Achar, B. N. Narahari. 1997. "A Note on the Five-Year Yuga of the Vedāṅga Jyotiṣa." *Electronic Journal of Vedic Studies* 3, no. 4: 21–28.

———. 2000. "Searching for Nakṣatras in the Ṛgveda." *Electronic Journal of Vedic Studies* 6, no. 2. http://ejvs.laurasianacademy.com/ejvs0602/ejvs0602.txt.

Adorno, Theodor Wiesengrund. 1994. *The Stars Down to Earth and Other Essays on the Irrational in Culture.* London: Routledge.

Ahern, Emily M. 1979. "The Problem of Efficacy: Strong and Weak Illocutionary Acts." *Man*, n.s., 14, no. 1: 1–17.

Allocco, Amy L. 2009. "Cacophony or Coherence: Ethnographic Writing and Competing Claims to Ritual and Textual Authority." *Method and Theory in the Study of Religion* 21, no. 1: 3–14.

———. 2014. "The Blemish of "Modern Times: Snakes, Planets, and the Kaliyugam." *Nidān* 26, no. 1: 1–21.

Alter, Joseph S. 1992. *The Wrestler's Body: Identity and Ideology in North India*. Berkeley: University of California Press.

———. 1998. "Hanuman and the Moral Physique of the Banarsi Wrestler." In *Living Banaras: Hindu Religion in Cultural Context*, edited by Bradley R. Hertel and Cynthia Ann Humes, 127–144. Delhi: Manohar.

Avdeeff, Alexis. 2014. "Les feuilles de palme et le stylet: l'art de la prédiction astrologique chez les Valluvar du pays tamoul (Inde du Sud)." PhD dissertation, École des Hautes Études en Sciences Sociales, Toulouse.

Bachelard, Gaston. 2002 [1938]. *The Formation of the Scientific Mind: A Contribution to a Psychoanalysis of Objective Knowledge*. Manchester: Clinamen.

Bailly, Jean Sylvain. 1787. *Traité de l'astronomie indienne et orientale*. Paris: Debure l'aîné.

Balaudé, Jean-François. 1997. "La 'part' de l'homme: entre destin et nécessité." In *Le Destin: Défi et Consentement*, edited by Catherine Chalier, 19–33. Collection Morales 21. Paris: Éditions Autrement.

Banerjea, J. N. 1948. "Surya, Aditya and the Navagrahas." *Journal of the Indian Society of Oriental Art* 16: 47–100.

Banerjee, Paulomi, and Malini Banerjee. 2007. "Star Turn: Astrologers Are Reinventing Themselves to Keep Up with the Modern Times." *Telegraph, Sunday Supplement*, May 13.

Bayly, Christopher A. 1996. *Empire and Information: Intelligence Gathering and Social Communication in India (1780–1870)*. Cambridge: Cambridge University Press.

Beinorius, Audrius. 2008. "Astral Hermeneutics: Astrology and Medicine in India." In *Astro-Medicine: Astrology and Medicine, East and West*, edited by Anna Akasoy, Charles Burnett, and Ronit Yoeli-Tlalim, 189–208. Micrologus's Library 25. Florence: Sismel Edizioni del Galluzzo.

———. 2015. "Transformations of the Social and Religious Status of Indian Astrologer at the Royal Court." In *Astrology in Time and Place: Cross-Cultural Questions in the History of Astrology*, edited by Nicholas Champion and Dorian Gieseler Greenbaum, 53–66. Cambridge: Cambridge Scholars.

Bellamy, Carla. 2014. "The Age of Śani in Modern Delhi." *Nidān* 26, no. 1: 22–41.

Bentley, John. 1825. *A Historical View of the Hindu Astronomy: From the Earliest Dawn of That Science in India, to the Present Time*. London: Smith Elder.

Benveniste, Émile. 1969. *Le Vocabulaire des institutions indo-européennes, 2: Pouvoir, droit, religion*. Le sens commun. Paris: Éditions de Minuit.

Bergaigne, Abel. 1963 [1878–1897]. *La religion védique d'après les hymnes du Rig-Veda*. 4 vols. Bibliothèque de l'École des hautes études 36, 53, 54, and 117. Paris: Honoré Champion.

Berti, Daniela. 1992. "Il karma in un villaggio dell'India del Nord: Aspetti e Problemi Antropologici." *Studi e Materiali Di Storia Delle Religioni* 16, no. 2: 53–69.

———. 2001. *La parole des dieux: rituels de possession en Himalaya indien*. Monde indien. Paris: CNRS Éditions.

Bharati, Agehananda. 1961. *The Ochre Robe*. London: George Allen & Unwin Ltd.

Bhasin, J. N. 1981. *Medical Astrology: A Rational Approach*. New Delhi: Sagar.

———, ed. 1986. *Sarvārthacintāmaṇi, with English Translation*. Delhi: Sagar.

Bhat, Ramakrishna. 1967. *Fundamentals of Astrology*. New Delhi: Motilal Banarsidass.

———. 1992. *Essentials of Horary Astrology or Praśnapadavī*. Delhi: Motilal Banarsidass.

Billard, Roger. 1971. *L'astronomie indienne: investigation des textes sanskrits et des données numériques*. Publications de l'École française d'Extrême-Orient 83. Paris: École française d'Extrême-Orient.

Biot, Jean-Baptiste. 1862. *Études sur l'astronomie indienne et sur l'astronomie chinoise*. Paris: Michel Lévy frères.

Biswas, D. K. 1949. "The Maga Ancestry of Varāhamihira." *Indian Historical Quarterly* 25: 175–183.

Borges, Jorge Luis. 1942. "El idioma analítico de John Wilkins." *La Nación*, February 8. Text and English translation available on http://www.ldc.upenn.edu/myl/wilkins.html.

Boudet, Jean-Patrice. 2006. *Entre science et nigromance: astrologie, divination et magie dans l'Occident médiéval (XIIe–XVe siècle)*. Histoire ancienne et médiévale 83. Paris: Publications de la Sorbonne.

Boutier, Jean, Jean-Claude Passeron, and Jacques Revel, eds. 2006. *Qu'est-ce qu'une discipline ?* Enquête 5. Paris: Éditions de l'Ehess.

Bronkhorst, Johannes. 2016. *How the Brahmins Won: From Alexander to the Guptas*. Handbook of Oriental Studies, Section 2, South Asia 30. Leiden: Brill.

Brunner, Hélène. 1986. "*Maṇḍala* et *yantra* dans le śivaïsme āgamique." In *Mantras et Diagrammes Rituels Dans l'hindouisme*, edited by André Padoux, 11–31. Paris: CNRS Éditions.

Burgess, James. 1893. "Notes on Hindu Astronomy and the History of Our Knowledge of It." *Journal of the Royal Asiatic Society of Great Britain and Ireland* 25, no. 4: 717–761.

Chalier-Visuvalingam, Élisabeth. 1986. "Bhairava: Kotwāla of Vārāṇasī." In *Varanasi Through the Ages*, edited by T. P. Verma et al., 241–260. Varanasi: Bhartiya Itihas Sankalan Samiti.

Chanda, Sudhendu. 2002. *Astrologers and Palmists in Contemporary Society*. Kolkata: Anthropological Survey of India.

Charak, K. S. 1997. *Essentials of Medical Astrology*. Delhi: UMA.

Chaturvedi, Shukdev. 2007. *Jyotiṣ Śāstra mẽ Rog Vicār*. Delhi: Motilal Banarsidass.

Chaudhary, Kapileshvara, ed. 1953. *Jātakapārijātaḥ*. Kashi Sanskrit Series 10. Varanasi: Chowkhamba Sanskrit Sansthan.

Chenet, François. 1985. "Karma and Astrology: An Unrecognized Aspect of Indian Anthropology." *Diogène* 33, no. 129: 101–126.

———. 1998a. "Astrologie: Inde," "Astrologie consultative: Inde," "Astrologie des 'élections': Inde," "Astrologie naturelle: Inde." In *Dictionnaire Critique de l'ésotérisme*, 147–159 and 178–183. Paris: Presses universitaires de France.

———. 1998b. "Divination par le souffle de vie." In *Dictionnaire Critique de l'ésotérisme*, 432–434. Paris: Presses universitaires de France.

Chowbe, Umashankar. 2008. "Garbhāśay kainsar." In *Akhil Bhāratīya Jyotiṣa Sammelan*, edited by Chandrama Pandey and Sacchidanand Mishra, 310–311. Varanasi: Banaras Hindu University.

Ciurtin, Eugen. 2004. "À propos du 'temps opportun' (*kāla*, *kṣaṇa*) en Āyurveda." In *Du corps humain, au carrefour de plusieurs savoirs en Inde: Mélanges offerts à Arion Roşu*, edited by Eugen Ciurtin, 197–234. Bucharest: De Boccard.

Claveyrolas, Mathieu. 2003. *Quand le temple prend vie: atmosphère et dévotion à Bénarès*. Paris: CNRS Éditions.

Clémentin-Ojha, Catherine. 1990. "Image animée, image vivante: L'image du culte hindou." In *L'image divine: Culte et méditation dans l'hindouisme*, edited by André Padoux, 115–132. Paris: CNRS Éditions.

———. 2000. "Être un brahmane *smārta* aujourd'hui." *Bulletin de l'École Française d'Extrême-Orient* 87, no. 1: 317–339.

Colas, Gérard. 2012. *Penser l'icône en Inde ancienne*. Bibliothèque de l'École des Hautes Études—Sciences religieuses 158. Turnhout: Brepols.

Courtright, Paul B. 1985. "On This Holy Day in My Humble Way: Aspects of Pūjā." In *Gods of Flesh, Gods of Stone: The Embodiment of Divinity in India*, edited by Joanne Punzo Waghorne and Norman Cutler, 33–50. Chambersburg: Anima.

Curry, Patrick, ed. 1987. *Astrology, Science, and Society: Historical Essays*. Woodbridge: Boydell & Brewer.

———. 1989. *Prophecy and Power: Astrology in Early Modern England*. Princeton: Princeton University Press.

Dalmia, Vasudha. 1996. "Sanskrit Scholars and Pandits of the Old School: The Benares Sanskrit College and the Constitution of Authority in the Late Nineteenth Century." *Journal of Indian Philosophy* 24, no. 4: 321–337.

———. 1997. *The Nationalization of Hindu Traditions: Bhāratendu Hariśchandra and Nineteenth-Century Banaras*. Oxford: Oxford University Press.

Dange, Sadashiv Ambadas. 1986. *Encyclopaedia of Puranic Beliefs and Practices*. New Delhi: Navrang.

Daniel, Sheryl B. 1983. "The Tool Box Approach of the Tamil to the Issues of Moral Responsibility and Human Destiny." In *Karma: An Anthropological Inquiry*, edited by Charles F. Keyes and E. Valentine Daniel, 27–61. Berkeley: University of California Press.

Daniel, E. Valentine 1983. "Conclusion: Karma, the Uses of an Idea." In *Karma: An Anthropological Inquiry*, edited by Charles F. Keyes and E. Valentine Daniel, 287–300. Berkeley: University of California Press.

———. 1984. *Fluid Signs: Being a Person the Tamil Way*. Berkeley: University of California Press.

Daniélou, Alain. 1982. *Le Shiva-Svarodaya: la naissance du souffle de vie révélé par le dieu Shiva*. Bibliothèque de l'unicorne 21. Milan: Archè.

Dar, Shivanand Lal, and S. Somaskandan. 1966. *History of the Banaras Hindu University*. Banaras: Banaras Hindu University Press.

Dayananda Saraswati, Maharishi. 2008 [1875]. *Satyārthaprakāśa*. Delhi: Arsh Sahitya Prachar Trust.

Defouw, Hart, and Robert Svoboda. 1996. *Light on Life: An Introduction to the Astrology of India*. New Delhi: Penguin Books.

Delambre, Jean-Baptiste. 1817. *Histoire de l'astronomie ancienne*. 2 vols. Paris: Mme Ve Courcier.

DeNapoli, Antoinette E. 2009. " 'By the Sweetness of the Tongue': Duty, Destiny, and Devotion in the Oral Life Narratives of Female Sādhus in Rajasthan." *Asian Ethnology* 68, no. 1: 81–109.

Department of Jyotish. 1999–2000. *Śrīkāśīviśvanātha Pañcāṅgam Śrīhṛṣīkeśa Pañcāṅgam (śrīsaṃvat 2056)*. Varanasi: Kashivishavanath Panchang Karyalay.

Descombes, Vincent. 2001. "Les individus collectifs." *Revue du MAUSS* 18, no. 2: 305–337.

Devduta, S. Das. 2006. "Ārbud rog kā prāmāṇik vivecan." *Jyotiṣa Vaijñānikī* 4: 46–47.

Diehl, Carl Gustav. 1956. *Instrument and Purpose: Studies on Rites and Rituals in South India*. Lund: C. W. K. Gleerup.

Dikshit, Sankara Balakrshna. 1969. *Bharatiya Jyotish Sastra: History of Indian Astronomy*. Translated by R. V. Vaidya. Delhi: Manager of Publications.

Dodson, Michael S. 2002. "Re-Presented for the Pandits: James Ballantyne, 'Useful Knowledge,' and Sanskrit Scholarship in Benares College during the Mid-Nineteenth Century." *Modern Asian Studies* 36, no. 2 (2002): 257–298.

———. 2007. *Orientalism, Empire and National Culture: India 1770–1880*. New York: Palgrave Macmillan, 2007.

Drévillon, Hervé. 1996. *Lire et écrire l'avenir: l'astrologie dans la France du Grand siècle, 1610–1715*. Époques. Seyssel: Champ Vallon.

Dreyer, Ronnie Gale. 1990. *Indian Astrology*. Delhi: Harper Collins.

———. 1997. *Vedic Astrology: A Guide to the Fundamentals of Jyotish*. York Beach: S. Weiser.

Duchesne-Guillemin, Jacques. 1990. "The Dragon and the Lunar Nodes." *Bulletin of the Asia Institute*, no. 4: 17–19.

Dumézil, Georges. 1952. *Les Dieux souverains des Indo-Européens*. Paris: Gallimard.

———. 1956. *Déesses latines et mythes védiques*. Brussels: Latomus.

Dumont, Louis. 1979. *Homo hierarchicus: le système des castes et ses implications*. Collection Tel 39. Paris: Gallimard.

———. 1980 [1966]. *Homo Hierarchicus: The Caste System and Its Implications.* Chicago: University of Chicago Press.

———. 1983. "The Debt to Ancestors and the Category of *Sapinda.*" In *Debt and Debtors*, edited by C. Malamoud, 1–20. New Delhi: Vikas.

Dumont, Paul-Emile. 1954. "The Iṣṭis to the Nakṣatras (Or Oblations to the Lunar Mansions) in the Taittirīya-Brāhmaṇa: The First Prapāṭhaka of the Third Kāṇḍa of the Taittirīya-Brāhmaṇa with Translation." *Proceedings of the American Philosophical Society* 98, no. 3: 204–223.

Dvivedi, Krishna Chandra, ed. 1996. *Bṛhatsaṃhitā, with Bhaṭṭotpala's Commentary.* 2 vols. Sarasvatībhavana Granthamālā 97. Varanasi: Sampurnanand Sanskrit Viswavidyalay.

Eck, Diana L. 1993. *Banaras: City of Light.* New Delhi: Penguin Books.

Einoo, Shingo, and Jun Takashima, eds. 2005. *From Material to Deity: Indian Rituals of Consecration.* Delhi: Manohar.

Endres, Kirsten W. 2008. "Engaging the Spirits of the Dead: Soul-Calling Rituals and the Performative Construction of Efficacy." *Journal of the Royal Anthropological Institute* 14, no. 4: 755–773.

Esnoul, Anne-Marie. 1959. "Les songes et leur interprétation dans l'Inde." In *Les songes et leur interprétation*, edited by Serge Sauneron, Anne-Marie Esnoul, et al., 207–247. Sources Orientales 2. Paris: Éditions du Seuil.

———. 1968. "La divination dans l'Inde." In *La Divination*, edited by A. Caquot and M. Leibovici, 115–139. Paris: Presses universitaires de France.

Fahd, Toufic. 1987. *La divination arabe: Études religieuses, sociologiques et folkloriques sur le milieu natif de l'Islam.* Paris: Sindbad, 1987.

———. 1992. "La connaissance de l'inconnaissable et l'obtention de l'impossible dans la pensée mantique et magique de l'Islam." *Bulletin d'Études Orientales, Sciences Occultes et Islam* 44: 33–44.

Festinger, Leon, Henry W. Riecken, and Stanley Schachter. 1964 [1956]. *When Prophecy Fails: A Social and Psychological Study of a Modern Group That Predicted the Destruction of the World.* Researches in the Social, Cultural, and Behavioral Sciences. New York: Harper & Row.

Foucault, Michel. 1970 [1966]. *The Order of Things: An Archaeology of the Human Sciences.* New York: Pantheon Books.

Frawley, David. 1990. *The Astrology of the Seers: A Comprehensive Guide to Vedic Astrology.* New Delhi: Motilal Banarsidass.

Freed, Ruth S., and Stanley A. Freed. 1964. "Calendars, Ceremonies, and Festivals in a North Indian Village: Necessary Calendric Information for Fieldwork." *Southwestern Journal of Anthropology* 20, no. 1: 67–90.

Friedman, Barry Steven. 1986. "Negotiating Destiny: The Astrologer and Its Art in Bengali Cultural History." PhD dissertation, University of Chicago.

———. 1989. "The Astrologer in Medieval Bengali Culture." In *Shaping Bengali Worlds: Public and Private*, edited by Tony K. Stewart, 47–56. East Lansing: Michigan State University.

Fuller, Christopher J. 1980. "The Calendrical System in Tamilnadu (South India)." *Journal of the Royal Asiatic Society of Great Britain and Ireland* 112, no. 1: 52–63.

———. 2003. *The Renewal of the Priesthood: Modernity and Traditionalism in a South Indian Temple*. Princeton: Princeton University Press.

Gaborieau, Marc. 1982. "Les fêtes, le temps et l'espace: structure du calendrier hindou dans sa version indo-népalaise." *L'Homme* 22, no. 3: 11–29.

———. 1992. "L'ésotérisme musulman dans le sous-continent indo-pakistanais: Un point de vue ethnologique." *Bulletin d'études Orientales, Sciences Occultes et Islam* 44: 191–209.

Gail, Adalbert. 1980. "Planets and Pseudoplanets in Indian Literature and Art with Special Reference to Nepal." *East and West* 30, no. 1/4: 133–146.

Gansten, Martin. 2003. *Patterns of Destiny: Hindu Nāḍī Astrology*. Lund Studies in the History of Religion 17. Stockholm: Almqvist & Wiksell International.

———. 2012. "Some Early Authorities Cited by Tājika Authors." *Indo-Iranian Journal* 55: 307–319.

———. 2017. "Notes on Some Sanskrit Astrological Authors." *History of Science in South Asia* 5, no. 1: 117–133.

Gansten, Martin, and Ola Wikander. 2011. "Sahl and the Tājika Yogas: Indian Transformations of Arabic Astrology." *Annals of Science* 68, no. 4: 531–546.

Garin, Eugenio. 1983. *Astrology in the Renaissance: The Zodiac of Life*. Translated by Carolyn Jackson, June Allen, and Clare Robertson. London: Routledge & Kegan Paul.

Gaur, Ashok Kumar. 1997. *Navagraha Rahasyam*. Varanasi: Savitri Thakur Prakashan.

Gerke, Barbara. 2012. *Long Lives and Untimely Deaths: Life-Span Concepts and Longevity Practices among Tibetans in the Darjeeling Hills, India*. Brill's Tibetan Studies Library 27. Leiden: Brill.

Geslani, Marko. 2011. "Appeasement and Atonement in the Mahādānas, the Hindu 'Great Gifts.'" *Journal Asiatique* 299, no. 1: 133–192.

———. 2016. "Astrological Vedism: Varāhamihira in Light of the Later Rituals of the Atharvaveda." *Journal of the American Oriental Society* 136, no. 2: 305–323.

———. 2018. *Rites of the God-King: Śānti and Ritual Change in Early Hinduism*. Oxford Ritual Studies. New York: Oxford University Press.

Geslani, Marko, Bill Mak, Michio Yano, and Kenneth Zysk. 2017. "Garga and Early Astral Science in India." *History of Science in South Asia* 5, no. 1: 151–191.

Grimaud, Emmanuel. 2014. *L'étrange encyclopédie du docteur K.: Portraits et horoscopes d'un astrologue indien*. Nanterre: Société d'ethnologie.

Guenzi, Caterina. 1997. "Brahmani astrologi: I Śākadvīpīya di Benares." MA thesis, University of Sienna.

———. 2005. "L'influence (*prabhāva*) de la planète et la colère (*prakopa*) du Dieu: Śani (Saturne) entre astrologie et pratiques de culte à Bénares." *Bulletin d'études indiennes* 23: 391–446.

———. 2008. "Planètes, remèdes et cosmologies: La thérapeutique astrologique à Bénarès." In *Divins remèdes: Médecine et religion en Asie du Sud*, edited by Ines G. Zupanov and Caterina Guenzi, 191–217. Puruṣārtha 27. Paris: Éditions de l'Ehess.

———. 2012. "The Allotted Share: Managing Fortune in Astrological Counseling in Contemporary India." Special Issue, *Future and Fortune: Contingency, Morality, and the Anticipation of Everyday Life*, edited by G. Da Col and C. Humphrey, *Social Analysis* 56, no. 2: 39–55.

———. Forthcoming. "When Useful Knowledge Is Not 'Useful Knowledge': Astrology at Universities in Banaras (c. 1800–2000)." Special Issue, *Indigenous Knowledges and Colonial Sciences in South Asia*, edited by M. Menon, *South Asian History and Culture*.

Guenzi, Caterina, and Sunita Singh. 2009. "The Smell of Soil: Geomantic Practices among Banaras Astrologers." In *Territory, Soil and Society in South Asia*, edited by Daniela Berti and Gilles Tarabout, 175–202. Delhi: Manohar.

Guérin, J. M. F. 1847. *Astronomie indienne*. Paris: Imprimerie royale.

Guichard, Sylvie. 2010. *The Construction of History and Nationalism in India: Textbooks, Controversies and Politics*. New York: Routledge.

Gupta, Chitrarekha. 1983. *The Brahmanas of India: A Study Based on Inscriptions*. Delhi: Sundeep Prakashan.

Halbfass, Wilhelm. 1980. "Karma, Apūrva, and 'Natural' Causes: Observations on the Growth and Limits of the Theory of Saṃsāra." In *Karma and Rebirth in Classical Indian Traditions*, edited by Wendy Doniger O'Flaherty, 268–302. Berkeley: University of California Press.

Harrison, Mark. 2000. "From Medical Astrology to Medical Astronomy: Sol-Lunar and Planetary Theories of Disease in British Medicine, c. 1700–1850." *British Journal for the History of Science* 33, no. 1: 25–48.

Hayashi, Takao. 1987. "Varāhamihira's Pandiagonal Magic Square of the Order Four." *Historia Mathematica* 14, no. 2: 159–166.

———. 2003. "Indian Mathematics." In *Blackwell Companion to Hinduism*, edited by Gavin D. Flood, 360–375. London: Blackwell.

Heesterman, J. C. 1959. "Reflections on the Significance of the 'Dakṣiṇā.'" *Indo-Iranian Journal* 3, no. 4: 241–258.

———. 1985. *The Inner Conflict of Tradition: Essays in Indian Ritual, Kingship, and Society*. Chicago: University of Chicago Press.

Heim, Maria. 2004. *Theories of the Gift in South Asia: Hindu, Buddhist, and Jain Reflections on Dāna*. Religion in History, Society, and Culture 9. London: Routledge.

Humphrey, Caroline, and James Laidlaw. 1994. *The Archetypal Actions of Ritual*. Oxford: Clarendon Press.

Hüsken, Ute, ed. 2007. *When Rituals Go Wrong: Mistakes, Failure and the Dynamics of Ritual*. Leiden: Brill.

Inden, Ronald B. 1985. "Kings and Omens." In *Purity and Auspiciousness in Indian Society*, edited by J. Carman and F. Marglin, 30–39. Leiden: Brill.

———. 1992. "Changes in Vedic Priesthood." In *Ritual, State and History in South Asia*, edited by A. W. Van den Hoek et al., 556–577. Leiden: Brill.

Iyengar, H. V. R. 2007. "Recalling the Historical Midnight Scene." *The Hindu*, August 15.

Jha, Achyutanand, ed. 2011. *Bṛhatsaṃhitā, with Hindi Translation*. Varanasi: Chowkhamba Vidyabhavan.

Jha, Chandra Mohan. 2008. "Kainsar abhijñān tathānidān mẽ jyotiṣ tathā āyurvijñān kī bhūmikā." In *Akhil Bhāratīya Jyotiṣa Sammelan*, edited by Chandrama Pandey and Sacchidanand Mishra, 68–74. Varanasi: Banaras Hindu University.

Jha, Dinesh. 2006. "Jyotiṣ śāstrānusār rogõ kā nidān." *Jyotiṣa Vaijñānikī* 4: 30–36.

Jha, Kunal Kumar. 2003. "Grahõ ke prabhāv se rogõ kī utpatti." *Jyotiṣa Vaijñānikī* 1: 51–53.

Jha, Sitaram, ed. 1974. *Bṛhajjātakam, with Bhaṭṭotpala's Commentary and Hindi Translation*. Varanasi: Jyotish Prakashan.

Johnson-Roehr, Susan N. 2011. "The Spatialization of Knowledge and Power at the Astronomical Observatories of Sawai Jai Singh II, c. 1721–1743 CE." PhD dissertation, University of Illinois.

Joshi, Keval Anand. n.d. *Saṃpūrṇa Ratna Vijñān*. Delhi: Manoj Panket Books.

Joshi, Kedardatta, ed. 1992. *Muhūrtacintāmaṇiḥ*. Varanasi: Motilal Banarsidass.

Kakar, Sudhir. 1982. *Shamans, Mystics and Doctors: A Psychological Inquiry into India and Its Healing Traditions*. Delhi: Oxford University Press.

Kane, Pandurang Vaman. 1968–1977. *History of Dharmaśāstra*. 5 vols. Pune: Bhandarkar Oriental Research Institute.

Kapadia, Karin. 1995. *Śiva and Her Sisters: Gender, Caste, and Class in Rural South India*. Boulder: Westview Press.

Kassell, Lauren. 2005. *Medicine and Magic in Elizabethan London: Simon Forman—Astrologer, Alchemist, and Physician*. Oxford Historical Monographs. Oxford: Clarendon Press.

Katre, S. L. 1942. "Śivadāsa's Jyotirnibandha: The Work and Its Date." *New Indian Antiquary* 5: 275–279.

Kaye, George Rusby. 1924. *Hindu Astronomy*. Memoirs of the Archaeological Survey of India 18. Calcutta: Govt. of India, Central Publication Branch.

Kemper, Steven. 1979. "Sinhalese Astrology, South Asian Caste Systems, and the Notion of Individuality." *Journal of Asian Studies* 38, no. 3: 477–497.

———. 1980. "Time, Person, and Gender in Sinhalese Astrology." *American Ethnologist* 7, no. 4: 744–758.

Keul, István, ed. 2017. *Consecration Rituals in South Asia*. Numen Book Series 155. Leiden: Brill.

Keyes, Charles F., and E. Valentine Daniel, eds. 1983. *Karma: An Anthropological Inquiry*. Berkeley: University of California Press.

Khankhoje, Vasudev Sadashiv. 1997. *Sulabha-Jyautiṣa-Jñāna*. Varanasi: Chowkhamba Vidyabhavan.

Khare, R. S. 1967. "Prediction of Death among Kanya-Kubja Brahmans: A Study of Predictive Narratives." *Contributions to Indian Sociology*, n.s., 1, no. 1: 1–25.

Kolenda, Pauline Mahar. 1964. "Religious Anxiety and Hindu Fate." *Journal of Asian Studies* 23: 71–81.

Krishan, Yuvraj. 1983. "The Doctrine of Karma and Phalita Jyotisa." *Vishveshvaranand Indological Journal Hoshiarpur* 21, no. 1–2: 53–67.

Kuhn, Thomas Samuel. 1962. *The Structure of Scientific Revolutions*. Chicago: University of Chicago Press.

Kumar, Nita. 1997. *The Modernization of Sanskrit Education*. Occasional Paper 60. Calcutta: Centre for Studies in Social Sciences.

Kuppanna Sastry, T. S., and K. V. Sarma, eds. 1985. *Vedāṅga Jyotiṣa of Lagadha in Its Ṛk and Yajus Recensions*. New Delhi: Indian National Science Academy.

Kusuba, Takanori. 1993. "Combinatorics and Magic Squares in India: A Study of Nārāyaṇa Paṇḍita's Gaṇitakaumudī, Chapters 13–14." PhD dissertation, Brown University.

Langford, Jean M. 2002. *Fluent Bodies: Ayurvedic Remedies for Postcolonial Imbalance*. Durham: Duke University Press.

Lepenies, Wolf. 1990. *Les trois cultures: Entre science et littérature, l'avènement de la sociologie*. Paris: Éd. de la Maison des sciences de l'homme.

Leutgeb, Anna. 2000. *Das indische Wissen um den günstigen Augenblick*. Pune: Sanjay Godbole Oriental Research Foundation.

Lock, Margaret. 2005. "Eclipse of the Gene and the Return of Divination." Supplement, *Current Anthropology* 46: 47–70.

Long, Bruce J. 1980. "The Concepts of Human Action and Rebirth in the Mahābhārata." In *Karma and Rebirth in Classical Indian Traditions*, edited by Wendy Doniger O'Flaherty, 38–60. Berkeley: University of California Press.

Macaulay, Thomas Babington. 1935. *Speeches by Lord Macaulay, with His Minute on Indian Education, Selected with an Introduction and Notes by G. M. Young*. London: Oxford University Press.

Mahias, Marie-Claude, ed. 2011. *Construire les savoirs dans l'action: Apprentissages et enjeux sociaux en Asie du Sud*. Puruṣārtha 29. Paris: Editions de l'Ehess.

Mak, Bill M. 2013. "The Transmission of Greek Astral Science into India Reconsidered: Critical Remarks on the Contents and the Newly Discovered Manuscript of the Yavanajātaka." *History of Science in South Asia* 1: 1–20.

———. 2014. "The 'Oldest Indo-Greek Text in Sanskrit' Revisited—Additional Readings from the Newly Discovered Manuscript of the Yavanajātaka." *Journal of Indian and Buddhist Studies* 62, no. 3: 37–41.

———. 2018. "The First Two Chapters of Mīnarāja's *Vṛddhayavanajātaka*." *Zinbun* 48: 1–31.

———. 2019a. "Greco-Babylonian Astral Science in Asia: Patterns of Dissemination and Transformation." In *East-West Encounter in the Science of Heaven and Earth* 天と地の科学—東と西の出会い, edited by T. Tokimasa and B. M. Mak, 14–34. Kyoto: Institute for Research in Humanities, Kyoto University.

———. 2019b. "Vedic Astral Lore and Planetary Science in the *Gārgīyajyotiṣa*." *History of Science in South Asia* 7: 52–71.

Malamoud, Charles. 1976. "Terminer le sacrifice: remarques sur les honoraires rituels dans le Brahmanisme." In *Le sacrifice dans l'Inde ancienne*, Madeleine Biardeau and Charles Malamoud, 155–204. Paris: Presses universitaires de France.

———, ed. 1983. *Debts and Debtors*. Delhi: Vikas.

———. 1993. "Retours à l'écriture, détournements de l'écriture: remarques sur une cérémonie védique dans l'Inde de 1990." In *Les retours aux écritures: Fondamentalismes présents et passés*, edited by Évelyne Patlagean and Alain Le Boulluec, 157–174. Bibliothèque des Hautes Études 99. Louvain: Peeters Press.

———. 1996. *Cooking the World: Ritual and Thought in Ancient India*. Translated by David G. White. Delhi: Oxford University Press.

———. 1997. "Croyance, crédulité, calcul politique: Présentation et traduction commentée de l'Arthaçâstra de Kautilya, Livre XIII, Chapitres I et III." *Multitudes: Futur Antérieur*, 41–42. https://www.multitudes.net/Croyance-credulite-calcul.

Mallmann, Marie-Thérèse de. 1963. *Les enseignements iconographiques de l'Agni Purāṇa*. Paris: Presses universitaires de France.

Mandelbaum, David G. 1964. "Introduction: Process and Structure in South Asian Religion." *Journal of Asian Studies* 23: 5–20.

———. 1966. "Transcendental and Pragmatic Aspects of Religion." *American Anthropologist* 68, no. 5: 1174–1191.

Markel, Stephen. 1990. "The Imagery and Iconographic Development of the Indian Planetary Deities Rāhu and Ketu." *South Asian Studies* 6: 9–26.

———. 1995. *Origins of the Indian Planetary Deities*. Lewiston, NY: Edwin Mellen Press.

Marriott, McKim. 1976. "Hindu Transaction: Diversity without Dualism." In *Transactions and Meanings: Directions in the Anthropology of Exchange and Symbolic Behavior*, edited by Bruce Kapferer, 109–142. Philadelphia: Institute for the Study of Human Issues.

Marriott, McKim, and Ronald B. Inden. 1975. "Caste Systems." In *Encyclopaedia Britannica*, 982–991. Chicago: Benton.

———. 1977. "Toward an Ethnosociology of South Asian Caste System." In *The New Wind: Changing Identitites in South Asia*, edited by Kenneth Davis, 227–238. The Hague: Mouton.

McArthur, Brian. 1992. *Penguin Book of Twentieth-Century Speeches*. London: Penguin Viking.

Merrey, Karen L. 1982. "The Hindu Festival Calendar." In *Religious Festivals in South India and Sri Lanka*, edited by Guy R. Welbon and Glenn E. Yocum, 1–25. Delhi: Manohar.

Meulenbeld, Gerrit Jan. 1999–2002. *A History of Indian Medical Literature*. 5 vols. Groningen Oriental Studies 15. Groningen: Forsten.

Michaels, Axel, ed. 2001. *The Pandit: Traditional Scholarship in India*. New Delhi: Manohar.

Minkowski, Christopher Z. 2001. "The Pandit as Public Intellectual: The Controversy over Virodha or Inconsistency in the Astronomical Sciences." In *The Pandit: Traditional Scholarship in India*, edited by Axel Michaels, 79–96. Delhi: Manohar.

———. 2002. "Astronomers and Their Reasons: Working Paper on Jyotiḥśāstra." *Journal of Indian Philosophy* 30: 495–514.

———. 2004. "Competing Cosmologies in Early Modern Indian Astronomy." In *Ketuprakāśa: Studies in the History of Exact Sciences in Honor of David Pingree*, edited by Charles Burnett et al., 349–385. Leiden: Brill.

———. 2008. "Meanings Numerous and Numerical: Nīlakaṇṭha and Magic Squares in the Ṛgveda." In *Indologica, T. Ya. Elizarenkova Memorial Volume*, edited by L. Kulikov and M. Rusanov, 315–328. Moscow: Russian State University of the Humanities.

———. 2010. "Sanskrit Scientific Libraries and Their Uses: Examples and Problems of the Early Modern Period." In *Looking at It from Asia: The Processes That Shaped the Sources of the History of Science*, edited by Françoise Bretelle, 81–114. Boston Studies in Philosophy of Science 206. New York: Springer.

———. 2014. "Learned Brahmins and the Mughal Court: The Jyotiṣas." In *Religious Interactions in Mughal India*, edited by Vasudha Dalmia and Munis D. Faruqui, 102–134. New Delhi: Oxford University Press.

Mishra, Satyendra, ed. 1993. *Laghujātaka, with Bhaṭṭotpala's Commentary and Hindi Translation*. Kashi Sanskrit Series 279. Varanasi: Chowkhamba Sanskrit Sansthan.

Mishra, Shivakant. 2008. "Kainsar abhijñān tathā nidān mẽ jyotiṣ tathā āyurvijñān kī bhūmika." In *Akhil Bhāratīya Jyotiṣa Sammelan*, edited by Chandrama Pandey and Sacchidanand Mishra, 51–62. Varanasi: Banaras Hindu University.

Mishra, Vibhuti Bhushan. 1973. *Religious Beliefs and Practices of North India during the Early Medieval Period*. Leiden: Brill.

Mitchiner, John E. 1986. *The Yuga Purāṇa: Critically Edited, with an English Translation and a Detailed Introduction*. Calcutta: Asiatic Society.

Mitra, Debala. 1965. "A Study of Some Graha-Images of India and Their Possible Bearing on the Nava-Devās of Cambodia." *Journal of the Asiatic Society of Calcutta* 7, no. 1–2: 13–37.

Mohapatra, Satyen. 2008. "Feeling Ill? It Could Be the Planets, Says Govt Study." *Hindustan Times*, September 6. http://www.hindustantimes.com/India-news/NewDelhi/Feeling-ill-It-could-be-the-planets-says-govt-study/Article1-335986.aspx.

Monier-Williams, Monier. 1994. *A Sanskrit-English Dictionary*. Delhi: Munshiram Manoharlal.

Morin, Edgar, et al. 1981. *La croyance astrologique moderne: Diagnostic sociologique*. Cheminements. Lausanne: L'Âge d'homme.

Mukharji, Projit. 2016. *Doctoring Traditions: Ayurveda, Small Technologies, and Braided Sciences*. Chicago: University of Chicago Press.

Müller, Friedrich Max. 1862. *On Ancient Hindu Astronomy and Chronology*. Oxford: Oxford University.

Nanda, Meera. 2003. *Prophets Facing Backward: Postmodern Critiques of Science and Hindu Nationalism in India*. London: Rutgers University Press.

Nayak, Anand. 1997. "Les deux roues du chariot." In *Le destin: Défi et consentement*, edited by Catherine Chalier, 125–139. Collections Morales. Paris: Éditions Autrement.

Neufeldt, Ronald W., ed. 1986. *Karma and Rebirth: Post Classical Developments*. Albany: State University of New York Press.

Neugebauer, Otto, and David Edwin Pingree, eds. 1970–1971. *The Pañcasiddhāntikā of Varāhamihira*. 2 vols. Copenhagen: Munksgaard.

Nicholas, Ralph W. 2003. "The Bengali Calendar and the Hindu Religious Year in Bengal." In *Fruits of Worship: Practical Religion in Bengal*, 13–27. Delhi: Chronicle Books.

Nicholls, George. 1907 [1848]. *Sketch of the Rise and Progress of the Benares Patshalla or Sanskrit College, Now Forming the Sanskrit Department of the Benares College*. Allahabad: Govt. Press.

Nichter, Mark. 1992. "Of Ticks, Kings, Spirits, and the Promise of Vaccines." In *Paths to Asian Medical Knowledge*, edited by Charles Leslie and Allan Young, 224–253. Berkeley: University of California Press.

Nichter, Mark, and Mimi Nichter. 2010. "Revisiting the Concept of Karma: Lessons from a Dhanvantari Homa." Special Issue, *The Efficacy of Rituals*, *Journal of Ritual Studies* 24, no. 2: 37–55.

Nuckolls, Charles W. 1981. "Interpretation of the Concept of Karma in a Telugu Fishing Village." *Eastern Anthropologist* 34, no. 2: 95–106.

Obeyesekere, Gananath. 1968. "Theodicy, Sin, and Salvation in a Sociology of Buddhism." In *Dialectic in Practical Religion*, edited by Edmund R. Leach, 7–40. Cambridge: Cambridge University Press.

O'Flaherty, Wendy Doniger. 1976. *The Origins of Evil in Hindu Mythology*. Berkeley: University of California Press.

———, ed. 1980. *Karma and Rebirth in Classical Indian Traditions*. Berkeley: University of California Press.

———. 1984. *Dreams, Illusion, and Other Realities*. Chicago: University of Chicago Press.

O'Hanlon, Rosalind, and Christopher Minkowski. 2008. "What Makes People Who They Are? Pandit Networks and the Problem of Livelihoods in Early Modern Western India." *Indian Economic and Social History Review* 45, no. 3: 381–416.

Ōhashi, Yukio. 2015. "Astronomy of the Vedic Age." *Handbook of Archaeoastronomy and Ethnoastronomy*, edited by Clive L. N. Ruggles, 1949–1958. New York: Springer Science & Business Media.

Oldenberg, Hermann. 1903. *La religion du Véda (traduit de l'allemand par Victor Henry)*. Paris: F. Alcan.

Olivelle, Patrick. 2013. *King, Governance, and Law in Ancient India: Kauṭilya's Arthaśāstra*. New York: Oxford University Press.

Padoux, André, ed. 1986. *Mantras et diagrammes rituels dans l'hindouisme*. Paris: CNRS Éditions.

Pal, P., and D. P. Bhattacharya. 1969. *The Astral Divinities of Nepal*. Varanasi: Prithivi Prakashan.

Palmié, Stephan. 2007. "Genomics, Divination, 'Racecraft.'" *American Ethnologist* 34, no. 2: 205–222.

Pandey, Chandrama and Sacchidanand Mishra, eds. 2008. *Akhil Bhāratīya Jyotiṣa Sammelan (16–17 March 2007): Smārikā. Pro. Rājmohan Upādhyāy Samsmṛti*. Varanasi: Publications of the Banaras Hindu University.

Pandey, Nagendra, ed. 2002–2005. *Bṛhatsaṃhitā*. 2 vols. Gaṅgānāthajhā granthamālā 20. Varanasi: Sampurnanand Sanskrit Viswavidyalay.

Pandey, Rajbali. 1994. *Hindu Saṃskāras: Socio-Religious Study of the Hindu Sacraments*. Delhi: Motilal Banarsidass.

Pandey, Ram Chandra, ed. 1992. *Muhūrtacintāmaṇiḥ, with Hindi Translation*. Krishnadas Sanskrit Series 73. Varanasi: Chowkhamba.

———. 2003. "Vyādhinidān mẽ jyotiṣaśāstra kī bhūmikā." *Jyotiṣa Vaijñānikī* 1: 8–11.

Pandit, Vasant Kumar R. 1951. "Ṭikanikayātrā of Varāhamihira." *Journal of the University of Bombay* 20, no. 2: 40–63.

Parry, Jonathan. 1980. "Ghosts, Greed and Sin: The Occupational Identity of the Benares Funeral Priests." *Man*, n.s., 15, no. 1: 88–111.

———. 1986. "The Gift, the Indian Gift and the 'Indian Gift.' " *Man*, n.s., 21, no. 3: 453–473.

———. 1994. *Death in Banaras*. The Lewis Henry Morgan Lectures, 1988. Cambridge: Cambridge University Press.

Pathak, Ganeshadatta, ed. 1972. *Bṛhatpārāśarahorāśāstra, with Hindi Translation*. Varanasi: Thakur Prasad and Sons.

Pathak, Ramchandra, ed. 2013. *Bṛhajjātakam, with Bhaṭṭotpala's Commentary and Hindi Translation*. Varanasi: Chowkhamba.

Pellissero, Alberto. 1991. *Tecniche indiane di divinazione (Śivasvarodaya)*. Turin: Promolibri.

Perinbanayagam, R. S. 1981. "Self, Other and Astrology: Esoteric Therapy in Sri Lanka." *Psychiatry* 44: 69–79.

———. 1982. *The Karmic Theater: Self, Society and Astrology in Jaffna*. Amherst: University of Massachusetts Press.

Pingree, David Edwin. 1963. "Astronomy and Astrology in India and Iran." *ISIS* 54, no. 176: 229–246.

———. 1970–1994. *Census of the Exact Sciences in Sanskrit (series A. 1–5)*. 5 vols. Memoirs of the American Philosophical Society. Philadelphia: American Philosophical Society.

———, ed. 1976. *Vṛddhayavanajātaka of Mīnarāja*. Gaekwad's Oriental Series 162. Baroda: Oriental Institute.

———, ed. 1978a. *The Yavanajātaka of Sphujidhvaja*. Harvard Oriental Series 48. Cambridge: Harvard University Press.

———. 1978b. "History of Mathematical Astronomy in India." In *Dictionary of Scientific Biography*, vol. 15, 533–633. New York: Charles Scribner & Sons.

———. 1978c. "Indian Astronomy." *Proceedings of the American Philosophical Society* 122, no. 6: 361–364.

———. 1981. *Jyotiḥśāstra: Astral and Mathematical Literature*. A History of Indian Literature, vol. 6, Scientific and Technical Literature. Wiesbaden: O. Harrassowitz.

———. 1989. "Indian Planetary Images and the Tradition of Astral Magic." *Journal of the Warbourg and Courtauld Institutes* 52: 1–13.

———. 1990. "The Purāṇas and Jyotiḥṣāstra: Astronomy." *Journal of the American Oriental Society* 110, no. 2: 274–280.

———. 1992. "Hellenophilia versus the History of Science." *ISIS* 83, no. 4: 554–563.

———. 1997a. *From Astral Omens to Astrology: From Babylon to Bīkāner*. Serie orientale Roma 78. Rome: Istituto italiano per l'Africa e l'Oriente.

———. 1997b. "Two Karmavipāka Texts on Curing Diseases and Other Misfortunes." *Journal of the European Āyurvedic Society* 5: 46–52.

———. 1999. "An Astronomer's Progress." *Proceedings of the American Philosophical Society* 143, no. 1: 73–85.

———. 2001. "I professionisti della scienza e la loro formazione." In *Cina, India, Americhe: Storia della scienza*, vol. 2, 690–707. Rome: Istituto della enciclopedia italiana.

Plofker, Kim. *Mathematics in India*. Princeton: Princeton University Press, 2009.

———. 2012. "Indian Exact Sciences in Sanskrit Manuscripts and Their Colophons." In *Aspects of Manuscript Culture in South India*, edited by Saraju Rath, 173–185. Brill's Indological Library 40. Leiden: Brill.

Podemann Sørensen, Jørgen. 2006. "Efficacy." In *Theorizing Rituals: Issues, Topics, Approaches, Concepts*, edited by Jens Kreinath et al., 523–31. Numen Book Series 114/1. Leiden: Brill.

Pollock, Sheldon. 1985. "The Theory of Practice and the Practice of Theory in Indian Intellectual History." *Journal of the American Oriental Society* 105, no. 3: 499–519.

———. 2008. "Is There an Indian Intellectual History?" *Journal of Indian Philosophy* 36, no. 5–6: 533–542.

———. 2011. "The Languages of Science in Early Modern India." In *Forms of Knowledge in Early Modern Asia: Explorations in the Intellectual History of India and Tibet, 1500–1800*, edited by Sheldon Pollock, 19–48. Durham: Duke University Press.

Polo, Marco. 2016. *The Description of the World*. Translated, with an introduction and annotations by Sharon Kinoshita. Indianapolis: Hackett.

Potter, Karl H. 1980. "The Karma Theory and Its Interpretation in Some Indian Philosophical Systems." In *Karma and Rebirth in Classical Indian Traditions*, edited by Wendy Doniger O'Flaherty, 241–267. Berkeley: University of California Press.

Prakash, Gyan. 1999. *Another Reason: Science and the Imagination of Modern India*. Princeton: Princeton University Press.

Prasad, Rajendra. 1989. *Karma, Causation and Retributive Morality: Conceptual Essays in Ethics and Metaethics*. New Delhi: Munshiram Manoharlal.

Pugh, Judy F. 1981. "Person and Experience: The Astrological System of North India." PhD dissertation, University of Chicago.

———. 1983a. "Astrology and Fate: The Hindu and Muslim Experience." In *Karma: An Anthropological Inquiry*, edited by Charles F. Keyes and E. Valentine Daniel, 131–146. Berkeley: University of California Press.

———. 1983b. "Astrological Counseling in Contemporary India." *Culture, Medicine and Psychiatry* 7: 279–299.

———. 1983c. "Into the Almanac: Time, Meaning and Action in North Indian Society." *Contributions to Indian Sociology* 25, no. 2: 27–49.

———. 1984. "Concepts of Person and Situation in North Indian Counseling." *Contributions to Asian Studies* 18: 85–105.

———. 1988. "Divination and Ideology in the Banaras Muslim Community." In *Sharī'at and Ambiguity in South Asian Islam*, edited by Katherine P. Ewing, 288–306. Berkeley: University of California Press.

Quack, Johannes, and William S. Sax, eds. 2010. Special issue, *The Efficacy of Rituals*, *Journal of Ritual Studies* 24, 1–2 vols.

Raheja, Gloria Goodwin. 1988. *The Poison in the Gift: Ritual, Prestation, and the Dominant Caste in a North Indian Village*. Chicago: University of Chicago Press.

Raina, Dhruv. 1999. "Nationalism, Institutional Science and the Politics of Knowledge: Ancient Indian Astronomy and Mathematics in the Landscape of French Enlightenment Historiography." PhD dissertation, Göteborgs Universitet.

———. 2000. "Jean-Baptiste Biot on the History of Indian Astronomy (1830–1860): The Nation in the Post-Enlightenment Historiography of Science." *Indian Journal of History of Science* 35, no. 4: 319–346.

———. 2001. "Disciplinary Boundaries and the Civilizational Encounter: The Mathematics and Astronomy of India in Delambre's Histoire (1800–1820)." *Studies in History* 17, no. 2: 211–243.

———. 2003. "Betwixt Jesuit and Enlightenment Historiography: The Context of Jean-Sylvain Bailly's History of Indian Astronomy." *Revue d'histoire des mathématiques* 9, no. 2: 101–153.

Raman, Bengalore Venkata. 1992. *Astrology for Beginners*. 26th ed. New Delhi: UBS Publishers' Distributors.

Renold, Leah. 2005. *A Hindu Education: Early Years of the Banaras Hindu University*. New Delhi: Oxford University Press.

Renou, Louis. 1978. "Connexion en védique, cause en bouddhique." In *L'Inde Fondamentale*, 149–153. Paris: Hermann.

Renou, Louis, and Jean Filliozat. 1985. *L'Inde classique: manuel des études indiennes*, vol. 1. Paris: Maisonneuve.

———. 1996. *L'Inde classique: manuel des études indiennes*, vol. 2. Paris: École française d'Extrême-Orient.

Rochberg, Francesca. 2004. *The Heavenly Writing: Divination, Horoscopy, and Astronomy in Mesopotamian Culture*. Cambridge: Cambridge University Press.

Roşu, Arion. 1986. "Mantra et yantra dans la médecine et l'alchimie indiennes." *Journal Asiatique* 274, no. 3/4: 203–268.

———. 1989. "Les carrés magiques indiens et l'histoire des idées en Asie." *Zeitschrift Der Deutschen Morgenländischen Gesellschaft* 139, no. 1: 120–158.

Sachau, Carl Eduard, ed. 2000 [1910]. *Alberuni's India: An Account of the Religion, Philosophy, Literature, Geography, Chronology, Astronomy, Customs, Laws and Astrology of India about A.D. 1030*. Trübner's Oriental Series 45–46. London: Routledge.

Sahana, Udupa. 2016. "Fast Time Religion: News, Speculation, and Discipline in India." *Critique of Anthropology* 36, no. 4: 397–418.

Saliba, George. 1992. "The Role of Astrologer in Medieval Islamic Society." *Bulletin d'études Orientales, Sciences Occultes et Islam* 44: 45–67.

Santhanam, R., ed. 1984. *Bṛhat Pārāśara Horā Śāstra, with English Translation*. New Delhi: Ranjan.

———, ed. 1996. *Saravali of Kalyana Varma, with English Translation*. 2 vols. New Delhi: Ranjan.

Sarma, Sreeramula Rajeswara. 1995. "Sanskrit as Vehicle for Modern Science: Lancelot Wilkinson's Efforts in the 1830s." *Studies in History of Medicine and Science* 14: 189–199.

———. 2008. *The Archaic and the Exotic: Studies in the History of Indian Astronomical Instruments*. New Delhi: Manohar.

Sax, William S., Johannes Quack, and Jan Weinhold, eds. 2010. *The Problem of Ritual Efficacy*. New York: Oxford University Press.

Schaffer, Simon. 2009. "The Asiatic Enlightenments of British Astronomy." In *The Brokered World: Go-Betweens and Global Intelligence, 1770–1820*, edited by Simon Schaffer, Lissa Roberts, Kapil Raj, and James Delbourgo, 49–104. Sagamore Beach, MA: Watson Publishing International.

Sen, Joydeep. 2014. *Astronomy in India, 1784–1876*. London: Pickering & Chatto Ltd.

Sen, Samarendra Nath, and Kripa Shankar Shukla. 1985. *History of Astronomy in India*. New Delhi: Indian National Science Academy.

Sharma, Bulbul. 1995. "Rites of Passage." In *In Other Words: New Writing by Indian Women*, edited by Urvashi Butalia and Ritu Menon, 81–91. New Delhi: Kali for Women.

Sharma, Kalyanadatta. 1992. *M. M. Śrī Sudhākara Dvivedī Vedhaśālā Paricaya*. Varanasi: Publications of the Sampurnananda Sanskrit University.

Sharma, Kisanlal. n.d. *Jyotiṣ aur Rog*. Delhi: Manoj Punket Books.

Sharma, R. S. 1977. "Conflict, Distribution and Differentiation in Rg Vedic Society." *Proceedings of the Indian History Congress* 38: 177–191.

Sharma, Thakur Prasad, and Shivadatta Mishra, eds. 1999. *Sāmudrikarahasyam, with Hindi Translation*. Varanasi: Jyotish Prakashan.

Sharma, Ursula. 1973. "Theodicy and the Doctrine of Karma." *Man*, n.s., 8, no. 3: 347–364.

Sharma, Vasudev. 2008. "Jyotiṣ-āyurved dṛṣṭyā 'kainsar ' (vidradhi) rogasya nidānam." In *Akhil Bhāratīya Jyotiṣa Sammelan*, edited by Chandrama Pandey and Sacchidanand Mishra, 15–21. Varanasi: Banaras Hindu University.

Sharma, Vishwadath Deva. 1973. *Astrology and Jyotirvidya: The Fundamental Principles and the System of Prognosis*. Calcutta: Vishwa Jyotirvid Samgha.

Shastri, Girija Shankar. 2006. "Oṣadhiyō kā grahō evam nakṣatrō se sambandh." *Jyotiṣa Vaijñānikī* 4: 12–15.

Shastri, Jagannath. n.d. *Navagraha Upāsanā*. Delhi: Dehati Pustak Bhandar.

Shrivastava, C. M. 2001. *Śani kā Prakop: Usse Bacāv*. Delhi: Manoj.

Shukla, Shatrughnalal. 1993. *Navagraha Anukūlan Tantra*. Mathura: Hindi Seva Sadan.

Silburn, Lilian. 1989. *Instant et cause: Le discontinu dans la pensée philosophique de l'Inde*. Paris: De Boccard.

Simon, Gérard. 1992. *Kepler: astronome, astrologue*. Bibliothèque des sciences humaines. Paris: Gallimard.

Singh, Prahlad, and Kalyanadatta Sharma. 1978. *Stone Observatories in India, Erected by Maharaja Sawai Jai Singh of Jaipur, 1686–1743 A.D., at Delhi, Jaipur, Ujjain, Varanasi, Mathura*. Varanasi: Bharata Manisha.

Singh, Rana P. B., ed. 1993. *Banāras (Vārāṇasī): Cosmic Order, Sacred City, Hindu Traditions*. Banaras: Tara Book Agency.

Sircar, D. C. 1952. "The Astrologer at the Village and the Court." *Indian Historical Quarterly* 28: 342–349.

Sivapriyananda, Swami. 1990. *Astrology and Religion in Indian Art*. New Delhi: Abhinav.

Smith, Brian K. 1989. *Reflections on Resemblance, Ritual, and Religion*. Oxford: Oxford University Press.

Smith, Frederick M. 2006. *The Self Possessed: Deity and Spirit Possession in South Asian Literature and Civilization*. New York: Columbia University Press.

Stengers, Isabelle, ed. 1987. *D'une science à l'autre: des concepts nomades*. Science ouverte. Paris: Éditions du Seuil.

Stietencron, Heinrich von. 1966. *Indische Sonnenpriester: Sāmba und die Sākadvīpīya-Brāhmana—Eine textkritische und religionsgeschichtliche Studie zum indischen Sonnenkult*. Universität Heidelberg—Schriftenreihe 3. Wiesbaden: Harrassowitz.

———. 2005. "Orthodox Attitudes towards Temple Service and Image Worship in Ancient India." In *Hindu Myth, Hindu History, Religion, Art, and Politics*, 51–63. New Delhi: Orient Blackswan.

Stone, Philip A. 1981. *Hindu Astrology: Myths, Symbols and Realities*. New Delhi: Select Books.

Subbarayappa, B. V., and Debi Prasad Chattopadhyaya. 2008. *The Tradition of Astronomy in India: Jyotiḥśāstra*. Vol. 4. History of Science, Philosophy, and Culture in Indian Civilization. New Delhi: Center for Studies in Civilization.

Sundar, Nandini. 2002. " 'Indigenise, Nationalise and Spiritualise'—an Agenda for Education?" *International Social Science Journal* 54, no. 3: 373–383.

Supreme Court of India. 2004. "Judgment of the Case No. 5886 (Appeal) of 2002. Petitioner: P. M. Bhargava & Ors.; Respondent: University Grant

Commission & Anr.; Bench: J.P. Mathur," Date of Judgment May 5, 2004. http://judis.nic.in/supremecourt/qrydisp.asp?tfnm=26188.

Svoboda, Robert. 1998. *The Greatness of Saturn: A Therapeutic Mythic*. Noida: Rupa & Co.

Tambiah, Stanley J. 1979. "A Performative Approach to Ritual." Radcliffe-Brown Lecture in Social Anthropology. *Proceedings of the British Academy* 65: 113–169.

Tarabout, Gilles. 1999. "'Psycho-Religious Therapy' in Kerala as a Form of Interaction between Local Traditions and (Perceived) Scientific Discourse." In *Managing Distress: Possession and Therapeutic Cults in South Asia*, edited by Marine Carrin, 133–154. Delhi: Manohar.

———. 2002a. "Résonances et métaphores corporelles dans l'astrologie appliquée au temple (Kérala)." In *Images du corps dans le monde hindou*, edited by Véronique Bouillier and Gilles Tarabout, 135–159. Paris: CNRS Éditions.

———. 2002b. "Élaborations indiennes du temps." In *Les Calendriers: Leurs Enjeux Dans l'espace et Dans Le Temps*, edited by J. Le Goff et al., 193–204. Paris: Somogy Éditions d'art.

———. 2007. "Authoritative Statements in Kerala Temple Astrology." *Rivista Di Studi Sudasiatici* 2: 85–120.

———. 2012. "Sin and Flaws in Kerala Temple Astrology." In *Sin and Sinners: Perspectives from Asian Religions*, edited by Phyllis Granoff and Koichi Shinohara, 309–323. Numen Book Series 139. Leiden: Brill.

———. 2015. "Religious Uncertainty, Astrology and the Courts in South India." In *Of Doubt and Proof: Legal and Ritual Practices of Judgment*, edited by Daniela Berti, Anthony Good, and Gilles Tarabout, 59–75. London: Routledge.

Thibaut, George. 1899. *Astronomie, Astrologie und Mathematik*. Grundriss der Indo-arischen Philologie und Altertumskunde. Strassburg: K. J. Trübner.

Thomas, Keith. 1971. *Religion and the Decline of Magic*. New York: Charles Scribner's Sons.

Thomas, Paul. 1958. *Epics, Myths and Legends of India*. Bombay: D. B. Taraporevala.

Tiwari, Srinivas. 2006. "Grahajanya rog evam grahauṣadhiyō kā vivecan." *Jyotiṣa Vaijñānikī* 4: 58–65.

Toffin, Gérard. 1989. "La vie des 'héros': Tantrisme et héritage védique chez les brāhmanes Rājopādhyāya du Népal." In *Prêtrise, Pouvoir et Autorité En Himalaya*, edited by Véronique Bouillier and Gérard Toffin, 19–40. Puruṣārtha 12. Paris: Éditions de l'Ehess.

Tripathi, Shatrughna. 2008. "Stan-kainsar kā jyotiṣaśāstrīya nidān." In *Akhil Bhāratīya Jyotiṣa Sammelan*, edited by Chandrama Pandey and Sacchidanand Mishra, 197–208. Varanasi: Banaras Hindu University.

Trivedi, Mridula. 1996. *Śani Śaman*. Delhi: Motilal Banarsidass.

Trivedi, Mridula, and Prakash Trivedi. 2008. *Foretelling Widowhood*. Delhi: Motilal Banarsidass.

Udupa, Sahana. 2016. "Fast Time Religion: News, Speculation and Discipline in India." *Critique of Anthropology* 36, no. 4: 397–418.

University Grants Commission. 2004. *Annual Report 2003–4*. Delhi: University Grants Commission.

Upadhyay, Chandra Mauli. 2008. "Kainsar rog-vimarś." In *Akhil Bhāratīya Jyotiṣa Sammelan*, edited by Chandrama Pandey and Sacchidanand Mishra, 182–191. Varanasi: Banaras Hindu University.

Upadhyay, Kameshwar. 1996. *Svapnavidyā*. Varanasi: Triskandha Jyotisham.

Van Buitenen, Johannes A. B. 1981. *The Bhagavadgītā in the Mahābhārata*. Chicago: University of Chicago Press.

Van der Veer, Peter. 1988. *Gods on Earth: The Management of Religious Experience and Identity in a North Indian Pilgrimage Centre*. London: Athlone.

Varma, Ramacandra. 1965. *Mānak Hindī Koś*. Prayag: Hindi Sahitya Sammelan.

———. 1971. *Saṅkṣipt Hindī Śabdasāgar*. Varanasi: Nagaripracarini Sabha.

Vatsa, Shyam Sundar Lal. 1996. *Śani Graha Pīṛa Nivāraṇ Vidhi*. Noeda: Paras.

Vernant, Jean-Pierre. 1991. *Mortals and Immortals: Collected Essays*. Edited by Froma I. Zeitlin. Princeton: Princeton University Press.

Vogel, Claus. 2007. "The Propitiation of the Planets in Indian Ritual and Allied Literature with Special Reference to Colours and Flowers." In *Indica et Tibetica (Festschrift Für Michael Hahn)*, edited by K. Klaus and J.-U. Hartmann, 587–606. Wiener Studien Zur Tibetologie Und Buddhismuskunde 66. Vienna: Arbeitskreis für Tibetische und Buddhistische Studien Universität Wien.

Wadhwa, Soma. 2004. "Astrology: The Future Is Big." *Outlook India*.

Wadley, Susan S. 1975. *Shakti: Power in the Conceptual Structure of Karimpur Religion*. Chicago: Dept. of Anthropology, University of Chicago.

———. 1983a. "The Rains of Estrangement: Understanding the Hindu Yearly Cycle." *Contributions to Indian Sociology* 17, no. 1: 51–85.

———. 1983b. "Vrats: Transformers of Destiny." In *Karma: An Anthropological Inquiry*, edited by Charles F. Keyes and E. Valentine Daniel, 147–162. Berkeley: University of California Press.

Wadley, Susan S., and Bruce W. Derr. 1989. "Eating Sins in Karimpur." *Contributions to Indian Sociology* 23, no. 1: 131–148.

Weiss, Mitchell G. 1980. "Caraka Saṃhitā on the Doctrine of Karma." In *Karma and Rebirth in Classical Indian Traditions*, edited by W. Doniger O'Flaherty, 90–115. Berkeley: University of California Press.

White, David G. 1996. *The Alchemical Body: Siddha Traditions in Medieval India*. Chicago: University of Chicago Press, 1996.

———. 2008. "Amulettes et lambeaux divins: 'superstition,' vraie 'religion' et 'science' pure à la lumière de la démonologie hindoue." In *Divins Remèdes:*

Médecine et Religion En Asie Du Sud, edited by I. Zupanov and C. Guenzi, 135–162. Puruṣartha 27. Paris: Éditions de l'Ehess, 2008.

Wilkinson, Lancelot. 1834. "On the Use of Siddhāntas in the Work of Native Education." *Journal of the Asiatic Society of Bengal* 3: 504–519.

Woods, Julian F. 2001. *Destiny and Human Initiative in the Mahābhārata*. McGill Studies in the History of Religions. Albany: State University of New York Press.

Yano, Michio. 2003. "Calendar, Astrology, and Astronomy." In *The Blackwell Companion to Hinduism*, edited by Gavin D. Flood, 276–292. Malden, MA: Blackwell.

———. 2004. "Planet Worship in Ancient India." In *Studies in the History of the Exact Sciences in Honour of David Pingree*, edited by Charles Burnett, 331–348. Leiden: Brill.

———. 2005. "Medicine and Divination in India." *East Asian Science, Technology and Medicine* 24: 44–61.

———. 2006. "Oral and Written Transmission of the Exact Sciences in Sanskrit." *Journal of Indian Philosophy* 34, no. 1–2: 143–160.

Yongjia, Liang. 2008. "Between Science and Religion: An Astrological Interpretation of the Asian Tsunami in India." *Asian Journal of Social Science* 36, no. 2: 234–249.

Young, Richard Fox. 1981. *Resistant Hinduism: Sanskrit Sources on Anti-Christian Apologetics in Early Nineteenth-Century India*. Vienna: De Nobili Research Library.

Zimmermann, Francis. 1980. "Ṛtu-Sātmya: The Seasonal Cycle and the Principle of Appropriateness." *Social Science and Medicine* 14B, no. 2: 99–106.

———. 1981. "Les aspects médicaux du *Yavanajātaka* (Traité Sanskrit d'astrologie)." *Suddhoffs Archiv* 64, no. 3: 299–305.

Zysk, Kenneth G. 2016. *The Indian System of Human Marks, with Editions, Translations and Annotations*. 2 vols. Sir Henry Wellcome Asian Series 15. Leiden: Brill.

Index

adultery: astrological research on, 70; in the horoscope, 204, 333n43; planetary influence and, 179, 183, 185–87

aggressiveness, 225, 278

agriculture: astrology and, 31, 35–36; astrological research on, 70; *muhūrtas* and, 118, 120, 124, 326n24; potatoes harvest, 114–16, 326; vocation for, 160

Aishwarya Rai, actress, 78, 228, 320n6, 320n7

almanac (*pañcāṅga* or *pañcāṅg*): academic publication, 65, 68–69, 99, *plate 3*, 327n29; astronomical schools and, 43; during colonial times, 60; *kumbha-vivāha* and, 338n24; *muhūrtas* and, 79, 118–26, 133–34, 326n24; syllabi and, 293; treatises on, 27; used during consultations, 19, 49, 113, 116, 226–27

amethyst, 175, 256, 266, 274, 280, 342n10, 344n29

amulets (*jantar*), 249, 261–63; as cheap remedies, 252; *dakṣiṇā* and, 85–86; dogs and, 108, 323n27; Muslims clients and, 21; *prāṇa pratiṣṭhā* and, *plate 17*; sold in shops or sent by post, 96, 99; sorcery attacks and, 143

ariṣṭa (fatal signs at birth), 30, 188–91, 333n3; *balāriṣṭas*, 201

Arya Samaj, 63–64, 316n23–25

asthma, 70, 72

astral conjunctions (*see*: *yog*)

auspicious times (see: *muhūrtas*)

Banaras Hindu University: alumni becoming astrologers, 97, 99, 109; astrologers working at, 5–6, 78, 95, 315–16n22; astrological research, 55–57, 69–75, 286, 313n2; Professor Katt's case, 116–18; scientists consulting astrologers 231, 271–72, 278; teaching of astral sciences, 60–61, 65–69, 291–96, 312n41, 313n4, 317n28–29

Benares Sanskrit College (*see*: Sanskrit College)

bhāgya (fortune, destiny): concerning lands, 108; family connections and, 187–88, 198, 206, 208, 215–16; forehead and, 131; hand's line, 128–29; house of the horoscope, 110; in horoscope reading, 156–64, 166, 168, 170, 226, 243; karma and, 147–49, 152–53, 176–77,

Yog or *yoga* (astral conjunction), 30, 44, 84, 112, 163, 170–76, 181, 193, 205, 328n50; *akhaṇḍa saubhāgya yog*, 338n25; *aṣṭa grahī yog*, 177, 333n31; *candrādhiyoga*, 207, 335n23; for house or land, 170, 173; for marriage, 6, 138, 170–74; for promotion, 175–76; for sons, 173, 184, 201, 232; for traveling abroad, 127, 138; good or bad, 174–75; *kāl sarp yog*, 222, 224, 239, 241–44, 336n3, 340n47; *kamāndh yog*, 179; *nīc karm yog*, 181; *rāj yog* (or *rājayoga*), 44, 137; *rogayoga*, 72, 318n39

Zimmermann, Francis, 31, 71
zodiacal signs (*rāśi*), 37, 43, 48, 108, 112, 127, 179, 236–38, 277–78, 333, 339

www.ingramcontent.com/pod-product-compliance
Lightning Source LLC
Chambersburg PA
CBHW030635270326
41929CB00007B/81